Cover Photo by John Rizzo

A Menu Guide to the Top 200
Restaurants in New York City
& Vicinity

PETER KUMP

This has been compiled for all who love fine food
and beverages wherever they may find it, knowing, when found,
it is certainly one of life's most enhancing experiences.
I hope this helps you in our shared mission.

ACKNOWLEDGMENTS

Several people assisted in this guide: My special appreciation goes to Phyllis Isaacson who organized the restaurants, my assistant Stephen Kelley who coordinated the effort, Len Pickell who offered his advice with New Jersey, and Caroline Stuart who offered hers for Upstate New York and Connecticut, and also to Jeanne Wilensky, Dorie Greenspan, and Bonnie Lee Black who offered many invaluable suggestions.

ISBN 0-9628274-4-4

PRINTED IN THE UNITED STATES OF AMERICA

Printed on Recycled Paper with Soy Based Inks

Cover Design & Illustrations
by Heather Kier

733 NW Everett St., Box 12, Studio 5E
Portland, Oregon 97209
(503) 226-6233

Restaurants by Cuisine

W 15
NO STAND
X24
X20

Historically, New York City has been a leader in dining out in America. Home of one of the first great restaurants in America, Delmonico's, it has remained on the cutting edge of what is happening in this country ever since. Though the Delmonico family was Italian-Swiss, from the start, its cooking was French, and fine dining in New York has been mostly based on those foundations ever since.

Whatever their place of origin, chefs in New York are quick to embrace various ethnic influences, whether out of an artistic curiosity or in order to attract customers. New York has looked more to western Europe, Italy most recently, just as California has looked to the far East. Yet with the second largest Chinatown outside of Asia and an enormous Japanese community served by over 400 restaurants, eastern influences are deeply felt. Few would argue that there is probably a greater diversity of cuisines available to the diner in New York than in any other city in the world today.

The sometimes contradictory tugs of health-promoting diets, exciting flavors and tastes, and "new" cuisines affect cooking trends today. Foreign chefs have begun to lighten their cooking and cooks in the American tradition quickly assimilate foreign techniques and flavors. The result produces Italian food not quite like it is in Italy and American food rapidly achieving the high quality we used to think was only possible in the temples of gastronomy on the French three-star circuit.

In my opinion, food cooked in America, for Americans and using our ingredients, is American cooking. It may be a Chinese immigrant cooking Chesapeake Bay soft shell crabs, a native-born American who puts foie gras on his menu or lemon grass in her bouillon, or an Austrian making pizzas with goat cheese and cilantro. Whether the cooking borrows more or less from one cuisine or several others, it is what we eat. And it is, overall, very good. New York City is a prime example of this. Certainly New York presents the most diverse, vibrant cooking found anywhere in the world.

With an immediate population of over 8,000,000 and a greater metropolitan population of well over 15,000,000, New York is never at a loss for diners. Although an alarming number of restaurants have gone out of business in recent years, statistics show that an even larger number have opened. The recession has merely hastened an already occurring trend — restaurants which appeal to contemporary tastes and offer good value.

Although I eat out five to six times a week, obviously it is not possible to visit all of the top restaurants in New York on any sort of a regular basis. As head of The James Beard Foundation, as well as a professional cooking school, I have had the opportunity to become familiar with a large number of chefs and their culinary endeavors. However, attempting to select 200 restaurants out of the tens of thousands that abound is a challenging feat.

My selections are all personal. Some are my most favorite restaurants, others I enjoy for special occasions, and some are "institutions" that simply should not be missed. In some instances, mostly out of town establishments, I have relied on the opinions of very good friends whose taste I trust.

This guide is a book for New Yorkers and for those who want to visit the restaurants New Yorkers enjoy. Those we consider to be New Yorkers are an odd lot: Few are native born; many live in the suburbs (mostly New Jersey, Connecticut, and Westchester County) and work in Manhattan, and many of those who live in Manhattan spend their weekends "in the country" (which usually translates to the Hamptons, upstate New York, and parts of Connecticut). I have, therefore, used those areas as the base for Metropolitan New York.

I hope you find my selections useful. If you have any suggestions, I would enjoy hearing from you.

Peter Kump
307 East 92nd Street
New York City, NY 10128

Publisher's Note

Everyone's a critic. No experience more perfectly echoes that sentiment than dining out. It never fails — whenever someone finds out that I publish restaurant guides, they immediately proceed to tell me about their favorite places to eat. My mouth waters as they describe, in vivid detail, the dish they ordered, as well as what everyone else in their party ordered. In other words, they describe the restaurant's menu.

It follows that a great way to choose a restaurant would be to read its menu, provided the place is well recommended. In the last few years, it has been my pleasure to discover that literally thousands of readers like yourself share this same conclusion. As you enjoy using this book, please keep three items in mind:

1. NO ONE PAID TO BE IN THIS BOOK.
   Neither Peter Kump nor the publisher, nor any of their associates, allow fees to be charged to any of the restaurants featured in the book, nor is inclusion in the book subject to any favors, trade-outs, book purchases, or any such promotional fees whatsoever.
2. MENUS AND PRICES CHANGE.
   Most all of the restaurants in this book change their menu and/or prices frequently, many even daily. We have tried to feature menus that accurately reflect the style and approach of the chef.
3. YOU CAN'T PLEASE EVERYONE.
   Even with no strings attached, we do (on rare occasion) encounter a restaurant who is either unwilling or unable to provide us with menus and other information, and thus, reluctantly, must be excluded.

Putting this book together was no small task. My heartfelt thanks go out to Deanna Demaree, Cordy Jensen, Heather Kier, Susan Fishback, Frank Alvey, Lynn Burgess, Alicia Geiger, Rex Nurnberg, Scott Deusebio, Jeannette Schilling, Barbara Disciascio, John Rizzo, and especially Peter Kump.

We are continually striving to improve our product. To do so, we need your feedback. To that end, you will find a tear-out Reader Survey inside the back cover. Please take a moment to fill it out and mail it (pre-paid) to my attention. I would love to hear from you.

Here's hoping that, as a fellow food lover, you not only find *THE MENU* to be a useful handbook of your favorite places, but also a tempting map to new gastronomical discoveries.

Tom Demaree
Publisher

The following table will answer the most often asked questions about the services offered by a particular restaurant. Please keep in mind that just as menus and prices change, so do amenities. It is always best to confirm those features important to you when making your reservation.

A few explanatory notes:

Types of Cuisine — The restaurants are grouped alphabetically by type of cuisine, starting with *American*, all the way through *Thai*. The cuisine category is referenced at the top right of each two-page spread. Index by Cuisine can be found on page 424.

Geographic Location — The address of the restaurant is located at the bottom of the left page on each menu. When there are additional locations, the best known or original location address is given, followed by the statement: (call for additional locations). Restaurants located in New York City are listed by their district or neighborhood, all others by their city name. Geographical index begins on page 428.

Hours — Dinner hours are listed at the bottom of the right page on each menu. A quick reference icon appears at the bottom right showing which meals a restaurant serves. See icons on next page.

100% Non-Smoking — Restaurants that do accommodate smoking guests generally offer non-smoking areas as well.

Wheelchair access — Most all of the restaurants without full wheelchair access are still able and happy to accommodate the special needs of any of their guests.

Dress — The three categories of dress referred to are only an indication of how *most* people dress for dinner. If you have a question, call ahead.

Personal Checks — Restaurants which accept personal checks require proper I.D.

On each lower right-hand page you will notice a row of symbols that represent certain features or services that a particular restaurant may offer. These "icons" are designed to give you a quick reference to the features that you may be looking for in a restaurant—at a glance.

Below is a list of the icons and what they represent:

— Wheelchair Access

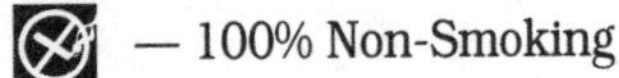
— 100% Non-Smoking

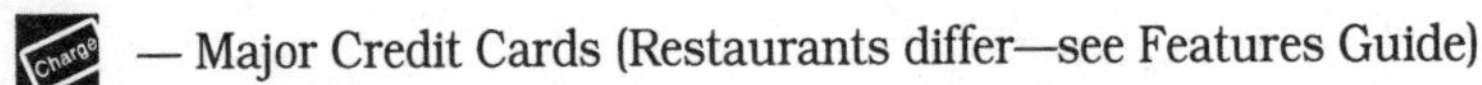
— Major Credit Cards (Restaurants differ—see Features Guide)

— Full Bar

— Breakfast

— Lunch

— Dinner

— Sunday Brunch

— Jacket/Tie (May be required - call to be safe)

— Live Entertainment

Features Guide

Restaurant	Pg.	Wheelchair Access	100% Non-Smoking	Visa/Master Card	American Express	Discover	Diners Club	Checks Accepted	Beer & Wine	Full Bar	Live Entertainment	Sunday Brunch	Breakfast	Lunch	Dinner	High Chairs	Take Out	Valet Parking	Private Parties	Informal Dress	Casual Dress	Jacket/Tie	Reserv. Recom.	Reserv. Required	Reserv. Not Taken
"21" Club	24	◆		◆	◆		◆		◆	◆				◆	◆				◆			◆	◆	◆	
Adrienne	164			◆	◆	◆	◆	◆		◆		◆	◆	◆	◆			◆				◆	◆		
Alison on Dominick Street	166	◆		◆	◆					◆					◆				◆			◆	◆		
Ambassador Grill	26			◆	◆	◆	◆		◆	◆	◆	◆	◆	◆	◆			◆	◆			◆	◆		
American Hotel, The	168	◆		◆	◆	◆	◆	◆	◆	◆	◆	◆	◆	◆	◆				◆			◆		◆	
An American Place	28	◆		◆	◆		◆		◆	◆				◆	◆				◆		◆	◆	◆		
Aquavit	384			◆	◆		◆			◆				◆	◆		◆		◆	◆		◆		◆	
Arcadia	30	◆		◆	◆		◆		◆	◆				◆	◆				◆			◆	◆		
Arizona 206 and Cafe	116	◆		◆	◆	◆	◆			◆	◆			◆	◆						◆		◆		
Arqua	278			◆	◆					◆				◆	◆				◆	◆	◆		◆		
Aureole	32	◆		◆	◆		◆		◆	◆				◆	◆							◆		◆	
Ballroom, The	134	◆		◆	◆		◆	◆	◆	◆	◆	◆		◆	◆		◆		◆	◆	◆		◆		
Bangkok House	420			◆	◆					◆					◆		◆				◆		◆		
Barbetta	280			◆	◆	◆	◆	◆	◆	◆	◆			◆	◆				◆			◆	◆		
Barocco	282			◆	◆	◆	◆			◆				◆	◆		◆		◆		◆		◆		
Basilico	284				◆					◆					◆						◆	◆		◆	
Becco	286			◆	◆	◆	◆			◆				◆	◆				◆	◆			◆		
Beekman 1766 Tavern, The	34	◆		◆	◆		◆	◆	◆	◆	◆	◆	◆	◆	◆	◆	◆		◆	◆			◆		
Bertrand	170			◆	◆		◆	◆	◆	◆				◆	◆		◆		◆			◆	◆		
Bice	288	◆		◆	◆		◆		◆	◆				◆	◆					◆	◆		◆		
Bistro du Nord	172			◆	◆		◆			◆		◆		◆	◆		◆		◆		◆			◆	
Bouley	174			◆	◆	◆	◆			◆				◆	◆				◆			◆		◆	
Bridge Cafe, The	36	◆		◆	◆		◆	◆	◆	◆		◆		◆	◆		◆		◆	◆	◆	◆	◆		
Cafe Botanica	38	◆		◆	◆	◆	◆	◆	◆	◆		◆	◆	◆	◆	◆			◆		◆		◆		
Cafe Crocodile	372				◆			◆		◆					◆				◆		◆		◆		
Cafe des Artistes	176	◆		◆	◆		◆			◆		◆		◆	◆							◆		◆	
Cafe Loup	178	◆		◆	◆	◆	◆		◆	◆		◆		◆	◆	◆	◆		◆		◆		◆		
Cafe Luxembourg	180	◆		◆	◆		◆		◆	◆		◆		◆	◆				◆		◆		◆		
Cafe Pierre	182	◆		◆	◆		◆		◆	◆	◆	◆	◆	◆	◆	◆		◆	◆		◆	◆	◆		
Cafe Trevi	290			◆	◆					◆					◆						◆		◆		
Cal's	40	◆		◆	◆		◆		◆	◆				◆	◆	◆	◆		◆		◆		◆		
Canton	118							◆	◆					◆	◆		◆				◆		◆		
Capsouto Freres	184			◆	◆		◆		◆	◆		◆		◆	◆				◆	◆	◆		◆		
Carlyle Dining Room	136	◆		◆	◆		◆		◆	◆		◆	◆	◆	◆							◆	◆		
Carnegie Deli	160								◆				◆	◆	◆	◆	◆		◆		◆				◆
Cellar in the Sky	138	◆		◆	◆	◆	◆		◆	◆	◆				◆				◆			◆		◆	
Cent'Anni	292	◆			◆				◆	◆				◆	◆						◆		◆		
Chanterelle	186	◆		◆	◆		◆			◆				◆	◆				◆			◆		◆	
Chefs & Cuisiniers Club	42	◆		◆	◆				◆	◆				◆	◆		◆		◆		◆		◆		
Chez Catherine	188			◆	◆		◆	◆	◆					◆	◆				◆				◆		
Chez Jacqueline	190	◆		◆	◆		◆			◆				◆	◆		◆		◆		◆	◆	◆		
Chez Michallet	192			◆	◆		◆		◆			◆			◆				◆		◆			◆	
Chiam	120	◆		◆	◆		◆		◆	◆		◆		◆	◆		◆		◆			◆	◆		
Chin Chin	122	◆		◆	◆		◆	◆	◆	◆				◆	◆	◆	◆		◆		◆		◆		
China Grill	124	◆		◆	◆		◆		◆	◆				◆	◆		◆		◆		◆		◆		

Features Guide

Restaurant	Pg.	Wheelchair Access	100% Non-Smoking	Visa/Master Card	American Express	Discover	Diners Club	Checks Accepted	Beer & Wine	Full Bar	Live Entertainment	Sunday Brunch	Breakfast	Lunch	Dinner	High Chairs	Take Out	Valet Parking	Private Parties	Informal Dress	Casual Dress	Jacket/Tie	Reserv. Recom.	Reserv. Required	Reserv. Not Taken
Christ Cella	404	◆		◆	◆		◆			◆				◆	◆				◆			◆	◆		
Cité	194	◆		◆	◆		◆		◆	◆		◆	◆	◆	◆		◆		◆	◆			◆		
City Cafe	44	◆		◆				◆		◆		◆		◆					◆		◆		◆		
Claire	386			◆	◆		◆			◆		◆		◆	◆		◆		◆		◆		◆		
Coco Pazzo	294	◆		◆	◆		◆		◆	◆				◆	◆				◆			◆		◆	
Corrado	296			◆	◆		◆			◆				◆	◆		◆		◆		◆		◆		
Coyote Grill	46	◆		◆	◆				◆	◆	◆	◆		◆	◆	◆	◆	◆	◆		◆		◆		
Culinary Institute America	196	◆	◆	◆	◆		◆		◆	◆				◆	◆	◆			◆			◆		◆	
Da Pietro's	298	◆		◆	◆		◆			◆					◆		◆		◆		◆		◆		
Da Silvano	300	◆		◆	◆					◆				◆	◆						◆		◆		
Da Umberto	302				◆				◆	◆				◆	◆						◆		◆		
Darbar	274	◆		◆	◆	◆	◆		◆	◆				◆	◆	◆	◆		◆		◆		◆		
Dawat	276	◆		◆	◆		◆	◆	◆	◆				◆	◆	◆	◆		◆	◆			◆		
Della Femina	304			◆	◆					◆					◆		◆		◆		◆		◆		
Dennis Foy's Townsquare	140	◆		◆	◆	◆	◆	◆	◆	◆	◆			◆	◆	◆			◆			◆	◆	◆	
Dock's Oyster Bar	388	◆		◆	◆		◆			◆		◆		◆	◆				◆		◆		◆		
Dominick's	306									◆				◆	◆		◆			◆					◆
Duane Park Cafe	48	◆	◆	◆	◆		◆		◆	◆				◆	◆				◆	◆			◆		
E.A.T.	50				◆				◆				◆	◆	◆		◆		◆	◆			◆		
East Hampton Point	52			◆	◆					◆		◆		◆	◆			◆	◆		◆		◆		
Ecco	308			◆	◆	◆	◆		◆	◆				◆	◆		◆		◆		◆		◆		
Elaine's	310	◆		◆	◆	◆			◆	◆					◆				◆		◆		◆		
Erminia	312				◆			◆	◆						◆				◆			◆		◆	
Felidia	314			◆	◆	◆	◆		◆	◆				◆	◆				◆			◆		◆	
Follonico	316	◆	◆	◆	◆		◆		◆	◆				◆	◆						◆	◆	◆		
Four Seasons, The	54			◆	◆	◆	◆		◆	◆				◆	◆				◆			◆	◆		
Frank's	406			◆	◆		◆			◆				◆	◆				◆	◆			◆		
Fu's	126			◆	◆		◆		◆	◆				◆	◆		◆					◆	◆		
Gabriel's	318	◆		◆	◆					◆				◆	◆				◆		◆		◆		
Gallagher's	408	◆		◆	◆	◆	◆		◆	◆				◆	◆				◆	◆			◆		
Gascogne	198			◆	◆				◆	◆					◆						◆		◆		
Girafe	320			◆	◆		◆		◆	◆				◆	◆				◆			◆	◆		
Gotham Bar & Grill	56			◆	◆		◆			◆				◆	◆							◆			
Halcyon	142	◆		◆	◆	◆	◆		◆	◆	◆	◆	◆	◆	◆	◆		◆	◆			◆	◆		
Harrald's	144	◆	◆					◆	◆	◆					◆				◆			◆		◆	
Harry Cipriani	322	◆		◆	◆	◆	◆	◆	◆	◆		◆	◆	◆	◆		◆					◆		◆	
Honmura An	366			◆	◆		◆			◆				◆	◆						◆			◆	
Hudson River Club	58	◆		◆	◆	◆	◆		◆	◆	◆	◆		◆	◆				◆			◆	◆		
Il Cantinori	324			◆	◆		◆		◆	◆				◆	◆						◆		◆		
Il Giglio	326	◆		◆	◆					◆				◆	◆			◆			◆	◆	◆		
Il Nido	328			◆	◆		◆			◆				◆	◆							◆		◆	
Inn at Ridgefield, The	146	◆		◆	◆			◆		◆		◆		◆	◆				◆			◆	◆		
John's Pizzeria	330	◆							◆					◆	◆		◆			◆	◆				
JoJo	200			◆	◆					◆				◆	◆				◆		◆			◆	
La Boite en Bois	202							◆		◆					◆				◆		◆		◆		

Features Guide

Restaurant	Pg.	Wheelchair Access	100% Non-Smoking	Visa/Master Card	American Express	Discover	Diners Club	Checks Accepted	Beer & Wine	Full Bar	Live Entertainment	Sunday Brunch	Breakfast	Lunch	Dinner	High Chairs	Take Out	Valet Parking	Private Parties	Informal Dress	Casual Dress	Jacket/Tie	Reserv. Recom.	Reserv. Required	Reserv. Not Taken
La Caravelle	204	◆		◆	◆		◆	◆	◆	◆				◆	◆				◆			◆	◆		
La Colombe d'Or	206			◆	◆		◆			◆				◆	◆				◆	◆			◆		
La Cote Basque	208			◆	◆		◆	◆	◆	◆				◆	◆				◆			◆	◆		
La Metairie	210	◆		◆	◆		◆		◆			◆		◆	◆				◆		◆				
La Panetiere	212			◆	◆		◆		◆	◆				◆	◆			◆	◆			◆		◆	
La Reserve	214	◆		◆	◆		◆	◆		◆				◆	◆				◆			◆	◆		
Lattanzi	332				◆			◆	◆	◆				◆	◆				◆		◆		◆		
Laundry Restaurant	60	◆		◆	◆		◆	◆	◆	◆					◆		◆				◆				◆
Le Chantilly	216	◆		◆	◆		◆	◆		◆				◆	◆				◆			◆		◆	
Le Cirque	218	◆		◆	◆	◆	◆		◆	◆				◆	◆				◆			◆	◆		
Le Madri	334			◆	◆		◆		◆	◆				◆	◆			◆	◆			◆		◆	
Le Perigord	220		◆	◆	◆	◆	◆	◆	◆	◆				◆	◆				◆			◆	◆		
Le Pistou	222	◆		◆	◆		◆	◆	◆					◆	◆						◆		◆		
Le Regence	224	◆		◆	◆		◆		◆	◆		◆	◆	◆	◆	◆			◆			◆	◆		
Les Celebrites	226	◆	◆	◆	◆	◆	◆		◆	◆					◆				◆			◆		◆	
Les Halles	228	◆		◆	◆		◆			◆		◆		◆	◆	◆			◆	◆			◆		
Lespinasse	230	◆		◆	◆	◆	◆		◆	◆			◆	◆	◆							◆	◆		
Lola	62			◆	◆				◆	◆	◆	◆		◆	◆	◆	◆		◆		◆		◆		
Lutèce	232	◆		◆	◆		◆		◆	◆				◆	◆				◆			◆		◆	
Manhattan Ocean Club	390			◆	◆		◆		◆	◆				◆	◆				◆	◆			◆		
March	64			◆	◆		◆		◆	◆					◆				◆			◆		◆	
Mark's Restaurant	234	◆		◆	◆	◆	◆		◆	◆		◆	◆	◆	◆	◆			◆		◆		◆		
Maxime's	236	◆		◆	◆	◆	◆	◆	◆	◆		◆		◆	◆				◆			◆	◆		
Mayflower Inn, The	66	◆		◆	◆			◆	◆	◆	◆		◆	◆	◆			◆	◆		◆		◆	◆	
Mesa Grill	68	◆		◆	◆		◆			◆		◆		◆	◆						◆		◆		
Mezzogiorno	336	◆						◆		◆		◆		◆	◆		◆			◆	◆	◆	◆		
Mi Cocina	376	◆		◆	◆		◆		◆	◆		◆		◆	◆						◆		◆		
Michael's	70			◆	◆		◆		◆	◆			◆	◆	◆		◆		◆		◆	◆	◆		
Mirabelle	238			◆	◆		◆	◆	◆	◆				◆	◆		◆		◆			◆	◆		
Montrachet	240	◆			◆					◆									◆			◆	◆		
Nanni's	338			◆	◆		◆			◆				◆	◆							◆	◆		
Nick & Toni's	374	◆			◆			◆		◆		◆			◆		◆		◆		◆			◆	
Nippon	368	◆		◆	◆		◆			◆				◆	◆		◆		◆			◆	◆		
Nosmo King	72		◆	◆	◆	◆	◆			◆	◆	◆		◆	◆						◆		◆		
Oceana	392			◆	◆	◆	◆			◆				◆	◆							◆	◆		
Odeon	74	◆		◆	◆		◆			◆		◆		◆	◆		◆				◆		◆		
One Fifth Avenue	394	◆		◆	◆		◆		◆	◆		◆		◆	◆				◆		◆		◆		
One if by Land	148	◆		◆	◆		◆	◆		◆	◆				◆				◆			◆	◆		
Orso	340			◆						◆				◆	◆						◆	◆	◆		
Oyster Bar, The	396	◆		◆	◆	◆	◆		◆	◆				◆	◆	◆	◆		◆		◆		◆		
Palio	342	◆		◆	◆	◆	◆		◆	◆				◆	◆				◆			◆	◆		
Palm, The	410	◆		◆	◆		◆	◆	◆	◆				◆	◆		◆	◆	◆		◆		◆		
Paola's	344	◆			◆				◆			◆		◆	◆		◆						◆		
Parioli Romanissimo	346			◆	◆					◆									◆			◆		◆	
Park and Orchard	76	◆		◆	◆	◆	◆		◆	◆				◆	◆	◆	◆				◆				◆

Features Guide

Restaurant	Pg.	Wheelchair Access	100% Non-Smoking	Visa/Master Card	American Express	Discover	Diners Club	Checks Accepted	Beer & Wine	Full Bar	Live Entertainment	Sunday Brunch	Breakfast	Lunch	Dinner	High Chairs	Take Out	Valet Parking	Private Parties	Informal Dress	Casual Dress	Jacket/Tie	Reserv. Recom.	Reserv. Required	Reserv. Not Taken
Park Avenue Cafe	78	◆		◆	◆		◆		◆	◆		◆		◆	◆				◆	◆			◆		
Park Bistro	242			◆	◆	◆	◆			◆				◆	◆				◆		◆		◆		
Peacock Alley	244	◆		◆	◆	◆	◆	◆	◆	◆	◆	◆	◆	◆	◆	◆		◆	◆			◆	◆		
Periyali	272			◆	◆		◆		◆	◆				◆	◆				◆	◆		◆	◆		
Petaluma	348			◆	◆	◆	◆	◆	◆	◆		◆		◆	◆	◆	◆				◆		◆		
Peter Luger	412	◆						◆	◆	◆				◆	◆	◆	◆		◆		◆		◆		
Petrossian Paris	246			◆	◆		◆			◆		◆		◆	◆				◆			◆	◆		
Poiret	248	◆		◆	◆		◆		◆	◆		◆			◆				◆		◆		◆		
Polo, The	150	◆		◆	◆	◆	◆		◆	◆		◆	◆	◆	◆	◆						◆	◆		
Positano	350	◆		◆	◆		◆		◆	◆				◆	◆		◆		◆		◆		◆		
Post House, The	414			◆	◆		◆		◆	◆				◆	◆					◆			◆		
Primavera	352	◆		◆	◆		◆			◆					◆				◆			◆	◆		
Provence	250			◆	◆					◆		◆		◆	◆		◆		◆		◆		◆		
Quatorze Bis	252	◆		◆	◆					◆		◆		◆	◆				◆		◆		◆		
Rainbow Room, The	152	◆			◆				◆	◆	◆	◆			◆				◆			◆		◆	
Raoul's	254	◆		◆	◆				◆	◆					◆				◆		◆		◆		
Regency, The (540 Park)	80			◆	◆		◆		◆	◆	◆	◆	◆	◆	◆	◆			◆		◆		◆		
Remi	354	◆		◆	◆		◆			◆				◆	◆		◆		◆			◆	◆		
Restaurant Daniel	256	◆		◆	◆		◆		◆	◆			◆	◆	◆				◆			◆		◆	
Restaurant Jean-Louis	258			◆	◆		◆	◆		◆					◆		◆		◆			◆		◆	
Restaurant Lafayette	260	◆		◆	◆		◆		◆	◆				◆	◆				◆		◆	◆	◆		
Restaurant Raphael	262			◆	◆		◆			◆				◆	◆				◆	◆		◆		◆	
River Cafe, The	82	◆		◆	◆		◆	◆	◆	◆	◆	◆		◆	◆			◆	◆			◆	◆		
Rosa Mexicano	378			◆	◆		◆			◆					◆		◆				◆		◆		
Rosemarie's	356			◆	◆					◆				◆	◆	◆	◆		◆		◆		◆		
Russian Tea Room	382			◆	◆	◆	◆		◆	◆	◆	◆		◆	◆				◆			◆	◆		
Ryland Inn, The	264			◆	◆	◆	◆		◆	◆				◆	◆	◆		◆	◆			◆	◆		
Saddle River Inn	154	◆		◆	◆									◆	◆				◆			◆		◆	
San Domenico	358	◆		◆	◆	◆	◆	◆	◆	◆				◆	◆				◆			◆	◆		
Sapore di mare	360			◆	◆					◆				◆	◆		◆	◆	◆		◆		◆		
Sarabeth's	84	◆	◆	◆	◆		◆			◆		◆	◆	◆	◆	◆			◆		◆		◆		
Savoy	86							◆	◆					◆	◆						◆		◆		
Scarlatti	362	◆		◆	◆		◆	◆	◆	◆				◆	◆		◆		◆			◆	◆		
Sea Grill, The	398	◆		◆	◆		◆		◆	◆				◆	◆	◆			◆			◆	◆		
Second Avenue Deli	162	◆			◆			◆	◆											◆					◆
Shun Lee Palace	128	◆		◆	◆		◆		◆	◆				◆	◆		◆	◆	◆			◆	◆		
Sign of the Dove, The	88	◆		◆	◆	◆	◆			◆	◆	◆		◆	◆	◆			◆			◆	◆		
Silverado Bar & Grill	90	◆		◆	◆		◆			◆		◆	◆	◆	◆				◆		◆		◆		
Smith & Wollensky	416	◆		◆	◆		◆		◆	◆		◆		◆	◆				◆	◆	◆		◆		
Solera	402	◆		◆	◆		◆	◆	◆	◆				◆	◆				◆			◆		◆	
Sonia Rose	92	◆		◆	◆	◆	◆	◆	◆	◆				◆	◆				◆			◆	◆		
Sparks Steak House	418			◆	◆	◆	◆			◆				◆	◆							◆	◆		
Sushisay	370			◆	◆		◆		◆					◆	◆		◆		◆		◆			◆	
Sylvia's	94	◆			◆				◆	◆	◆	◆	◆	◆	◆	◆	◆		◆		◆		◆		
Taliesin	96	◆		◆	◆	◆	◆		◆	◆			◆	◆	◆	◆		◆				◆	◆		

Features Guide

RESTAURANT	PG.	Wheelchair Access	100% Non-Smoking	Visa/Master Card	American Express	Discover	Diners Club	Checks Accepted	Beer & Wine	Full Bar	Live Entertainment	Sunday Brunch	Breakfast	Lunch	Dinner	High Chairs	Take Out	Valet Parking	Private Parties	Informal Dress	Casual Dress	Jacket/Tie	Reserv. Recom.	Reserv. Required	Reserv. Not Taken
Tatou	98	◆		◆	◆				◆	◆	◆			◆	◆				◆			◆	◆	◆	
Tavern on the Green	156	◆		◆	◆			◆		◆	◆	◆		◆	◆	◆		◆	◆		◆	◆	◆		
Terrace, The	266	◆		◆	◆		◆	◆	◆	◆	◆			◆	◆			◆	◆		◆	◆	◆	◆	
Trattoria dell'Arte	364			◆	◆				◆	◆		◆		◆	◆				◆		◆			◆	
TriBeCa Grill	100	◆		◆	◆		◆		◆	◆		◆		◆	◆				◆		◆		◆		
Trois Jean	268	◆		◆	◆				◆	◆		◆		◆	◆		◆		◆		◆		◆		
Tropica	102	◆		◆	◆		◆		◆	◆				◆	◆				◆		◆		◆		
Tse Yang	130	◆		◆	◆		◆		◆	◆				◆	◆				◆			◆	◆		
Union Square Cafe	104		◆	◆	◆		◆		◆	◆				◆	◆						◆		◆		
Vince and Eddie's	106			◆	◆	◆			◆	◆		◆		◆	◆		◆		◆		◆	◆	◆		
Vong	270	◆		◆	◆		◆		◆	◆				◆	◆						◆			◆	
Water Club, The	108	◆		◆	◆		◆	◆	◆	◆	◆	◆		◆	◆			◆	◆			◆	◆		
West Broadway	110	◆		◆	◆		◆		◆	◆					◆	◆			◆		◆		◆		
Wilkinson's Seafood Cafe	400			◆	◆		◆			◆					◆		◆				◆	◆	◆		
Windows on the World	158	◆		◆	◆	◆	◆		◆	◆		◆		◆	◆				◆			◆	◆		
Xaviar's	112	◆						◆	◆	◆		◆		◆	◆				◆			◆		◆	
Zarela	380				◆		◆			◆	◆			◆	◆		◆		◆		◆		◆		
Zen Palate	132	◆	◆	◆	◆							◆		◆	◆		◆			◆	◆		◆		
Zoë	114	◆		◆	◆		◆		◆	◆		◆		◆	◆	◆			◆		◆		◆		

The Restaurants

"21" has been a New York institution since Prohibition. Although it went through a decline a number of years ago, owner Ken Aretsky has totally upgraded the food and decor and it shines once again.

Menu Changes Seasonally

The '21' Club Dinner

Appetizers

Oysters or Clams on the Half Shell 15.00
Jumbo Lump Crabmeat Cocktail 17.00
'21' Shrimp Cocktail 16.50
Our Own Tequila-Cured Salmon Gravlax 17.50
Fresh Mozzarella and Tomato-Basil Salad 15.00
Asparagus or Artichoke Vinaigrette 16.00
Oak Smoked Salmon with Chive Vinaigrette 17.50
Caesar Salad 12.50
Salad of Mixed Baby Greens 10.00
Chicory, Blue Cheese and Bacon Salad 12.50
Maryland Crab Cake with Horseradish Cream 18.00
Fresh Foie Gras with Roasted Shallots, Sweet and Sour Cabbage and Pepper Bread 21.00
Goat Cheese Ravioli with Fresh Roma Tomato Sauce 15.00
Shrimp, Scallop and Squid with Ginger Rice and Noodles in Curry Broth 16.00
Grilled Rabbit Loin Salad with Truffle Oil 17.00
Endive, Radicchio and Arugula Salad 11.50
Beluga Caviar Service 70.00 per ounce

Soups

9.00

Cold Curried Senegalaise
Gazpacho with Smoked Shrimp
Spicy Cuban Black Bean
Chunky Lobster Bisque

Entrees

SEARED SALMON FILET with Yukon Gold Potatoes, Calamata Olives and Capers 36.00
HERB ROASTED NATURAL CHICKEN with Sugar Snap Peas and Turnip Home Fries 29.00
FARM RAISED STRIPED BASS, Crisply Fried with Sesame-Ginger Vegetable Sauce 34.00
ROASTED CALIFORNIA SQUAB with Cumin scented Couscous, Foie Gras Nuggets and Zinfandel Sauce 38.00
PAN ROASTED MAINE LOBSTER with Littleneck Clams, Sweet Corn and Tarragon Biscuits 39.00
VEAL FILET with Asparagus, Leeks, Wild Mushrooms and Port Wine Sauce 38.00
PEPPERED TUNA STEAK with Seared Tomatoes and Fine Green Beans 37.00

21 West 52nd St • Midtown West Side • (212) 582-7200

DRY AGED BLACK ANGUS PORTERHOUSE STEAK (for two only, please) 39.00 per person

GRILLED SWORDFISH with Tuscan White Beans, Fresh Herbs, Applewood Smoked Bacon and Natural Juices 37.00

MUSCOVY DUCK BREAST with Balsamic Vinegar Glaze, Pecan Wild Rice and Cherry-Confit Salad 36.00

VEAL CHOP or DRY AGED BLACK ANGUS SIRLOIN or RIBEYE with Mashed Potatoes and Onion Rings 39.00

GRILLED VENISON LOIN on Green with Sage Potato Crisp and Peppercorn Vinaigrette 39.00

MARINATED LAMB RACK with Grilled Eggplant, Zucchini and Rosemary Flatbread 39.00

GRILLED ATLANTIC HALIBUT with Roasted Leeks and Tomatoes, Thyme and Vermouth 35.00

ENGLISH DOVER SOLE with Asparagus and Fingerling Potatoes - Grilled or Sauteed 39.00

'21' TRADITIONS

"SPEAKEASY" STEAK TARTARE - discreetly prepared tableside to your taste 30.00

COLD WHOLE MAINE LOBSTER SALAD with Avocado, Tomatoes and Herb Potatoes 33.00

THE '21' BURGER on Grilled Sourdough Bread 24.00

'21' SUNSET SALAD - Jack and Charlie's Chopped Barroom Salad 26.00

CHICKEN HASH with Wild Rice, Sherry and Wilted Spinach 26.00

Side Orders

8.50

French Fries Hash Browns Pommes Souffle Gratin Potatoes
Creamed Spinach Fried Zucchini Strings Onion Rings Mashed Potatoes
Sauteed Spinach Baked Potato

'21' TRIM MENU

Jumbo Asparagus with Lemon-Thyme Vinaigrette 12.00

Venison Carpaccio with Ancho Chili Remoulade 15.00

GRILLED QUAIL SALAD with Tabbouleh and Port Vinaigrette 29.00

ROASTED VEGETABLE TART with Whole Wheat Crust 22.00

HALIBUT steamed with Lemon Grass and Thai Curry 29.00

on the lighter for those Nutritionally concerned

Appetizer or Soup Served as entree, or Entrees shared, additional 50%.

Dinner: M - F 5:30 - 11:30

The only major hotel near the United Nations, it has an important clientele, dramatic decor, and consistently excellent cuisine.

AMBASSADOR GRILL

Menu Changes Seasonally

Prix Fixe $ 24.93
includes First, Main Course and Dessert

FIRST COURSES

Crawfish Gazpacho *with a splash of tequila*

Tomato and Mozzarella *with a basil vinaigrette*

Seared Yellowfin Tuna *with marinated vegetables*

Lemon-Soy Grilled Shrimp *over warm succotash salsa*

Prosciutto Quesadilla *with jack cheese and sun dried tomatoes*

Smoked Trout and Gravlax *with dill-horseradish sauce*

Bundle of Chilled Asparagus *with sesame and orange dressing*

Carpaccio of Venison *with blueberries and three cabbage slaw*

Lambs Lettuce and Pear Salad *with pecans and cheddar dressing*

Salad of Baby Lettuces *with balsamic vinaigrette*

UN Plaza-Park Hyatt Hotel • 1 UN Plaza • Midtown East Side • (212) 702-5014

MAIN COURSES

Grilled Swordfish Steak *with peppered beet vinaigrette*

Seared Salmon in a Mushroom Crust *with lemon sauce*

Coriander Seed Roasted Striped Bass *with green curry oil*

Roasted Monkfish in a Tortilla Crust *with horseradish sauce*

Pan Roasted Scallops *with ginger-scallion vinaigrette*

Armagnac Roasted Grouper *with carrot-citrus broth*

Char-Grilled Angus Rib Steak *with red wine-mushroom butter*

Grilled Tenderloin of Pork *with roasted sweet pepper coulis*

Grilled Rack of Lamb *with goat cheese-tequila sauce*

Sauteed Duck Breast *with caramelized onions and ginger*

Peanut Roasted Chicken *with thai apple and melon salad*

VEGETARIAN

Grilled and Steamed Vegetables *with mustard or tomato vinaigrette*

Cold Buckwheat Noodles *in a spicy peanut sauce*

Wild Mushroom Linguini *with broccoli, pine nuts, garlic and olive oil*

Chef de Cuisine Walter Houlihan

Dinner: 7 Days a Week 6 - 11

Chef/owner Larry Forgione was one of the first chefs in New York to reinvent American cuisine and promote local food products. His spacious restaurant remains one of New York's most popular.

An American Place

Menu Changes Seasonally

DINNER MENU

Appetizers

GRILLED SPRING ASPARAGUS WITH A SPRING SHALLOT VINAIGRETTE
with grilled farmhouse bread and field cress 8.00

CHARRED TUNA CARPACCIO
with a choyote, red pepper and pineapple salad and drizzled with a chile oil 9.50

FIELD SALAD WITH BABY LETTUCE AND SEASONAL GREENS
shaved Hudson Valley aged goat cheese
and a charred tomato vinaigrette 7.50

HOUSE SMOKED SALMON AND POTATO CRISP "NAPOLEON"
with chive oil and sturgeon caviar 12.50

SLOW ROASTED VIDALIA ONION SALAD
with specially aged New York State Prosciutto with a warm sherry vinaigrette 9.50

GRILLED FRESH GULF SHRIMP WITH A RED PEPPER HONEY GLAZE
and cilantro corn cakes, roasted red pepper cream
and avocado corn salsa 10.50

SALAD OF ROMAINE HEARTS, FRISEE AND ENDIVE
tossed with a caesar dressing, smokehouse bacon,
shaved aged Monterey Jack cheese and croutons 8.00

SOUP OF THE DAY 7.50

Fish and Shellfish

FISH OF THE DAY
priced accordingly

CRISP SOFT SHELL CRAB WITH A WARM CHARLESTON VEGETABLE SLAW
and a spicy she crab sauce 12.00/23.00*

GRILLED FRESH MAINE LOBSTER TAILS
BASTED WITH A BARBECUE LIME MARINATE
served with a diced spring vegetable
and toasted bread salad with fresh herbs 15.00/29.00*

2 Park Ave • Murray Hill/Kips Bay • (212) 684-2122

Grilled, Cedar Planked or Pan Roasted

ATLANTIC SALMON 24.00

YELLOW FIN TUNA 25.00
DAY BOAT FRESH COD 19.50
MAHI-MAHI 22.00

With your Choice of

CREAMY SORREL WHIPPED POTATOES AND A ROASTED TOMATO FISH BROTH WITH BASIL

TOASTED CORN AND MOREL SAUCE ON A BED OF WILTED SPRING GREENS

SOFT CORN PUDDING WITH SPRING VEGETABLES AND A WILD LEEK VINAIGRETTE

STRAW POTATOES AND LEMON OREGANO SAUCE

Meat, Poultry and Game

CRISP PINEAPPLE-CHILE BASTED BARBECUED FREE RANGE DUCK BREAST
slow roasted with a black bean cake
field cress and a tropical fruit salsa 24.00

HERB RUBBED ROAST FREE RANGE POUISSIN WITH SAUTEED SPRING VEGETABLES
served semi-boneless with creamer potatoes and a natural jus 24.00

ROAST RACK OF ORGANIC LAMB WITH A CRISP MOREL AND POTATO PANCAKE
carmelized young fennel and fresh artichoke hearts
and a fresh mint lamb jus 32.00

GRILLED NEW YORK SHELL STEAK SMOTHERED WITH SAUTEED SWEET ONIONS
mild-west smashed new potatoes and California cabernet sauce 29.50
certified organic Colorado beef, dry aged for two weeks

*** Denotes price as Appetizer or Main Course**

Pipe and Cigar Smoking are allowed in the Bar Area only

An 18% gratuity will be added to all parties of eight or over

Larry Forgione
Chef-Proprietor

Richard D'Orazi
Executive Chef

Dinner: Sat 5:30 - 9:30

Arcadia

Arcadia has always been one of the top restaurants in New York because of its elegant setting (a charming mural runs around the small room) and creative, trend-setting food from one of this country's most renowned chefs.

ARCADIA

Menu Changes Seasonally

smoked salmon tart with sweet onion jam & spring lettuces

caesar salad with arrugula & brioche croutons

lobster crème brûlée with sweet water prawn toast

corn cakes with crème fraîche & caviars $5.

field greens with fresh herb vinaigrette

soup of the spring season

gâteau St. Honoré with grilled shrimps, tomato confit, & sea urchin cream

---

crispy roast chicken with a wild mushroom hash

chimney smoked lobster with tarragon butter & Chinese noodle cakes $7.

---

21 East 62nd St • Upper East Side • (212) 223-2900

slow roasted duck with a fig & shallot compote,
& chick pea polenta

sauté of skate with celery root purée, red wine, & frizzled leeks

loin of rabbit with hazelnut crumbs, asparagus, & beet oil

salmon in rice paper with pink grapefruit & rice croquettes

coriander crusted rib-eye with a mashed potato napoleon

---

frozen mango mousse in a coconut tuile

blackberry shortcake with blackberry ice cream

chocolate sharpei cake

warm peach tart with vanilla ice cream

strawberry & rhubarb charlotte

warm chocolate bread pudding with brandy custard sauce

litchi & ginger ice cream in an Earl grey broth with melon

prix fixe $58.

Chef/owner Charles Palmer is one of America's top chefs and helped to recreate American cooking, using local ingredients and creative combinations. The elegant bi-level townhouse setting is decorated in soothing shades of off-white.

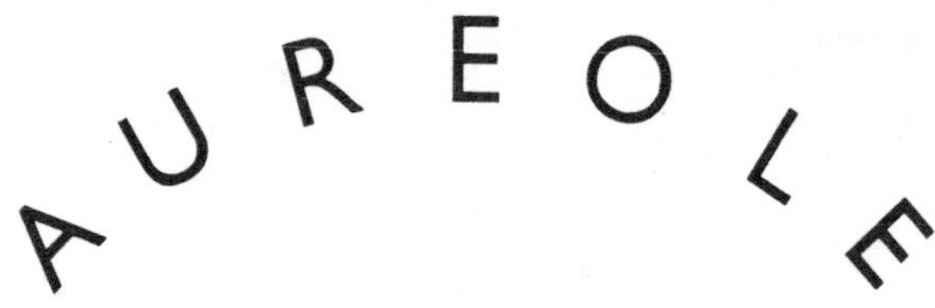

Appetizers

Asparagus Vinaigrette with Toasted Walnut and Goat Cheese Savory
essence of tarragon and celeriac shavings
$10

Grilled Eggplant and Cured Sirloin Salad
thinly sliced over marinated artichokes and tomato compote
$11

Tartare of Yellowfin Tuna with Fennel-Chive Oil
pickled cucumber salad, cultured cream, brioche toasts
$11

Terrine of Natural Foie Gras with Pressed Duck Confit
salad of new potatoes, confiture of plum fruits
$13

Salmon and Lobster Wontons in Tomato Herb Consommé
cold pressed olive oil, marinated leeks and grilled shitake
$10

Smoked Shrimp and Sweet Corn Chowder
melted leeks, fresh thyme and toasted quinoa
$9

Salad of Seasonal Lettuces and Herbs
vinaigrette with essence of shallot
$7

Oak Smoked Salmon with Cucumber Salad
double cultured cream and Michael's sourdough toasts
(or served naturally)
$12

Market Select Oysters over Shaved Ice
with shallot mignonette and caraway crisps
$11

(Please refrain from cigar and pipe smoking. Thank you.)

34 East 61st St • Midtown East Side • (212) 319-1660

Main Course

Braised Monkfish "Pot au Feu" with Saffron Broth
couscous roulade and winter vegetables
$18

Sauté Grouper Escalopes with Fricasée of Wild Mushroom
puree of new potatoes, basil oil, cured plum tomato
$19

Pan Seared Salmon Filet with Citrus and Fresh Sage
crisped potato "jimmy's" and baby spinach
$19

Sauté Soft Shell Crabs with Lemon Confit and Tiny Capers
Kail Farm asparagus and chive scented potato cake
$22

Warm Fruitwood Grilled Ginger-Prawn Salad
light curry and papaya vinaigrette
$22

Seared Veal Medallions with Herb Braised Stuffed Turnip
madiera essence sauce, country potatoes, oyster mushrooms
$24

Sauté Calves Liver with Roasted Shallot and Pinot Noir
a braise of wild mushrooms, spinach flan
$18

Simple Grills over Oak Charcoal

accompaniment of grilled season vegetables and crisp potato tart
$19

Bell's Farm Chicken Breast
◆
Black Angus Sirloin Paillard
◆
Escalope of Norwegian Salmon
◆
"Minute" of Yellowfin Tuna

Complement of Steamed Vegetables
$5

(Please note our fish is prepared slightly underdone.)

Dinner: Mon - Thurs 5:30 - 10:30, Fri - Sat 5:30 - 11

Beekman 1766 Tavern, The

Larry Forgione has breathed new life into what is the oldest continually operating inn in America. The charming colonial tavern rooms now serve excellent contemporary American fare, featuring food products from the Hudson Valley.

Menu Changes Seasonally

APPETIZERS

Jerk Spiced Grilled Chicken Wrapped in Roti
with a banana tamarind salsa and field greens 8.50

Field Salad of Tossed Lettuces and Greens
with a fresh herb vinaigrette or an Iowa Blue cheese dressing 5.95

The Beekman Caesar Salad
with shaved aged jack and croutons 6.95

Charred Carpaccio of Beef Tenderloin
drizzled with roast garlic oil, shaved asiago cheese, and spring dandelion salad with olives 9.95

House Smoked Salmon and Potato Crisp "Napoleon"
layered with lemon cream and drizzled with chive oil 9.95

Roasted Local Vegetable Terrine with Coach Farms Goat Cheese
with a red pepper coulis 8.50

Hudson Valley Camembert Crisp with Local Venison Proscuitto
served with a cherry gooseberry chutney and field greens 10.95

Summer Salad
vine ripened local tomatoes, sweet vidalia onions, roast garlic,
white beans and fresh oregano with black olive crostini 6.95

4 Mill St • Rhinebeck, NY • (914) 871-1766

MAIN COURSES

Cedar Planked Atlantic Salmon with a Charred Tomato Vinaigrette
served with an Indian flatbread 'pizza' of plum tomatoes and wilted arugula 21.95

Grilled Montauk Yellowfin Tuna " Brick "
with adobo splashed New Mexican Yellow Mole, black bean puree and tortilla crisps 22.95

Pan Seared Day Boat Cod with Black Olive Whipped Potatoes
served with fresh fava beans and tomato fondue scented with basil 17.95

Pan Roasted Maine Sea Scallops with a Tomato Thyme Oil
and a white bean salad with preserved lemons and smoked tomatoes 19.95

Fresh Cavatelli Pasta with Summer Squashes
stewed local tomatoes, fresh basil, and aged sonoma jack cheese 15.95

Herb Rubbed Whole Roasted Free Range Poussin with Natural Jus
atop a springtime ragout of morels, asparagus and fiddlehead ferns with roasted red bliss potatoes 18.95

Roast Adirondack Free Range Duck
with spring vegetables, orzo pilaf and plumped figs in a natural jus 20.50

Wood Grilled Double Lamb Chops with Merguez
and a baby vegetable skewer on a bed of couscous and natural lamb jus 22.00

Grilled Center Cut Pork Scallopini with Potato Pancakes
with a curried Hudson Valley apple chutney and spring vegetables 16.95

Charred Filet of Beef with Braised Spring Shallots
on a bed on horseradish spiked whipped potatoes with roasted baby carrots and a Pinot Noir sauce 24.00

Larry Forgione, Proprietor ***Melissa Kelly, Chef***

James Beard
'The truth is one must be inspired to cook. For you know, we always learn from others and end up teaching ourselves.'
Friend and Mentor

Dinner: Mon - Thurs 5:30 - 9, Fri - Sat 5:30 - 9:30, Sun 3:30 - 8:30

Bridge Cafe, The

Long before the South Street Seaport became a tourist mecca, this authentic, circa 1850 pub-style restaurant (with tin ceiling, wooden floor, and room-length mirrored bar) attracted people to the waterfront. The fare is "modern" American.

BRIDGE CAFE

Menu Changes Every Five Weeks

DINNER

Consomme Christina / lemongrass, bean thread noodles & julienne vegetables $4.95

Sorrel, Lemon & New Potato Chowder $4.95

Seasonal Salad / shallot vinaigrette $5.95

Buffalo Mozzarella & Tomato / black & green olives $6.50

Savory Lamb Turnover / moroccan spices, red pepper & chickpea salad $6.95

Herb Breaded Calamari / spicy tomato mayonnaise $6.95

Five Grain Salad / asparagus, morels & pecan dressing $7.25

John's Fennel Stuffed Clams $7.25

Medallions of Swordfish / tomato, eggplant & black olive oil $7.95

Smoked Scottish Salmon / pickled sea beans $8.95

* * * * * *

279 Water St • TriBeCa/Downtown/Chinatown • (212) 227-3344

Prince Edward Island Mussels
steamed in white wine, shallots & basil

appetizer	entree
$5.95	$11.95

* * * * * *

Penne Pasta / *tiny meatballs & vodka sauce* $11.95

Egg Linguine / *spring vegetables, olive oil & herbs* $12.95

Lemon Tagliatelle / *artichokes, olives & parsley* $12.95

Warm Asparagus Salad / *baby red field lettuce & tarragon vinaigrette* $13.95

Angel Hair Pasta / *parmesan cream, fresh peas & bacon* $13.95

Roulade of Chicken / *ricotta, zucchini & herbs* $14.50

Grilled Medallions of Chicken / *saffron, roasted garlic & red pepper rice* $14.50

Grilled Red Trout / *fennel & onion salad* $15.50

Spring Lamb Stew Moroccan Style / *preserved lemons, olives & cous cous* $15.95

Grilled Lamb Loin Chops / *red wine, mint & asparagus* $15.95

Roast Duck / *green peppercorn sauce* $16.25

Soft Shell Crab / *scallion butter & lemon* $17.50

Poached Halibut / *ginger broth with watercress, lemon balm & squash blossoms* $17.50

Grilled N.Y. Strip Steak / *madeira sauce & herbed potato puree* $17.95

Pan Seared Buffalo Steak / *served sliced on a bed of fancy greens with blackberries & grilled portobello mushrooms* $18.95

* *Special dietary requests gladly accommmodated*

Dinner: Sun - Mon 4:45 - 10, Tues - Sat 4:45 - 12

Cafe Botanica

As part of its multmilion dollar upgrade of the Essex House, the Nikko hotel chain installed this beautiful, flower-filled and themed restaurant in the front, with views of Central Park. It's most popular for breakfast and lunch.

Menu Changes Weekly & Seasonally

LUNCH

Appetizers and Salads

Maryland Crabcake with Corn Salad,
Roasted Peppers and Tomato Vinaigrette $12.00

Ragout of Scallops, Shrimp, Clams and Mussels $10.50

Roasted Chicken Salad with Watercress, Walnuts,
Red Peppercorns, Raspberry Vinaigrette $14.00

Pizza and Sandwiches

Vegetable Calzone with Asparagus, Wild Mushrooms,
Zucchini and Goat Cheese $14.00

Pancetta, Fresh Tomatoes and Sage Pizza $16.00

Shrimp Sausage and Black Olives Pizza $16.00

Grilled Sirloin Steak Sandwich on Olive Baguette with
Mixed Field Greens $18.00

Main Courses

Capellini with Morrell Mushrooms, Fava Beans and Asparagus,
Herbs de Provence and Shaved Aged Parmegiano $17.00

Sauteed Grouper with Ratatouille,
Coulis of Fennel $19.00

Seared Tuna with Confit of Endives $19.50

Grilled Salmon with Spaghetti of Yellow Squash and Zucchini,
Fresh Thyme Sauce $18.50

Sauteed Breast of Chicken with
Ragout of Young Vegetables $18.00

Essex House • 160 Central Park South • Midtown West Side • (212) 484-5120

DINNER

Appetizers

Carpaccio of Tuna with New Potatoes Salad $11.50

Ragout of Scallops, Shrimp, Clams and Mussels $10.50

Capellini with Morell Mushrooms, Fava Beans and Asparagus, Herbs de Provence and Shaved Aged Parmegiano $9.00

Couscous Salad with Julienne of Duck and Confit of Kumquats $9.50

Maryland Crabcake with Corn Salad, Roasted Pepper and Tomato Vinaigrette $12.00

Purse of Phyllo Dough with Shiitaki Mushrooms and Goat Cheese $9.00

Cold Melon Soup $7.00

Soup of the Day $6.50

Main Courses

Grilled Salmon with Spaghetti of Yellow Squash and Zucchini, Fresh Thyme Sauce $18.50

Sauteed Jumbo Shrimp and Radicchio Risotto $19.00

Sauteed Grouper with Ratatouille, Coulis of Fennel $19.00

Seared Tuna with Confit of Endives $19.50

Pan Fried Veal T-Bone with Roasted Peppers, Broccoli, Raisins and Pignoli Nuts $23.00

Sauteed Breast of Chicken with Ragout of Young Vegetables $18.00

Grilled Porterhouse Steak with Mashed Potatoes and Chives $27.00

Roasted Rack of Lamb with Eggplant Gratin $25.00

We would appreciate your refraining from cigar or pipe smoking while in the restaurant

Dinner: 7 Days a Week 5:30 - 12

Those who've been there (it's relatively new) think this is one of the best restaurants in the city. The room is comfortable and the food is delicious, creative, and beautifully presented.

RESTAURANT & BAR

Menu Changes Seasonally Along With Daily Specials

DINNER APPETIZERS

SOUP DU JOUR

MIXED MESCLUN SALAD 6.00
seasonal lettuces, extra virgin olive oil,sage and lemon juice

WARM GOAT CHEESE TART 6.75
with grilled eggplant and tomato

GRILLED PORTOBELLO AND ARUGULA SALAD 7.50

CRABMEAT AND AVOCADO FILLED ENDIVE 7.50
scallion vinaigrette

CALAMARI AND CHICKPEA SALAD 6.50
baby frisee, cumin mint dressing

CEASAR SALAD 7.50
garlic croutons

"CARPACCIO" OF BEEF, COFFEE BEAN MARINATED SIRLOIN 8.50
house cured wild mushrooms, tomato concassé

FRESH OYSTERS ON THE HALF SHELL ***
sauce mignonette

CHILLED MIXED SHELLFISH PLATTER FOR TWO 24.50
lobster, shrimp, oysters and mussels

SAUTEED SALMON CAKE, JALAPENO TARTAR SAUCE 8.75
marinated red cabbage

55 W 21st St • Chelsea • (212) 929-0740

DINNER ENTREES

SEARED TUNA SALAD 14.50
on arugula, endive in pineapple, ginger, soy and lime juice

GRILLED JUMBO SHRIMP 16.50
cous cous salad with celantro, mint and harissa sauce

TRICOLOR FETTUCCINI AND SAUTEED SEA SCALLOPS 14.50
roasted peppers, basil cream sauce

LINGUINI AND GRILLED SHRIMP 14.50
tossed with arugula, radicchio, lemon, ginger and extra virgin olive oil

PAN SEARED, HERB CRUSTED SWORDFISH 18.75
niçoise olives, tomato and scallion sauce

FILO WRAPPED SALMON FILLET 18.50
citrus supremes and fried baby eggplant crisps

BRAISED CODFISH PROVENÇAL 16.75
in white wine and herbs, served on mashed potatoes

FREE RANGE POUSSIN TAGINE 16.25
onion, zucchini, new potatoes, raisins

HONEY AND HERB GLAZED DUCK 18.50
wild rice croquettes, white turnip confit

BRAISED RABBIT 17.50
in white wine with preserved lemon and green olives

STEAMED MARINATED BABY LAMB 19.75
moroccan spices, cous cous

STEAK FRITES 19.50
grilled, aged sirloin au pôivre or plain

WIENERSCHNITZEL 15.50
breaded veal paillard with parsley potatoes and cucumber salad

MEDITERRANEAN VEGETABLE PLATE 12.75
marinated in herbs, lemon juice, olive oil, minted tabouleh salad

SAFFRON RISOTTO PRIMAVERA 14.50
celery and tomato broths, garden vegetables

Dinner: Sun - Thurs 5:30 - 11, Fri - Sat 5:30 - 12

A few years ago a number of chefs decided that what was needed was a restaurant where they could hang out after hours. The result was Chefs & Cuisiniers Club. It's still popular with chefs, who come after work, and the rest of us.

CHEFS • CUISINIERS • CLUB

APPETIZERS

Braised Veal and Sage Raviolis
drizzled with sage brown butter and tomato concasee
$7.50

Chefs Club Daily Soup
$6.00

Tasting Plate of Babaghanough, Hommous and Tabbouleh
$8.50

Summer Tuscan Bread and Tomato Salad
panzenella style with fresh basil and shaved ricotta
$8.00

Duck Terrine and Duck Liver Mousse Pairing
with plum fruits and spicy greens
$9.00

Sautéed Fresh Sardines with Basil Potatoes and Nicoise Olives
$8.00

Simple Salad with Spicy Greens and Red Wine Vinaigrette
$6.00

Crisped Calamari with Spicy Coriander Mayonnaise
$8.00

Composed Duck Confit Salad with Lentil Vinaigrette
$7.50

Half Dozen Market Oysters
with traditional migonette
$9.00

Carpaccio of Yellowfin Tuna with Lemongrass Vinaigrette
bed of frisée and wasabe cream
$9.00

36 East 22nd St • Murray Hill/Kips Bay • (212) 228-4399

MAIN COURSE

Pasta Special

Grilled Tuna Steak with Crisp Polenta Cakes
caramelized fennel hash and warm balsamic jus
$17.50

Wood Grilled Salmon with Roast Eggplant-Potato Purée
cured tomatoes and fresh basil
$18

Sautéed Soft Shell Crabs over New Asparagus
roast sweet pepper and caper pan sauce
$16.50

Pan Seared Duck Breast with Confit Potato Cake
duck essence with citrus and green pepper corns
$19

Grilled N.Y. Sirloin with Classic French Fries
roasted vegetables
$19.50

SIDE DISHES

$3.50

Roasted Vegetables, Puree Potato, Sauté Spinach, French Fries

◆◆◆

MONDAY: Calves Liver
TUESDAY: Bouillabaisse
WEDNESDAY: Grilled Leg of Lamb
THURSDAY: Crabcakes
FRIDAY: Fulton Market Special
SATURDAY: Veal Chop

PLEASE NOTE: THEY TOW AT 11 P.M. (Special Parking Rates Available Next Door)

Dinner: Mon - Sat 5:30 - 12

City Cafe

This bright white, contemporary newcomer is very popular with its neighbors on the Upper East Side, and the owners seem to know everyone. The upscale American food is delicious and creatively presented.

Menu Changes Periodically

Marc Salonsky
Chef de Cuisine
Eric Miller
Chef/Proprietor

APPETIZERS

Oyster Mary	2.50
Cold spring asparagus soup with fresh chive	6.00
Seasonal green salad with balsamic vinaigrette and potato crisps	6.00
Salad of chopped greens and vegetables with baked goat cheese/roast pepper cake and fried red onion rings	8.00
Steamed Manilla clams with bacon, broccoli rape and ginger broth	9.00
Grilled gulf shrimp with avocado/corn salsa and fried wontons	10.00
Jumbo lump crab and salmon cake with crisp fried zucchini	10.00

1481 York Ave • Upper East Side • (212) 570-9810

PASTA

Ravioli of wild mushrooms with sun-dried tomatoes and rosemary	9.00/17.00
Farfalle with Italian sausage, sweet peppers, black olives and warm mozzarella	9.00/16.00
Capellini with bay scallops, grilled fennel and fresh tomato	10.00/19.00

MAIN COURSES

Herb roasted chicken with whipped potatoes and spring vegetables	16.00
Grilled loin of pork with crispy onions and honey-mustard sauce	19.00
Crisp-roasted duckling with brandied cherry polenta and cinnamon jus	20.00
Filet of lamb with crispy potato fries, wilted greens and ginger peppercorn sauce	20.00
Grilled filet mignon with apple pancake, shoestring yams and balsamic glaze	22.00
Grilled hamburger with jack cheese, red cabbage slaw and crispy potato fries	11.00
Tarragon seared steak cod with roast Portabellos and raspberry-shallot coulis	18.00
Spiced salmon in phyllo with baby artichokes and citrus vinaigrette	20.00
Sea scallops with minestrone vegetables, couscous and cured olive compote	20.00
Rare grilled yellowfin tuna with curried vegetable vermicelli and cilantro jus	22.00

PLEASE: NO CIGAR OR PIPE SMOKING
MASTERCARD AND VISA ACCEPTED
WE DO NOT SERVE GENETICALLY ENGINEERED FOODS

Dinner: Mon - Sat 6 - 11, Sun 6 - 10

Brendan Walsh made culinary history in New York when he created Southwestern style cuisine at Arizona 206. His next move was to this restaurant on Long Island, where he remains as consulting chef, lending his star quality to the endeavor.

Menu Changes Seasonally

Coyote's Summer Menu

Appetizers

HOUSE SMOKED SALMON SOFT TACO *w/ lime crema* $8.50
SOUTHWESTERN CHICKEN WINGS *w/ cilantro jelly* $6.50
VEGETABLE RELLENO *w/ gazpacho coulis* $6.50
BLUE CORN FRIED OYSTERS *w/ charred tomato salsa* $7.50
CHICKEN AND RED CHILE SAUSAGE *w/ sweet pepper puree* $6.50
GULF SHRIMP AND SCALLION QUESADILLA $7.50
GUACAMOLE AND CHIPS *w/ blue and yellow corn chips* $6.50
SEAFOOD ESCABECHE *(shrimp, scallop, squid and crab)* $9.00
MARKET SALAD *w/ citrus vinaigrette* $5.50
COYOTE CAESAR SALAD $6.50
w/ crispy fried hominy and queso blanco

Bowls of Soup

BLACK BEAN SOUP *w/ sour cream and salsa cruda* $4.00
SOUP OF THE DAY $3.50

104 Waterview Rd • Island Park, NY • (516) 889-8009

Entree Salads

GRILLED FILLET OF SALMON $18.50
w/ vegetable couscous and roast pepper vinaigrette

PAN SEARED DUCK SALAD $15.50
w/ wild mushrooms, spinach and orange

WARM LOBSTER SALAD *w/ grilled herb brioche* $19.50

Grills

SOUTHWESTERN RIB-EYE STEAK (16oz) *w/ herb marinade* $19.50

SKIRT STEAK TORTILLA *w/ slow-cooked onions and chiles* $16.50

FREE RANGE LAMB TENDERLOIN $19.50
w/ mushroom tamale and red chile tomatoes

HICKORY GRILLED VEAL CHOP $21.50
w/ coriander sauce and vegetable tart

From the Range

SEARED SEA SCALLOPS AND PASTA $16.50
w/ tomato-cumin sauce and pumpkin seed pesto

CHILE RUBBED CHICKEN $15.50
w/ corn, black bean and sour grass stew

ROASTED WHOLE LOBSTER .... (Market)
w/ lime butter and corn stuffing

CHICKEN QUESADILLA *w/ grilled vegetables and salsa* $14.50

FRESH SEAFOOD SPECIALS .... (Prepared Daily)

Sides

SUMMER VEGETABLE $3.50

HELL'S FIRE FRIES $4.00

TEXAS MASHED POTATOES $2.50

TOBACCO ONION RINGS $4.00

B.B.Q. BEANS $2.50

Coyote Grill is available for private parties.

Charge Lun Din Sun Bru

Dinner: Mon - Thurs 5 - 10, Fri - Sat 5 - 11

Lots of people have been talking about this new place in TriBeCa. They serve a more contemporary than traditional menu, with seasonal produce that's fresh from the farm and a large variety of pasta dishes.

DUANE PARK CAFÉ

Menu Changes Seasonally

Appetizers

Grilled Miso Marinated Duck Salad with Arugula 8.

Grilled Shrimp and Calamari with Skordalia and Olives 7.

Sauteed Sweetbreads with Polenta, Porcini and Cabernet 8.

Mixed Baby Field Greens with Shaved Fennel and Reggiano Parmesan 6.

Tea Smoked Chicken and Shiitake Salad with Hazelnut-Leek Vinaigrette 8.

Crispy Quail with Pumpkin Spaetzle and Roasted Garlic Cream 9.

House Cured Basil Gravlax with Cucumber and Creme Fraiche 9.

Warm Red Cabbage Salad with Gorgonzola, Bacon and Pecans 7.

Pastas

Fresh Herb Pappardelle with Wild Mushroom Sauce 13.

Rigatoni with Duck Confit, Artichokes and Ovendried Tomatoes 15.

Butternut Squash Agnolotti with Mascarpone, Sage and Toasted Almonds 13.

Pistachio Tagliatelle with Asparagus and Parmesan 14.

Entrees

Crispy Skate with Ponzu Dipping Sauce 17.

Boneless Catskill Trout with Mushroom Risotto 20.

Roasted Rack of Lamb with Garlic Potato Ravioli 21.

Seared Salmon with Rosemary-Citrus Essence and Orange Lentil Pilaf 19.

Herb Crusted Chicken with Bruschetta Stuffing and Whipped White Beans 16.

Roasted Halibut with Fresh Herb Crust and Tomato-Horseradish Coulis 18.

Pan Blackened Cajun Ribeye Steak with Roasted Potatoes 22.

Mustard Grilled Tuna with Potato- Leek Gratin 19.

Desserts

Goat Cheesecake with Fresh Blackberries and Coulis 6.

Cherry Fitters with Vanilla Ice Cream and Apricot Caramel 7.

Bittersweet Chocolate Strudel with Hazelnut Praline Ice Cream 7.

Cornmeal Savarin with Strawberries, Lemon and Kirsch 6.

Warm Banana-Pecan Tartlet with Banana-Rum Caramel 6.

Assorted Sorbets: Lemongrass, Tangerine, Pomegranate, Spearmint and Crenshaw Melon...choice of three 5.

Dinner: Mon - Fri 5:30 - 10, Sat 5:30 - 11

E.A.T.

Notorious for its high prices, this Upper East Side cafe is nonetheless popular with a tony crowd for excellent omelettes, salads, and baked goods. Owner Eli Zabar is one of the premier bread bakers in the city.

Menu Changes Seasonally

SOUP

Carrot $8.00
Chicken Vegetable $8.00
Mushroom Barley $8.00
Mediteranean Vegetable $8.00

SANDWICH PLATES

Focaccia Sandwich $12.00
P.L.T. Sandwich $12.00
Country Sandwich $12.00
Egg Salad $14.00
Chopped Liver on Raisin Nut. $14.00
*Cucumber & Chevre $12.50
*Tomato & Mozzarella $14.00
Meat Loaf $14.50
Tower of Bagel $16.00
Chicken Salad $16.00
Whitefish Salad $16.00
Turkey Club $18.00
Smoked Salmon $18.00
Grilled Cheese $14.00
Grilled Ham & Cheese $14.50

*only available on Eli's Bread

SALADS

Choice of Two Salads $14.50
Choice of Three Salads $18.00

- Cucumber & Dill
- French Potato
- Confetti Rice
- Celeri Remoulade
- Beets
- Lentil
- Tuscan Salad
- Mushrooms w/-Grilled Leek Garnish
- Tomato & Proscuitto
- Tomato & Mozzarella
- Egg Salad
- Four Bean Salad
- Broccoli & Garlic
- Avocado & Endive
- Haricots Vert
- Potato, Fennel & Haricot Vert
- Asparagus
- Pasta with Tomato & Basil
- Chicken Salad

E.A.T.S.

Quiche & Salad $14.00
Ratatouille Pizza & Salad $14.50
Omelet & Salad $14.50
Fruit & Cheese $16.00
Melon & Proscuitto $12.00
Potato Pancakes & Applesauce $14.50
Scrambled Eggs & Salmon $12.00
Field Salad & Warm Chevre $12.00
Grilled Chicken Salad $16.00
Grilled Free Range Chicken $16.00
Salad Nicoise w/-Swordfish $22.00
Smoked Salmon $24.00
Grilled Salmon $24.00
Smoked Fish Plate $24.00

BELUGA CAVIAR

Omelet ....
Blinis ....
Potato Skins w/-Creme Fraiche

SIDE ORDERS

Cup of Soup $6.00
Field Salad $7.00
Side Salad $8.00
Side of Whitefish Salad $10.00
Side of Calamari Salad $10.00
Parmesan Toast $6.00

TO DRINK

Coffee $2.50
Expresso $3.00
Cappucino $4.50
Tea $2.00
Orange Juice $3.00
Unsweetened Lemonade $2.00
Berry Spritzer $3.00
Saratoga Water $2.00
Mineral Water $2.00

1064 Madison Ave • Upper East Side • (212) 772-0022

DINNER

SOUPS
Chicken Vegetable $8.00
Mushroom Barley $8.00
Carrot $8.00
Mediterrean Vegetable $8.00
Potato Leek $8.00

COLD APPETIZERS
Tomato & Mozzarella $8.00
Pickled Herring w/-Onions & Cream $8.00
Field Salad w/-Warm Chevre $12.00
Grilled Vegetables $12.00
Prosciutto & Melon $12.00
Calamari Salad $12.00
Whitefish Salad $12.00
Mussels Remoulade $10.00
Smoked Salmon $20.00
Three Salad Plate ....$1200/$18.00
- •cucumber & dill
- •french potato
- •celeri remoulade
- •beets
- •three bean
- •mushrooms W/- grilled leek garnish
- •tomato & prociutto
- •egg & dill
- •broccoli & garlic
- •avocado & endive
- •haricots vert
- •asparagus
- •pasta w/-tomato & basil
- •chicken
- •grilled artichokes
- •potato, fennel & haricots vert

HOT APPETIZERS
Warm Lentil Salad $8.00
Ratatouille Pizza $10.00
Steamed Mussels $14.00
Fried Calamari $14.00
Fried Clams w/-Tartar Sauce... $14.00
Potato Skins & Beluga Caviar.. $28.00

COLD PLATES
Grilled Chicken Salad $16.00
Smoked Fish Plate $24.00
Turkey Club Sandwich $18.00
Fruit & Cheese $16.00
Spinach Salad w/-Feta & Tomatoes $12.00

PASTA
Pasta w/-Tomato & Basil......... $14.00
Pasta w/-Broccoli & Basil Puree. $14.00
Pasta w/-Fresh Vegetables $16.00
Pasta w/-Calamari Marinara... $16.00
Pasta w/-Clam Sauce $18.00
Seafood Marinara $20.00

SEAFOOD
Grilled Swordfish w/-Cornichons. $24.00
Grilled Stuffed Salmon $24.00
Fresh Grilled Shrimp $24.00
Crab Cakes w/-Field Salad....... $24.00
Salmon Paillard w/-Spinach $24.00

POULTRY
Chicken Breast -Spinach & Ricotta Stuffing . $18.00
Grilled Chicken w/-Mashed Potatoes $22.00
Barbequed Chicken w/-Cole Slaw .. $18.00

MEAT
Pot Roast, Potatoes & Carrots . $24.00
Meat Loaf w/-Fresh Tomato Sauce . $22.00
Veal Chop w/-Garlic Cloves...... $28.00
Steak & Onion Rings $24.00
Hamburger & Onion Rings $18.00

SIDE ORDERS
Green Salad $7.00
Mashed Potatoes $5.00
Fried Onion Rings $8.00
Kasha Varnishkas $8.00
Macaroni & Cheese $8.00
Potato Dauphinoise $8.00
Applesauce $5.00

SUPPER
Omelet & Field Salad............... $14.00
Beluga Caviar Omelet............... $28.00
Fried Eggs & Country Ham $14.00
Scrambled Eggs & Smoked Salmon $12.00
Scrambled Eggs & Chicken Livers $14.00
Potato Pancakes & Applesauce... $12.00
Grilled Ham & Cheese Sandwich. $14.50

Service Is Not Included • We Only Accept The American Express Card
EVERYTHING COMES WITH ELI'S BREAD

Dinner: 7 Days a Week until 10

East Hampton Point

Although this restaurant just opened in the past few months, it's already a huge success because of the professional clout and capabilities of Drew Nieporent. He's also hired a very talented chef, Jerry Hayden, with an excellent background, so it's got all the right credentials.

EAST HAMPTON POINT

Menu Changes Seasonally Along With Daily Specials

Sweet Corn and Clam Chowder 6.

Roasted Vegetable Terrine with Mushroom Vinaigrette 7.

Crab and Cod Cakes with Celery Root Remoulade 8.

Country Salad with Pancetta and Parmesan 7.

Seared Tuna Tart with Marinated Tomato and Sweet Basil 9.

Spicy Duck Salad with Honey Lime Dressing 8.

Field Green Salad 6.

Clams on the Half Shell 8.

Oysters on the Half Shell 9.

Mustard Glazed Chicken, Whipped Parsnips, Roast Shallot Sauce 17.

Barbequed Braised Lamb Shanks over Red Onion and Corn Risotto 17.

295 Three Mile Harbor Rd • East Hampton, NY • (516) 329-2800

Charcoal Grilled Long Island Duck Breast, Caramelized Apples, Calvados Sauce 21.

Seared Swordfish, Vegetable Couscous, Tomato Curry Vinaigrette 22.

Roasted "Cape" Cod with Eggplant Fondue 19.

Market Fish, Plain Grilled p/a

Steamed Red Snapper with a Vegetable Pistou Broth 22.

Sirloin Steak with a Sweet Onion and Dark Beer Sauce, Potato Pancake 22.

Bonacker Shellfish Stew with Fresh Herbs 23.

Shelled Two Pound Lobster with Lemon Butter p/a

Roast Chicken with Whipped Potatoes 17.

Pasta Special p/a

Creme Brulee 5.

Chocolate Hazelnut Torte 5.

Seasonal Berry Tart 5.

Ice Cream and Sorbet Selection 5.

Jasmine and Citrus Napoleon 5.

Carmelized Banana Financier 5.

Chef: Gerard Hayden Sous Chefs: Joseph Fortunato Robert Kirchhoff

Pastry Chef: Chad Vanderslice

Dinner: 7 Days a Week 5:30 - 11

The Four Seasons still retains its cachet, even after more than a quarter century. It remains on the cutting edge of food presentation and service. Stefano Battastini is the talented new chef. No list would be complete without this legendary star.

THE FOUR SEASONS

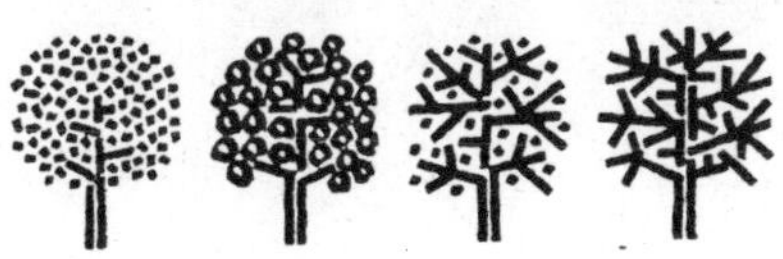

Menu Changes Daily

COLD APPETIZERS

A Service of SHRIMP	18.50
LITTLENECKS, A Platter	10.50
Cherrystone CLAMS	10.50
CRAB Lump Cocktail	18.50
A Selection of OYSTERS	13.50
Smoked Scottish SALMON	25.00
Beluga CAVIAR	
Parma PROSCIUTTO with Red Papaya	15.50
A FOIE GRAS Terrine	25.00
Smoked Scottish SALMON Roulade with Caviar	25.00
Marinated Spring VEGETABLES with Mozzarella and Basil	15.00
TUNA Carpaccio with Ginger and Coriander	14.00

HOT APPETIZERS

Rabbit RAVIOLI	16.00
Braised FROGS' LEGS on Savoy Cabbage	14.50
Sautéed Fresh FOIE GRAS	25.00
Crisp SHRIMP with Mustard Fruits	18.50

SOUPS

SORREL and CRAYFISH Chowder	11.50
DUCK Consommé	9.50
Chilled ASPARAGUS and CRABMEAT	11.00

SPA CUISINE ®

APPETIZERS:
A Lambs Lettuce and Crayfish SALAD 14.00
MUSSELS in Green Chili Sauce 13.00

MAIN COURSES:
Roast Loin of RABBIT with Asparagus and Bulgur 32.00
Grilled SEA SCALLOPS with Fava Beans 33.00

99 East 52nd St • Midtown East Side • (212) 754-9494

THIS EVENING'S ENTREES

Pan Fried SOFT SHELL CRABS with Herb Lemon Butter and Crisp Snow Peas 35.00
Filet of RED SNAPPER with Green Asparagus and Red Merlot Sauce 37.00
CRABMEAT Cakes with Crisp Taro Root 35.00
Maine LOBSTER: Broiled, Poached or Steamed 40.00
DOVER SOLE Meunière or Broiled 45.00
Roast Loin of Spring LAMB with Morels 37.00
Grilled LAMB CHOPS with Truffled String Beans 36.50
Sautéed CALF'S LIVER with Smothered Sweet Onions 34.00
VEAL Four Seasons with Porcini Dumplings and Spring Carrots 39.00
Aged Prime SIRLOIN STEAK, Bordelaise Sauce and Cannelini Beans 39.00
Grilled FILET MIGNON, Béarnaise and Snow Peas 39.00
Barbecued Whole SWEETBREADS with Zucchini and Pepper Tart 35.00
A Skewer of Grilled VEGETABLES and WILD MUSHROOMS, Bulgur and Avocado 29.00

FOR TWO (PER PERSON)

Baked Whole SEA BASS with Roasted Peppers and Spring Vegetables 39.00
Roast Darn of SALMON with Herb Sauce 38.50
Crisp Farmhouse DUCK: Au Poivre or with Rhubarb Compote 39.00
Roast Rack of LAMB with Zucchini and Pepper Timbale 40.00
CHATEAUBRIAND with Béarnaise, Snow Peas and Wild Mushrooms 45.00

SALADS, VEGETABLES AND POTATOES

Raw MUSHROOMS, Pepper Dressing	8.50
Wilted SPINACH and Bacon	9.00
Spring GREENS	8.50
Steamed GREEN ASPARAGUS	10.00
Spring CARROTS	8.00
Baked CANNELINI BEANS with Herbs	7.00
WILD RICE with Pine Nuts	9.00
Sautéed WILD MUSHROOMS	9.50
SNOW PEA Pods with Shoyu	8.00
Baked POTATO	6.00
ROESTI	6.50

DESSERTS

A Selection from the DESSERT WAGON	8.50
SHERBETS and ICE CREAMS	6.50
Choice of STRAWBERRY, MACADAMIA COCONUT or GRAND MARNIER Soufflé	8.50
Frozen MOCHA Soufflé	8.50

Dinner: Mon - Sat 5 - 11:30

Gotham is one of the finest restaurants in New York City. Chef Alfred Portale, one of New York's most talented, turns out exceptionally creative, original dishes and the spacious, modern interior is very "New York." Everyone loves Gotham.

First Course

Menu Changes Seasonally

SELECT OYSTERS AND CLAMS
Served Chilled with Cocktail Sauce and Champagne Mignonette Priced Daily

SAUTÉED SKATE WINGS
Artichoke Bottom, White Bean Salad and Browned Butter $10.50

DUCK TERRINE
Haricot Vert and Green Lentil Salad, Pickled Onion and Port Glaze $12.50

SAUTÉED SEA SCALLOPS
Napa Cabbage, Caviar and Crème Fraîche $13.50

WILD MUSHROOM RAVIOLI
Served in Mushroom Broth, with Chervil and White Truffle Oil $12.50

ASPARAGUS SALAD
Fingerlings, Quail Eggs, and Croutons, dressed in Lemon and Extra Virgin Olive Oil $11.00

WARM SQUAB AND FOIE GRAS
With Fingerling Potatoes and Wild Huckleberry Sauce $18.00

SEARED ATLANTIC MACKEREL
Grilled Tomatoes, Arugula and Chickpea Salad $11.50

COLD SMOKED SALMON WITH WARM POTATO GALETTE
Crème Fraîche, Salmon Roe, Chives and Chervil $14.00

SEAFOOD SALAD
Scallops, Squid, Japanese Octopus, Shrimp and Avocado, dressed in Lemon and Extra Virgin Olive Oil $12.50

GOAT CHEESE SALAD
Grilled Spring Leek, Lettuces, Sweet Peas and Beet $12.50

OREGON MOREL RISOTTO
With Roasted Quail, Savory, Asparagus and Pea Leaves $16.00

12 East 12th St • Greenwich Village • (212) 620-4020

Second Course

SAUTÉED HALIBUT
Grilled Fennel, Braised Artichoke, Dill and Green Pepper Vinaigrette $28.50

SEARED YELLOW FIN TUNA
Rosemary, Savory, Pappardelle and Caponata $28.50

ROAST MONKFISH
Manila Clams, Linguiça, Chard and Confit Tomato $26.50

GRILLED SWORDFISH
Fennel, Tomato, Green Olive Tapenade and Puréed Potatoes $29.00

RED SNAPPER
Roasted Potatoes, Whole Garlic, Olive Oil and Rosemary $27.50

SAUTÉED SOFT SHELL CRABS
Grilled Yellow and Green Squash, Cous-Cous and Arugula $28.00

SHELLFISH BOUILLABAISSE
Scallops, Prawns, Mussels, Squid and Crayfish in a Saffron-Shellfish Stock $28.50

GRILLED ATLANTIC SALMON
Served with Asparagus, Morels, Spring Onions and Chervil $28.50

SELECT GRILLED, STEAMED AND BRAISED VEGETABLES
Served with Pappardelle, White Beans and Oregon Black Truffle $25.00

MUSCOVY DUCK BREAST
In Red Wine Sauce, with Turnip, Parsnip, Bunch Carrots and Potato Purée $28.00

SADDLE OF RABBIT
Grilled, with Steamed Spinach, White Beans and Young Fennel $28.50

GRILLED SQUAB
Roasted Garlic, Pancetta, Crimini and Ratatouille $27.00

ROAST FREE RANGE CHICKEN
With Broccoli Rabe and Shoestring Potatoes $26.50

RACK OF LAMB
Spinach, Flageolet, Mustard and Sweet Garlic Custard $29.50

VEAL CHOP
Mustard Greens, Fava Beans and Rostï Potato $32.00

GRILLED NEW YORK STEAK
Crushed White Peppercorns, a Marrow Mustard Custard and Deep Fried Shallots $29.50

Chef de Cuisine: Alfred Portale

Dinner: Mon - Thurs 5:30 - 10, Fri - Sat 5:30 - 11, Sun 5:30 - 9:30

Hudson River Club

Located in the eye-catching World Financial Center, this place boasts a spectacular view overlooking the marina, Battery Park City and the Hudson River. In addition, it has an elegant, bi-level interior and creative American cuisine, by chef Waldy Malouf, with an emphasis on fresh ingredients from New York State.

HUDSON RIVER CLUB

Menu Changes Seasonally

APPETIZERS

GRILLED SWEETWATER PRAWNS
red pepper vinaigrette 16.

MINT CURED and APPLE SMOKED SALMON
caviar cream and black dirt red onion relish 14.

SMOKED QUAIL and GRILLED SHEEP'S MILK CHEESE
over greens with wild mushrooms 15.

ROASTED EAST COAST OYSTERS
stewed leeks and black peppercorns 14.

PUMPKIN APPLE SOUP with SMOKED HAM
spiced croutons 9.

SAUTÉED HUDSON VALLEY FOIE GRAS
"Tear of the Clouds" wine reduction 15.

ICE PLATE of GRILLED SHRIMP and LOCAL OYSTERS
tomato–horseradish sorbet 15.

SEARED TUNA and CRISP SQUID SALAD
candied lemon vinaigrette 15.

SCALLOP & YELLOW LENTIL SOUP
rosemary oil 9.

4 WFC • 250 Vesey St • TriBeCa/Downtown/Chinatown • (212) 786-1500

MAIN COURSES

STEWED FREE RANGE CHICKEN
wild mushrooms, foie gras sausage and red beet risotto 26.

BRAISED & ROASTED BEEF
caramelized onions and carrots, Rivendell Merlot sauce 29.

BRAISED SNOWSHOE HARE & MORELS
house made herbed noodles 27.

"WILD SHOT" PHEASANT in a NEW YORK PORT SAUCE
braised cabbage and napoleon of blue cheese 28.

SWORDFISH in a MUSTARD SEED CRUST
celeri-root potato cake and vegetable confetti 29.

RED SNAPPER wrapped in BACON
roasted garlic potato puree and braised fennel 27.

HALIBUT poached with WINTER ROOT VEGETABLES
carrot & leek vinaigrette 27.

MILLBROOK VENISON CHOPS
chestnut stuffing and Millbrook Cabernet vinaigrette 33.

VEAL CHOP with CHANTERELLES
pumpkin & acorn squash dumplings 31.

FILET of SALMON in WOVEN POTATOES
herb & lemon butter sauce 27.

RACK of LAMB
coriander & hard cider sauce, sweet potato and red cabbage 29.

GRILLED BLACK ANGUS 16oz. SIRLOIN
crisped onions and marinated shallots 34.

Dinner: 7 Days a Week 5 -10

The Laundry is a relaxed establishment located in central East Hampton where Hamptonites enjoy very good food in the welcoming and informal atmosphere that, indeed, was once a laundry.

LAUNDRY restaurant

Menu Changes Daily

APPETIZERS:

LOCAL OYSTERS ON THE HALF SHELL WITH TWO SAUCES $7.50

LOCAL LITTLE NECK CLAMS ON THE HALF SHELL $6.50

QUESADILLA OF BLACK BEANS, GARLIC SAUSAGE AND JACK CHEESE $5.50

GRILLED PORTABELLO MUSHROOMS WITH GARLIC, SAGE AND PARMESAN $7.00

SPINACH AND CHEESE FILLED RAVIOLI WITH MUSHROOMS AND HERBS $6.00

SMOKED ATLANTIC SALMON, OSSETRA CAVIAR, SOUR CREAM AND SEVEN GRAIN BREAD $10.50

CHILLED ASPARAGUS VINAIGRETTE $6.50

GRILLED BARBECUED BABYBACK RIBS $8.00

SWEET POTATO SKINS WITH YOGURT, HONEY AND MINT $5.50

SHRIMP COCKTAIL WITH TWO SAUCES $9.50

CARPACCIO OF AGED BEEF WITH MUSTARD VINAIGRETTE $8.50

FRESH MELON WITH PARMA PROSCIUTTO $8.50

SLICED TOMATO AND RED ONION WITH SHALLOT VINAIGRETTE AND FRESH BALSAMIC $8.00

FRESH MOZZARELLA WITH ROASTED PEPPERS, VIRGIN OLIVE OIL AND BALSAMIC $7.50

TAPAS: CHOICE OF TWO $10.50

: GRILLED BEEF WITH GINGER AND GARLIC

: FRIED CALAMARI WITH LEMON-HERB DIPPING SAUCE

: GRILLED SPICY CHICKEN TENDERS

: GRILLED APPLE CHICKEN SAUSAGES WITH ONION

SOUPS: MANHATTAN CLAM CHOWDER $4.50

SALADS: FARM SALAD WITH HOUSE VINAIGRETTE $6.50

: FARM SALAD WITH SHALLOT VINAIGRETTE AND CRUMBLED ROQUEFORT $7.50

: FARM SALAD WITH WARM GOAT CHEESE $7.50

: CAESAR SALAD $7.50

: GRILLED EGGPLANT, ENDIVE, SWEET PEPPERS, ZUCCHINI, FENNEL AND ONIONS WITH ARUGULA AND SHALLOT VINAIGRETTE $8.50

VEGETABLES: THE LAUNDRY'S MASHED POTATOES $4.00

: BASKET OF LAUNDRY FRENCH FRIES $3.50

: FRESH BAKED IDAHO POTATO $2.00

: FRESH SPINACH SAUTEED WITH GARLIC AND OLIVE OIL $4.00

MAIN COURSES:

PASTA: FRESH TAGLIATELLE TOSSED WITH ROASTED SWEET PEPPERS, FRESH GARLIC HOT RED PEPPER, WHITE WINE AND OLIVE OIL $16.50

: PENNE TOSSED WITH SUNDRIED TOMATOES, MUSHROOMS, FRESH HERBS, CHOPPED SHALLOTS AND BUTTER $17.00

LOBSTER CASTLEBAY $26.00

ROASTED SALMON WITH ZUCCHINI "SPAGHETTI" TOSSED WITH FRESH BASIL, THYME AND EXTRA VIRGIN OLIVE OIL; ROASTED POTATOES $21.00

GRILLED SWORDFISH STEAK WITH BACON, LETTUCE AND TOMATO, LAUNDRY TARTAR SAUCE; SAFFRON RICE $18.50

POACHED LOCAL STRIPED BASS SERVED CHILLED WITH SAUCE VERT AND FRESH GREENS WITH CUCUMBER AND TOMATO TOSSED IN VINAIGRETTE $21.00

ROASTED MEDALLIONS OF PORK WITH JAMAICAN JERK SPICE, AVOCADO SALSA AND GARLIC BUTTER SAUCE; SAFFRON RICE $18.00

SAUTEED CALVES LIVER WITH LOCAL RHUBARB; MASHED POTATOES $17.50

PAN ROASTED CHICKEN WITH FRESH ROSEMARY AND GARLIC; MASHED POTATOES $17.50

GRILLED NEW YORK SIRLOIN STRIP DRY AGED 14 DAYS; LAUNDRY FRIES $23.00

LAUNDRY HAMBURGER ANY STYLE; LAUNDRY FRIES $11.50

Dinner: 7 Days a Week 5:30 - 12

Lola

This place is wild and wacky, and serves great American food with a Caribbean accent. A band usually plays nightly, and it's very popular on Sunday when they feature a Gospel Jazz Brunch.

Menu Changes Seasonally

DINNER

First Plates

Fried Louisiana Shrimp *Asian barbecue sauce & peanut sauce*	$9.00
Gnocchi *prepared with seasonal items*	OPEN
Arugula & Frisee Salad *shaved pepper cheese & balsalmic vinaigrette*	$6.50
Cayenne Ribbon Onion Rings *Lola's original recipe*	$7.00
Crisp Calamari *spicy Thai sauce*	$6.50
Warm Wild Mushroom Salad *baby greens & mushroom vinaigrette*	$8.50
Seafood Puffed Pizza *shrimp, scallops, calamari, lobster, goat cheese, & basil*	$8.50
Seasonal Greens *sherry shallot vinaigrette*	$6.00
Caesar Salad & Garlic Poppyseed Breadsticks *baby red & green romaine with caesar vinaigrette*	$7.50
Jumbo Lump Blue Crab Cake *lime oil & mache*	$8.50
Mustard Glazed Quail & Vegetable Fried Rice	$9.00

30 West 22nd St • Chelsea • (212) 675-6700

D I N N E R

Second Plates

Grilled Veal Chop & Parsley Mashed Potatoes *wild mushroom, sweet corn, & fava bean ragout*	$24.00
Lola's 100 Spice Caribbean Fried Chicken *creamed corn & warm greens*	$19.50
Yellowfin Tuna & Crispy Baby Artichokes *white beans, red onion, & red wine vinaigrette*	$19.50
Grilled Free Range Chicken & Potato Dumplings *oyster mushrooms, green beans, & ginger broth*	$16.50
Spicy Short Ribs & Coo Coo *onion chile sauce & spinach*	$17.50
Grilled Lamb Chops & Beet Risotto *wilted spinach & cardamom infused sauce*	$24.50
Spicy Seared Swordfish & Tempura Oysters *fermented black bean sauce & leeks*	$24.00
Seared Snapper & Sea Scallops *tomato horseradish broth, leeks, & roasted red pepper rouille*	$22.50
Dry Aged Sirloin & Potato Gnocchi *roasted red onion, crisp arugula, & black pepper jus*	$25.50
Mustard Seed & Fennel Crusted Salmon *saffron sauce & blood orange glaze*	$20.00
Wild Mushroom Risotto & Field Greens *seasonal mushrooms*	$16.50
Sauteed Sea Scallops & Creamy Polenta *roasted shallot sauce & peas*	$19.50

Executive Chef Lynne Aronson

Dinner: Sun - Wed 6 - 12, Thurs - Sat 6 - 1

Chef Wayne Nish opened this restaurant a couple of years ago to great critical acclaim. He serves creative, stylish American food in a lovely, intimate townhouse setting - it's very popular and always crowded.

MARCH
NEW YORK

Menu Changes Seasonally

mesclun salad with herbs and baby tomatoes

tuna tart and tartare with roast vegetables

maine scallops with tomato coulis and gaufrette potatoes

napoleon of smoked trout with artichokes and ricotta cheese

open ravioli with crab in ginger and tomato broth

charred venison salad with wild mushrooms

confit of chicken salad with foie gras and morels

---

atlantic salmon with middle eastern spices and wild mushrooms

filet of grey sole with black truffles and white asparagus

shrimp tempura with pomegranate and spicy carrot sauces

($5.00 supplement)

405 East 58th St • Midtown East Side • (212) 838-9393

poached breast of chicken with thai oyster sauce and baby bok choy

confit and grilled duck with sweet and savory chutneys

aged sirloin of beef with garlic potatoes and caramelized shallots

rack of lamb with sweet mustard and herbed crust (\$5.00 supplement)

---

lemon and raspberry gratin with sesame wafer

crispy pancake with vanilla ice cream, mango and berries

warm walnut tart with hazelnut ice cream

spiced pear cake with lemon curd and cranberry sauce

warm valrhona chocolate cake with whipped cream

grapefruit and grapefruit sorbet in gin syrup with coriander seed

dessert sampler (\$10.00 supplement)

---

dinner price is fixed at \$50.00

wayne nish, chef/proprietor **joseph scalice,host/proprietor**

Dinner: Mon - Thurs 6 - 10, Fri - Sat 6 - 10:30

Mayflower Inn, The

The Mayflower Inn has the air of a British-style country house à la Ralph Lauren. The dining room is exquisite, with custom-made tableware and a view of the gracious, landscaped grounds; the food is as good as it gets - anywhere.

Menu Changes Seasonally

STARTERS

Mixed Seasonal Greens with a Balsamic Vinaigrette	5.25
Tomato Fish Soup with Macaroni and Pecorino Cheese	5.50
Steamed Snug Harbor Mussels	8.25
Rock Shrimp Cakes with Tomato Herb Aioli	8.75
Pizza with Roasted Shallots, Red Pepper, Taleggio and Mozzarella	8.50
Grilled Rabbit Strip Loin Salad with Coach Farm Chevre and Pancetta	7.75
Mayflower Smoked Salmon with Traditional Service	9.75
Grilled Marlin Pastrami with Fennel and Lobster Oil	8.25

PASTA

	Starter	Main Course
Linguine with Baby Artichokes, Rapini and Roma Tomatoes	7.50	15.00
Penne with Roasted Barbarie Duck Breast, Seared Foie Gras and Leeks	7.75	18.25

118 Woodbury Rd, Rt 47 • Washington, CT • (203) 868-1632

MAIN COURSES

Spring Vegetable Risotto with Asiago Cheese	16.00
Grilled Atlantic Swordfish with Tomato Cucumber Relish and Pommes Frites	19.75
Roasted Mahi Mahi on Red Lentils with Fava Beans, Lobster and Roasted Pearl Onions	21.00
Herb Roasted Natural Chicken with Mayflower Mashed Potatoes	15.50
Medallions of Lamb with Creamed Spinach and Morels	23.00
Grilled Veal Chop with Rhubarb Pepper Sauce and Pancetta Potatoes	24.00
Grilled New York Strip Steak with Spice Island Butter and Pommes Frites	23.00

DESSERTS

Mayflower Chocolate Mousse Tart with English Cream	6.75
Strawberry Sundae with Mayflower Cookies	6.75
Coffee Ice Cream Profiterolles and Caramel Bananas	7.25
Apricot Amaretto Cheesecake with Apricot Amaretto Ice Cream	6.75
Haagen Dazs Vanilla, Chocolate or Coffee Ice Cream	5.75
Mayflower Fruit Ices	5.75

We feature organically raised meats, grains and produce from local New England farms when possible. A surcharge of $1.50 will be added for split plates. Pipe and cigar smoking is permitted on the porch.

Dinner: 7 Days a Week 6 - 9:30

Mesa Grill

Mesa Grill is the result of a winning combination of factors and has been a hit from the day it opened. The decor is wild Western, the owner is a well-known figure and restaurateur, chef Bobby Flay is one of the best in New York and his interpretation of Southwestern cooking has become the standard.

GRILL

Menu Changes Seasonally

Chef: BOBBY FLAY

APPETIZERS

ZUCCHINI + CORN QUESADILLA
with Smoked Tomato Salsa + AvocadoRelish
$10.50

ROMAINE SALAD
with Spicy Caesar Dressing + Red Chile Croutons
$6.25

TOMATO TORTILLA SOUP
garnished with Avocado, White Cheddar Cheese + Cilantro
$6.75

GRILLED TUNA TOSTADA
with Black Bean-Mango Salsa + Avocado Vinaigrette
$10.00

CORNMEAL COATED PACIFIC OYSTERS
with Red Curry Sauce + Corn Relish
$12.00

FRISEE SALAD
with Chorizo, Asiago Cheese, Tomatoes + Roasted Garlic Vinaigrette
$7.00

BARBECUED RIBS
with Chipotle-Peanut Sauce + Corn-Tomatillo Relish
$9.00

CRISPY QUAIL SALAD
with Mango-Red Onion Relish + Spicy Pecans
$10.00

SHRIMP + ROASTED GARLIC CORN TAMALE
$10.25

CORNMEAL COATED CHILE RELLENO
filled with Goat Cheese + *served with* Black Bean Sauce
$8.75

RED CHILE DUCK
with Papaya Green Onion Relish, Sweet Onion Salad, Flour Tortillas
$9.50

GRILLED RABBIT + GOAT CHEESE ENCHILADA
with Wild Mushroom-Ancho Chile Sauce
$10.75

102 Fifth Ave • Gramercy Park/Union Square • (212) 807-7400

ENTREES

Grilled Pork Chops Adobo
with Spicy Apple Chutney + Chickpea Polenta + Asparagus
$19.75

Grilled Salmon
with a Red Chile Honey Glaze
served with Cornmeal Coated Eggplant and Spinach
$22.00

Grilled Swordfish Steak
with Papaya-Tomatillo Salsa, Sweet Potato Tamale + Green Beans
$22.00

Grilled Whole Red Snapper
with Charred Jalapeño-Basil Vinaigrette
served with Beet-Goat Cheese Torta + Spinach
$22.50

Black Angus Steak
with House Made Mesa Steak Sauce,
Potato-Corn Taco + Creamed Kale
$24.50

Roasted Chicken
with Red Chile Oil, Fresh Sage Sauce,
Cous Cous with Smoked Peppers + Roasted Onions
$19.00

Ancho-Rubbed Game Hen
with Cilantro Pesto + Roasted Garlic Mashed Potatoes,
Sauteed Mushrooms + Corn
$22.50

Grilled + Marinated Vegetable Salad
with Tender Greens, Goat Cheese Croutons + Balsamic Vinaigrette
$16.50

Grilled Loin of Lamb Chops
with Jalapeño Preserves, Asparagus + Sweet Potato Gratin
$20.50

Pan Roasted Venison
with a Spicy Black Grape Sauce, Horseradish Potatoes + Spinach
$23.50

Grilled Mahi Mahi
with Pineapple-Ancho Chile Barbecue Sauce,
Napa Cabbage + Wild Rice Pancake
$19.50

Blue Corn Striped Bass
in a Smoked Yellow Tomato Broth +
Cilantro Risotto Cake
$20.25

Dinner: 7 Days a Week 5:30 - 10:30

This is a branch of Michael McCarty's popular Los Angeles restaurant, and it has proved to be a winner here as well. The original artwork on the walls is offset by a simple, quiet decor and the food is what you would expect - lots of fresh salads, pastas, and grills.

MICHAEL'S

Menu Changes Seasonally

APPETIZERS

Skookum Oysters or Littleneck Clams on the Half Shell with Walnut Toast, Lemon and NYC Cocktail Sauce	10.00
Garden State Bresaola (Air-Dried Beef) with Arugula Bufalo Mozzarella, Grilled Peppers, Basil and Monini Extra Virgin Olive Oil	12.00
House Cured Gravlax with Mustard Dill Sauce and Brioche Toast	12.00
Risotto with Shiitake Mushroom, Pancetta and Baby Asparagus	12.50
Fettucine with Canadian Salmon, Vine - Ripened Tomatoes, Reggiano Parmesan, Doubled Blanched Garlic, Monini Olive Oil	14.00

SALADS

Limestone, Arugula, Radicchio, Mache, San Fernando Valley Greens and Basil with Vine Ripened Tomatoes, Balsamic Vinegar and Monini Extra Virgin Olive Oil	8.00
Watsonville Curly Endive and Iowa Bacon with Dijon Mustard and Chive Vinaigrette	9.50
Oregon State Shiitake, Chantrelles and Oyster Mushrooms with Double Blanched Garlic, Pancetta, Herbs and Pinenuts on Baby Greens with Sherry Wine Vinegar	11.50
Radicchio with Belgian Endive, Watercress, Laura Chenel Crotin De Chevre and Pommery Walnut Vinaigrette	12.50
Grilled Squab with California Frisee, Raspberry Vinegar Sauce Spinach, Walnuts and Fresh Raspberries	12.50
Colorado Prime Lamb Filet with Onion Confit, Wild Rice, Vine Ripened Tomatoes and Belgian Endive on Baby Greens with Balsamic Vinegar and Monini Extra Virgin Olive Oil	14.50
East Coast Sea Scallops with Grilled Onions, Haricot Verts Papaya, Avocado, Vine-Ripened Tomatoes on Baby Greens with Balsamic Vinegar and Monini Extra Virgin Olive Oil	14.50

MICHAEL'S — THE BIG EATS MENU

Iowa Center Cut Pork Chop	25.50
Illinois Veal Porterhouse Chop	28.50
Colorado Lamb Porterhouse Chops	28.50
Kansas City Beef Porterhouse	29.50
Grilled Maine Cull Lobster *2 lb*	29.50

All Big Eats Items are Served with Michael's Famous Frites

24 West 55th St • Midtown West Side • (212) 767-0555

MICHAEL'S — 1993 MAINS

Canadian Salmon with Vine - Ripened Tomato Vinaigrette, Grilled Peppers and Onions on Baby Greens with Balsamic Vinegar and Monini Extra Virgin Olive Oil	22.50
Eberly Farms Chicken and Montrachet Goat Cheese with Grilled Peppers, Grilled Onions and Vine - Ripened Tomatoes on Baby Greens with Jalapeno, Cilantro Lime and Monini Extra Virgin Olive Oil	22.50
Nicoise Salad with Pacific Blue Fin Tuna, Nicoise and Calamata Olives, Capers, New Potatoes, Hard Boiled Egg Reggiano Parmesan, Grilled Peppers, Vine - Ripened Tomato and Tarragon Vinaigrette on Baby Mixed Greens	22.50
Cobb Salad with Maytag Bleu Cheese, Juliennes of Bacon Hard Boiled Egg, Cherry Tomato, Avocado, Balsamic Vinaigrette and Chicken Filets on Baby Mixed Greens	22.50
Mixed Grilled Onions, Fennel, Leeks, Peppers, Japanese Eggplant Baby Squash, Baby New Potatoes, Jicama, Yucca, Asparagus and Flagelots	22.50
***	
Canadian Salmon with Beurre Blanc and American Caviar	23.50
East Coast Sea Scallops with Watercress, Julienne Bacon and Beurre Blanc	23.50
Striped Sea Bass with Leek Vinaigrette and Chervil	24.50
Atlantic Swordfish with Tomato Basil Vinaigrette	24.50
***	
Eberly Farms Poulet Frites with Tarragon Butter	18.00
Griggstown Quail with Fresh Lime Thyme Butter	22.50
D'artagnan Duck with Bouchant and California Blood Oranges	23.50
Chicago Sweetbreads with Lemon, Capers and Parsley Butter	23.50
Roasted Eberly Farms Chicken Breast with Muscovey Foie Gras and Fresh Oregon St. Chantrelles	24.50
Squab with Raspberry Vinegar Sauce and D'artagnan Foie Gras	24.50
***	
Iowa Pork Tenderloin with Double Blanched Garlic, Lemon Sage and Extra Virgin Olive Oil	22.50
Kansas City Dry Aged Prime Steak with Frites	24.50
Illinois Veal with Caramelized Lemon	24.50
Colorado Lamb with Cabernet Sauvignon, Black Currants and Fresh Thyme	24.50

DESSERTS

Tarte Tatin - Caramelized Red Delicious Apples in Pastry Puff	7.00
Blackberry and Browned Butter Tart - Sweet Pastry Crust Browned Butter Filling and Fresh Blackberries	8.00
Chocolate Raspberry Mousse Cake - Alternate Layers of Genoise, Raspberries and Chocolate Mousse Laced with Framboise	9.00
Strawberry Bagatelle - White Chocolate Mousse, Almond Biscuit,	9.00

Charge Bre Lun Din

Dinner: Mon - Sat 5:30 - 10:30

Nosmo King

Although a little difficult to find for most New Yorkers, this place has gained a reputation for the creative use of fresh, organic ingredients. Chef Alan Harding's mission is to make food that's delicious - and healthy besides.

FIRST COURSE

Black Bean Soup
Tomatillo Cilantro Chutney 5.

Mixed Green Salad
Toasted Sesame Cumin Vinaigrette and Chickpeas 6.

Calamari and Octopus Salad
Ratatouille, Basil and Black Olive Puree 7.

Thai Fun
Spicy Rice Noodles with Vegetables and Green Curry 7.

Country Salad
Chicory, Portobello Mushrooms, Fennel and Roasted Garlic 7.

Coach Farm Goat Cheese Tart
Beets, Potatoes and Citrus Vinaigrette 7.

MAIN COURSE

Grilled Rainbow Trout
Roasted Potatoes, Jerusalem Artichokes, Escarole and Balsamic Vinegar 17.

Roasted Chicken
Spring Vegetables, Mushrooms and Whipped Potatoes 17.

Mushroom Spinach Lasagna
Mushroom Caper Marinara and Basil Oil 15.

Grilled Vegetables
Herb Polenta, White Bean Stew and Black Olive Vinaigrette 14.

54 Varick St • TriBeCa/Downtown/Chinatown • (212) 966-1239

Moo Shu Vegetables
Bok Choy, Sesame Pancakes, Hoisin and Chinese Mustard 13.

Pan Roasted Duck
Warm Chicory Lentil Salad and Foie Gras Pancakes 17.

Smoked Skate Burrito
Refried Beans, Avocado Jicama Salad and Spicy Grains 15.

Seared Tuna
Escarole, White Beans and Lime-Marjoram Vinaigrette 18.

SPECIALS

FIRST COURSE

Chilled Asparagus
On Gazpacho with Horseradish Oil 7.

Salmon and Yam Cakes
Mixed Lettuces and Cilantro Yogurt Fraiche 8.

MAIN COURSE

Truffled Risotto
Morel Ragout, Spinach, Parmesan Reggiano 17.

Grilled Mahi-Mahi
Black Bean Cake, Grilled Okra and Mango Salsa 18.

SIDE PLATES 5. / 4.

Sauteed Spinach *Roasted Herb Polenta*

Sauteed Garlic Greens *Refried Beans*

Whipped Potatoes *Spicy Sweet Potato Home Fries*

Roasted Head of Organic Garlic 3.

CHEF: Alan Harding PROPRIETOR: Steve Frankel

Dinner: Mon - Sat 6 - 11, Sun 5:30 - 10

Odeon practically coined the term "trendy." Opened in 1980, it drew "the beautiful" people to the then-desolate downtown area (now called TriBeCa), offering a unique interpretation of culinary basics in a renovated cafeteria. It's still very good and very popular.

Ask Waiter For Daily Specials

Menu Changes Seasonally

Full Menu Served at the Bar

APPETIZERS

FRIED CALAMARI 6.50 SOUP DU JOUR 5.00
MIXED GREEN SALAD 5.50 with warm goat cheese 7.25
ARTICHOKE and FENNEL SALAD 6.50
MUSSELS steamed in wine and garlic 6.75
COUNTRY SALAD with Roquefort, bacon lardons and sweet garlic 7.75
GRILLED PORTOBELLO MUSHROOMS with arugula 7.50
BRUSCHETTA tomatoes on toasted garlic bread with chickpea salad 6.50

ENTREES

SAUTEED RAINBOW TROUT with red peppers, tomatillo salsa 17.50
GRILLED SALMON with corn and cilantro 18.50
SEARED MARINATED TUNA with mixed greens 18.50
ASPARAGUS RISOTTO 12.00
RICOTTA RAVIOLI with butter & Parmesan cheese or tomato sauce 12.50
PIZZA with tomatoes, mozzarella and basil 11.50
GRILLED HALF FREE RANGE CHICKEN with mashed potatoes and spinach 16.00
STEAK FRITES 20.00 STEAK au POIVRE 21.00
WARM DUCK SALAD with haricots verts & beets 17.50
FUSILLI with fresh tomatoes, zucchini & arugula 11.00
ROAST LEG of LAMB with sauteed artichokes 18.00
STEAMED ASPARAGUS, ROAST PEPPERS & COUSCOUS 11.50

145 West Broadway • TriBeCa/Downtown/Chinatown • (212) 233-0507

SIDES

VEGETABLE DU JOUR 4.50 FRENCH FRIES 4.00
SAUTEED SPINACH 4.50 MASHED POTATOES 4.50

BRASSERIE MENU

AVAILABLE AT ALL TIMES

GRILLED LAMB and LEEK SANDWICH 11.00 SOUP DU JOUR 5.00
RICOTTA RAVIOLI with butter & Parmesan
cheese or tomato sauce 12.50
MIXED GREEN SALAD 5.50 with warm goat cheese 7.25
MUSSELS steamed in wine and garlic 6.75
FRENCH FRIES 4.00
GRILLED PORTOBELLO MUSHROOMS &
MOZZARELLA SANDWICH 9.00
STEAMED ASPARAGUS, ROAST PEPPERS & COUSCOUS 11.50
FUSILLI with fresh tomatoes, zucchini & arugula 11.00
HAMBURGER, CHEESEBURGER or BACONBURGER 7.50
COUNTRY SALAD 7.75 FRIED CALAMARI 6.50
STEAK FRITES 20.00
PIZZA with tomatoes, mozzarella and basil 11.50
OMELETTE:
fine herbs, spinach, onion, bacon, Swiss or Cheddar
cheese any two 6.50 any three 7.00

DESSERTS

TRIPLE CHOCOLATE PUDDING 5.25
MIXED BERRY SHORTCAKE 4.75 CREME BRULEE 4.75
CHOCOLATE TORTE 5.50 LEMON TART 5.00
FRESH FRUIT, priced accordingly
PROFITEROLES 5.75
ICE CREAM 4.50 SORBET 4.50
DESSERT OF THE DAY, priced accordingly
HOT FUDGE SUNDAE 5.00
FIG & BUTTERSCOTCH SUNDAE 5.00

Stephen Lyle - Chef

Dinner: 7 Days a Week 6 - 2am

Park and Orchard Restaurant

Not too far from the Meadowlands Sports Complex, this spacious restaurant serves very non-macho, "natural" American food, i.e., pastas, grilled fish and poultry - no red meat. It's very popular with restaurant critics and residents.

DINNER MENU

The idea behind our restaurant is simple: to please your palate and provide you with the best, freshest, whole food. We know that you who come here expect that and we aim to have something for all food philosophers.

Many of our dishes can be tailored to your dietary needs — made salt-free, fat-free, etc. Just ask!

We serve absolutely nothing that contains refined sugar, bleached white flour, preservatives, colorings, or any other artificial ingredients in our food. We serve only the freshest grown vegetables and fruits. We only cook in stainless steel and iron pots, and only bake in tin and glass pans. This assures you that the nutrients will not be leached from your food, or you, via the utensils.

All our foods are prepared to order......................Please bear with us.

APPETIZERS

Hummus — Chicken, Tahini Pate $3.95
Shrimp Cocktail $3.95
Park Platter (A Sampling of our Cold Appetizers) $3.95
Ratatouille $3.95
Stuffed Mushrooms $3.95
Baba Ganoush — Eggplant Pate $3.95

SOUPS

(Prepared fresh daily)

Miso Soup or Soup Du Jour Cup .... $1.95 Bowl $2.50

SALADS

(Choice of Dressing)

Spinach — Tender leaves generously laced with Mushrooms, Apple and Egg $6.95
Seafood Salad — Our Large Garden Salad topped with Shrimp $10.95
Large Garden Salad — A variety of Fresh Vegetables with Crisp Lettuce $6.95
Dinner Salad — Romaine — Tomato $3.25

Dressings:
Oriental — Vinegar and Oil with Ginger, Onion, Tamari, Tomato, Lemon and Orange
Basil — Vinegar and Oil with Basil, Garlic and Sea Salt
Tofu — Blended Tofu with Garlic and Herbs
Blue Cheese - Extra Small .... $.50 Large $1.00

PASTA

Choice of **Whole Wheat** or **Italian Pasta**. Either:

Alfredo $8.50
Marinara $6.95
Pesto — Parsley, Basil, Garlic, Nuts and Cheese $7.50
Marinara Pesto $8.50
Antine Special — Cold Pasta with raw Tomato Sauce and lots of Garlic and Basil $6.95

240 Hackensack St • East Rutherford, NJ • (201) 939-9292

ENTREES

Mexican Specials
(Served with a cup of Soup **or** Salad)

Cheese Enchiladas — Served with Pinto Beans and Rice $10.95
Shepherd's Casserole — Rice, Pinto Beans, Enchilada Sauce topped with Cheese $9.95

STIR-FRIES

(Fresh in Season, Served over Rice or Pasta, with a Cup of Soup or Salad)

Mixed Vegetables $11.95
Chicken & Mixed Vegetables $14.95
Shrimp & Mixed Vegetables $16.95
Scallops & Mixed Vegetables $16.95
Plain Steamed Vegetables $10.95
Buttered Vegetables $11.95
Steamed Vegetables with Tahini Sesame Butter $11.95

Available with any one of the following sauces:
Oriental — With Ginger, Tamari, Garlic and Orange Peel
Italian — With Garlic, Oil, Italian Seasonings; Tomato Sauce on Request
Indian — A unique dish, served with our own special Curry. Spicy if you like
Mongolian — A delicious Semi-sweet Barbecue Flavor from the Orient
Szechwan — For those who like their Vegetables Hot and Spicy
Mild Szechwan — For those who like Szechwan flavor but not Hot and Spicy
Chinese — Tamari and Garlic

PARK & ORCHARD SPECIAL STIR-FRIES

(Served over Rice or Pasta, with a Cup of Soup or Salad)

Chicken, Broccoli, Fettucine, Mushrooms, Snowpeas, White Wine Sauce $14.95
Chicken, Stringbeans, Broccoli, Mushrooms — Very spicy Shanghai Specialty Sauce $14.95
Chicken, Broccoli, Apples, Walnuts — Mongolian or Szechwan Style $14.95
Chicken, Broccoli, & Mushrooms — Any Style $14.95
Shrimp, Broccoli & Mushrooms — Any Style $16.95
Shrimp, Snap peas, Mushrooms — Sherry Ginger Sauce $16.95
Tofu, Broccoli, Snowpeas, Mushrooms & Scallions — Any Style $12.95

FOWL

(Our Fowl have not been abused with injections of antibiotics or hormones.
They're just naturally fed -- you'll taste the difference. Served with Rice, Vegetable, with a Cup of Soup or Salad)

Chicken Parmesan — Served with Pasta and Sauce $13.95
Chicken Piccata — Lightly sauteed boneless Breast of Chicken, prepared with a light Butter or Lemon Sauce. A delicate treat $13.95

SEAFOOD

(Served with Rice, Vegetable, with a Cup of Soup or Salad)

Shrimp .... $16.95 **Scallops** .... $16.95 **Filet of Fish** $14.95

Choose one of the above, served Baked or Broiled to your liking in any of the following ways:
Japanese — Baked with Mushrooms in a Ginger, Onion, Garlic and Tamari Sauce
Scampi — Baked with White Wine, Garlic, Olive Oil, Butter and Spices
Butter and Lemon
Parmesan — Baked with Tomato Sauce and covered with Mozzarella
A La Buddy — Baked with Mixed Vegetables and Mushrooms in a slightly Sweet Oriental Sauce
A La Faye — Baked with Dijon Mustard Sauce
A La Ken — Baked with Tomatoes, Butter and Lemon
Bananas & Nuts & Heavy Cream — Sauteed with Butter and Cashews with a touch of Heavy Cream (Best with Scallops and Filet)
Park & Orchard Special — Baked with Mushrooms and Mozzarella

Dinner: Mon - Sat 5 - 10, Sun 2 - 9

Park Avenue Cafe

As the latest showcase for master chef David Burke, Park Avenue Cafe became an immediate hit. His beautiful, complex presentations have legions of fans. Restaurateur Alan Stillman is behind the venture, which makes it a real contender.

Menu Changes Daily

APPETIZERS

Carpaccio of Marinated Tuna with
Seaweed Wrapped Noodles 11.50

House Smoked Salmon with
Warm Corn Blini 12.50

Tuna & Salmon Tartare with
Pertossian Caviar 12.50

Hand Made Cavatelli with
Wild Mushrooms & White Truffle Oil 11.50/21.00
or
Simply with Tomato, Basil & Parmesan 9.50/19.00

Barbecued Squab with
Foie Gras & Corn Cake 12.50

SOUP & SALADS

Lobster Wonton Soup 9.50

Gazpacho with
Smoked Shrimp & Jack Cheese Quesadilla 9.50

Country Salad with Walnuts &
Coach Farms Goat Cheese 9.50

Salad of Mixed Organic Greens 7.50

100 East 63rd St • Upper East Side • (212) 644-1900

SIDE DISHES

Whipped Potatoes with Basil Oil 6.50

Stir Fried Vegetables 7.50

Wild Mushroom Hash 6.75

Creamed Spinach & Leeks 6.50

ENTREES

Soy Glazed Brook Trout with
Manila Clams, Sticky Rice & Nori 19.50

Park Avenue Cafe Swordfish Chop(tm) 29.50
Save the Tag...! .... (Market Availability)

Seared Salmon with Ginger, Cracked Pepper
& Shitake Dumpling 26.50

Sautéed Red Snapper with Shrimp
& Lemon Pepper Noodle Cake 27.50

Halibut Steak with
Artichoke Ravioli & Shaved Fennel 25.50

Mrs. Ascher's Steamed Vegetable Torte 19.00

Pan Roasted Chicken with
Grilled Eggplant "Parmesan"
& Balsamic Sauce 19.50

Spiced Veal Chop with
Mango, Celery & Leeks 29.50

Rack of Baby Lamb with
Honey Mustard & Rosemary 28.50

Sirloin of Aged Beef with
Wild Mushroom Hash 29.50

All of Our Entrées Available
Simply Grilled or Steamed.

Dinner: Mon - Fri 5:30 - 10:30, Sat - Sun 5:30 - 11:15

Regency Dining Room, The (540 Park)

This is where the term "power breakfast" (or "power" any meal) originated; in the morning it's full of the city's movers and shakers, with limos lining the street outside. Although the food isn't fabulous, it's not bad, and the room is elegant.

Menu Changes Seasonally Along With Daily Specials

LUNCH

Main Courses

Fresh Tuna or Salmon Nicoise 16.50
with haricot verts, tomatos, potatos, artichokes, olives and anchovies

Caesar Salad 7.00/12.00
with herb-parmesan chicken croutons
appetizer 8.00 main course 14.00
with lobster
appetizer 9.75 main course 17.50

Classic Cobb Salad
with apple-wood smoked bacon, tomato, avocado and Maytag blue cheese
with chicken 15.50 with lobster 18.00

Loews Santa Monica Beach Hotel Spicy Grilled Chicken Salad 14.50
with Mango, Papaya and Pineapple

Thick Crust Pizza with Mixed Greens
with roast eggplant, red pepper, bermuda onion, zucchini and goat cheese 12.50
or
with smoked chicken, proscuitto, tomato, onion, mozzarella and thyme 14.50
or
simply with tomato and mozzarella 11.50

Penne with Smoked Chicken 16.00
with roasted red pepper, tomato and snow peas, pesto

Fettucini with Grilled Vegetables 16.00
with julienne of jicama and snow peas, chunky tomato sauce

Smoked Norwegian Salmon Club Sandwich 14.50
with cucumber, Jersey tomato and boursin cheese on raisin bread

Park Avenue Burger 12.50

Regency Club Sandwich 12.50
with grilled chicken breast, apple-wood smoked bacon, lettuce and tomato, herb aoili

The Regency Hotel • 540 Park Ave • Upper East Side • (212) 759-4100

DINNER

Appetizers

Cold

Classic Shrimp 12.50 or Crab Cocktail 14.50
with cocktail Sauce

Green and White Asparagus Salad 8.50
with mozzarella
and shaved proscuitto di parma

Red Snapper Napoleon 11.00
with shoestring potato
and onion tomato salad

Mixed Spring Greens 8.50
with toasted hazelnuts
and shallot vinaigrette

Hot

Crispy Gulf Shrimp 9.00
on paella risotto

Sauteed Soft Shell Crab 12.00
on tomato, onion and rosemary tart,
basil oil

Regency Spring Roll 7.50
with shitake mushrooms
and crispy plummed pancake

Duck Strudel 8.50
with Jack cheese and corn,
yellow and red pepper coulis

Main Courses

Sauteed Florida Grouper 21.00
with fresh herb crust and parsley oil

Roasted Lobster 28.00
in the shell with Chinese spice, celery risotto and lemon thyme

Bowtie Pasta with Grilled Salmon 18.00
with peas, garlic and basil, tomato sauce

Penne with Goat Cheese 19.50
& Jersey tomato, haricot vert and cilantro, extra-virgin olive oil

Roast Free Range Chicken 18.00
with scallion mashed potatoes

Grilled Moscovy Duck Breast 21.00
with duck and spinach pastilla, cherry sauce

Mixed Grill of Lamb, Veal, Chicken and Sausage 21.50
with mediterranean rice caviar

Seared Veal Chop 28.00
with roasted baby corn, fava beans,
tomato confit and provencal herb sauuce

Roasted Rack of Lamb 25.00
with vegetable couscous and spicy lamb sausage

Grilled Certified Angus NY Strip or Filet Mignon 25.00
with green tomato fritters, mixed greens and red wine sauce

Dinner: Mon - Sun 6 - 10:30

Overlooking the East River and all lower Manhattan, the River Cafe probably has the best view in New York. It also is the most romantic restaurant and under Chef John Loughran it has some of the best food in the city.

The River Café

Menu Changes Seasonally

Appetizers

Salad of Mixed Seasonal Greens
herb vinaigrette

Chilled Sweet Roasted Pepper Consommé
grilled shrimp and pepper bow ties

Smoked Salmon and Halibut with Capers
toasted black bread

Sea Scallops en Croute
asparagus butter sauce

Tuna and Salmon Tartares
osetra and salmon caviar $6.00 supp.

Nori Crusted Salmon with Red Onion Puree
ginger and soy vinaigrette

Chilled Lobster Salad, Grilled Vegetables and Orzo
lobster oil and coriander vinaigrette $6.00 supp.

Cheese Ravioli with Grilled Vegetables
tomato roast garlic sauce

Roast Soy and Honey Marinated Squab
stir fried vegetable

Chilled Foie Gras Terrine with Apple Chutney
toasted walnut bread

1 Water St • Brooklyn • (718) 522-5200

Entrees

Salmon Seared with Cracked Pepper and Fried Oysters
horseradish butter sauce

Moroccan Glazed Monkfish and Smoked Shrimp Falafel
charred eggplant, fennel broth

Roast Garlic Crusted Yellowfin Tuna
mushroom polenta, tomato seed vinaigrette

Grilled Swordfish with Corn and Mushroom Polenta
shiitake mushroom hash, red wine vinegar

Pan Roasted Lobster with Cucumber Linguine
roast corn and chive broth $ 12.00 supp.

Special Duck Preparation

Pan Seared Poussin Breast with Foie Gras Corn Cake
wild mushrooms, sherry wine natural sauce

Grilled Veal Chop with Sautéed Foie Gras
red wine natural sauce

Seared Rack of Lamb with Farmers Cheese, Eggplant Charlotte
rosemary mustard sauce

Grilled Prime Sirloin of Beef

Pheasant Steak with Grilled Artichoke Ravioli
thyme artichoke broth

Six Course Tasting Menu, Limited to the Entire Table

Fixed Price 58.00
Tasting Menu 78.00

gratuity and 8.25% sales tax not included

Chef John Loughran and staff

Dinner: Mon - Sat 6 - 11, Sun 6:30 - 11

These spots are popular primarily for lunch and brunch, with excellent baked goods, soups, and Sarabeth's famous jams and jellies.

Menu Changes Seasonally

APPETIZERS

VELVETY CREAM OF TOMATO SOUP ...4.25

MIXED GREEN SALAD with balsamic vinaigrette ...5.00

ARUGULA & FRIED TOMATO SALAD with sliced red onions & red wine-oregano vinaigrette ...6.25

SAVORY SOURDOUGH "FRENCH TOAST" topped with sauteed wild mushrooms, roasted tomatoes and baby green beans ...6.50

CAESAR SALAD of romaine, anchovy dressing, aged parmesan & brioche croutons ...6.25

COLD LINGUINE PASTA tossed with grilled shrimp, avocado, tomato salsa, parsley and mint ...6.50

SMOKED WHITEFISH SALAD with grilled tomato croutons, baby lettuce and red onion vinaigrette ...6.50

PASTAS & RISOTTO

FUSILLI PASTA with asparagus, fresh corn, basil-leek sauce & ricotta cheese ...14.50 (Vegetarian)

SPAGHETTI with fresh grilled tuna, mushrooms, garlic, capers, roasted red peppers, olive oil & rosemary ...16.00

FRESH FETTUCINE with tomatoes, spinach, Virginia country ham, sweet onions & parsley ...15.00

"JAMBALAYA" RISOTTO of roasted chicken, rock shrimp, and smoked duck sausage with sweet peppers, onions tomatoes & garlic ...16.00

(Above pastas may be split for two or more as appetizer. No half orders, please.)

1295 Madison Ave • Upper West Side • (212) 410-7335 • (Call For Other Locations)

FISH & MEAT

HERB-ROASTED SALMON with mixed toasted grains, sauteed spring greens and a pan sauce of lemon, white wine & olive oil ...18.25

LOUISIANA SHRIMP & ARUGULA SALAD - Fresh Louisiana shrimp (cornmeal-fried or grilled) with an andouille-roasted tomato dressing in a tossed salad of arugula, baby lettuces, grilled red onions, roasted peppers, lemon & olive oil ...17.75

GRILLED YELLOWFIN TUNA on a warm salad of roasted potatoes, arugula, fennel and sun-dried tomatoes ...18.25

SAUTEED MAINE SEA SCALLOPS with basil whipped potatoes, julienned vegetables & basil oil ...18.00

MAHI-MAHI with a thin nut crust over sliced potatoes & sauteed fresh corn, tomato and scallions ...17.75

GRILLED CHICKEN BREAST with traditional Boston baked beans, asparagus and cornsticks ...15.75

CHICKEN POT PIE - Braised chicken, assorted vegetables and herbs in a light cream sauce with a crisp pastry crust ...16.25

GRILLED AGED RIBEYE STEAK with roasted garlic mashed potatoes & a saute of green peas and mushrooms ...18.75

GRILLED LEG OF LAMB SALAD - Sliced leg of lamb drizzled with garlic sauce and served with baby green beans, grilled tomatoes, lacy fried Vidalia onions and seasonal greens in herb vinaigrette ...16.50

SIDE DISHES ...3.00 each

Mixed Julienned Vegetables - Steamed or Sauteed

Whipped Potatoes - Plain or with Basil

Warm Toasted Grain Salad

Boston Baked Beans

Fresh Asparagus - Grilled or Steamed

Crisp Fried Onion Rings

Steven Picker, Executive Chef

Dinner: Mon - Fri 6 - 10:30, Sat 6 - 11, Sun 6 - 9:30

Savoy was an immediate hit with SoHo gallery owners and artists. The room is perfect "New York": brick-walled with a pressed tin ceiling, and the food is an inspired American with Mediterranean influences.

Menu Changes Seasonally

LUNCH

Wild Leek Soup with Spring Radish Salad and Rye Croutons .... $ 6.00

Artichoke and Grilled Onion Salad with Arugala, Toasted Pecorino and Semolina-Raisin Focaccia .... $ 7.75

Mixed Green Salad with Roasted Creminis and Shaved Parmesan .... $ 6.00

Potato and Celery Root Pancake with One Baked Egg and a Frisee, Bacon and Apple Salad .... $ 7.75

Salad of Smoked Chicken, Lentils, Radicchio and Green Cabbage with Oregano Pan Bread .... $ 8.00

Salmon Gravlax with Avocado, Braised Leeks and Almond Caper Dressing $10.00

Flank Steak with Sauteed Morels, Asparagus and Onion Rings $11.00

Grilled Shrimp with Asian Greens, Lentil Salad and a Shrimp Oil Vinaigrette .... $ 9.50

Grilled Eggplant Sandwich with Sheep Cheese and Roasted Onion and a Moroccan Carrot Salad .... $ 8.00

Braised Rabbit with Cremini Mushrooms, Green Olives and Polenta .... $ 9.75

Orecchiette with Sea Scallops, Saffron-Onions and Belgian Endive $10.00

Sauteed Shad Roe with Roasted Fingerling Potatoes, Arugala and a Mushroom Vinaigrette .... $ 9.50

Open Face Sausage Sandwich with Black Beans, Wilted Spinach and Pickled Vegetables .... $ 9.50

DINNER

Appetizers

Antipasto Plate $10.50

Mixed Green Salad with Roasted Creminis and Shaved Parmesan .... $ 6.50

Wild Leek Soup with Spring Radish Salad and Rye Croutons .... $ 7.00

Rosemary Marinated Flank Steak with Red Pepper Ketchiap and Corn Fritters .... $ 7.50

70 Prince St • Greenwich Village • (212) 219-8570

Carrot and Jicama Salad With Shredded Duck and Mole .... $ 8.00
Penne with Roasted Shad in a Caper, Mint and Green Olive Sauce .... $ 8.50
Sauteed Morels with French Fries Tossed in Capers and Garlic Chives .... $ 9.00
Shad Roe Salad with Fingerling Potatoes and a Mushroom Vinaigrette .... $ 8.50
Seasonal Shellfish and Marinated Seafood Plate $10.50
Grilled Shrimp with Asian Greens, Lentil Salad and a Curry Vinaigrette .... $ 8.00
Salmon Gravlax Salad with Almond Caper Dressing and Matchstick Potatoes .... $ 8.50

Entrees

Grilled Baby Chicken with Moroccan Lamb Sausage and Chickpea Olive Stew $16.00
Grilled Salmon with Spanish Almond Garlic Sauce and Potato Tortilla $19.50
Mushroom Dusted Skate with Apple, Celery Root and Baby Onions $17.00
Risotto with Smoked Duck, Asparagus and Orange Shallot Gremolata $16.00
Fennel Stuffed Rabbit with Black Beans and Kale $18.50
Grilled Leg of Lamb in a Persian Marinade with Eggplant Slippers and Bulghur $19.00
Grilled Sea Scallops in a Provencal Stew with White Beans and Rouille $19.50
Salt Crust Baked Duck with Dried Cherry-Red Wine Sauce and Polenta $17.00

Side Orders

Tortilla with Romescu .... $ 3.50
Black Beans and Kale .... $ 3.50
Corn Fritters .... $ 3.50

DESSERTS $5.00

Susan's Choice
Chocolate Hazelnut Ganache Torte
Espresso Chocolate Chip Ice Cream
Assorted Cookies
Fresh Fruit Sorbet

BEVERAGES

Sparkling Mineral Water-Lurisia .... $ 5.00
Duche de Longueville Sparkling Cider 2.5% .... $ 4.50
China Cola .... $ 3.00
Orangina .... $ 3.50
Cappucino .... $ 2.75
Espresso .... $ 2.50
Coffee and Tea .... $ 2.00

Dinner: Mon - Thurs 6 - 10:30, Fri - Sat 6 - 11

Sign of the Dove, The

The Sign of the Dove has been synonymous with romantic dining for years and one of New York's most beautiful restaurants. With chef Andrew D'Amico, the quality of the food has steadily increased to the point where it is now on a par with the decor.

Menu Changes Seasonally

FIRST COURSES

CRISPY PAN FRIED OYSTERS
Cabernet Veal Glace and Lime-Shallot Oil 10.

ROAST VEGETABLE TERRINE
Feta, Cucumber and Pepper Salad 8.

DILL, CILANTRO & LIME CURED SALMON
Beets, Potatoes and Mustard Oil 10.

STAR ANISE QUAIL Cooked Two Ways
Stir Fried Vegetables with Sichuan Flavors 12.

HEARTS OF ROMAINE
Caesar Dressing and Aged Goat Cheese 8.

PAN SEARED TUNA WITH PANCETTA
Ragout of Vegetables in Warm Vinaigrette 12.

FAVA BEAN AND PARMESAN RAVIOLI
Braised Rabbit, Mushrooms and Truffle Oil 10.

MIXED GREENS AND BABY LETTUCES
Red Wine Vinaigrette 8.

GRILLED HERB MARINATED SHRIMP
Tuscan Bread Salad with Fennel & Orange 14.

1110 Third Ave • Upper East Side • (212) 861-8080

MAIN COURSES

STEAMED HALIBUT WITH SHIITAKES
Sweet Pea Broth and Crisp Leeks 20.

GROUPER WITH CHINESE SAUSAGE
Potato Broth with Watercress and Clams 24.

GRILLED MOROCCAN SPICED SALMON
Roast Asparagus, Tabouleh and Pepper Oils 22.

RED SNAPPER WITH BLACK BEAN SALAD
Ragout of Peppers, Roast Tomato and Scallion 26.

HERB MARINATED CHICKEN
Tomato-Ginger Tart and Lemon Thyme 20.

MUSCOVY DUCK WITH COUS COUS
Poached Pears, Grapes and Salsify 26.

GRILLED BARBECUE GLAZED VENISON
Onion Spaetzle and Rhubarb Sauce 28.

BEEF RIB-EYE WITH SEMOLINA PUDDING
Grilled Radicchio and Portobella Mushroom 30.

VEAL MEDALLION WITH ROESTI POTATOES
Rosemary Rubbed Sweetbreads and Fava Beans 32.

LAMB LOIN WITH BRAISED ARTICHOKES
Crisp Risotto Cake and Pearl Onions 28.

PRE AND AFTER THEATRE MENU SAMPLING
(Available Monday through Friday at 6:00 p.m. and at 10:00 p.m.)

FISH SOUP WITH EGGPLANT AND LEEKS
Sun-Dried Tomato Aioli

MIXED GREENS WITH SHERRY-WALNUT VINAIGRETTE
Avocado, Fennel, Sun-dried Tomato and Egg

TANDOORI MARINATED LEG OF LAMB
Preserved Lemon and Mint Sauce

Dinner: Mon - Fri 6 - 11, Sat 5:30 - 11:30, Sun 6 - 10

Chef/owner Richard Krause has tried his hand at a number of culinary adventures; this time he's gone southwest. Although this is a new restaurant, there is no reason to doubt that it will also be successful.

Menu Changes Seasonally

$5.95

1. Black Bean Soup with avocado, cilantro, sour cream and chilis.
2. Chilled Avocado Soup with lemon and cilantro.
3. Tortilla Avocado Soup with chicken and pozole.
4. Spring Tostada Green Salad with tomato, jicama, roasted peppers, green avocado and a choice of dressings.
5. Steamed Asparagus served with jalapeno cornbread and cilantro creme fraiche and black bean sauce.
6. Mizzuna salad with pinto beans, hominy & jicama - goat cheese dressing.

$7.95

1. Vegetable Burrito Roll with red peppers, grilled scallions, eggplant, tomatillos, refried beans & chihuahua cheese - served with roasted pepper cream.
2. Fried Calamari served with chipotle mayonnaise and cucumber, jicama orange salsa.
3. Grilled Shrimp and Chilled White Bean Salad with grilled summer squash and lemon.
4. Guacamole - hecho a la mesa - ask.
5. Acapulco Sopes - shrimp, oyster, or chorizo with black beans, salsas, and queso blanco.

$9.95

1. Duck Chili Molé with tortillas and corn salsa.
2. Red Pepper Cornmeal Griddle Cakes with grilled shrimp, avocado and cilantro creme fraiche.

99 East 19th St • Gramercy Park/Union Square • (212) 505-5500

3. Grilled Sagebread Pizza with poblano chilis, tomatillos, fennel, chihuahua cheese and chorizo.
4. Crisp Potato Pancakes with seasoned creme fraiche and 3 caviars.
5. Braised Atlantic Grouper Soft Tacos served with tomatillo salsa and plantain chips.

$12.95

1. Shrimp Quesadilla with mozzarella and queso blanco - avocado - red chili sauce and corn salsa.
2. Two Chili Rellenos, one with seasoned crab meat stuffing and the other with cheese and chilies - served with green chili sauce, yellow rice and refried beans.
3. Santa Fe Vegetable Assortment with grilled squashes and mushrooms, white bean chili, asparagus, salsas, roasted peppers and yellow rice served with tortillas.
4. Veracruz Crab Cakes with roasted red pepper sauce served with grilled squashes and yellow rice.

$14.95

1. Grilled Atlantic Salmon with yellow tomato salsa.
2. Grilled Sea Scallops on black bean salsa with red pepper griddle cakes and cilantro creme fraiche.
3. Chili Rubbed Skirt Steak with grilled pineapple salsa and crisp shoestring fries.
4. Chicken Paillard Salad on mixed baby greens with grilled eggplant and fennel, tomato - mint vinaigrette and crisp tortilla croutons.
5. Chili Rubbed Grilled 1/2 Chicken with ancho mustard cream and garlic mashed potatoes.

$16.95

1. Grilled Florida Red Snapper served on plantain chips and fried leeks with sweet yellow pepper sauce - rice and beans side.
2. Southwestern Peking Duck with ancho - plum sauce, scallions, cucumber and homemade tortillas.
3. Santa Fe pesto seared loin of lamb served with a mache, corn and tomato salad and sweet potato puree.
4. Rare Charred Tuna with green mango, tomato and spring onion salsa.
5. N.Y. Sirloin Steak served on mango - chili BBQ sauce with grilled vegetables and crisp shoestring fries.

Dinner: Mon - Fri until 11, Sat 5 - 12, Sun 5 - 10

New Yorkers love this intimate, quiet restaurant that serves a unique, eclectic take on American standards. It hasn't made a lot of waves with the press, but those who know it keep going back.

Menu Changes Daily

DINNER

Salad of Organically Grown Baby Greens
Tarragon Vinaigrette

Oysters in Cornmeal - Dennis Foy *3.75

Thai Corn & Crabmeat Soup *1.75

Smoked Scottish Salmon - Creme Fraiche & Caviar *3.75

Duck Pate with Orange & Duck Pate with Cherries
Lingonberry, Dijon Mustard, Mango Chutney & Celery Root

Warm Asparagus - Puff Pastry *4.00

Raw Bar - Fisher's Island Oysters *1.75

Breast of Cavendish Quail - En Croute *5.25

Breaded Sweetbreads - Sauce Supreme

132 Lexington Ave • Murray Hill/Kips Bay • (212) 545-1777

Breast of Free Range Hen - Tarragon Sundried Tomato Sauce

Poached Fillet of Norwegian Salmon - Lobster Buerre Blanc

Tenderloin of Beef - Wild Mushroom Sauce *3.75

Roast Leg of Lamb - Fine Herb Sauce

Aged Entrecote of Beef - Smitane Sauce *6.00

Fillet of Lotte - Tomato Crabmeat Sauce

Grilled Fillet of Red Snapper - Compound Butter *3.75

Sauteed Fillet of Skate - Classic Burnt Butter Caper Sauce

Dessert Assortis

Chocolate Truffle Cake & Dessert Wine Elysium *5.00

Raspberries, Strawberries & Blackberries *6.00

Sorbet - Cassis & Grapefruit *4.75

Water Processed Decaffeinated Swiss Blend

Selection of Fine Teas

Espresso *3.00 Sonia Rose Cappucino *4.00

PRIX-FIXE-MENU — $29.50 PP

*SUPPLEMENTAL CHARGES

Dinner: Mon - Sat 6 - 10:30

Sylvia's

Although there must be equally as good African-American-owned southern soul-food restaurants in New York, this is the one that is the best known. Manhattanites feel safe coming here for their fried chicken, ribs, black-eyed peas and collard greens, and Sylvia Wood has become a spokesperson for the industry and the community.

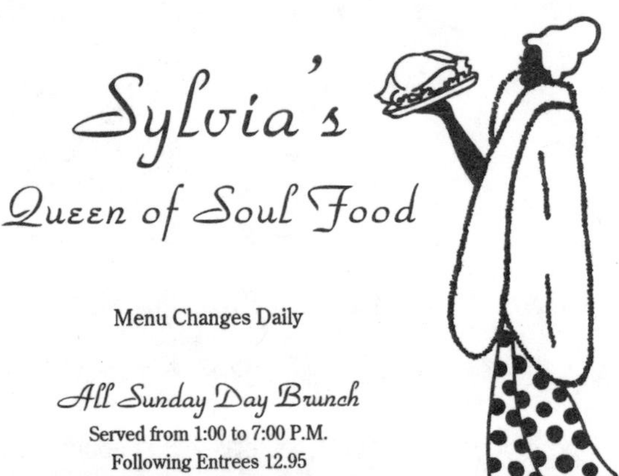

Menu Changes Daily

All Sunday Day Brunch

Served from 1:00 to 7:00 P.M.
Following Entrees 12.95

SOUTHERN FRIED or SMOTHERED CHICKEN
GOLDEN BROWN FRIED or SMOTHERED PORK CHOPS
SHORT RIBS of BEEF with Our Secret Brown Gravy
SYLVIA'S WORLD FAMOUS, TALKED ABOUT BAR-B-QUE RIBS
with Her Sweet and Sassy Sauce
GLAZED BAKED CHICKEN
SIRLOIN STEAK, Grilled to Perfection ...15.00
All Day Brunch Served with Two Vegetables of Your Choice and Cornbread

Choice of Vegetables

Collard Greens with Smoked Turkey Cheesey Macaroni & Cheese Potato Salad
Blackeyed Peas Candied Yams String Beans Steamed Rice Tossed Salad

PLEASE ASK YOUR SERVER ABOUT TODAY'S HOMEMADE DESSERTS
MINIMUM CHARGE 8.00 PER PERSON

Entrees

SYLVIA'S DOWN HOME FRIED or
SMOTHERED CHICKEN (Leg) ...8.00
(Breast) ...8.50
TWO GOLDEN BROWN FRIED or
SMOTHERED PORK CHOPS ...10.00
ONE PORK CHOP ...7.50
SHORT RIBS of BEEF in Sylvia's Special Brown Gravy, Made to Perfection ...10.50
BAKED GLAZED HAM ...8.50
BEEF LIVER SAUTE with ONIONS ...7.50
SAUTE CHICKEN LIVERS with Onions and Green Pepper ...7.00
TWO SALMON CROQUETTES ...9.50

328 Lenox Ave • Upper West Side • (212) 996-2669

Sylvia's Daily Specials

Sunday

SYVIA'S WORLD FAMOUS, TALKED ABOUT, BAR-B-QUE RIBS
SPECIAL with Her Sweet and Spicy Sauce ...9.75
All of the Above Served with Two Vegetables

Monday

STEWED CHICKENand DUMPLINGS ...8.50
CHICKEN LIVERS & ONIONS ...7.00
SYLVIA'S WORLD FAMOUS, TALKED ABOUT,
BAR-B-QUE RIBS
SPECIAL with Her Sweet and Spicy Sauce ...9.75

Tuesday

ROAST BEEF ...9.95
CHICKEN GIBLETS ...3.75
OXTAIL ...7.95
SYLVIA'S WORLD FAMOUS, TALKED ABOUT, BAR-B-QUE RIBS
SPECIAL with Her Sweet and Spicy Sauce ...9.75

Wednesday

MEAT LOAF ...7.95
OXTAIL ...7.95
SMOTHERED STEAK ...12.00
SYLVIA'S WORLD FAMOUS, TALKED ABOUT, BAR-B-QUE RIBS
SPECIAL with Her Sweet and Spicy Sauce ...9.75

Thursday

TURKEY WINGS with that Down Home Dressing ...7.95
SYLVIA'S
WORLD FAMOUS, TALKED ABOUT, BAR-B-QUE RIBS
SPECIAL with Her Sweet and Spicy Sauce ...9.75

Friday

DEEP FRIED FISH
with Tartar Sauce ...8.00
PORK CHITTERLINGS ...10.95
SYLVIA'S WORLD FAMOUS, TALKED ABOUT,
BAR-B-QUE RIBS
SPECIAL with Her Sweet and Spicy Sauce ...9.75

Saturday

DEEP FRIED FISH
with Tartar Sauce ...7.95
PORK CHITTERLINGS ...10.95
GRILLED RIB STEAK ...12.00
SYLVIA'S WORLD FAMOUS, TALKED ABOUT,
BAR-B-QUE RIB
SPECIAL with Her Sweet and Spicy Sauce ...9.75

Dinner: Mon - Sat until 10:15, Sun 1 - 7

Taliesin

Located in the only new hotel in the Wall Street area, Taliesin's interior was designed on a Frank Lloyd Wright theme. The American cuisine has received very good notices from the restaurant critics and from the lawyers and bankers who frequent it.

Menu Changes Daily and Seasonally

APPETIZERS

Spring Vegetable Soup
with Basil Pesto and Asiago Cheese — *$5.50*

Clam and Corn Chowder
with Essence of Fresh Clams, Vegetables and Thyme — *$5.50*

Chilled Watercress Soup
with Marinated Shellfish and Orange Zest — *$6.00*

Salad of Seasonal Greens and Baby Lettuces
with Balsamic Vinaigrette and Fresh Oregano — *$6.00*

Caesar Salad
Hearts of Romaine, Red Oak Leaf and Sweet Onions
with Focaccia Bread Croutons — *$6.50*

Bocconcini Salad
with Marinated Peppers, Mushrooms and Tomatoes — *$7.00*

New York State Goat Cheese and Parma Ham on Focaccia Bread
served warm with Grilled Vegetable Salad and Roasted Pepper Aioli — *$8.95*

Fresh Seasonal Oysters
with Taliesin Cocktail Sauce and Champagne Mignonette — *$9.95*

Salmon and Potato Knish
with Grilled Portobello and Chive Butter — *$9.95*

Grilled Louisiana Shrimp
with Spicy Great Northern Beans, Pancetta and Frisée Salad — *$11.95*

Grilled New Bedford Sea Scallops
with Smoked Lobster, Leeks and Black Truffle Sauce — *$12.95*

Hotel Millenium • 55 Church St • TriBeCa/Downtown/Chinatown • (212) 312-2000

ENTREES

Grilled Breast of Chicken
with Cilantro and Pignoli Nut Pesto, Shiitake Mushrooms and Natural Jus — *$16.95*

Gulf Shrimp and Baby Clams
with Sundried Tomatoes and Chinese Noodles — *$16.95*

Grilled Red Snapper
with Pencil Asparagus, Quinoa Grains, Red Pepper and Chinese Black Bean Sauce — *$19.95*

Seared Atlantic Salmon
with Blue Mussels, Yellow Tomatoes, Orzo Pasta and Basil — *$21.95*

Grilled Medallion of Tuna
with Warm Chinese Cabbage, Sake and Ginger Sauce — *$21.95*

Grilled Lamb Chops
with Pearl Barley, Roast Carrots and Natural Rosemary Jus — *$22.95*

Grilled Veal Chop
with Potato and Roasted Garlic Puree — *$24.00*

Grilled Certified Black Angus Steak
with Scallion Peppercorn Sauce and Fizzled Onions — *$24.95*

OUR CHEF'S SUGGESTIONS OF THE DAY:

Grilled Baby Chicken
with Artichoke, Creamer Potato Hash and Roasted Peppers served with Natural Jus scented with Fresh Oregano — *$21.95*

Health First:
Sauteed Soft-Shell Crabs
with Basmati Rice, Curried Onions and Scallion Sauce — *$23.95*

DESSERTS

Anise flavored Shortcake with Rhubarb and Strawberries
Vanilla Bean Ice Cream — *$5.50*

Flourless Bitter Chocolate Cake with Caramelized Beans
and Caramel Ice Cream — *$6.00*

Chef Albert DeAngelis

Charge Bre Lun Din

Dinner: 7 Days a Week 6 - 10:30

Chef Scott Cohen serves excellent contemporary American food at Tatou. People who realize the quality go for lunch or dinner, and others enjoy it very late in the evening when the place rocks to disco.

Menu Changes Seasonally

APPETIZERS

House Made Crab Ravioli *with Braised Fennel and Smokey Tomato Sauce*...$9.00
New England Chowder Style Steamed Clams...$11.50
Roasted Vegetable Tart *with Yellow Pepper Coulis*...$7.50
Maine Lobster Chowder...$6.50
Roasted Corn Chowder *with Corn Stick Crouton*...$5.50
Asparagus and Smithfield Ham *with Chili Spiked Olive Oil*...$7.50
House Smoked Salmon *with Dill Pancakes, Creme Fraiche, and Salmon Caviar*...$9.50
Grilled Boneless Quail *with Red Onion, Tomato, Arugula Oil, and Crispy Potato Ribbons*...$10.50
Terrine of Foie Gras on Country Bread *with Baby Greens and "Fresh Truffle Oil"*...$14.00

Seafood Cocktails:
Seafood Tasting...$24.00
Half Dozen Oysters Mignonette...$9.50

SALADS

Lightly Dill Cured Salmon - House Smoked Salmon, "Tartare Style" *with Country Bread Croutons*..$14.50
Jumbo Lump Crabmeat in a Crisp Potato Shell *with Avocado, Tomato, Mushroom and Chives, Mustard Vinaigrette*...$17.00
Mixed Seasonal Lettuces *with House Vinaigrette...$7.00*
with Blue Cheese and Freshly Shelled Walnuts or Roasted N.Y. State Goat Cheese...$9.00

ENTREES

Sauteed Scallops *with Cilantro, Grapefruit and Roasted Peppers*...$17.50
Honey Mustard Roasted Salmon *with Basil Vinaigrette*...$19.00
Oven Baked Sea Bass *with "Potato Scales" and Blue Point Oyster Sauce*...$19.50
Pan Roasted Halibut *with Crabmeat-Potato Crust and Oven Dried Tomato Vinaigrette*...$19.00
Broiled Free-Range Chicken *with Mushroom Dressing, Sweet Potato and Collard Green Crisps*...$16.50
Pan Roasted Loin of Lamb *with Okra and Tomato Stew*...$19.50
Roast Duck *with Sundried Cranberries, Wild Rice and Fresh Corn Fritters*...$18.50
Sauteed Veal Chop *with Savory Mushroom Pie*...$25.00
Angel Hair Pasta in a "Bouillabaisse Broth" *with Fresh Shellfish and Seafood*...$23.00
Roasted Vegetable, Wild Mushroom, Polenta Cake *with Roasted Red Bell Pepper Vinaigrette*...$15.00
Daily Pasta Preparation...$15.00
Fresh Fish of the Day...Priced Accordingly

FROM THE GRILL

Grilled Red Snapper *with Tomato Basil Saffron Broth, Artichokes, and Cous Cous*...$19.50
Iron Skillet Roasted Baby Chicken *with Cornbread Stuffing and Sage*...$16.50
Homemade Rye-Whole Wheat Pizza *with Fresh Buffalo Mozzarella, Oven Roasted Tomatoes, Black Olives, Fresh Basil and Extra-Virgin Olive Oil*...$13.50
Aged New York Shell Steak *with French Fries* - 14 oz...$24.50
Whole Maine Lobster in Shell...Market Price

Executive Chef
Scott Cohen

Dinner: Mon - Sat 5:30 - 11

Tribeca Grill

The fact that this restaurant is partially owned by Robert De Niro insured its success from day one. Drew Nieporent also has an outstanding track record and chef Don Pintabona has maintained the high quality of the menu, which consists mainly of light, grilled fare.

Menu Changes Seasonally

Field Green Salad	7.
Crisp Fried Oysters with Garlic Anchovy Aioli	10.
Endive, Watercress & Roquefort Salad	**8.**
Daily Soup	8.
Salad of Shrimp, Calamari & Bay Scallops, Citrus Juices	12.
Arugula Salad with Bocconcini & Basil Oil	10.
Grilled Vegetable Salad with Warm Goat Cheese	11.
Rare Seared Tuna with Sesame Noodles	**12.**

Roasted Chicken with Whipped Potatoes & Wild Mushrooms	**18.**
BBQ Breast of Duck with Bok Choy, Peanut Whipped Potatoes	24.
Angel Hair Pasta with Shrimp, Manilla Clams, Roast Pepper & Caper Broth	**21.**

375 Greenwich St • TriBeCa/Downtown/Chinatown • (212) 941-3900

Pan Seared Snapper, Warm Vinaigrette, Spinach & Plum Tomatoes	**22.**
Penne with Plum Tomatoes & Eggplant, Sausage Cheese Bread	18.
Grilled Salmon with Balsamic, Chive Oil, Shaved Fennel	22.
Pan Seared Veal Chop, Rosemary Essence, Provencal Vegetable Tart	26.
Grilled Rib Eye Steak, Potato & Leek Cake	**24.**
Potato Pancakes "Vonnas"	**5.**
Whipped Potatoes	4.
Provencal Vegetable Tart	5.
Fennel Sausage & Mozzarella Bread	5.
Banana Tart with Milk Chocolate Malt Ice Cream	**7.**
Chocolate Torte	**7.**
Almond Strudel with Stir Fried Pineapple & Coconut Brittle Ice Cream	7.
Ginger Poached Pears with Blueberries & Sugar Cookies	7.
Selection of Fresh Fruit	6.
Homemade Ice Creams & Sorbets	6.

Chef: Don Pintabona

Pastry Chef: George McKirdy

Dinner: Mon- Thurs 5:30 - 11, Fri - Sat 5:30 - 11:30, Sun 5:30 - 10

Located in the Pan Am building, Tropica sports a profusion of lush, tropical foliage with a Caribbean theme. The largely seafood menu of chef Edward Brown is very creative and extremely good.

TROPICA

Bar and Seafood House

Menu Changes Daily

TROPICA PRIX FIXE DINNER $29.50
Includes choice of small plate, main plate and dessert.

THE WINE TASTING DINNER $45.00
The wines by the glass have been specially matched to complement your choice of small plate, main plate and dessert. Both dinners served from 5pm -10pm.

SELECTED WINES

Dienhard Riesling Dry, QBA Rheinhessen 1990

Lakespring Sauvignon Blanc Napa 1991

Late Harvest Wine, New York State

Hugel Pinot Noir, Alsace 1990

Cabernet Sauvignon Cathedral Cellars KWV 1988, Coastal Region, South Africa

Raymond Chardonnay 1989

Late Harvest Wine, New York State

SMALL PLATES

Sesame Seared Tuna, Fennel Carrot Salad, Orange Glaze

Conch Chowder with Christophene and Okra

Grilled Foie Gras, Warm Cabbage, Truffles & Beet Oil

MAIN PLATES

Cod with Cous Cous, Sake Wine and Fermented Chinese Black Bean Sauce

Seared Black Angus Sirloin, Honey Mustard Spiced Oil and Crispy Taro

Grilled Mahi Mahi, Yucca Cake & Passion Fruit Sauce

DESSERT

Tropica Key Lime Fantasy

Coconut Creme Brulee

Warm Chocolate Ginger Cake, Vanilla Ice Cream & Ginger Crisp

200 Park Ave • Midtown East Side • (212) 867-6767

Small Plates and Soups

Olympia, Hama Hama, Little Skookum & Quilscene Oysters and North Carolina Clams — ea. 1.95

Salmon Carpaccio with Red Peppercorns and Lime Vinaigrette — 10.95

Crab Cake, Field Greens, Mustard Beurre Blanc — 9.95

Seared Baby Octopus, Pickled Plum Mayonnaise, Mitsuba, Root Vegetables & Crispy Noodles — 9.95

Lobster Ravioli, Lobster Consomme — 9.95

Conch Chowder with Christophene and Okra — 6.75

White Miso Soup with Lobster, Shrimp & Sea Vegetables — 6.95

Black Bean Soup with Andouille Sausage — 6.75

Salads and Vegetables

Butternut Lettuce, Roquefort Cheese and Spicy Cashew Nuts — 6.95

Baby Greens, Olive Oil & Vintage Vinegar Dressing — 6.75

Steamed Rice and Beans — 4.50

Grilled Vegetables Aioli — 7.00

Hawaiian Rice — 4.95

Plantain Chips — 4.50

Spiral Potato Chips — 4.50

Maine Lobsters

Baked, Grilled or Steamed
served with Spaghetti Vegetables

1 1/2 lbs and 2 1/2 lbs — 17.00 per pound

Today's Fish Selections

Bluenose Walu		*Soft Shell Crabs*	32.75
Arctic Char		*Sea Bass*	
Cobia		*Nairagi*	
Cod	23.50	*Salmon*	
Grouper		*Sturgeon*	
John Dory		*Swordfish*	27.00
Mong Chong	27.00	*Trigger*	
Opa		*Wahu*	

Fish selections are indicated by price

Main Plates and Specialties

Salmon Steamed in Kombu, Dulce, Sea Urchin Butter Sauce and Sevruga Caviar — 24.75

Two Crab Cakes, Field Greens and Mustard Beurre Blanc — 24.75

Grilled Mahi Mahi, Sweet Plantains and Pink Peppercorn Sauce — 21.00

Seared Marinated Tuna Loin, Potato Puree & Chive Sauce — 24.75

Grilled New Bedford Sea Scallops, Fettuccine & Cilantro Pesto — 21.50

Caribbean Bouillabaisse, 1 lb Lobster, Clams, Mussels and Scallops — 26.00

Marinated Barbecued Shrimp, Szechuan Peppercorns, Sugar Cane with Ginger Lime Sauce & Hawaiian Rice — 23.00

Hawaiian Red Snapper, Leeks, Napa Cabbage & Wild Mushrooms, Pumpkin Sauce — 24.50

Grilled Breast & Roasted Leg of Chicken Marinated with Jerked Spices, Red Pepper Corn Bread — 19.75

Chef Edward G. Brown

Dinner: Mon - Fri 5:30 - 10

New Yorkers are in love with Danny Meyer and the Union Square Cafe because Michael Romano's food is always excellent and the service is gracious, friendly, and informed. It takes weeks to get a reservation.

Menu Changes Seasonally Along With Daily And Weekly Specials

Michael Romano
Executive Chef

OYSTERS AND LUNCH SELECTIONS

Iced Oysters on the Half-Shell -- Please See Below for Today's Varieties.
--All Oysters are Shucked to Order and are Served with Shallot Vinaigrette and Fresh Lemon--

Roast Vegetable Sandwich on Grilled Seven-Grain Bread with Fresh Mozzarella, Arugula, Garlicky Chick Pea Spread and Cucumber-Sprout Salad	14.95
Tuna Club Sandwich with Garlic Potato Chips -- A Triple-Tiered Sandwich on Tom Cat White with Yellowfin Tuna Salad, Slab Bacon, Arugula and Aioli	13.95
Chicken Salad "Deluxe" -- Lightly Smoked, with Crispy Vegetables, Pancetta, Arugula & Peppers	13.95
U.S.C. Hamburger -- Grilled and Served on a Homemade Poppy Seed Roll with French Fries, and includes your choice of Melted Cheddar or Slab Bacon	9.75

APPETIZERS

Homemade Sheep's Milk Cheese Ravioli with Black Pepper and Sage Butter	7.95
Linguini ai Frutti di Mare -- with Tomatoes, Shrimp, Clams, Calamari & Mussels	8.95
Pasta Primavera -- with Spring Vegetables, Pecorino Romano and White Bean Sauce	7.50
Roast Garlic Gnocchi *all' Amatriciana* - with Tomatoes, Basil, Pancetta and Pecorino Romano	7.95
Risotto ai Fegatini -- Simmered with Seared Chicken Livers, Snow Peas, Moscato d'Asti and Parmigiano	7.50
Ciabatta Crostini with Charred Sweet Peppers, Portobello Mushrooms and Taleggio Cheese	8.50
Roast Eggplant, Zucchini and Tomato Terrine with Goat Cheese, Arugula & Chili Oil	7.95
Union Square Cafe's Fried Calamari with Spicy Anchovy Mayonnaise	7.95

21 East 16th St • Gramercy Park/Union Square • (212) 243-4020

SALAD AND SOUP

Union Square Cafe's Black Bean Soup with Lemon and a Shot of Australian Sherry	5.95
Arugula, Endive and Radicchio Salad with Tuscan Olive Oil and Fresh Oregano Vinaigrette	7.50
Cracked Wheat "*Panzanella*" Salad -- with Tomatoes, Basil, Olives, Onions, Pine Nuts and Mizuna	6.95
Red Oak Leaf and Bibb Lettuce Salad with Grated Gruyere and Dijon Vinaigrette	7.50
Union Square Cafe Greens Salad with Garlic Croutons and Sherry Vinaigrette	6.95
House-Smoked Salmon Salad with Radish, Cucumber and Watercress	8.50

WEEKLY SPECIAL ENTREES

Monday:	Baked Lobster "Shepherd's Pie" -- with Mushrooms, Spinach, Carrots and Lobster Sauce	24.50
Tuesday:	Grilled Black Angus Rib Steak for Two with Sautéed Spinach & Grilled Red Onions	24.00pp
Wednesday:	"Porchetta Arrosta" -- Roast Suckling Pig with Rosemary and Garlic, Served with Sautéed Greens and Herb-Roasted Potatoes	23.50
Thursday:	Roast Stuffed Breast of Veal with Grilled Zucchini and White Corn Polenta	21.50
Friday:	*Cacciucco di Pesce* -- Mediterranean Seafood Stew with Tomatoes, Fennel and Orange	22.00
Saturday:	Roast Baby Lamb Chops with Sweet Peas, Pearl Onions, Escarole, Mushrooms & Mint	23.50
Sunday:	Roast Guinea Hen with Mushrooms, Prosciutto, Asparagus and Mashed Potatoes	22.50

MAIN COURSES

Herb-Roasted Chicken with Creamy Polenta and Tomato-Sourdough *Panzanella*	18.95
Grilled Smoked Black Angus Shell Steak with Creamy Mashed Potatoes and Frizzled Leeks	23.50
Crisp Roasted Lemon-Pepper Duck with Rhubarb Chutney, Shiitake-Quinoa Pilaf and Spicy Greens	21.00
Grilled Salmon Fillet with Rosemary-Lemon Vinaigrette, Fennel Mashed Potatoes and Spring Vegetables	22.50
"Earth & Surf"- Baby Artichokes, Roast Fennel, Caponata, Tomato Mashed Potatoes & Seared Sea Scallops	19.50
Grilled Marinated Fillet Mignon of Tuna with Eggplant-Mashed Potatoes and Gingered Vegetable Slaw	24.50
Grilled Venison Paillard with Warm *Insalata Tricolore* and Zucchini, Eggplant & Parmigiano Tortino	23.50
Steamed Halibut with Orange Vinaigrette, Minted Bean Pureé, Pea Shoots and Asparagus	19.50

VEGETABLES AND CONDIMENTS

Union Square Cafe's Hot Garlic Potato Chips	4.50
Creamy Polenta with Mascarpone, Toasted Walnuts and Crumbled Gorgonzola	4.50
"Rice & Beans" -- Basmati Rice and Adzuki Beans Simmered with Ginger, Lime Juice & Miso	4.25
Fagioli alla Toscana - Simmered White Beans with Savory Herbs, Tuscan Olive Oil and Pecorino	4.95
Bruschetta Rossa - Garlic-Rubbed Grilled Sourdough with Tomatoes, Basil & Tuscan Olive Oil	4.95
Sautéed Spinach with Lemon and Tuscan Olive Oil	4.95
Creamy Mashed Potatoes with Frizzled Leeks	4.25
Grilled Slices of Sweet Red Onion	3.25

Charge Lun Din

Dinner: Mon - Thurs 6 - 10:30, Fri - Sat 6 - 11:30, Sun 5:30 - 10

Vince and Eddie's

This place has been crowded since it opened about two years ago because Chef Scott Campbell's food is inventive and very good, it's a small, "intimate" townhouse setting, and it's near Lincoln Center.

Menu Changes Seasonally, Specials Change Daily

LUNCH

SANDWICHES

Grilled Vegetable Sandwich 9.50
Grilled Tuna Sandwich with Cole Slaw 11.95
Grilled Chicken Club Sandwich 10.50
Grilled Salmon Sandwich with Avocado and Watercress 10.95

ENTREE SALADS

Curried Chicken and Apple Salad 9.95
Spinach, Roquefort and Bacon Salad 9.75
Seasonal Fruit Salad and Sorbet 9.95

DINNER

FIRST COURSE

Mussel and Corn Chowder 5.95
Field Green Salad 5.75
Smoked Salmon on Rosti Potato 9.95
Gravlax Salad 6.95
Crabcakes with Cilantro Oil 11.95

70 West 68th St • Lincoln Center • (212) 721-0068

Caesar Salad 6.75
Fried Calamari 7.25
Fresh Lump Crabmeat Cocktail 11.95
Warm Montrachet Salad 7.25
String Bean Salad 6.95
Fried Oysters Diablo 8.75

ENTREE SALADS

Grilled Chicken Kabob Salad 14.95
Herbed Shrimp Salad 16.75

MAIN COURSES

Calves Liver and Onion Rings 15.25
Pepper Crusted Tuna 17.95
Grilled Salmon and Asparagus 18.95
Panroasted Chicken 14.95
Grilled Shell Steak and French Fries 18.95
Broiled Scrod and Frizzled Leeks 16.75
Braised Lamb Shank and Dried Cherry Sauce 16.95
Sesame Crusted Swordfish and Snow Peas 19.95
Seafood Stew 18.95
Grilled Quail and Sweet Potato Fries 17.95
Spring Vegetable Plate 13.95

VEGETABLES

Broccoli 4.65
Spinach 4.75
Asparagus 5.50
Haricot Verts 5.50
Mashed Potatoes 4.25
French Fries 5.50
Onion Rings 4.75
Sweet Potato Fries 4.50
Mashed Turnips and Shallot Crisps 4.75
Savoy Cabbage and Escarole 3.95

DESSERTS

Desserts and Homemade Ice Creams 5.50

Executive Chef: Scott Campbell and Staff

Dinner: Mon - Sat 5 - 12, Sun 5 - 11

Situated on a barge in the East River, the Water Club is a popular location for parties, weddings, etc. Most people seem to come for the view and ambiance, but chef Rick Moonen's food is innovative and happens to be very good.

Menu Changes Seasonally

APPETIZERS

Water Club Smoked Salmon
with creme fraiche, red onions, capers, eggs and toasted brioche
12.00

Fresh Basil Polenta
served warm with melted roquefort and baby vegetables
9.00
Entree Size 15.00

Chesapeake Bay Jumbo Lump Crabcakes
avocado tartare sauce and cucumber slaw
12.00

Seasonal Oysters on the Half Shell
sherry vinegar mignonette
12.00

New England Farmed Littleneck or Cherrystone Clams
cocktail sauce
10.00

SOUPS

Spring Vegetable Minestrone with Tomato Bruschetta
7.00

Lobster Gazpacho with Crisp Wontons
7.00

Fresh Asparagus Soup with Rye Croutons
7.00

Water Club Seafood Gumbo
12.00

500 East 30th St • Murray Hill/Kips Bay • (212) 683-3333

ENTREES

Grilled Yellowfin Tuna Steak on Arugula
with salsa cruda and lobster potato pancakes
25.00

Seared Salmon Filet with Fresh Basil Crust
on spinach with citrus vinaigrette
24.00

Roasted Cod on Sweet Corn Purée
red pepper coulis and vegetable frisee
19.00

Maine Lobster
steamed to order with lemon butter or
infused cold pressed olive oil
** priced according to daily market **

Grilled Marker Swordfish Steak on Cous Cous
lemon confit, caper and roast garlic oil
26.00

Pan Seared Skate Wing Filet on Snow Peas and Turnips
ginger lemon grass vinaigrette and grilled prawns
19.00

Steamed Spaghetti Squash with Seasonal Vegetables
toasted pignolis, chunk tomato sauce and basil
16.00

Roasted Rack of Lamb with Mustard Herb Crust
ratatouille vegetables and mixed grains
28.00

Certified Organic Amish Chicken with Taro Purée
natural pan juices and fresh fava bean succotash
19.00

Dry Aged Sirloin Steak
grilled with gratin potatoes and tomato onion salad
28.00

Spinach and Cheese Filled Pasta Twists
with grilled fennel, black olives and reggiano cheese
and vine ripe tomato coulis
19.00

Cigar and pipe smoking are welcome in our lounge

Executive Chef Rick Moonen

Pastry Chef Loren Ramirez

Dinner: Mon - Sat 5:30 - 10:30, Sun 5:30 - 10

No one has anything but great things to say about this relatively new place in SoHo. The food is exceptional and the dramatic bi-level interior has been upgraded from its recent past as a Tex-Mex hangout.

WEST BROADWAY

RESTAURANT-BAR

Menu Changes Seasonally

Appetizers

West Broadway Soup of the Day
priced accordingly

Heart of Romaine Salad
with feta cheese, black beans and marjoram, cayenne toasts
7.50

Warm Skate Salad
with red pepper chick pea salad and fried carrots,
tumeric and cilantro vinaigrette
7.50

Unagi and Potato Terrine
with watercress, wasabi and baby lettuces.
8.00

Grilled Octopus Salad
with lemon rice dolmas and fava beans
8.00

Asparagus Salad
with grilled leeks, roasted beets, roquefort vinaigrette, baby lettuces
8.00

Grilled Stuffed Squid
with cous cous and merguez sausage,
spicy tomato cumin broth
7.50

Fried Shrimp
with cucumber and seaweed salads, sesame - soy vinaigrette
9.50

Chile Dusted Quail
with lentil and carrot salads, red chili sauce
8.75

349 West Broadway • SoHo • (212) 226-5885

Entrées

Seared Sea Scallops
with corn, spinach, fried leeks and salmon caviar
17.50

Sauteed Trout
with gnocchi and collard greens, bacon and black peppercorn broth
15.00

Roast Red Snapper
with warm potato salad, roasted shiitake mushrooms,
rosemary viniagrette
18.00

Lobster and Green Chile Stew
with mussels, clams and scallops, coconut milk,
and cilantro chutney
20.00

Grilled Tuna
on marinated arugula, cannelini bean and celery salad
with tapenade-stuffed tomato
17.50

Fried Soft Shell Crabs
with haricot verts, fennel and roasted red pepper, tarter sauce
18.50

Roast Cod
with mashed potatoes, celery root chips and roast carrots
16.00

Grilled Muscovy Duck Breast
with soft polenta, wild mushrooms and sugar snap peas
19.50

Roast Amish Chicken
with morels, baby artichokes and fava beans
18.00

Grilled Steak
dry-aged shell with onion rings, grilled potatoes and rosemary
22.00

Dinner: Mon - Thurs 6 - 11, Fri - Sat 6 - 12

This restaurant is exceedingly popular and serves excellent contemporary, French-influenced American food. Everyone, patrons and restaurant critics alike, raves about the creative cookery and elegant service.

Menu Changes Weekly

Dinner

Prixe Fixe - Sixty Five Dollars

Menu

Oyster & Champagne Soup
Snipped Chives

Irish Smoked Salmon Salad
Haricot Vert & cucumber

Saddle Of Rabbit
Apricots & Asparagus Flan

Lemon Sorbet

Grilled Entrécote Of Beef
Roasted Shallots & Pommes Frites

Banana Stonehenge
With Caramel

Petits Four
Coffee - Tea - Espresso

Menu

Saddle Of Lamb
Goat Cheese & New Potato Tart

Melon Steeped in Port

Maine Diver Scallops
Seaweed Salad & Chive Oil

Roasted Alaskan Halibut
Pesto Crust & Preserved Tomato

Guinea Hen Breast
Sundried Cherries & Crispy Noodles

Hot Chocolate Soufflé
Créme Anglaisé

Petits Four
Coffee - Tea - Espresso

Wine

Bellini Cipriani

Fieldstone
Sauvignon Blanc 1991

Bernardus
Chardonnay 1991

Fieldstone
Sauvignon Blanc 1991

Dalla Valle
Carbernet Sauvignon 1986

Beaumes de Venise
J. Vidal Fleury 1990

Rioja
Conde De Valdemar Reserva 1986

Route 9D • Garrison, NY • (914) 424-4228 • (Call For Other Locations)

Dinner

Prixe Fixe - Sixty Five Dollars

Menu

Grilled Jumbo Shrimp
Honey, Balsamic Vinegar & Parsley

Seared Norwegian Salmon
Consummé with Coriander & Caviar

Roasted Baby Pheasant
Chanterelles & Brussel Sprouts

Melon Steeped In Port

Tournedos of Beef
Galette Potatoes & Sour Mash Sauce

Hot Praline Soufflé
Crème Anglaise

Petits Four
Coffee - Tea - Espresso

Menu

Nantucket Bay Scallops
Orange & Crisp Leeks

Seawood-Wrapped Rare Tuna
Warm Cucumber & Wasabi Dressing

Quail with Foie Gras & Apple
Field Lettuce Salad & Toasted Pignoli

Lemon Sorbet

Roast Saddle of Venison
Spaetzle & Casis

Tartelet of Anjou Pears
Prune & Armagnac Ice Cream

Petits Four
Coffee - Tea - Espresso

Wine

Pouilly-Fumé
"Les Bascoin" Domaine Blondelet 1990

Trefethen
Estate Bottled Chardonnay Napa Valley 1990

Domaine Ste. Michelle
Blanc de Blac

Acacia
Pinot Noir 1990

Justin Vineyards
Cabernet Sauvignon 1986

Château du Cros
Loupiac 1988

Dinner: Fri & Sat 6 - 9:30

The food at Zoe ("contemporary" American) continues to get better and better, to the point that it's very difficult to get a reservation. The restaurant is especially popular with gallerygoers and shoppers in SoHo.

Menu Changes Weekly

DINNER

Wines-by-the Glass
(6 oz. glass)

-Bonny Doon Vineyards, Dry Pacific Riesling '91
Santa Cruz $5.25

-Caymus Vineyards, Sauvignon Blanc '91
Napa $6.00

-Whitcraft Vineyards, Chardonnay '90
Bien Nacido Vineyard, Santa Maria Valley $7.75

-Whitehall Lane Winery, Cabernet Sauvignon '88
Napa $6.75

-Rabbit Ridge Winery, Zinfandel '91
Russian River, Sonoma $5.00

-Byron Vineyards, Pinot Noir '91
Santa Barbara $7.00

-Iron Horse Vineyards, Blanc De Noir
"Wedding Cuvee", Green Valley-Sonoma '88 $7.25

First Plates

Crispy Calamari with a Vietnamese Dipping Sauce...$8.75

Salmon Tartar with Chili Potato Chips and Wasabi...$7.50

Bar-B-Que Quail with a Foie Gras Popover & Plum Chutney...$9.75

House Smoked & Ginger Cured Salmons with Squash Latkes,
Sheeps Milk Yogurt and Salmon Caviar...$11.00

Crisp Noodle-Wrapped Shrimp with Soy & Toasted Peanut Oil Dressing...$8.75

Salad of Seasonal Greens with Aged Sonoma Jack Cheese,
Shaved Fennel & Sherry-Shallot Vinaigrette...$6.75

Wild Mushroom & Multi-Grain Soup with Fresh Herbs & Crisp Shallots...$6.50

Main Plates

Ginger Crust Mahi Mahi in an Herbed Vegetable Broth
with Asparagus Tempura...$19.00

Black Pepper Pappardelle with Braised Rabbit, Tomatoes, Garlic & Herbs...$16.25

Grilled Yellowfin Tuna on Wok-Charred Vegetables
with Jasmine Rice and Chinese Chili Sauce...$19.00

Grilled 13 oz. Angus Ribeye Steak with Red Wine Hunter-Style Sauce
& Oak Barrel Baked Potato with Truffle Butter....$25.00

Wood-Oven Braised Lamb Shank with Fennel, Kale, Tomatoes and Herb Gnocchi...$16.50

Long Island Duck Breast from the Rotisserie
with a Thai Coconut Stuffing & Crisp Spring Roll...$19.75

Oven-Crisped Free Range Chicken with Pesto Grilled Eggplant & Feta Polenta...$16.00

Grilled Salmon with Moroccan Spices, Basil Mashed Potatoes, and
Charred Tomato Compote...$19.50

Seared Maine Halibut on Oxtail Risotto
with Morel Mushrooms & White Truffle Oil...$23.00

The Vegetarian Sampler...$15.50

Side Plates

Crisp Duck Spring Roll...$4.50
Basil Mashed Potatoes...$4.50
Feta Polenta...$3.50
Beer-Battered Onion Rings..$3.50
Oak Barrel Baked Potato with Truffle Butter...$5.50
RoastedVegetables...$3.50
Squash Latkes...$3.50

Chef: Steven Levine

Please refrain from pipe & cigar smoking
Minimum per person...$20.00
(042993)

Dinner: Tues - Sat 6 - 10:30, Sun 5:30 - 9:30

Arizona 206 and Cafe

This was the first place in New York to offer Southwest cooking (as opposed to Tex-Mex), with a charming adobe/cactus/chili-style decor. The quality of the food by David Walzog is currently on a real high and the place is packed.

Menu Changes Seasonally

PRE THEATRE
- $24.93 PRIX FIXE -

Mixed Greens w/ Rabbit Empanadas

Fish Soup w/ Red Snapper, Clams and Shrimp in a Red Chile Shellfish Broth

Roast Chicken Breast w/ Potato Puree and Chicken Sausage

Sauteed Grouper w/ Roast Garlic, Corn and Guero Chilies

Cherry Pecan Sundae w/ Chocolate Ancho Ice Cream

Cinnamon Tostada w/ Apple Spice Sorbet and Warm Stewed Fruit

The items above are available every night from 5:30 - 6:15pm only.

206 East 60th St • Midtown East Side • (212) 838-0440

- DINNER -

Black Bean Terrine w/ Pear Tomato Salad & Grilled Bread 7-

Vegetable Relleno w/ Yellow Mole 6-

Grilled Chile Rubbed Quail w/ Bulgur Wheat Salad & Cuitlacoche 9-

Pan Seared Sea Scallops w/ Roast Garlic, Spinach & Pumpkin Seed Pesto 8-

Red Chile Duck Ham w/ Mixed Grains, Wood Grilled Fruit & Cinnamon Oil 10-

Tequila-Cured Salmon w/ Tomatillo Salsa, Pickled Vegetables, and Salmon Roe 8-

Skate Salad w/ Roast Corn-Mushroom Salsa and Caperberries 8-

Mixed Green Salad w/ Cilantro-Balsamic Vinaigrette and Green Chile Croutons 6-

Ancho Glazed Poussin w/ Buckwheat Sourdough Pancake, Wilted Beet Greens & Roasted Garlic 19-

Grilled Rabbit Loin w/ Cilantro Oil, Habanero and Braised Leg in a Crisp Tortilla 25-

House Aged N.Y. Strip w/ Wild Mushrooms, Cuitlacoche, and Roasted Potato 28-

Roasted Red Snapper in a Light Broth of Pickled Shallots and Serranos w/ Grilled Onion & Orzo Salad 23-

Grilled Atlantic Salmon w/ Jicama Tangerine Salsa & Zucchini Potato Galette 21-

Roasted Free Range Chicken w/ Chicken-Serrano Sausage & Creamy Polenta 18-

Grilled Maine Lobster w/ Stuffed Squid & Clams in a Red Chile Shellfish Broth 27-

Cinnamon Rubbed Pork Loin w/ Carnitas, Spinach & Root Vegetables 20-

Muscovy Duck Breast w/ Whole Wheat - Vegetable Tortilla, Bitter Greens, Smoked Chile - Peanut Sauce 25-

Charge Lun Din

Dinner: Mon - Thurs 5:30 - 11, Fri - Sat 5:30 - 11:30, Sun 5:30 - 10:30

Canton is where uptowners come when they want to feel adventurous and experience Chinatown. The owner makes everyone feel welcome and offers familiar dishes in an upscale, modern room. The food happens to be very good, too.

Menu Changes Seasonally

Soups

wonton	2.25
chicken egg drop	2.25
mushroom egg drop	2.25
canton's hot and sour	6.95
diced wintermelon	6.95
chicken corn	6.95
soup of the day	*

Appetizers

lettuce wrap	*
dim som	6.95
spring roll	2.75
egg roll	2.75
stuffed clams	*
spareribs	6.95

45 Division St • TriBeCa/Downtown/Chinatown • (212) 226-4441

Entrees

fish - catch of the day	*
special chicken - crispy boneless chicken with scallions	13.95
herb chicken	13.95
beef with seasonal vegetables	*
scallion loin pork	13.95
jumbo shrimps with bacon and onions	*
jumbo shrimps with canton sauce	*
peking duck	*
ginger scallion noodles	9.95
canton's fried rice	10.95
fresh vegetables of the day	*

Desserts

seasonal fruits　　　ice cream

* special dishes prepared upon request

$10.00 minimum per person

Dinner: Fri - Sat until 11, Wed - Thurs, Sun until 10

Chiam

An extensive wine list is not ordinarily something you equate with a Chinese restaurants, but this is where Chiam differs from the norm. In a short time it has become very popular for its excellent Chinese food, exceptional wine list, and upscale decor.

Menu Changes Seasonally

HOT APPETIZERS

海棠雞餃	*Steamed Chrysanthemum Chicken Dumplings (4)*	5.50
蝦皇蝦餃	*Steamed Shrimp Dumplings Imperiale (4)*	6.50
仙竹卷	*Steamed Beef Rolls (2)*	5.50
乾蒸燒賣	*Steamed Pork Dumplings (4)*	5.50
蒸雞餃	*Steam Chicken Dumplings (4)*	5.50
正宗春卷	*Cantonese Egg-Roll*	3.50
百花小卷	*Baby Shrimp Rolls (6)*	5.50
龍蝦卷	*Lobster Roll*	16.95
酥炸蝦丸	*Crispy Shrimp Balls (4)*	6.50

LIGHT SPECIALS

銀芽雞絲	*L-1*	*Julienne Chicken w. Beansprouts*	12.50
松米雞絲	*L-2*	*Chicken w. Pinenuts*	12.50
清蒸全魚	*L-3*	*Steamed Catch of The Day w. Ginger & Scallion*	17.95
素菜叉燒片	*L-4*	*Roast Pork Steak*	15.50
清蒸龍蝦	*L-5*	*Steamed Lobster w. Lemon & Ginger*	21.95
素菜雞片	*L-6*	*Sliced Chicken w. Seasonal Vegetables*	12.50
素菜牛肉	*L-7*	*Beef Tender Loin w. Seasonal Vegetables*	13.50

160 East 48th St • Midtown East Side • (212) 371-2323

PASTA & RICE

海鮮炒麵	*Pan-Fried Angel Hair w. Seafood*	15.95
豉椒乾炒牛河	*Beef Fettuccini (Chow Fun)*	9.95
鮮蜆薑葱撈麵	*Angel Hair w. Clams & Black Bean Sauce*	10.95

POULTRY & MEAT

荷葉蒸雞	*Steamed Lotus Wrapped Chicken*	14.50
胡桃雞丁	*Boneless Walnut Chicken*	13.50
鳳凰雞	*Wok-Grilled Stuffed Chicken*	14.50
西檸炸軟雞	*Lemon Chicken*	13.50
京都肉排	*Beijing Pork Filets*	13.50
本樓叉燒	*Roast Pork ala Chiam*	15.50
蘆筍牛柳	*Beef Tenderloin w. Asparagus*	13.50
陳皮牛柳	*Crispy Beef L'Orange*	15.50
燒菲利球	*Filet Mignon Kew*	19.95
中式牛柳	*Hong Kong Marinated Steak*	15.50
梅子鴨	*Roast Duck w. Plum Sauce*	14.50
樟茶鴨	*Smoked Duck w. Campor*	14.50

CHIAM'S SPECIALS SEAFOOD

椒鹽鮮魷	*Salt-Baked Calamari Kowloon*	13.50
紅油爆鮮魷	*Sauteed Squid with Spicy Sauce*	13.50
黑椒帶子	*Scallop Meunier w. Black Peppercorn*	15.95
四川大明蝦	*Szechuan Prawns*	17.95
干煎釀明蝦	*Grilled Stuffed Prawns*	17.95
素菜蝦球	*Prawns w. Fresh Garden Vegetable*	17.95
菓汁大明蝦	*Grand Marnier Prawns*	17.95
豉汁炒龍蝦	*Lobster w. Black Bean Sauce*	21.95
乾燒龍蝦	*Lobster w. Hot Chili Sauce*	21.95
三鮮龍糊	*Oceanic Treat of Assorted Seafood*	22.95

Dinner: Fri - Sat until 1am, Sun - Thurs until 12

Chin Chin

This is one of the handful of "gourmet" Chinese restaurants in New York. Top quality ingredients, complex preparations of new dishes, refined traditional ones, and a simple interior, accented by sepia photos of Jimmy Chin's family, are the highlights.

MENU CHANGES SEASONALLY

APPETIZERS - HOT

SNAILS W. CORIANDER & GARLIC BROTH $7.50
STEAMED SHANGHAI DUMPLINGS (PORK) $7.00
STEAMED VEGETABLE DUMPLINGS $7.00
PAN FRIED DUMPLINGS (PORK) $7.00
SZECHUAN WONTONS $6.00
BBQ SPARE RIBS $9.75
SWEET AND SOUR SPARE RIBS $8.50
CRISPY FRIED SQUID $7.50
SPRING ROLLS $4.00
SCALLION PANCAKES $4.00
VEGETABLE DUCK PIE W. CREPES $6.00
CHICKEN SOONG IN LETTUCE POCKET $8.50
STEAMED SHRIMP DUMPLINGS $8.50
STEAMED CHICKEN DUMPLINGS $7.00

APPETIZERS - COLD

SHREDDED JELLYFISH $7.50
THOUSAND YEAR OLD EGG
W. PICKLED SHALLOT $7.50
COLD NOODLES
W. HOT SESAME SAUCE $8.00
COLD NOODLE W. CHILLED SEAFOOD $12.00
TOSSED AGAR SALAD $7.00
SHREDDED ROAST DUCK SALAD $9.00
COLD BEAN CURD W. TWO SAUCES $7.00
HONG KONG SHRIMP COCKTAIL $9.00

VEGETABLES & RICE

EGGPLANT W. GARLIC SAUCE $8.00
POACHED WATERCRESS W. GARLIC $8.00
DRY SAUTEED STRING BEANS $7.50
CHINESE BROCCOLI W. OYSTER SAUCE $8.50
POACHED SPINACH W. GARLIC $7.50
BUDDIST DELIGHT $8.50
ABALONE MUSHROOM W. PEA PODS $8.50
COUNTRY STYLE BEAN CURD $8.00
TEN INGREDIENTS FRIED RICE $8.50
MANDARIN FRIED RICE $8.00
TOYSAN FRIED RICE $8.50

216 East 49th St • Midtown East Side • (212) 888-4555

FOWL

PEKING DUCK - ONE OR TWO WAYS $ 33.00
THREE GLASS CHICKEN $13.50
SHREDDED CHICKEN WITH
GARLIC SAUCE $ 12.50
TUNG ON CHICKEN $12.50
LEMON CHICKEN $12.50
COUNTRY STYLE CHICKEN W. SPINACH $13.50
DICE CHICKEN W.
WALNUTS AND LEEKS $13.50
SESAME CHICKEN $13.50
GRILLED BABY QUAILS $13.50
TEA SMOKED DUCK W.
SCALLION PANCAKE $ 15.50

BEEF

VEAL MEDALLIONS W. SPICY PEPPERCORN SAUCE $ 15.50
CRISPED ORANGE BEEF $ 15.50
CHIN CHIN STEAK W. ASPARAGUS $ 16.00
FILET MIGNON W. MUSHROOM AND BROCCOLI $ 16.00
SHREDDED BEEF W. HOT
PEPPERS AND BLACK BEAN SAUCE $ 13.50
SLICED STEAK W. BROCCOLI SPEARS $ 13.50

PORK & LAMB

SAUTEED LEG OF LAMB W. LEEKS $ 15.00
CURRIED LAMB STEW $ 14.00
SHREDDED PORK W. GARLIC SAUCE $ 12.50
MOO SHU PORK W. CREPES $ 13.50
HONG KONG PORK FILETS $ 13.50
MONGOLIAN SHREDDED PORK $ 13.50
PORK AND BEANS $ 13.50

SEAFOOD

LOBSTER W. GINGER AND SCALLIONS $19.50
STEAMED LOBSTER W. LEMON $19.50
OLD FASHIONED LOBSTER CANTONESE $19.50
STEAMED OR CRISPY SEABASS $17.50
JUMBO PRAWNS SZECHUAN $16.00
JUMBO PRAWNS W. LOBSTER SAUCE $16.00
STEAMED SALMON W. BLACK BEAN SAUCE $16.00
CHIN CHIN SHRIMP SCAMPI $16.00
CLAMS W. BLACK BEAN SAUCE $12.50
SAUTEED MUSSELS $ 12.50
APHRODESIA LOVE NEST $17.00
KING CRAB MEAT W. ABALONE MUSHROOM $19.00

PASTA

BROAD FUN NOODLES W. BEEF $10.00
LO MEIN (BEEF OR CHICKEN) $10.00
CHOPPED BEEF W. VERMICELLI NOODLES $9.50
SINGAPORE RICE NOODLES (MAI FUN) $11.00
CRISPY PAN FRIED EGG NOODLES $ 13.00
ANGEL HAIR PASTA W. FRESH GREENS $9.50
ANGEL HAIR PASTA W. ASSORTED SEAFOOD $15.00

Din

Dinner: 7 Days a Week until 12 am

China Grill serves California Chinese food - unique in New York. It also has a sleek, stylized decor in a soaring, multi-level space next door to the American Craft Museum and across the street from the Museum of Modern Art.

Menu Changes Seasonally

APPETIZERS

SAKE CURED SALMON ROLLS
with lemon grass vinaigrette
11.50

LAMB SPARERIBS
plum and sesame spiced
12.50

STIR FRIED SESAME CITRUS NOODLES
with spicy chicken
13.50
or seasonal vegetables
11.50

CHINA GRILL TRI-STAR
chefs choice of three appetizers
15.00

ORIENTAL ANTIPASTO
daily selection includes grilled and roasted vegetables, scallion mozzarella and more
13.50
with meat or seafood
16.00

TEMPURA SASHIMI
with hot mustard champagne sauce
12.50

SALADS

CRACKLING CALAMARI SALAD
with lime miso dressing
7.50/12.50

GRILLED BARBECUED PRAWNS
with fennel-bean-salad and asian pesto
12.50

PEKING DUCK SALAD
served crispy with tangerine orange sauce
8.50/14.00

THAI BEEF SATAY
with soba noodles and spicy peanut sauce
12.00

60 West 53rd St • Midtown West Side • (212) 333-7788

Entrees

Cantonese Sliced Steak
with scallions, sweet soy and Napa cucumber salad
25.00

Lamb T-Bones
in shitake mushroom sauce with roasted red pepper polenta
21.00

Grilled Organic Chicken
with tempura sweet onions
18.00

Tea Steamed Whole Flounder
with ribboned vegetables
20.50

Rice Stick Noodles and Smoked Salmon
with chili shallot cream sauce
21.00

Barbecued Salmon
with a Chinese mustard sauce and stir fried greens
20.50

Grilled Sea Scallops
with carrot-corn rissotto and zuccini crisps
19.00

Pan Seared Spicy Tuna
served rare with avocado sashimi
21.00

Shanghai Lobster
with ginger, curry, and crispy spinach
market

Grilled Dry Aged Szechuan Beef
with sake, soy, spicy shallots and cilantro
26.50/39.50

Crispy Duck
in a carmelized black vinegar sauce with scallion pancakes
21.00/33.00

Sizzling Whole Fish
with a Chinese black bean and red chile sauce
22.00/34.00

Grilled 38oz Porterhouse Steak
with roasted garlic and shallots and chinese black vinaigrette sauce
52.00

Angel Hair Pasta and String Vegetables
with red pepper tempura
19.00

Grilled Garlic Shrimp
on black fettucini in red curry coconut sauce
21.00

Lobster Perciatelli
with ginger and orange
22.00

Dinner: Mon - Thurs until 11, Fri until 12, Sat 5:30 - 12, Sun 5 - 10

Fu's serves reliable, top-quality Chinese food to a loyal neighborhood following. It is one of the few Chinese places on the Upper East Side in a genteel setting, so it is always crowded.

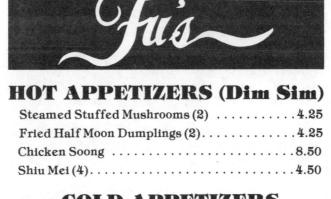

HOT APPETIZERS (Dim Sim)

Steamed Stuffed Mushrooms (2) 4.25
Fried Half Moon Dumplings (2). 4.25
Chicken Soong 8.50
Shiu Mei (4). 4.50

COLD APPETIZERS

Jelly Fish 9.50
★Tangy Spicy Shrimp 9.50

POULTRY

★Sesame Chicken 11.95
Chicken with Cashew Nuts 11.95
Fu's Duckling with Black Bean Sauce 13.95
Pineapple Duck 13.95

BEEF

★Fillet of Beef in Sesame Sauce 13.95
★Fillet of Beef Hong Kong Style 13.95
★Crispy Dry Shredded Beef Hunan Style 13.95
Shredded Beef with String Beans 13.95

FORGOTTEN MENU

Steamed Vegetable Dumplings (2) 3.25
Steamed Chicken with Black Mushrooms 11.95
Moo Shu Vegetables 11.95

1395 Second Ave • Upper East Side • (212) 517-9670

SEA FOOD

Sweet & Sour Shrimp 16.95
★Shrimp with Garlic & Scallion Sauce 16.95
Lobster with Black Bean Sauce 18.95
(Out of Shell) 20.95
★Ocean Flavor Scallops 16.95
Sweet & Sour Crispy Sea Bass ...... market price

VEGETABLES

★Szechuan Broccoli 9.95
★Eggplant Family Style 9.95
Snow Pea and Water Chestnuts 9.95

CHEF'S SPECIALTIES

PEKING DUCK 32.95
A young duckling slowly grilled until crispy and golden, sliced in front of you then served wth homemade crepes, spring onion brushes, fresh cucumbers and Hoisin sauce.

★HOMESTYLE CHICKEN 14.95
Large chunks of fresh chicken slightly breaded, then fried until crispy, sauteed with fresh red pepper and scallions in a hot spicy sauce.

★CRISPY ORANGE BEEF 15.95
Sliced fillet of beef done to a crisp, glazed with a tangy sauce with a touch or orange essence.

JUMBO SHRIMP FU'S STYLE 16.95
Large prawns sauteed with mushrooms, snow peas, water chestnuts, ginger and scallions in a rice wine. Baked in aluminum foil for a few extra minutes to seal in the sauce for exquisite flavor.

PAN FRIED FLOUNDER .... market price
Whole flounder pan fried to crispy golden brown with ginger, scallions and parsley, even the bones crunch when munched.

★HOT & SPICY

Dinner: 7 Days a Week 4 - 11:30

Shun Lee Palace

This restaurant has long been rated among the top Chinese in the city. It has remained consistently excellent and extremely popular.

S H U N L E E

Menu Changes Seasonally

HOT APPETIZERS

SPRING ROLLS (2) 4.75
VEGETABLE SPRING ROLLS (2) 4.75
CRAB CLAW WITH CHICKEN (2) 7.00
BARBEQUE SPARE RIBS 12.75
GRILLED SCALLOPS (4) 8.25
CRISPY SHRIMP BALLS (4)........................ 9.75

COLD APPETIZERS

JELLY FISH 10.50
*TANGY SPICY KIDNEY 10.25
*COLD DUCK WITH SPICY HUNAN SAUCE.................................... 11.25

FROM THE GARDENS

TRIPLE FRAGRANCE 11.95
Sugar snap peas, lotus root, fresh water chestnuts; these refreshing vegetables lightly sauteed with ginger.

BUDDHA'S DELIGHT 10.75
A mixture of fresh water chestnuts, Chinese mushrooms, bamboo shoots, snow peas, tree mushrooms, gingko nuts, dried bean curd, Chinese cabbage and carrots.

SHUN LEE SPECIALTIES

***SWEETBREADS WITH BLACK MUSHROOMS 16.75**
Chunks of fresh sweetbreads stir fried with scallions, black mushrooms and water chestnuts in a hot peppery Szechuan sauce.

RACK OF LAMB, SZECHUAN STYLE 20.25
Four individual chops grilled with garlic and scallions; served with broccoli and carrots in a Szechuan sauce.

SOLE ON ITS CRISPY BONE 22.50
Fresh fillet of sole sauteed, then placed on the crispy frame. Served with Chinese vegetables. (Frame can be eaten like a french fry.)

BARBECUED SQUAB (1) 14.50
Squab marinated in soy sauce and 5 spices; roasted to golden perfection.

155 East 55th St • Midtown East Side • (212) 371-8844

DUCK

***SLICED DUCKLING WITH YOUNG GINGER ROOT 16.75**
Tender sliced barbecued boneless duckling served with sweet young ginger root and hot pepper.

CRISPY DUCK WITH WALNUTS ... 17.75
Boneless Long Island duckling without skin and fat, marinated in five spices and steamed; then coated with a light batter and fried till crispy.

POULTRY

***CHAN-DO CHICKEN 15.25**
Chicken nuggets marinated with 5 spices; sauteed with ginger, hot pepper, garlic and scallions.

CHICKEN WITH THREE DIFFERENT NUTS 14.75
Chicken breast garnished with water chestnuts, bamboo shoots and snow peas; cooked in a brown sauce with sauteed walnuts, peanuts and cashew nuts.

MEAT

***ORANGE BEEF 17.25**
Sliced fillet of beef fried till crisp; sauteed with hot sweet preserved orange.

BEEF WITH SUGAR SNAP PEAS 15.95
Sliced fillet of beef, sugar snap peas, water chestnuts and bamboo shoots gently sauteed in oyster sauce.

FROM THE RIVER AND THE SEA

BEIJING PRAWNS 18.75
Large shrimp marinated in egg white and sauteed in rice wine; garnished with sugar snap peas and fresh water chestnuts.

***PRAWNS WITH GARLIC AND SCALLIONS 18.75**
Prawns sauteed with finely diced bamboo shoots and scallions mixed with Szechuan sauce.

LOBSTER IN SZECHUAN OR BLACK BEAN SAUCE 20.50
Chunks of Maine lobster simmered in lobster sauce with egg and black beans. Or *cooked in hot pepper sauce.
(Out of shell) 20.95

SIZZLING SCALLOPS 18.75
Tender scallops dipped in lotus flour and pan fried till crispy. Served with Chinese vegetables on a sizzling platter.

NEPTUNE'S NET 22.50
Fresh lobster chunks, sliced shrimp, scallops and fresh sea bass all sauteed together in a tasty wine sauce. Served in a potato basket.

HEAVENLY SEA BASS FILLET 16.75
Fresh sea bass fillets, water chestnuts and snow peas cooked in a rice wine sauce.

***HOT AND SPICY** *The degree of spice can be altered to your taste*

Dinner: 7 Days a Week 3 - 11:30

This is a beautifully decorated, expensive Chinese restaurant that largely appeals to an expense-account crowd. It has a great location near midtown shopping and also happens to serve excellent food.

TSE YANG

Soups

Our favorite Soup "TSE-YANG" *Notre Potage préféré «TSE-YANG»*	6.25	**Borneo's Swallows' nests** *Les Nids d'Hirondelles de Bornéo*	8.25
Pekinese Hot-Sour *Le Suprême Pékinois*	4.75	**"SOUTH-PACIFIC" Sharks' Fins** *Les Ailerons de Requins de «SUD-PACIFIQUE»*	12.50
South Pacific Vermicelli *Potage de Vermicelles*	4.75		

Appetizers

"RAINBOW" colored Appetizers *Les Hors-d'Oeuvre «ARC-EN-CIEL»*	12.50	**Pekinese Delicacies steamed or grilled min 2 pers.** *Les Délices de Pékin à la vapeur ou grillés*	8.25
Crab Legs Delicious Salad *Les Pattes de Crabe en Salade*	12.75	**Baby Spareribs** *Les Travers de Porc laqués*	11.75
"TSE-YANG" Fresh Smoked Salmon *Le Saumon Frais Fumé «TSE-YANG»*	12.50	**"TSE-YANG" Frog's Legs** *Grenouilles au roti*	18.00
Spring and Autumn Rolls *Les Rouleaux de Printemps et d'Automne*	6.25		

Sea foods

Ambrosia Sea Food *L'Offrande Des Dieux De La Mer*	29.50	**Crab "SHANGHAI STYLE"** *Les Pinces de Crabe Rouge farci*	32.75
"JADE PHOENIX" giant Shrimps *Les Crevettes géantes «PHOENIX DE JADE»*	25.75	**Frogs Legs "IMPERIAL SAUCE"** *Grenouilles a l'Imperial*	26.75
Shrimps in green Lemon sauce *Les Queues de Crevettes au Citron vert*	25.75	**"YANG-TSEU" style Sole** *Les Filets de Sole «YANG-TSEU»*	22.50
"SZECHUAN" style Lobster *Les Langoustines à la mode de «SZECHUAN»*	32.75	**Sole in spicy sauce** *Les Filets de Sole sauce piquant*	22.50
Scallops in tasty sauce *Les Coquilles St-Jacques dans leur sauce ravigote*	25.75	**Seasonal Fish cooked as you Wish** *Le Poisson de Mer à votre Façon*	S.GR

Fowl

"SZECHUAN" style Chicken *Les Filets de Poulets à la mode de «SZECHUAN»*	18.50	**Roasted Duck in Chinese Tea** *Le Canard rôti au Thé de Chine*	23.50
"HANTCHEU" style Chicken *Les Blancs de Poulet «HANTCHEU»*	18.50	**Loquat Duckling** *Le Caneton au Loquat*	23.50
Your favorite "TSE-YANG" Chicken *Votre Poulet préféré «TSE-YANG»*	21.50	**Sliced Duck in spicy sauce** *Les Filets de Canard sauce piquante*	22.75
Sauteed Tea-Smoked Chicken *l'Emince de poulet au Thé de Chine*	21.50	**Roasted Duck served Peking style** *Le véritable Canard laqué comme à Pékin*	52.00
Green Lemon flavored Chicken *La Poitrine de Poulet au Citron vert*	18.50		

Vegetables

Chinese Mushrooms in Oyster sauce *Les Champignons de Chine sauté au Jus d'Huître*	13.75	**"TSE-YANG" selected Vegetables** *Les Légumes sélectionnés «TSE-YANG»*	12.75

34 East 51st St • Midtown East Side • (212) 688-5447

Meats

Veal in Spicy sauce 25.75
L'Emincé de Veau poêlé dans sa sauce piquant
Sauteed Veal with green Onions 25.75
Les Mignons de Veau sautes aux Çiboulettes
"TSE-YANG" style Calf's liver 27.50
Le sauté de Foie de Veau «TSE-YANG»
Peking Style Beef Filet 29.50
Le Filet de Boeuf à la mode de «PEKING»
SZECHUAN style Beef 25.75
Le Pave de Boeuf à la mode de «SZECHUAN»
"TSE-YANG" Beef Filet 27.50
Le Filet de Boeuf «TSE-YANG»
Chef's Sauteed Tenderloin of Pork 22.50
Filet de porc sauté du chef
Lemon Sweet-Sour Pork 19.50
Les Filets de Porc à la Citronelle
"TSE-YANG" style Pork 22.50
Les Filets de Porc sautés «TSE-YANG»
Chef's sauteed Lamb 25.75
Le Filet d'Agneau du Chef
Lamb Tse Yang Style 25.75
Le Filet d'Agneau «TSE-YANG»

Rice and Noodles

"YANG-TSE" fried Rice 11.00
Le Riz sauté «YANG-TSEU»
Steamed white Rice 1.50
Le Riz blanc dans son bain de vapeur
Rice Vermicelli SINGAPORE style 12.75
Les Vermicelles de Riz comme à SINGAPOUR
"TSE-YANG" style Noodles 14.75
Les Nouilles sautées «TSE-YANG»

Desserts

"TSE-YANG" Cup 7.50
La Coupe «TSE-YANG»
Special caramelized Apples min 2 pers. 9.75
Les Pommes au Caramel suprême
Almond Jelly 7.50
Le Lait d'Amande en gelée
Sorbet - Choice of flavors 5.50
Les Sorbets aux divers Parfums
Exotic and fresh Season's Fruits 9.75
Les Fruits frais et exotiques de saison

Our Chef's Suggestions

Our special Menu for two or more

Shanghai style Dinner

Asparagus with Crab meat soup
Shanghai style Dumplings
Sauteed Prawns
Boneless Chicken with "TSE-YANG" special sauce
Shredded Veal in five spices (Chili sauce)
Special Fried Rice
Ice Cream
$42.00 per person (min 2 pers.)

Peking style Dinner

Shark's Fin with Crab meat soup
Steamed Dumpling Peking style
Scallops Peking style
Fried Prawns in Spicy sauce
Peking Roasted Duck with Crepes
Shredded Duck in spicy sauce
Rice Vermicelli Singapore style
Special Caramelized Apple
$52.00 per person (min 2 pers.)

Dinner: 7 Days a Week 6 - 11

Unique in New York, or probably anywhere in this country, Zen Palate serves strictly vegetarian Chinese that's as tasty as anything made with meat. The restaurant itself is very sleek and elegant and dining there makes you feel good.

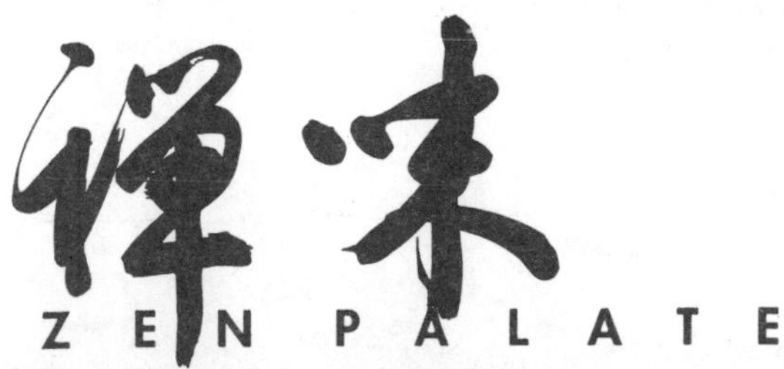

COLD STARTERS

Moo Shu Basil Rolls (2)	3.00
Marinated Seaweed	3.00
Sichuan Sesame Chips	4.00
Grilled Marinated Vegetarian Duck	6.50
Stuffed Mushroom Loaves	5.50
Smokey-Season Tofu with sesame seeds	5.50

MAIN COURSES

Jewel of Happiness 15.50
MINI MUSHROOM STEAKS WITH ENDIVE & SWEET PEAS

Stuffed Black Mushrooms 14.50

Moo-Shu Fantasia 9.50
SERVED WITH (4) CREPES

Festival-on-Roll 12.50
SEASONED SPINACH WRAPPED IN SOY BEAN CREPES STEAMED AND TOPPED WITH SPICY CHEF SAUCE

Eggplant Delight 9.00
STEAMED CHINESE EGGPLANT TOPPED WITH BASIL & BLACK BEAN SAUCE

West Lake 16.00
STEAMED SHITAKI MUSHROOMS TOPPED WITH SCALLIONS, GINGER & SHERRY

Sweet and Sour Divine 10.50
DEEP FRIED PECAN PUFFS SAUTEED WITH SWEET SOUR SAUCE & PEPPERS

663 Ninth Ave • Theater District • (212) 582-1669

Mushroom Forest *MINCED SHITAKI MUSHROOM, SOY BEAN GLUTEN & PINE NUTS WRAPPED WITH LETTUCE*	16.50
Dream-Land *LAYERS OF FRIED SPINACH LINGUINI, BEAN SPROUTS AND SHREDDED BLACK MUSHROOMS*	12.50
Rainbow Stuffed Chinese Cabbage *VEGETARIAN-BACON, CONJEX (JAPANESE VEGETABLE) & WATER CHESTNUTS WRAPPED WITH STEAMED CABBAGE AND GARLIC SAUCE*	13.50
Sauteed Fresh Mushrooms and Basil	12.50
Zen Retreat *PUMPKIN SHELL STUFFED WITH BEAN CREPE, TOFU PATE & VEGETABLE*	12.50
Zen Casserole *STUFFED TOFU STEWED WITH TOMATOES, BEAN THREADS AND PEAS*	12.50
Vegetables Bundles *ZUCCHINIS, BASIL, BLACK MUSHROOMS, BAMBOO SHOOTS AND WATER CHESTNUTS WRAPPED WITH VEGETARIAN-HAM*	14.50
Tofu Infinity *PAN FRIED TOFU WITH BASIL & SWEET TOMATO IN SIZZLING SPICE SAUCE*	9.50

DESSERTS

Tofu Pudding	4.00
Tofu Honey Pie with Berry topping	4.00
Coconut Tart	4.00
Cheese Cake	2.00
Water Chestnut Tart	4.00
Fresh Fruit Basket	4.00
Ice Cream	1.50
Coffee	1.50
Herb Tea	1.50

Dining Minimum Per Person 10.00

Dinner: 7 Days a Week until 11:45

Ballroom, The

Opened by the late Felipe Rojas-Lombardi, The Ballroom is known for its extensive tapas menu (Spanish-style hors d'oeuvres), which it introduced to New York, and its festive atmosphere, complete with carberet. The tapas bar remains one of the best bargains in New York.

The Ballroom®
Just 3 blocks south of Madison Square Garden

Menu Changes Seasonally

SOUPS

Tapas Soups (Three Flavors) 6.75

SALADS

Caesar Salad 8.50

Roast Sweet Pepper with Goat Cheese 8.50

Fennel with Grated Parmesan 6.75

Seasonal Mixed Greens 5.75

VEGETABLES

Baked Squash 5.75

Steamed Chayote with Dill Sauce 5.75

Platanos 5.75

Yuca Straws 5.75

Seasonal Vegetables

PAELLAS

Paella with Saffron 24.50

Paella Verde 24.50

Paella Negra 24.50

Paella Jardinera 24.50

253 West 28th St • Chelsea • (212) 244-3005

SEAFOOD

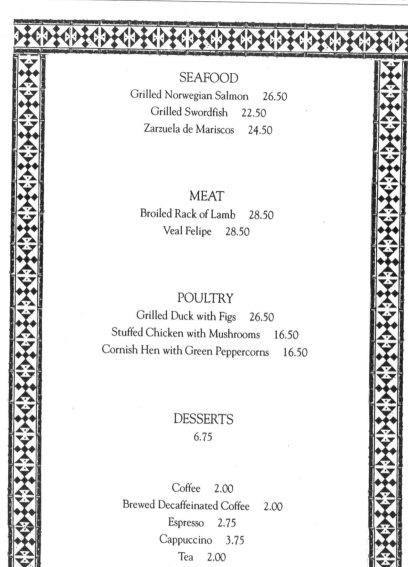

Grilled Norwegian Salmon 26.50

Grilled Swordfish 22.50

Zarzuela de Mariscos 24.50

MEAT

Broiled Rack of Lamb 28.50

Veal Felipe 28.50

POULTRY

Grilled Duck with Figs 26.50

Stuffed Chicken with Mushrooms 16.50

Cornish Hen with Green Peppercorns 16.50

DESSERTS

6.75

Coffee 2.00

Brewed Decaffeinated Coffee 2.00

Espresso 2.75

Cappuccino 3.75

Tea 2.00

Dinner: Tues - Sat 5 - 1

Carlyle Dining Room

Being in the Carlyle Hotel, one of the city's most prestigious, gives this restaurant its cachet. Although its food and decor have recently been overhauled and are said to be much improved, the real draw here is celebrity-sighting.

Menu Changes Seasonally Along With Daily Specials

HORS D'OEUVRE

Le Caviar de Beluga Malossol 85.00
Beluga Caviar Malossol

Le Mille Feuilles au Caviar de Sevruga 19.75
Mille-Feuille of Sevruga Caviar

La Terrine de Foie Gras de Canard sur sa Gelée au Sauternes 18.75
Terrine of Fresh Duck Foie Gras with Sauternes Aspic

La Salade de Champignons Sauvages à l'Huile de Truffes Blanches et Vinaigre de Balsam 14.50
Mixed Greens and Wild Mushrooms with White Truffle Oil and Balsamic Vinegar

Le Pâté de Faisan aux Truffes et Pistaches 12.75
Pheasant Pâte with Truffles and Pistachios

Le Saumon Fumé d'Ecosse 18.75
Scottish Smoked Salmon

Le Crabe de Maryland dans son Panier de Pommes Gaufrettes 17.50
Maryland Crabmeat served in a Potato Basket

Le Homard du Maine aux Shiitake à l'Huile Vierge et Citron 18.50
Maine Lobster with Shiitake, Lemon and Virgin Oil

Les Coquilles St. Jacques à la Compote d'Oignons Gratinée 12.75
Sea Scallops with a Gratin of Stewed Onions

LES PATES

Les Pâtes Fraîches Bolognese, Primavera ou à Votre Choix 23.75
Fresh Pasta, Bolognese, Primavera or Your Choice

Les Fettuccine aux Champignons Sauvages à l'Huile de Truffes Blanches 26.75
Fettuccine with Wild Mushrooms and White Truffle Oil

Les Ravioli de Homard sur un Lit d'Epinards "Sauce Corail" 32.50
Lobster Ravioli on a Bed of Spinach, "Coral Sauce"

Carlyle Hotel • 35 East 76th St • Upper East Side • (212) 744-1600

LES SPECIALTIES

La Sole de Douvre Meunière ou Grillée 36.00
Dover Sole, Sauteed or Grilled

L'Escalope de Saumon Grillée au Céleri Fondant à l'Aneth 28.75
Escalope of Grilled Salmon with Braised Celery and Dill Sauce

Le Filet de Bar Rayé aux Ecailles de Truffe et Concombre au Beurre de Noilly 29.50
Filet of Striped Bass with Truffle and Cucumber Scales, Noilly Butter Sauce

Le Suprême de Poulet aux Cèpes et Coulis de Foie Gras 29.00
Breast of Chicken with Porcini and Foie Gras Coulis

Le Magret de Canard aux Pommes Vertes, Poires et ses Galettes de Maïs 29.50
Magret of Duck with Green Apples, Pears and Corn Cakes

La Côte de Veau aux Lentilles et Oignons Nouveaux 32.00
Sauteed Veal Chop with Lentils and Pearl Onions

Le Filet d'Agneau à la Compote d'Aubergines et au Thym Frais 32.00
Loin of Lamb with Compote of Eggplant and Fresh Thyme

Les Mignonnettes de Boeuf Grillées et leur Pomme Purée aux Truffes 32.00
Grilled Medallions of Beef with Truffled Mashed Potatoes

La Poitrine de Faisan aux Châtaignes et Cassis 29.00
Breast of Pheasant with Chestnuts and Black Currants

LES ENTREES

Le Tournedos Grillé "Henri IV" 33.00
Grilled Tournedos "Henry IV"

Le Carré d'Agneau Rôti, Pommes Sarladaises 68.00
Rack of Lamb with Sarladaises Potatoes

Le Demi Poulet Rôti ou Grillé et ses Pommes Soufflées 23.50
Roasted or Grilled Half Chicken served with Soufflé Potatoes

Les Légumes Frais à Votre Choix 5.00
Your Choice of a Fresh Vegetable

Le Panier de Pommes Soufflées 6.00
Basket of Soufflé Potatoes

LES DESSERTS

Le Soufflé Chaud au Chocolat ou au Grand Marnier 10.00
Chocolate or Grand Marnier Soufflé

La Tarte Chaude aux Pommes 8.00
Warm Apple Tart

(Please order at time of entrée selection)

Dinner: 7 Days a Week 6 - 11

The deal here is NOT the view - it's the wine. Small parties are seated in the wine cellar (on the 107th floor) and are served a prix fixe 7-course meal, paired with the finest wines.

Menu Changes Bi-Weekly

CHEF'S CANAPES
Veuve Clicquot Brut n.v.

~

WARM HERB SALAD with BAKED SKATE and CRAYFISH
Chardonnay, Leeuwin Estate 1984

~

SAUTEED FOIE GRAS on CHANTERELLE RAGOUT with CHIVE CREPE

~

LOBSTER FRICASEE with CUCUMBER and MINT

~

ROASTED RACK of LAMB with PICKLED LIMES
Chappelle-Chambertin, Trapet 1985

~

INTERNATIONAL CHEESE SELECTION, CRUSTY FRENCH BREAD
Cabernet Sauvignon, Lakespring 1981

~

GLAZED CASSOULET of BAY SCALLOPS and OYSTERS, CHAMPANGE SABAYON
St. Aubin, Les Combes 1990

~

DUCK CONSOMME BAKED in BABY PUMPKIN

ROASTED VEAL LOIN on FOIE GRAS JUS,
BABY ARTICHOKE and VEGETABLE FEUILLETEE
Mazy-Chambertin, Rousseau 1987

~

FRESHLY SMOKED MALLARD DUCK BREAST on AUTUMN SALAD LEAVES,
RASPBERRY OIL
Auxey-Duresses, Duc de Magenta, Jadot 1988

~

SEA URCHIN and CRABMEAT GRATIN

~

FILET of TURBOTIN in POTATO CRUST with FAVA BEANS WITH TARRAGON

~

MARINATED LOIN of VENISON on JUNIPER BERRY BEURRE ROUGE,
CELERY ROOTS and WILD MUSHROOMS
Pesquera 1989

~

INTERNATIONAL CHEESE SELECTION, CRUSTY FRENCH BREAD
Chateau Gruaud Larose 1981

~

WARM CHOCOLATE SOUFFLE
Semillon Late Harvest, Chalk Hill 1986

~

WARM APPLE TART with CREME FRAICHE and GREEN APPLE SORBET
Robertson's Vintage Port 1977

~

COLOMBIAN COFFEE

~

FRIANDISE

Dinner: Mon - Sat, One Seating at 7:30

Any restaurant that Dennis Foy is involved in is a contender for top honors. He has gained an excellent reputation over the past few years for the creative flair he brings to Continental and French dishes.

Menu Changes Seasonally

Appetizers

Salad of Baby Lettuces, Truffle Vinaigrette
6.75

Spring Onion Soup, Crab Wonton, Lemon Gras
6.95

Tian of Crab, Thyme
12.50

Wild Mushroom Napoleon, Mustard, Shallots
9.25

Mussel Bouillabaisse, Aioli Baguette
7.75

Gravlox, Sauteed Spinach, Red Onion Lime Vinaigrette
10.25

6 Roosevelt Ave • Chatham, NJ • (201) 701-0303

Entrees

Grilled Salmon, Polenta, Jicama, Salsa
24.00

Sauteed Black Sea Bass, Herb Broth
23.75

Pan Roasted Monkfish, Scallion, Mushroom, Star Anise
21.75

Sauteed Halibut, Oyster Mushrooms, Asparagus
24.00

Roasted Sea Scallops, Cilantro, Ginger, Chili Oil
22.50

Grilled Muscovy Duck, Jasmine Rice, Melange of Vegetables
25.50

Roasted Guinea Hen, Potato Mango Compote, Field Greens
23.50

Roasted Pigeon, Portabello and Foie Napoleon, Peppered Cabbage
22.50

Sauteed Loin of Veal, Root Flours, Fava Beans Marineire
28.50

Rack of Baby Lamb, Cous Cous, Bayaldi
27.00

Roasted Sirloin, Roasted Vegetables, Au Jus
24.00

Dinner: Mon - Thurs 5:30 - 9:30, Fri - Sat 5:30 - 10:30

The owners of the Rihga Royal decided to make Halcyon a destination dining spot for other than hotel guests and they spent a lot of money on the place. It shows. The decor is elegant and the food very good - it's raised the level of hotel dining rooms in the city.

Menu Changes Seasonally

Starters

Today's Soup
$6.00

Watercress, Endive & Shiitake Mushroom Salad, Sliced Beets & Wild Mushroom Vinaigrette
$8.00

Heart of Romaine Casear Salad, Virgin Olive Oil, Dry Aged Monterey Jack Cheese
$8.50

Mixed Spring Greens, Baby Plum Tomatoes, Champagne Vinaigrette
$7.95

Arugula Salad, Candied Pecans, Corn & Roasted Peppers
$8.50

Fresh Pacific Oysters with Dill Marinated Salmon & Fresh Chive Mignonette
$12.00

Halcyon's Own Maple Cured Smoked Salmon Glazed New York Style Goat Cheese, Summer Greens, Apple Jack Vinaigrette
$12.50

Lightly Applewood Smoked Lobster Chili With White Beans, Virginia Ham & Chipotle Peppers
$12.50

Roasted Eggplant, Peppers & Wild Mushrooms Layered Between Thin Crisp Phyllo Chive And Basil Oil
$11.00

Pastas

Penne Pasta Tossed With Roasted Eggplant, Zucchini & Virgin Olive Oil, Glazed With A Sheeps Milk Cheese
$11.00 Appetizer
$16.50 Entree

Orecchiette Pasta With Plum Tomatoes, Olives, Buffalo Mozzarella & Basil
$11.00 Appetizer
$16.50 Entree

Lobster & Scallop Ravioli
Chardonnay Butter Sauce
$15.50

Rihga Royal Hotel • 151 West 54th St • Midtown West Side • (212) 468-8888

****$24.93 Dinner Special****

Soup or Salad
Grilled Breast Of
Chicken With Grilled Vegetables

or

Poached Halibut
Wilted Spinach
Lobster Butter

Choice Of A Fresh Fruit Tart or New York Style Cheese Cake

Entrees

Roasted Maine Lobster
Aromatic Lobster & Orange Broth
Capellini Pasta & Crispy Leeks
$24.00

Herb Crusted Jumbo Sea Scallops
Watercress & Endive, Charred Tomato &
Chipotle Pepper Vinaigrette
$22.00

Sauteed Paillard Of Salmon, Smoked
Apple & Grilled Red Onion Salad,
Vanilla & Apple Cream
$22.00

Grilled Tuna With Baby Spinach &
Macadamia Nut Pesto,
Southern Fried Morels
$23.00

From The Grill

Served With
Baked Rosemary New Potatoes &
Winter Vegetables

Black Angus Sirloin Steak
$24.00

Colorado Double
Lamb Chops,
$25.00

Herb Crusted Double
Breast of Chicken
$19.00

Swordfish Tournedo
$22.00

Dinner: 7 Days a Week 5:30 - 10:30

The voluble proprietor and his chef wife run their very attractive restaurant flawlessly, and the food is outstanding.

Menu Changes Seasonally

Prix Fixe $55.00

★★★

Smoked rainbow trout

Oeuf en cocotte

Escargots Alsacienne

Croustade du jour

Seafood en coquille

Galantine of veal

Quail Oriental

Onion tart Slavonian

★★★

Okroshka
(cucumber dill soup chilled)

Mushroom
(hot)

Onion
(w/Swiss emmenthaler cheese - served in a small crock)

Trout Blue or Sauteed
(Live from out tank Beaverkill rainbows)

Fresh Canadian Farm Grown Salmon
(Broiled or steamed in papillote)

Veal Madagascar

Zürcher Rahm Schnitzel w/roesti

Rack of Spring Lamb Bearnaise (for 2)

Breast of Duckling Calvados

Roast Young Duckling Cassis

Filet of Beef Dijon

Sirloin Steak au Poivre

Fresh Poussin
(Boned, stuffed, roasted)

★★★

Tossed green salad w/our house dressing
served before main course

★★★

A variety of cheeses, basket of fresh fruit and port wine
served after main course

★★★

For dessert - our own pastries and other sweets together with three different coffees *(two ground fresh daily)*

Dinner: Wed - Fri 6 - 9, Sat 5:30 - 9:15

Inn at Ridgefield, The

Consistent, excellent food and the contemporary elegance of an authentic country inn have made The Inn at Ridgefield a popular choice for years. Everyone loves it.

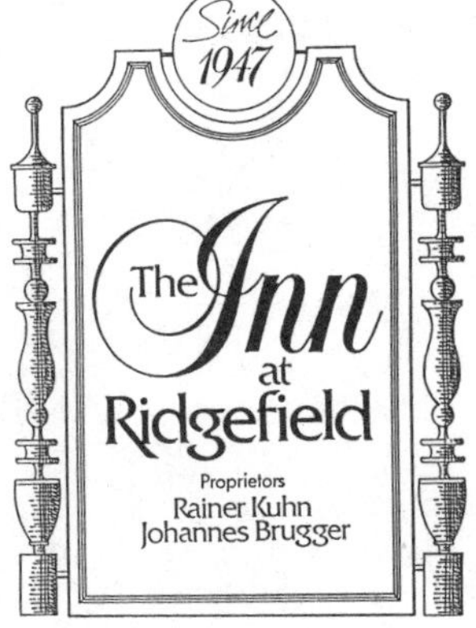

Menu Changes Seasonally

La Table D'Hote De L'Auberge

Les Hors D'Oeuvres

Pâté Aux Trois Poissons
Pâté of Salmon, Sole and Lobster, Fresh Basil Sauce

Melon Et Viande De Grisons, Romande
with Thinly Sliced Swiss Cured Beef

Coquille St. Jacques
Scallops, Shrimp and Mushrooms in Lobster Sauce

Cassolette D'Escargots A La Crème D'Ail
Snails in Cream with Herbs and Garlic Butter

Le Potage Ou La Soupe Du Jour

Filet De Sole, Caprice
Sautéed, with Kiwi and Fresh Fruits
Glazed with Béarnaise Sauce

Fricassé De Ris De Veau Et Homard Mélanie
Sautéed Lobster and Sweetbreads in Lobster Sauce,
Julienne of Vegetables

Suprême De Volaille, Aurora
Sautéed Breast of Chicken, Madeira Sauce Tiny Olives, Red and Yellow Peppers

20 West Ln, Rt 35 • Greenwich, CT • (203) 438-8282

Filets De Canard Au Poivre Vert Aigre Doux
Sliced Breast of Duck, Sweet and Sour Sauce and Green Peppercorns

Mignon De Boeuf, Bressane
Filet Mignon, Pistachio and Truffle Sauce

La Salade Verte

Les Desserts

Chariot De Pâtisseries *Les Glaces* *Les Sorbets* *Café* *Thé*

Prix Fixe $42.00

A La Carte

Hors D'Oeuvres Chaud

Coquille St. Jacques
9.50

Escargots de Bourgogne (1 Dz.)
10.50

Snails in Cream with Herbs and Garlic
9.25

Les Entrées

Filet of Sole, Normande
19.50

Jumbo Shrimp à La Chantal
25.75

Fresh Dover Sole, Sautée Belle Meunière
26.00

Whole Free-Range Chicken, Aurora
21.75

Medallions of Milk Fed Veal, Two Sauces
20.95

Wiener Schnitzel
20.75

Fresh Jumbo Sweetbreads, Sauce Béarnaise
22.50

N.Y. Sirloin Steak Vasco da Gama,
with green Peppercorns
25.50

Mignon of Beef, Bressane
25.75

Roast L.I. Duckling, à l'Orange, Flambé
39.00 for Two

Chateaubriand, Bouquetière
48.00 for Two

Rack of Baby Lamb, Rosemary
49.00 for Two

Les Plats Froid

Fresh Seafood Salad, Shrimp, Lobster and Crabmeat Julienne of Vegetables
21.00

Belgian Endive with Beets
4.95

The Inn's Special Seafood Platter on Ice
27.50

Bibb Lettuce and Watercress
4.95

Dinner: Mon - Thur 6 - 9:30, Fri - Sat 6 - 10:30, Sun 3 - 8

One if by Land

Its setting is a historic Village townhouse; its decor, brick walls, a roaring fireplace, profuse flower arrangements, and background piano music make it a favorite place with New Yorkers for that special, romantic occasion.

Two If By Sea

Menu Changes Seasonally And For Major Holidays

Hors d'Oeuvres

Poached Cold Maine Lobster Medallions, Saffron Cream	14.00
Roasted Portabello, with Zucchini Mousse	12.00
Lump Crab Cake, Sautéed, Tartar Sauce	14.00
Blue Point Oysters, Cocktail Sauce	12.00
Stuffed Mushrooms, Seafood Farcé	12.00
Cornucopia de Escargot, Thyme Cream	12.00
Shrimp Raviolis, Steamed, with Shrimp Cream Sauce	13.00

17 Barrow St • Chelsea • (212) 228-0822 • (Call for Summer Hours)

Salad & Soup

Soup du Jour	6.00
Lobster Bisque	7.00
Caesar Salad	9.00
Mixed Field Greens Salad	7.00
Montrachet Salad, Arugula, Extra Virgin Olive Oil & Balsamic Vinegar	8.00

Entrées

Individual Beef Wellington, Sauce Bordelaise	34.00
Roasted Rack of Lamb, Sour Cream Mashed Potatoes, Mint Sauce	31.00
Medallions of Veal, Wild Mushrooms, Cognac Sauce	32.00
Breast of Chicken, Fontina & Sautéed Spinach	26.00
Black Angus Filet Mignon, Pan Seared, Jack Daniels Peppercorn Sauce	32.00
Grilled Broadbill Swordfish, Vinaigrette	29.00
Norwegian Salmon, Sautéed, Dill Cream Sauce	28.00
Atlantic Red Snapper, Fresh Herbs, Basil Beurre Blanc	28.00

Dinner: 7 Days a Week 5:30 - 12

The ambiance at this hotel dining room is all you could ask for: pampering and elegant, with a view onto fashionable Madison Avenue. Chef Neil Murphy's food is a favorite with shoppers and gallery and museum-goers.

Menu Changes Seasonally

Dinner

Appetizers

Roast Monkfish, Field Greens, Truffle Madiera Vinaigrette and Crisp Tomato Chips
$14.00

Terrine of Fresh Foie Gras with Tiny Green Beans and Sundried Cherry Compote
$15.00

Seasonal Oysters on the Half Shell with Sherry Wine Mignonette and Basil Fritters
$12.00

Smoked Salmon with Cucumber and Citrus
$12.00

Lobster Chowder with Riesling and Lobster Gnocchi
$10.00

Pan Braised Vegetable Dumplings, Parmesan Broth, Cold Pressed Olive Oil and Fresh Herbs
$10.00

Foie Gras Sauteed
$15.00

Strudel Wrapped Shrimp with Shaved Fennel, Mesclun Greens and Tomato Nicoise
$13.00

The Westbury Hotel • 840 Madison Ave • Upper East Side • (212) 439-4835

Entrees

Pepper Crusted Grilled Salmon, Cabbage Charlotte and Champagne Sauce
$23.00

Carmelized Swordfish with Asparagus, Sweet Vegetable Pan Broth and Artichoke Crisps
$23.00

Braised Black Sea Bass with Grilled Shrimp, New Potatoes, Artichokes and a Lemon Herb Nage
$23.00

Grouper Sauteed with a Lobster Vinaigrette, Grilled Vegetables and Crisp Onion Rings
$21.00

Bells Farm Chicken Sauteed with Roast Garlic Pan Sauce, Crisp Potato Tart and Legfry
$19.00

Wood Grilled Spring Lamb, Saute Vegetable Provencale, Potato and Sweet Onion Napoleon, Barolo Vinegar Sauce
$24.00

Seared Veal Mignons with Oregon Morrels, Savory Corn Waffle and a Madiera Natural Sauce
$25.00

Black Angus Sirloin with Natural Jus, Fricasse of Wild Mushrooms and Roquefort Ravioli
$26.00

Neil Murphy
Executive Chef

Dinner: 7 Days a Week 6 - 10

Rainbow Room, The

The Rainbow Room is the most legendary, probably the most quintessential supper club in the country. Where else can you dine and dance in such elegance, with the lights of Manhattan surrounding you?

Menu Changes Seasonally

FIRST COURSES

Terrine of Quail and Foie Gras 12.00

Chilled Shrimp, zucchini chutney 13.00

Malpeque, Pemequid & Blue Point oysters 12.50

Norwegian Smoked Salmon 14.00

Beef Carpaccio, marinated artichokes and truffle oil 13.00

Tomato and Fresh Mozzarella, balsamic vinaigrette 11.00

Shellfish Extravaganza, Coast to Coast

for two 35.00 *for three* 50.00 *for four* 66.00

Caviar

Beluga 50.00/oz

Sevruga 28.00/oz

Caviar Sampler Plate 25.00

Cake of Steak Tartare, iced with sevruga 25.00

Spicy Salmon Tartare with salmon caviar 15.00

Oysters Rockefeller 15.00

Lump Crab Gratin with truffled orzo 13.00

Cake of Wild Mushrooms, watercress sauce 11.50

Seared Yellowfin Tuna on melted onion croustade 12.50

Asparagus and Leek Soup 8.50

30 Rockefeller Plaza • Midtown West Side • (212) 632-5000

MAIN COURSES

Mustard Glazed Salmon with asparagus, lemon chervil sauce 28.00

Grilled Swordfish Steak, spring vegetable and arugula sauce 29.00

Northwest Sturgeon Filet with potato, leeks and baby clams 27.50

Pan Roasted Red Snapper, roasted pepper ratatouille 28.00

Veal Loin Chop, sauteed artichokes and mushrooms 30.00

Roast Guinea Hen, potato galette and sweet garlic sauce 28.00

Farm Chicken braised with morels and new peas, rice pilaf 27.00

Grilled Double Lamb chops, plum tomato tart 29.00

Sirloin Steak, New York cut
grilled with mushrooms & onions 32.00
or *sauteed with Marchand de vin* 35.00

DISHES WITH TRADITION

Lobster Thermidor *first course* 17.00 *main course* 35.00

Fillet of Sole "Diamond Jim Brandy" 28.00

Tournedos Rossini, truffle sauce and pomme souffiees 35.00

Roast Rack of Lamb for two, herb roasted vegetables 58.00

ACCOMPANIMENTS

Mixed spring vegetables 6.50

Pommes souffiees 7.50

Baked potato 5.50

Creamed spinach 6.50

Field greens, mustard vinaigrette 8.00

Caesar salad for two 18.00

Frisse and Radicchio salad,
gorgonzola walnut dressing 8.50

Only Cigarette Smoking
Please No Photographs
Accepting Only One Card, American Express
Music Charge 15.00 Per Person

Dinner: Tues - Sat 5:30 - 12

Saddle River Inn is at the top of everyone's list of the best restaurants in New Jersey. Gourmet magazine just wrote it up as well. The reason is that it has a charming, woodsy setting and excellent food that has been consistent for many years.

The Saddle River Inn

Menu Changes Seasonally

LES HORS D'OEUVRES /Appetizers

Spaghettini al Pomodoro Secco e Gamberi 8.50
Spaghettini with sundried tomatoes, garlic and shrimp

Carousel 8.50
A selection of specialties

Cassolette d'Escargots en Croûte 7.00
Snails baked in herb butter with pastry crust

Cannelloni all'Emiliana 6.50
Cannelloni filled with meat, spinach and cheese topped with tomato sauce

Crevettes á la Créme d'Ail 9.00
Shrimp with a creamy garlic sauce

Crevettes au Sesame 9.00
Shrimp with sesame seeds and curry sauce

LES SALADES / Salads

Salade Maison 5.00
House salad

Salade Chinoise 9.00
Chiffonade of lettuce with crabmeat in a sesame oil vinaigrette

2 Barnstable Ct • Saddle River, NJ • (201) 825-4016

LES ENTREES / Main Courses

Saumon au Poivre *Salmon steak with peppercorn sauce*	22.00
Espadon aux Tomates Séches *Swordfish steak with olives and sundried tomatoes*	23.00
Carré d'Agneau aux Echalottes *Rack of lamb with shallots*	28.00
Tournedo de Boeuf, Beurre d'Ail *Filet of beef with garlic butter and portwine sauce*	23.00
Sûpréme de Saumon *Salmon filet baked in a potato crust*	23.00
Tournedo de Boeuf Maribar *Filet of beef with chestnut purée, bernaise and port wine sauce*	24.00
Filet de Veau Rôti aux Champignons *Roasted filet of veal with mushrooms*	24.00

LES DESSERTS / Desserts 6.00

Crêpes Pralinés
Crêpes with apples, raisins, cinnamon and praliné butter

Mousseline au Chocolat
Chocolate marquis with hazelnut cookies and vanilla cream

Méringue Glacée au Chocolat
Vanilla ice cream, meringues and chocolate sauce

Gratin aux Fruits
Fresh fruits overbaked with vanilla custard

Dinner: Tues - Sat 6 - 10

This is one of the most famous restaurants in New York. Located in Central Park, the decor is wondrous and the views, especially at night, are magical.

Menu Changes Seasonally Along With Daily Specials

Spring Dinner

Appetizers

GOAT CHEESE AND ARTICHOKE SALAD **8.50**
with Prosciutto and Spring Lettuce in Tarragon Vinaigrette

CARPACCIO **8.50**
Thin Slices of Raw Beef Garnished with Light Mustard Mayonnaise

ASPARAGUS **6.85**
Cold with Field Salad and Tarragon Vinaigrette or Hot with Hollandaise Sauce

JUMBO ARTICHOKE **6.85**
Cold with Herb Vinaigrette or Hot with Hollandaise Sauce

BRUSCHETTA **5.95**
Chopped Tomatoes with Garlic and Olive Oil on Toasted Italian Country Bread

GRILLED QUAIL SALAD **11.25**
with Duck Prosciutto, Haricots Verts, and Spring Lettuce in Balsamic Vinaigrette with Sauteed New Potatoes

LOBSTER SALAD **17.25**
with Citrus Vinaigrette, Asparagus, Haricots Verts, Tomatoes and Hearts of Palm

SCOTTISH SMOKED SALMON **12.50**
with Dill

SALMON TRIO **13.75**
Smoked Salmon with Horseradish Cream, Gravlax with Mustard-Dill Sauce and Cold Poached Salmon with Green Sauce

MARYLAND CRAB CAKES **12.75**
with Tartar Sauce

Pasta

CRESPELLE ALLA RICOTTA **9.85/19.50**
Italian Baked Crepes stuffed with Ricotta, Spinach, and Goat Cheese with Plum Tomato Sauce

ZITI WITH FOUR CHEESES **9.85/19.50**
(Fontina, Parmesan, Emmenthaler and Gorgonzola)

PAGLIA E FIENO **9.85/19.50**
Green and White Linguini with Peas and Prosciutto

TAGLIOLINI CON SCAMPI E ARUGULA **9.85/19.50**
Tagliolini with Shrimp and Arugula

SPAGHETTI PUTTANESCA **9.85/19.50**
Spaghetti with Tomatoes, Olives and Capers

Central Park West and W 67th St • Lincoln Center • (212) 873-3200

Seafood

SAUTEED JUMBO SHRIMP 24.00
with Lemon-Chive Sauce, Basmati Rice Pilaf and Crisp Fried Leeks

SAUTEED NORWEGIAN SALMON 26.00
with Asparagus, Red and Yellow Pepper Coulis and Wild Rice Pilaf

GRILLED SWORDFISH STEAK 26.00
with Sauteed Baby Artichokes, Lime Sauce and Basil

DOVER SOLE MEUNIERE 28.00
with Boiled New Parsley Potatoes and Vegetables

ROASTED LOBSTER 32.50
with Caramelized Fennel, Orange Anise Sauce and Pommes Maxim's

Main Courses

ROAST FREE-RANGE FRENCH CHICKEN 21.50
with Apricot-Cumin Sausage, Mashed Potatoes and Thyme Sauce

ROAST HONEY-GLAZED DUCK 24.50
with Blackcurrent Cassis Sauce, Haricots Verts and Roast New Potatoes

VEAL SCALOPPINE 25.50
with Wild Mushrooms, Sauteed New Potatoes and Asparagus

ROAST SPRING RACK OF LAMB 28.00
with Tapenade (Black Olive) Crust, Spring Vegetables and Sauteed New Potatoes

BRAISED LAMB SHANKS 23.50
with Spring Carrots and Flageolets

Grilled Meats

CLASSIC PRIME SIRLOIN STEAK 29.75
with Maitre d'Hotel Butter, Mashed Potatoes or French Fries

GRILLED FILET MIGNON 29.00
with Mashed Potatoes or French Fries and Bearnaise Sauce

GRILLED CHOPPED STEAK BURGER 12.75
with French Fries, on a Toasted Soft Roll with Lettuce, Pickles and Tomato or with Cheddar Cheese

Salads

CLASSIC CAESAR SALAD 6.50

MIXED GREENS 6.50
and Choice of Mustard Vinaigrette, Russian or Roquefort Cheese Dressing

SPECIAL SALAD 7.50
of young Spring Greens with Tarragon Vinaigrette

VEGETARIAN SALAD PLATE 17.00
with Young Lettuces, Asparagus, Avocado, Hearts of Palm, Tomatoes, Beets and Artichokes in Tarragon Vinaigrette

GRILLED CHICKEN SALAD 17.50
with Tarragon Mayonnaise, Tomatoes Basil and Young Lettuces

Desserts

TAVERN'S CREME BRULEE 6.75
Delicate Custard under Caramel with Praline Wafers

RED, SWEET, COLD AND CRISP 6.95
Raspberries and Strawberries in Crisp Filo Pastry with Macadamia-Vanilla Ice Cream

NEW YORK CHEESECAKE 6.50
with Strawberries

TIRAMI SU 6.50
with Espresso Coffee Sauce

CHOCOLATE FUDGE PECAN CAKE 6.50
with Chocolate Sauce and Whipped Cream

CHOCOLATE PLATE: 7.50
Dark Chocolate Cake with Chocolate Terrine, Chocolate Mousse and Chocolate Ice Cream with Schlag

CARAMEL PLATE: 7.50
Creme Caramel, Caramel Ice Cream and Caramel Nut Tart with Schlag

CARAMEL NUT TART 6.50
with Vanilla and Caramel Ice Creams

Dinner: Sun - Thurs 5:30 - 12, Fri - Sat 5:30 - 1

Windows on the World

Along with Tavern on the Green, Windows is the most flagrantly touristy of New York restaurants. The 107th floor of the World Trade Center affords a wonderful tri-state view on clear days.

Menu Changes Seasonally

PRIX FIXE

Oysters or Clams on the Half-Shell, Cocktail Sauce and Pepper Mignonette

Chilled Gulf Shrimp Cocktail

Sea Grill: Salmon, Scallops and Shrimp, Sauce Verte

Steamed Asparagus with Prosciutto di Parma

Romaine Lettuce in Garlic-Herb Dressing, Spicy Lump Crabmeat Fritters

House-made Duck Liver Mousse, Apple and Dried Cherry Relish

Cold Poached Half Lobster with Winter Vegetables ($8 additional)

Wild Mushroom Ravioli with Tomato, Sweet Peas and Shaved Romano Cheese

Cream of Mussels and Clams with Saffron and Smoked Salmon

Double Chicken Consomme with Watercress and Shiitaki Mushrooms

Potato-Leek with Roquefort

♦

Freshly Smoked Salmon Loin on Two-Caviar Cream with Chervil, Souffle Potatoes

Half Chicken Baked in Parchment with Winter Root Vegetables, Sage Jus

Black Peppered Sirloin of Beef, Pinot Noir Sauce, Potato-Leek Gratin

Sauteed Veal Scallopine in Lemon Persillade,
Wild Mushroom Ragout with Tomato-Basil Fettucine

♦

Salad Greens, Basil Vinaigrette

♦

Choice of Dessert

$37.00

1 World Trade Center, 107th Floor • TriBeCa/Downtown/Chinatown • (212) 938-1111

À LA CARTE

♦

APPETIZERS AND SOUPS

Oysters or Clams on the Half Shell, Cocktail Sauce and Pepper Mignonette 10.00

House-Smoked Salmon with Winter Greens, Sour Cream and Caviar 10.00

Grilled Sweet Water Prawns with Purple Potatoes, a l'Orientale 12.00

Baked Sea Scallops and Lobster Gratin 14.00

Dried Cured Duck Breast with Frisee Lettuce, Baked Onion Galette 9.00

Wild Mushroom Ravioli with Tomato, Sweet Peas and Shaved Romano Cheese 9.00

Double Chicken Consomme with Watercress and Shiitake Mushrooms 5.00

Cream of Mussels and Clams with Saffron and Smoked Salmon 6.00

♦

MAIN COURSES

Dover Sole (Grilled or Sauteed) with Tiny Green Asparagus, Lemon Butter 28.00

Filet of Baby Red Snapper with Fried Sweet Potato and Tarragon Beurre Rouge 26.00

Whole Grilled 1-1/4 lb. Lobster with Mussels, Clams and Prawns
in Saffron Court-Bouillon, Aioli and Garlic Croutons 36.00

Spicy Mallard Duck Breast on Dried Cherry Balsamic Jus,
Foie Gras and Cilantro Corncakes 28.00

Rack of Lamb, James Beard with Lavender, Sweet Garlic and Shallot Confit 31.00

Sauteed Medallion of Farm Venison, Red Wine Poached Pear and Celery Root Puree 32.00

Tournedo of Beef Tenderloin with Three-Peppercorn Mignonette,
Mashed Potatoes with Olive Oil and Garlic 30.00

Goat Cheese Risotto Tart Provencale with Grilled Baby Vegetable,
Lemon-Olive Oil Vinaigrette 24.00

GRILLED OVER CHARCOAL
with Garlic-Herb Butter

Salmon Steak 25.00   Swordfish Steak 27.00   Veal Chop 32.00

Filet Mignon 29.00   Sirloin Steak 29.00

Chef: Karl Otto Schmid

Dinner: Mon - Sat 5 - 10, Sun 5 - 9

New York "cuisine" used to be synonymous with deli. Carnegie remains one of the last and best of the breed, with the now-legendary communal tables, overstuffed corned beef and pastrami sandwiches and brusque waiters.

Menu Changes Yearly

CARNEGIE GARGANTUAN COMBOS

A MEAL IN ITSELF

No Substitutions Please

CARNEGIE HAUL Triple decker pastrami, tongue and salami, with Indian relish 14.95

FIFTY WAYS TO LOVE YOUR LIVER Chopped liver, hard boiled egg, lettuce and tomato and onion 11.45

AH, THERE'S THE REUBEN A savory grilled sandwich piled high with corned beef or pastrami with melted Swiss cheese and sauerkraut 16.95

SPOTLIGHT ON SANDWICHES

THE SANDWICH THAT MADE "BROADWAY DANNY ROSE" FAMOUS

"THE WOODY ALLEN" For the dedicated fresser only! Lotsa corned beef plus lotsa pastrami 12.45

NEW YORK'S BEST CORNED BEEF 9.45

HOT PASTRAMI 9.45

POTTED BRISKET OF BEEF 9.45

BEEF TONGUE 9.45

ROLLED BEEF (You don't find this everywhere!) 9.95

SHARING - $3.00 EXTRA

854 Seventh Ave • Midtown West Side • (212) 757-2245

IN THE HEAT OF THE SANDWICH

OPEN STYLE. SERVED WITH CREAMY COLE SLAW

NOSH, NOSH NANETTE Hot turkey with gravy, cranberry sauce, French fried potatoes or baked beans 14.75

BEEFAMANIA Hot roast beef, with gravy, French fried potatoes or baked beans 14.75

LI'L ABNER Hot brisket of beef, with gravy, French fried potatoes or baked beans 14.75

I LOVE MY BURGER

WE GRIND OUR OWN FRESH MEAT!

CARNEGIE'S FAMOUS HAMBURGER

Pure lean beef a' plenty. Grilled to a turn on a fresh baked Kaiser Roll 7.95

WITH MELTED CHEESE extra 1.50

WITH SLICED TOMATO, LETTUCE AND BERMUDA ONION extra 1.00

WITH CRISP BACON STRIPS extra 3.95

BIG HITS AT CARNEGIE DELI

WEST SIDE SPECIALTIES

Served with cole slaw

PRIME BRISKET OF BEEF POT ROAST
In rich brown gravy with potato pancake and fresh vegetable 16.95

BAKED MEATLOAF Mushroom gravy, choice of potato and fresh vegetable 11.95

HUNGARIAN GOULASH Served over broad noodles, with fresh vegetables jardiniere 11.95

OUR FAMOUS CHEESECAKE

YOUR TASTE BUDS WILL THROW A PARTY FOR YOUR MOUTH!

ENJOY IT PLAIN (BUT DELICIOUS) 4.95

TOPPED WITH BLUEBERRIES OR CHERRIES 5.45

ALL CHOCOLATE CHEESECAKE 5.45

FRESH STRAWBERRY CHEESECAKE (in season) 5.95

SUPER DELICIOUS RUGLACH CHEESECAKE TOPPED WITH CREAMY MILK CHOCOLATE 5.95

Bre Lun Din

Dinner: 7 Days a Week 5 - 3am

This and the Carnegie have maintained the Jewish delicatessen tradition in New York. It serves exceptional kosher stuffed sandwiches, chicken soup, chopped liver - all the items you associate with an authentic deli.

Entrees

Served with Vegetables, Bread and Relish (Kishka in place of Vegetable .35 Extra)

★ ***Except Entrees with Asterisk*** **A LA CARTE**

	Hungarian Beef Goulash *with noodles*	**11.85**
	Pepper Steak *with rice or egg barley*	**11.75**
	Stuffed Breast of Veal *with potato and vegetable*	**11.95**
★	**Boiled Beef in the Pot** *with noodles, carrots and matzoth ball*	**13.85**
★	**Boiled Beef in the Pot** *with mushroom barley soup*	**13.85**
	Mixed Platter *(meatball, derma and stuffed cabbage)*	**12.85**
★	**Corned Beef and Cabbage** *with boiled potato*	**12.85**
	Prime Veal Cutlet *breaded with fresh bread crumbs and sauteed in pure vegetable oil*	**15.35**
★	**Beef Lo Mein** *with Chinese vegetables*	**9.65**
	Roast Beef	**12.85**
	Boiled Beef Flanken	**12.35**
	Potted Meal Balls	**10.85**
	Potted Breast of Beef	**12.85**
	Meat Loaf	**10.85**
	Stuffed Cabbage	**12.85**

★ No Vegetables

Poultry

	CHICKEN CACCIATORE, *tender chicken simmered with onions, mushrooms, tomatoes herbs and spices, served with egg barley and vegetable*	**12.15**
★	**CHICKEN IN THE POT.** *A traditional Lower Eastside favorite, made the traditional way with noodles, carrots and matzoth ball*	**12.65**
★	**CHICKEN IN THE BASKET** *with french fries and cole slaw*	**11.35**
	ROAST TURKEY *with stuffing, cranberry sauce*	**12.85**
	BONELESS BREAST OF CHICKEN *with mushroom stuffing*	**12.85**
	BOILED or ROAST HALF SPRING CHICKEN	**11.35**
	STUFFED ROAST CHICKEN	**11.90**
	CHICKEN FRICASSEE	**10.70**
	BRAISED TURKEY LEG	**9.45**

Fish

BROILED FILET OF SOLE	**10.65**
GEFUILTE FISH WITH VEGETABLE AND POTATO	**8.90**
BOILED CARP *(Hot or Cold)* and vegetables	**10.25**
BROILED SALMON	**13.15**
BAKED CARP	**10.25**

Osso Buco Veal Shank Simmered in a Natural Gravy, Rice or Egg Barley......$12.95

Marinated Roumanian Tenderloin Steak......$16.95

★ Cholent Every Day......$5.25

156 Second Ave • Greenwich Village • (212) 677-0606

Broilings

ROUMANIAN TENDERLOIN STEAK *The Old-World Favorite* **15.35**
TURKEY KA-BOB *marinated chunks of turkey on a skewer, served with egg barley, lettuce, tomato and marinated onions* **11.75**
BROILED CHICKEN LIVERS *made only from livers of our own chickens* **11.00**
CHOPPED STEAK *freshly ground* **11.35**
PRIME RIB STEAK *broiled to your liking* **17.35**
SAUTE SLICED STEAK *fried onions, mushroom gravy* **13.05**

3 Decker Sandwiches

ROAST TURKEY and TONGUE, *cole slaw, Russian dressing, lettuce and tomato* **9.35**
ROAST TURKEY and BREAST OF BEEF, *Chicken fat, onion, cole slaw, Russian dressing* **9.35**
TONGUE, CORNED BEEF and SALAMI, *cole slaw and Russian dressing* **9.35**
HOT PASTRAMI, CORNED BEEF and CHICKEN SALAMI, *cole slaw, Russian dressing* **9.35**
ROLLED BEEF, GRILLED SALAMI and GRILLED BOLOGNA, *cole slaw, Russian dressing* **9.35**
TURKEY and CHOPPED LIVER, *cole slaw and Russian dressing* **9.35**
TONGUE TEMPTATION, *chicken salad, Russian dressing and cole slaw* **9.35**
ROAST BEEF, *Bermuda onion, chicken fat, lettuce and tomato* **9.35**
BREAST of BEEF, *Bermuda onion, chicken fat lettuce and tomato* **9.35**
SLOPPY JOE: *Everything but the Kitchen Sink* **9.35**
CHOPPED EGGS and CHOPPED LIVER, *lettuce and tomato* **9.35**

(Club Bread 50¢ Extra)

Hot Open Sandwiches

Served with our Deliciouse Gravy and French Fried Potatoes

Roast Turkey, with cranberry sauce 10.50
Roast Breast of Beef 10.50
Beef Tongue 10.50
Roast Prime Beef 10.50

Twin Double

Generous portion of
HOT CORNED BEEF and HOT PASTRAMI
on twin junior rolls
$9.05

Open Sandwich Medley

(Serves 3 - 4 persons) Consisting of
CORNED BEEF, TONGUE, ROAST BEEF, TURKEY, PASTRAMI, CHOPPED LIVER, EGGS and MUSHROOMS, SALAMI, *Garnished with Potato Salad*
$28.50

Favorite Deli Platters

CORNED BEEF, PASTRAMI, TONGUE, TURKEY AND SALAMI COMBINATION PLATTER **12.50**
SALAMI or (61) BOLOGNA PLATTER **9.25**
SLICED WHITE MEAT TURKEY, *with potato salad* **12.95**
HOT KNOBLE WURST PLATTER **9.25**
PRIME COLD ROAST BEEF PLATTER *with potato salad* **12.85**
HOT CORNED BEEF PLATTER **12.50**

Tempting Desserts

Pareve Cheese Cake *(A la Carte only)* **2.50**
Chocolate Devil Food Cake **2.50**
Marble or Sponge Cake **1.50**
Cherry or Blueberry Tart **2.00**
Ruglach **2.50**

Noodle Pudding *with fruit sauce* **2.75**
Fruit Compote **2.50**
Baked Apple *(extra on dinner .25¢)* **2.50**
Fresh Cut Fruit Salad **2.75**
Jello **1.75**

Dinner: 7 Days a Week 4 - 2am

Although the food has been inconsistent in the past, the current chef, Adam Odegard, is getting good notices and the decor of the restaurant and hotel are beautiful (art nouveau).

Menu Changes Seasonally

Appetizers

Crisp morel ravioli with asparagus $9.50
and champagne broth

Warm goat cheese salad with roasted red $10.00
peppers, opal basil vinegar and porcini oil

Seared sea scallops with eggplant terrine, young $14.50
greens and yellow pepper dressing

Portobello and potato napoleon with a $11.50
lemon vegetable broth and basil oil

Pan seared foie gras with spiced apple $17.50
fritter and sherry pan jus

House smoked salmon with warm corn pancake $16.50
and cilantro creme fraiche

Soups

Lobster minestrone with farfallini $6.00

Spring vegetable soup with marjoram $5.50

The Peninsula • 700 Fifth Ave • Midtown West Side • (212) 903-3918

Entrees

Grilled swordfish with pancetta $24.00
tomato-fennel roast and balsamic sauce

Pan-seared salmon and grilled scallops with $26.00
peashoots, crisp carrot and coriander seed broth

Lobster, Scallops, and Prawns, snow-pea butter, $30.00
rigati pasta and lobster oil

Breast of chicken with creamy aged goat cheese polenta $20.00
shallot confit and natural bay-leaf sauce

Grilled filet of beef with a potato knish, served with $28.00
green beans, bell pepper confetti and mustard sauce

Roasted spring lamb chops with crisp spice $27.50
onion rings and dill lamb jus

Miniature roasted loin of veal with spring $28.00
vegetables and thyme reduction

From the Grill

Chicken, Balsamic sauce $20.00

Sirloin, Port Wine sauce $28.00

Salmon, Champagne Reduction $26.00

Swordfish, Coriander Broth $24.00

Dinner: 7 Days a Week 5:30 - 10

A charming, romantic brownstone setting with universally praised food from chef Tom Valenti.

A L I S O N   O N   D O M I N I C K   S T R E E T

Menu Changes Seasonally

APPETIZERS

SMOKED COD
with friseé, lardons, and a poached egg in a bacon vinaigrette 11.00

OYSTER STEW
with braised pork, tomato, and black trumpet mushrooms 10.00

GRAVLAX
with a chickpea pancake and American caviar 12.00

TOMATO CONSOMMÉ
with fava beans and roasted mushrooms 9.00

CARPACCIO OF DUCK
served with a lentil salad 10.00

ROAST QUAIL
with wild rice, a dried fruit compote, and curry oil 11.00

MOSAIC OF FOIE GRAS
with mixed greens 15.00

CHARRED LAMB SALAD
with capers and a lemon cayenne mayonnaise 10.00

MINI "POT AU FEU"
Braised beef with smoked onions and spring vegetables in a beef broth 9.00

Salad of Asparagus, Beets, and Herbed Goat Cheese with wild greens 9.00

Salad of Wild & Baby Greens 8.00

Salad of Endive & Roquefort 7.00

ENTREES

SEARED TUNA "STEAK"
with white bean purée, mushroom broth and a parsley salad 26.00

ROAST HALIBUT
with pearl onions, tomato, lemon and shallots in a shellfish broth 25.00

SAUTEÉD CANADIAN SALMON
with poached vegetables in a basil broth 25.00

SAUTEED RED SNAPPER
with stewed leeks, whipped potatoes, and shrimp oil 24.00

ROAST GUINEA HEN
with creamy truffled polenta, diced root vegetables and rosemary 24.00

SAUTEED SQUAB
with roasted barley, smoked shallots, & and a wild mushroom pureé 26.00

HERB ROASTED VEAL CHOP
with roasted carrots, potato purée and onion rings 30.00

BRAISED LAMB SHANK
with white and fava beans, wilted chicory, and a sauce of roast garlic and parsley 21.00

PAN SEARED LIMOUSIN FILET MIGNON
with savoyard portatoes, sauteed arugula, and a madeira mushroom jus 27.00

Dinner: Mon - Thurs 5:30 - 10:30, Fri - Sat 5:30 - 11, Sun 5:30 -9:30

The American Hotel has the look and feel that you expect of a New England whaling establishment, because it's been that since Sag Harbor was one of our more important ports. The food and service can vary considerably, but the wine list is the best on Long Island.

The American Hotel

Menu Changes Seasonally

APPETIZERS

Calamari Fritti - Red and Green Aioli 6.50

Shrimp Cocktail 9.75

Maryland Crab Meat Cocktail 9.75

Special Cold-Smoked Canadian Trout 9.50
Dill-seasoned Creme Fraiche with Croutons

Saumon Frais Garni a l'Hotel 9.75

Chilled Small Lobster 12.00 each
Simply Split & Served with English Mustard Sauce

Local Littlenecks on the Half-Shell (8) 8.00

Fresh Foie Gras Sauterne Saute with Grilled Fennel 14.00

SOUPS

Chef's Cold Soup of the Day 5.00

Onion Soup 5.00

SALADS

Mixed Hotel Garden Lettuces Dijon Vinaigrette 5.50

Warm Chevre on Crouton with Watercress and Endive 7.25

SPA

Grilled Legumes 7.50

Minted Citrus Salad 6.50

Mediterranean Salad 12.00
Romaine, Dried Tomato, Mozzarella, Olives, Warm Homus

Main Street • Long Island • (516) 725-3535

Vegetarian Panache de Legumes 15.00
Vegetables, Mushrooms, Wild Rice

Grilled Swordfish 23.00
Vegetables en Salade

Grilled Tuna 21.00
Vegetables en Salade

Steamed Salmon with Dill and Lime 21.00
Grilled Vegetables

Warm Sage-Grilled Quails en Salade 21.00

SEAFOOD

Filet of Flounder Herb Saute or Grenobloise 17.95

Swordfish Ginger Beurre Blanc 23.00

Grilled Brook Trout Amandine 19.25

Seared Salmon with Tomato and Cilantro 23.50

Horseradish-Crusted Bluefish Lime Vinaigrette 19.75

Soft-Shell Crab with Brown Butter & Capers 20.00

Whole Long Island Lobster Steamed or Broiled 28.00

FOWL

Crisp Roasted Rosemary Chicken 19.50

Pintaudeau en Croute Monbazillac 23.00
Game Hen Stewed with Wild Mushrooms Pate Brisee

Roast Magret et Confit de Canard a l'Orange 21.00

Boned Marinated Duckling Breast & Leg Confit 21.00

Chestnut Lima Beans, Wild Mushrooms and Tomato and Sage

RED MEAT

Steak Fiorentina $30.00
Seasoned with Garlic, Seared in Olive Oil

Black Angus Filet Mignon aux Champignons Sauvages 26.00

Tournedos Rossini 30.00
Angus Filet Mignon, Foie Gras, Truffles Sauce Perigordine

Rack of Lamb Bouquetiere 28.50

Dinner: 7 Days a Week 4 - 12

Bertrand

Bertrand is the epitome of classic haute French cuisine, which chef/owner Christian Bertrand brought to the classy precinct of Greenwich from Lutece, France. Its formal, elegant room and service make it one of the best and most popular places in the state.

Menu Changes Seasonally

Des ses fourneaux Christian Bertrand et sa brigade vous souhaitent la bienvenue et vous proposent

Diner

LES HORS D'OEVRES FROIDS

Caviar russe sur sa galette de coquilles St. Jacques, beurre fondu au citron 35.00
RUSSIAN CAVIAR ON SEA SCALLOPS PANCAKE WITH LEMON BUTTER

Terrine de foie gras frais et pâté en croûte de canard en gelée 20.00
TERRINE OF FRESH FOIE GRAS AND DUCK PATE IN PASTRY WITH NATURAL ASPIC

Mousse de saumon fumé et saumon mariné a l'anêth au coeur de laitue 12.75
SMOKED SALMON MOUSSE AND MARINATED SALMON WITH HEART OF LETTUCE

LES HORS D'OEUVRES CHAUDS

Escargots de Bourgogne Landaise 9.50
SNAILS WITH DICED MUSHROOMS, SHALLOTS AND FRESH HERBS

Brioche de foie gras sauté au vinaigre de framboise 26.50
BRIOCHE OF FRESH FOIE GRAS, SAUTEED IN RASPBERRY VINEGAR

Cassolette de crabe et crevettes aux pistils de saffron et coriande frais 16.50
CASSOLETTE OF CRAB MEAT AND SHRIMP WITH SAFFRON AND FRESH CORIANDER

Salade tiède de filets de canard et haricots verts 15.25
WARM SALAD OF FILET OF DUCK AND FRENCH STRING BEANS

Escalope de saumon fumé tiède aux légumes de saison 14.75
FILLET OF WARMED, SMOKED SALMON WITH SEASONAL VEGETABLES

LES POTAGES

Soupe a l'oignon gratinée au confit de canard 7.25
ONION SOUP, GRATINE WITH DUCK CONFIT

Potage de petits pois frais aux dès de saumon et crevettes 8.25
FRESH GREEN PEA SOUP WITH DICED SALMON AND SHRIMP

253 Greenwich Ave • Greenwich, CT • (203) 661-4459

LES POISSONS ET CRUSTACES

Dover sole dorée aux macadamia et pain brioché sur un lit de pomme de terre à la créme 28.50
SAUTEED DOVER SOLE, BREADED WITH MACADAMIA AND BRIOCHE, SERVED ON A BED OF CREAMED POTATOES

Darne de bass Bohemienne, endives sautés 25.75
DARNE OF SEA BASS WITH WILD MUSHROOMS, MIXED PEPPERS AND SAUTEED ENDIVE

Râgout de homard et St. Jacques, sauce orange
Nouilles fraiches à l'huile d'olive au piment 27.75
RAGOUT OF LOBSTER AND SEA SCALLOPS, ORANGE AND GINGER SAUCE, FRESH PASTA IN OLIVE OIL 27.75

LES VIANDES ET VOLAILLES

Poitrine de volaille rôtie avec son feuilleté d'épinards aux
Champignons, jus à l'estragon 19.00
SAUTEED CHICKEN BREAST, PUFF PASTRY OF SPINACH AND MUSHROOMS IN NATURAL TARRAGON JUS

Fillet d'âgneau sauté paysanne, carottes, gousses d'ails
et oignons confits, pommes noisettes 25.75
SAUTEED FILLET OF LAMB, VEGETABLES, ONIONS AND GARLIC CONFIT

Râble de lapin au basillic, gâteau de nouilles grillées aux cêpes 24.50
ROAST SADDLE OF RABBIT WITH FRESH BASIL, GATEAU OF GRILLED PASTA WITH WILD MUSHROOMS

Médallion de veau poëlé, sauce cresson, galette de pommes de terre au persil 28.00
SAUTEED VEAL MEDALLION WITH WATERCRESS SAUCE, GALETTE OF POTATOES AND PARSLEY

Contre-filet Black Angus sauté à l'échalotte, vinaigre de vin, haricots verts fins 27.50
SAUTEED BLACK ANGUS STEAK WITH SHALLOTS AND WINE VINEGAR, FRENCH STRING BEANS

Confit de canard, sauce poivrade, julienne de cornichons, riz sauvage 23.75
CONFIT OF DUCK, PEPPERCORN SAUCE, WILD RICE

LES LEGUMES

Haricots verts fins au beurre 6.00
FRENCH STRING BEANS WITH ROASTED PIGNOLI NUTS

Nouilles fraîches maison 4.50
FRESH NOODLES MADE ON PREMISES

Champignons de bois en saison, sautés ou à la crème 9.50
WILD MUSHROOMS IN SEASON SAUTEED OR IN A CREAM SAUCE

Endives au jus de veau 5.50
SAUTEED ENDIVES

LES SALADES

Salade de mâche, vinaigrette aux betteraves rouges 8.75
FIELD SALAD WITH RED BEET, VINAIGRETTE DRESSING

Salade de cresson et julienne d'endive 8.75
WATERCRESS SALAD WITH JULIENNE OF ENDIVE

Salade de haricots verts fins et céleris rémoulade 11.50
SALAD OF FRESH STRING BEANS AND CELERY ROOT IN FRESH MUSTARD SAUCE

CHEF DE CUISINE — Christian Bertrand

Dinner: Mon - Sat 6 - 10

This is a popular destination for local residents and visitors to upper Fifth Avenue museums. The space is rather small, but charming, and they serve excellent bistro-style French food.

Bistro du Nord

Menu Changes Seasonally

~ Le Diner ~

Salade Bistro
grilled Shitake with bacon bits + walnuts

Poireaux Vinaigrette 8.95
warm leeks vinaigrette served on a mixed green salad

Salade de Tomate Et Mozzarella 8.95
tomato, basil + mozzarella

Jambon de Bayonne Et Parmesan 9.00
prosciutto, parmesan + arugola

Crottin de Chèvre Chaud 9.50
grilled goat cheese + roasted vegetables in filo crust

~

Salade de Jardin 7.25
mixed garden salad

1312 Madison Ave • Upper East Side • (212) 289-0997

Pasta Pagnol 16.95
fresh linguini fini with tomato sauce, sun dried tomatoes + thyme

Linguini Fini aux Champignons Sauvages 18.50
fresh pasta with wild mushrooms

Dorade de Floride Provençale 19.95
oven roasted red snapper with herb cous-cous

Saumon Bourgoise 20.75
filet of salmon wrapped with smoked salmon + encased in a fresh pasta sheet, served with braised endive + napa valley red wine sauce

Espadon au Beurre d'Anchois 20.75
grilled swordfish with anchovy butter served with roasted tomatoes provençale

Crevettes Indochine 19.95
sauteed shrimp with coconut milk + thai spices

Foie de Veau à l'Aigre Doux 18.95
sauteed calve's liver with sweet + sour sauce + mashed potatoes

Suprême de Poulet 18.
roast breast of chicken with lemon peppercorn sauce, rosemary + ginger + mashed potatoes

Confit de Canard Rouffignac 21.95
duck confit with frites

Souffle au Chocolat 8. must be advance ordered
Crème Caramel 6.
Mousse au Chocolat 6.25
Tarte du Jour 6.50
Fruits Frais 6.

Dinner: 7 Days a Week 5 - 12

Bouley is considered to be New York's best restaurant. A combination of the freshest ingredients, most creative French-inspired menu in town, and a soft, romantic, flower-filled room, reminiscent of the French countryside, make this a memorable dining experience.

BOULEY

Daily Specials Available

MENU DEGUSTATION

Fresh Pasta Ravioli with Maine Crabmeat and White and Green Celery Sauce
or
Atlantic Salmon with Roasted Sweet Onions and Wild Watercress Sauce

---

New York State Foie Gras Roasted with Lemon Thyme, Fresh Local Peaches, Fresh Organic Quince, and an Armagnac Sauce

---

Black Sea Bass Roasted with a 24 Hour Cooked Tomato, Green Basil, and Green Celery Sauce

---

Maine Day-Boat Lobster served with Tahitian Vanilla, Fresh Chervil, and a Fricassee of Vegetables in their Juices
or
Maine Halibut with Toasted Sesame seeds in Tomato Water

Roast Loin of Veal and Sweet Bermuda Onions Braised with Red Wine, Mustard Seeds, Yukon Gold Potato Puree, and Glazed Asparagus

---

Fresh Fruit Sorbets with Lemon Tea Cake

Pear and Fig Mirliton Tart served warm with Fresh Strawberry Sauce and Mint Almond Ice Cream
or
Hot Valrhona Chocolat Souffle with Chocolat Sauce, Maple Ice Cream, and Banana Tart

Seventy Dollars

ENTREES

Cape Cod Codfish with 24 Hour-Cooked Tomato, Italian Rose Olive Sauce, and Puree of Celery Root $26

Maine Salmon with Toasted Sesame in a Tomato Consomme $14

Big Eye Sashimi-Quality Tuna cured with Fresh Tarragon and Herb Oils and served with Fennel Julienne Salad $14

APPETIZERS

Maine Crab Meat with Fresh Asparagus, Leek, and Chive Vinaigrette, served warm $14

Creamless Asparagus Soup with Sweet Roasted Beets $8

Triangle of Fresh New York State Goat Cheese and Fresh Artichoke with a Sun Dried Tomato Dressing $10

DESSERTS

Roast Pigeon with Grilled Foie Gras and Braised Pigeon with Savoy Cabbage $28

Lavender Honey Glazed Organic Duckling with Roasted Shallots, Early Turnips, Sweet Peas, and Germinated Summer Wheat $24

Organic Guinea Hen Steamed Thigh with Brussel Sprout Leaves, Caraway Seeds, Roasted Breast in Almond Oil with a Fricassee of Wild Mushrooms $28

Hot Valrhona Chocolat Souffle with Hot Chocolat Sauce, Maple Ice Cream and Banana Tart $12

Creme Brulee with Fresh Tahitian Vanilla Beans $9
or
Chocolat Criollo Creme Brulee

Dinner: Mon - Sat 5:30 - 11

Cafe des Artistes

Famed for its murals of dancing naked nymphs by Howard Chandler Christy, this is one of the most romantic restaurants in New York. Under Jenifer Lang's direction, Cafe des Artistes turns out consistently good meals. Extremely popular.

EXEC. CHEF: THOMAS FERLESCH
CHEF EMERITUS: ANDRÉ GUILLOU

MENU CHANGES DAILY

FIRST COURSE

smoked or marinated fish

SALMON FOUR WAYS:
SMOKED, POACHED, DILL-MARINATED AND TARTAR
FOR ONE: 15.00 FOR TWO: 30.00

GRAVLAX SALMON, DILL-MARINATED 10.00

SALMON TARTAR IN AVOCADO, HERB TOAST 8.50

SMOKED SEA SCALLOPS 9.00

HERRING IN SOUR CREAM WITH APPLES AND ONIONS 8.50

SMOKED TROUT WITH A CUCUMBER-DILL-YOGURT DRESSING 9.00

salads

ARUGULA WITH LEMON-VIRGIN OLIVE OIL DRESSING AND PARMESAN SHAVINGS 6.00

BOSTON, ENDIVE, LAMB'S LETTUCE AND RADICCHIO 6.00

FRISÉE, RIPE PEARS AND WALNUTS WITH WARM GOAT CHEESE 10.00

VINE-RIPENED TOMATO WITH SNOW WHITE ANCHOVIES, BASIL AND ONIONS 10.00

shellfish appetizers

NEW ZEALAND MUSSELS WITH GARLIC BUTTER 9.00

OYSTERS SAUCISSE BORDELAISE 10.00

MR. FLOWER'S LONG ISLAND OYSTERS 8.50

CLAMS ON THE HALF SHELL TOPPED WITH MEXICAN RELISH 8.50

FIRST COURSE

charcuterie

ASSORTED PLANKED COCHONNAILLES WITH PÂTÉS AND OTHER CHARCUTERIES
FOR ONE: 12.00
FOR TWO: 22.00

CHEF ANDRÉ'S PÂTÉ WITH WALNUTS 7.50

RILLETTES 6.00

SWEETBREAD HEADCHEESE WITH PIQUANT VINAIGRETTE 6.00

another first course

ASPARAGUS VINAIGRETTE OR HOLLANDAISE 9.00

PROSCIUTTO DI PARMA WITH RIPE MELON 9.50

PASTA AS A FIRST COURSE 9.00

HOME CURED BRESAOLA WITH PEARS, PARMESAN SHAVINGS, AND ROSEMARY OLIVE OIL 10.00

SHIITAKE, OYSTER AND PORTOBELLO MUSHROOMS SAUTÉ WITH FRESH HERBS 9.00

BRANDADE DE MORUE - GARLIC MASHED POTATOES AND CODFISH, GRATINÉE 8.50

ARTICHOKE COLD, WITH SAUCE GRIBICHE 9.00

FOIE GRAS DE CANARD, WITH TOASTED BRIOCHE AND DUCK CRACKLINGS 14.00

BUFFALO MOZZARELLA, WITH VINE-RIPE TOMATO, BASIL, ARUGULA AND OLIVES NIÇOISE 12.00

1 West 67th St • Lincoln Center • (212) 877-3500

SECOND COURSE

cold entrees of the Café

RIPE CUT FRUIT, COTTAGE CHEESE AND *YOGURT DRESSING* 14.00

CHICKEN SALAD WALDORF, OUR OWN VARIATION, WITH SNOW PEA PODS, APPLES AND WALNUTS 16.00

SALADE NIÇOISE WITH FRESH TUNA AND PEELED BEEFSTEAK TOMATO 16.00

OUR OWN SMOKED CHICKEN WITH CUCUMBER SALAD 19.50

SALMON FOUR WAYS: SMOKED, POACHED, DILL-MARINATED, AND TARTAR 16.50

fish and crustaceans

SWORDFISH PAILLARD, LIGHTLY GRILLED, SAUCE MOUTARDE 19.50

FILLET OF SALMON, POACHED, GRILLED OR SMOKED TO ORDER, OVER NORWEGIAN SPRUCE CHIPS 25.00

SPICY HERB CRUSTED TUNA STEAK OR TUNA STEAK AU POIVRE 25.00

SWORDFISH PAILLARD, LIGHTLY GRILLED, SAUCE MOUTARDE 25.00

RED SNAPPER, WITH A CRISP HERB AND ORANGE ZEST COATING 25.00

VEGETARIAN

BUFFET PLATTER, MIDDLE EASTERN STYLE 21.00

chicken, duck and other birds

DUCK, ROASTED WITH DARK AND GOLDEN RAISINS IN GRAPPA, SERVED WITH MASHED POTATOES 27.50

DUCK CONFIT, POTTED AND CRISPED 27.50

ROASTED CHICKEN WITH ASPARAGUS, PROSCIUTTO AND GLAZED PEARL ONIONS 21.50

SECOND COURSE

veal

CALF'S LIVER SAUTÉ WITH BACON AND ONIONS 23.00

MEDALLIONS OF SWEETBREADS, IN A CRUST OF JAPANESE BREADCRUMBS, WITH SMOKED TENDERLOIN OF PORK 26.00

LONG BONE VEAL CHOP WITH ASPARAGUS, PROSCIUTTO AND GLAZED PEARL ONIONS 29.00

pork — lamb

RACK OF LAMB WITH BASIL CRUST 29.00

LENTIL CASSOULET WITH DUCK, LAMB AND HOMEMADE SAUSAGES 23.00

beef and game

STEAK, GRILLED OR AU POIVRE 29.00

POT AU FEU with marrow bone and traditional accompaniments 25.00

STEAK TARTAR, OUR OWN VERSION: CURRIED AND LIGHTLY TOASTED, WITH PINE NUTS 20.00

pies, cakes and pastries 6.00

SOUR CREAM APPLE WALNUT PIE

TOASTED ORANGE SAVARIN

CARROT CAKE

KEY LIME PIE

chocolate desserts 6.00

THE ORIGINAL ILONA TORTE

MOCHA DACQUOISE

CHOCOLATE RASPBERRY CAKE

a seasonal vegetable will be served with Second Courses

Dinner: Mon - Sat 5:30 - 12:30, Sun 5 -11

Cafe Loup can always be counted on for consistent, authentic French bistro cooking. Its charming townhouse setting and warm, conscientious servers also help to make it a neighborhood favorite.

Menu Changes Daily

APPETIZERS

MIXED GREENS - green leaf lettuces with sourdough croutons & a creamed anchovy-garlic dressing 5.00

SEVEN LETTUCE SALAD - arugula, tat-soi, baby mustard greens, frisee & mizuna tossed in a roasted pine-nut dressing, served on Belgian endive and radicchio 7.50

POMMES FRITES - hand-cut, twice-blanched russet potatoes served with dijon mayonnaise 3.50

PATE MAISON - country pate served with 2 mustard, cornichons and nicoise olives 6.00

ESCARGOTS - snails baked with butter, garlic, shallots & parsley - napped with hollandaise 6.50

CHAMPIGNON GRILLE - a grilled portobello mushroom set over leaf lettuce, topped with a radicchio-arugula salad, dressed with balsamic vinegar & extra-virgin olive oil 7.50

SALADE LYONNAISE - Belgian endive tossed in a strong roquefort dressing, garnished with organic beets, bacon lardons, chives & a warm poached egg 8.00

HUITRES - a tasting of long island 'flower' oysters & "chiloe's" from the rich, cold waters of the humbolt current - served with a champagne mignonette 9.00

105 W. 13th St. • Greenwich Village • (212) 255-4746

ENTREES

TUNA CARPACCIO - seared raw yellowfin tuna over lightly dressed greens with a soy-ginger sauce 14.00

EAR PASTA - tossed with various wild & cultivated mushrooms, scallions, garlic & basil, finished with a light stock, grated parmesan cheese & a touch of white truffle oil - garnished with tomato brunoise 14.50

VEGETABLE PLATE - assorted steamed & grilled seasonal vegetables 12.50

POUSSIN - roast baby chicken served with pommes frites 14.00

CALF'S BRAINS - sauteed & served with a brown butter & caper sauce 15.00

GRILLED SALMON - fillet of aqua-farmed Norwegian salmon, served over organic greens, topped with tomato brunoise, arugula & capers 15.50

CHICKEN PAILLARD - grilled chicken breast with grilled asian greens, sticky shiitake rice & a macadamia nut-roast pepper butter 15.50

BAVETTE FRITES - grilled marinated skirt steak served with pommes frites and a carmelized shallot glaze (served rare to medium rare) 15.50

CASSOULET TOULOUSE - confits of duck-leg & pork, sliced garlic sausage, and white haricot beans - baked in earthenware "cassole" with a crust of bread crumbs and bacon lardons 18.00

FILET MIGNON - grilled beef tenderloin steak brushed with dijon mustard and wasabi, set on a fanned portobello mushroom served with big fried potatoes and seasonal vegetables 19.50

PRIX FIXE OF THE EVENING; POISSON DU JOUR - ROTI DU JOUR - PATES FRAICHES

WE AT CAFE LOUP ALONG WITH OUR FARMERS, FISHERMEN, & PRODUCERS THANK YOU FOR YOUR CONTINUED SUPPORT OF LOCAL, SUSTAINABLE ORGANIC AGRICULTURE AND THE FAMILY FARM: LLOYD FEIT - chef owner

7 Days a Week until 12

Long a favorite with New Yorkers for French bistro food in the Lincoln Center area, it has an authentic bistro ambiance and menu.

DINNER

• APPETIZERS •

COUNTRY SALAD 9.25
frisee, Roquefort cheese, garlic croutons, bacon lardons with a mustard vinaigrette

GRAVLAX 10.50
with vodka, dill and honey mustard

SOUP DU JOUR 6.75

WARM LENTIL SALAD 7.00
with grilled chevre and arugula

MIXED GREEN SALAD 7.00
with boston lettuce, romaine, arugula and raddichio with a balsamic vinaigrette

ESCARGOTS 8.75
with garlic-herb butter

CRISP BABY ARTICHOKES 8.50
with olive tapenade

MARINATED OCTOPUS 9.50
marinated with fresh lime and jalapeno pepper

• ENTREES •

ROAST LEG OF LAMB 19.50
with spinach and white beans

GRILLED TUNA 23.50
with red pepper vinaigrette and couscous

200 West 70th St • Lincoln Center • (212) 873-7411

GRILLED SPRING VEGETABLES 15.50
with a spicy curry oil

PAN SAUTEED LIVER 17.50
with roast potatoes, bacon and sherry vinegar

HERB ROASTED CHICKEN 16.75
with mashed potatoes and spinach

GRILLED SQUAB 23.00
in grape leaves

LEMON RISOTTO 17.75
with fresh asparagus and parmesan

SAUTEED BROOK TROUT 17.50
with a pommery mustard sauce and summer squash

FISH DU JOUR PRICED ACCORDINGLY

STEAK FRITES 24.00

PROVENCALE VEGETABLE TART 15.75
with mixed grains

FRESH LINGUINE 16.50
with manila clams and fresh tomatoes

PASTA DU JOUR 16.50

FARM-RAISED STRIPED BASS 21.00
sauteed, with fresh herbs, garlic and olive oil

• ACCOMPANIMENTS •

Spinach **White Beans with Garlic and Olive Oil**

Mashed Potatoes **French Fries**

5.75

Dinner: Mon - Sat 5:30 - 12:30, Sun 6 - 11:30

Cafe Pierre is your basic hotel dining room, but it has excellent French food, correct, formal service, elegant decor, and high prices. Most New Yorkers go there for lunch or tea in the Atrium.

Menu Changes Seasonally Along With Daily Specials

Dinner

Spring 1993

Appetizers

Tuna Carpaccio with Sesame Cucumbers and Wasabi Cream 13.00

Caramelized Onion and Goat Cheese Tart, Marjoram Vinaigrette 11.00

Fricassee of Wild Mushrooms, Asparagus and Ricotta Gnocchi 12.00

Chili Marinated Shrimp with Watercress and a Roasted Pepper Relish 13.50

**Salad of Mushrooms Steamed in Bamboo with Apples, Celery Root and Truffles 12.00*

**An Assortment of Baby Field Greens 7.00*

New York State Foie Gras Terrine with a Green Bean and Potato Salad 16.00

**Norwegian Salmon Tartar with Sesame Tuilles, Lime Vinaigrette 10.00*

Entrees

Medallions of Salmon with Braised Canellini Beans, Citrus Vinaigrette 26.00

**Black Bass Filet served in an Artichoke Broth 22.50*

Sea Scallops with Parsley Risotto and a Ragout of Spring Vegetables 24.00

Herb Marinated Grilled Swordfish with Roasted Vegetables and Tomato Oil 23.00

Maine Lobster with Parsnip Puree and Crisp Potato Ravioli 32.50

Roast Baby Chicken with Sauteed Cepes, Green Beans and Fingerling Potatoes 23.50

Sliced Loin of Veal with Morels, Asparagus and Caramelized Shallots 27.00

Rack of Lamb with Basil Potato Puree and Garlic Chips 28.00

Pierre Hotel • 2 East 61st St • Midtown East Side • (212) 940-8185

Pastilla of Squab and Foie Gras with Turnip Confit and Pistacchio Oil 29.00

**Filet of Beef with a Grilled Crimini Mushroom and New Potato Brochette 26.50*

Lunch

Spring 1993

Appetizers

Caramelized Onion and Goat Cheese Tart, Marjoram Vinaigrette 10.00

Fricassee of Wild Mushrooms, Asparagus and Ricotta Gnocchi 12.00

Chili Marinated Shrimp with Watercress and a Roasted Pepper Relish 13.50

**Salad of Mushrooms, Steamed in Bamboo with Apples, Celery Root and Truffles 12.00*

Norwegian Salmon Tartar with Puppodums and Curry Vinaigrette 10.00

Penne with Sundried Tomatoes and Broccoli Rabe Pesto 11.00

Black Linguini with Sauteed Calamari, Roasted Peppers and Basil 12.50

**An Assortment of Baby Field Greens 7.00*

Entrees

Medallions of Salmon with Braised White Beans, Citrus Vinaigrette 25.00

Grilled Scallops with Herbed Polenta and Sauteed Escarole 23.00

**Cilantro Marinated Swordfish with a Charred Tomato and Cucumber Salsa 21.50*

Black Bass Filet served in an Artichoke Broth 21.00

Roast Baby Chicken with Sauteed Cepes and Fingerling Potatoes 22.00

Filet of Lamb with Broccoli Rabe and a Roasted Garlic Potato Cake 24.00

Sliced Loin of Veal with Morels, Asparagus and Caramelized Shallot Potato Puree 25.50

**Ragout of Spring Vegetables with Parsley Risotto and Garlic Chips 19.00*

Four Seasons Hotels Alternative Cuisine selections are nutritionally balanced, reduced in calories, cholesterol, sodium and have low fat levels.

Dinner: 7 Days a Week 6 - 10:30

Capsouto Freres

When you think of "real" New York, you think of this place; a funky location (the wholesale meat district) and comfortable setting (a high-ceilinged, brick-walled former warehouse with lace draperies) and very fine French food. Sunday brunch is always popular.

Menu changes daily and seasonally

Menu du Diner

Hors d'Oeuvre

Little Necks
1.10

Saucisson Chaud
Country style sausage with warm potatoes
7.00

Assiette de Pâtés
5.50

Oysters
1.50

Escargots Maison
Snails baked with garlic butter
7.50

Saumon Fumé au Caviar
Smoked salmon with caviar
12.50

Terrine Provençale
Layered eggplant, roasted peppers, and goat cheese
7.50

Salades

Belle Chaumière
An assortment of greens and fruit
5.00

Niçoise
Marinated Tuna with tomato, cucumber, egg, and anchovies
11.50

Arugula au Chèvre
6.50

Confit de Canard
Warm confit of duck with vegetables
13.00

Assiette Végétarienne
Seasonal assortment of vegetables on wild rice
12.00

Assiette de Fromages et de Fruits
9.00

Potages

Soupe à l'Oignon Gratinée
4.25

Poissons

Sole Meuniere ou Almandine
16.50

Ravioli de St. Jacques aux Champignons
Homemade ravioli with scallops and mushrooms
14.00

Saumon aux Herbes Fraîches
Poached salmon with a warm fresh herb vinaigrette
19.00

Crevettes Sautées Nimoise
Shrimps and scallops on fresh pasta
17.00

Viandes

Cailles Grillées à la Framboise
Grilled quails with a raspberry butter
18.50

Canard Rôti au Gingembre et Cassis
Roast duckling with a ginger and black currant sauce
17.50

Noisettes de Veau Poivre Vert
Saddle of veal with a green peppercorn sauce
25.00

Steak Frites
Grilled sirloin steak with french fries
24.00

Steak au Poivre
Sauteed sirloin steak with mixed peppercorns
26.00

Foie de Veau au Vieux Vinaigre de Jerez
Calfs liver sauteed with a sherry vinegar sauce
15.00

Rognons de Veau Moutarde
Veal kidneys with a mustard cream sauce
15.00

Tournedos Trois Frères
Filet of beef with a madeira sauce and mushrooms
24.00

Dinner: Mon - Thurs, Sun 6 - 11, Fri - Sat 6 - 12

Chanterelle pioneered the move downtown of top French restaurants. From its spare, elegant quarters in TriBeCa, it offers a personal interpretation of the classics. David Waltuck is one of the city's best chefs.

Chanterelle

Menu Changes Monthly

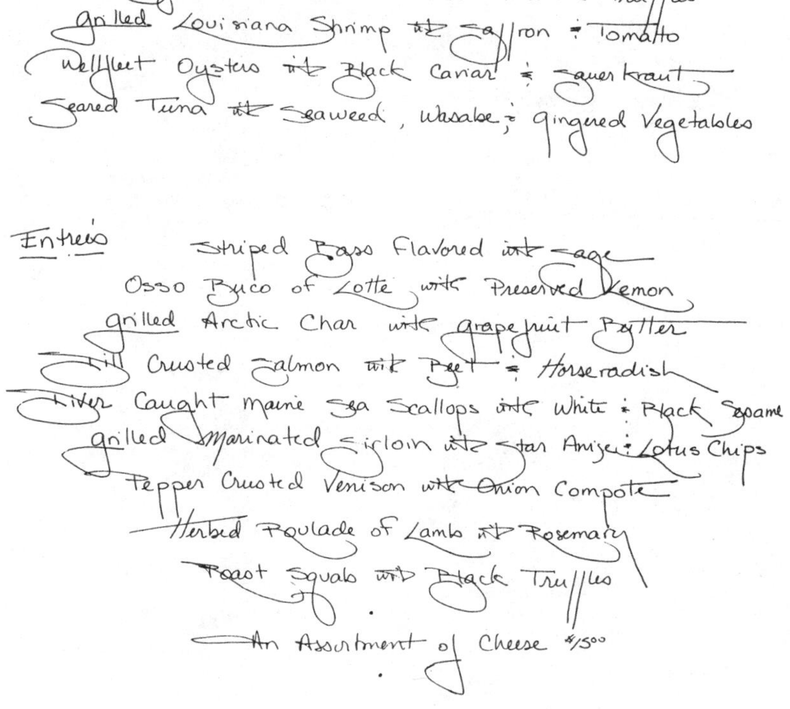

Appetizers

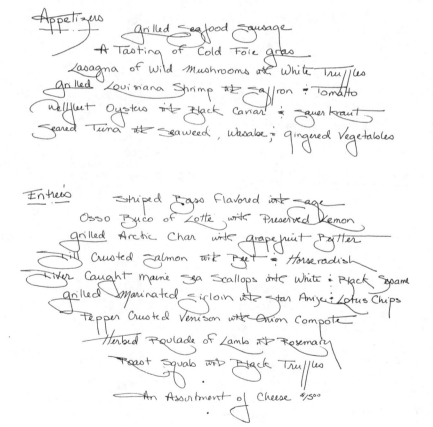

Grilled Seafood Sausage

A Tasting of Cold Foie Gras

Lasagna of Wild Mushrooms with White Truffles

Grilled Louisiana Shrimp with Saffron & Tomato

Wellfleet Oysters with Black Caviar & Sauerkraut

Seared Tuna with Seaweed, Wasabe & Gingered Vegetables

Entrées

Striped Bass Flavored with Sage

Osso Buco of Lotte with Preserved Lemon

Grilled Arctic Char with Grapefruit Butter

Dill Crusted Salmon with Beet & Horseradish

Diver Caught Maine Sea Scallops with White & Black Sesame

Grilled Marinated Sirloin with Star Anise & Lotus Chips

Pepper Crusted Venison with Onion Compote

Herbed Roulade of Lamb with Rosemary

Roast Squab with Black Truffles

An Assortment of Cheese $15.00

2 Harrison St • TriBeCa/Downtown/Chinatown • (212) 966-6960

Menu:

A Tasting of Cold Foie Gras

Wellfleet Oysters with Black Caviar & Sauerkraut

Dill Crusted Salmon with Beet & Horseradish

Roast Squab with Black Truffles

An Assortment of Cheese

Passionfruit Crepe Souffle with Raspberry Coulis

Coffee · Tea

petits fours

$87.00

Desserts

Ice Creams & Sherbets
Ginger Creme Caramel
A Medley of Chocolate Desserts
Gratin of Raspberries with Muscat Sabayon
Passionfruit Crepe Souffle with Raspberry Coulis
Pineapple Soup with Seasonal Fruit flavored with Thai Lime Leaves
Coffee $68.00 Tea

Dinner: Tues - Sat 6 - 10:30

Chef/owner Catherine Alexandrou has presided over her kitchen for thirteen years, which has established her as one of the preeminent chefs in New Jersey. Her restaurant is always listed as one of the top in the state.

Chez Catherine

Menu Changes Seasonally

"Dinner Complete"

Includes an Amuse-Gueule, an Appetizer, a Salad, a Main Course and a Homemade Dessert.

Prices vary according to the Entree selected.

Bon Appetit,
Catherine

Appetizers:

Stuffed "Calamar" with fresh salmon on a deglazing of green peppercorn.

Pizaïella gratinée with fresh mushrooms and light garlic.

Seafood with a "Concassé" of apples and celery in a lemon-grass, ginger, carrot and herb couli.

431 North Ave West • Westfield, NJ • (908) 232-1680

Smoked Poussin "émincé" with roasted garlic and red pepper.

Braised scrod on a bed of warm leeks in a champagne reduction.

Entrees:

Sauteed "Lotte" with lentils slightly smokey ...$41.95

Grilled boneless legs of chicken with apples and oranges ...$33.00

Diplay of at least Seven Vegetables with or without meat sauce ...$37.50

Shank of the day with its seasonal garniture ...$38.50

Beef "Aged Rib Eye" with potato Pierogi ...$40.00

Medallions of loin of lamb with a nut-crust and Fennel ...$42.95

Veal Chop sauteed, then grilled with fried shallots ...$43.50
or with Foie Gras, Madeira ...$45.25

Desserts:

A Choice of cut to order cheeses with nuts and Fruits
or a Choice of our freshly made desserts.

Dinner: Tues - Sat 5:30 - 9

This is a lovely Village spot that exudes Gallic charm. For years, it has served a traditional French menu that has remained consistently good.

Chez Jacqueline

cuisine provençale

Menu Changes Seasonally Along With Daily Specials

Nos Hors D'Oeuvres

Soupe De Poissons — $6.50
Traditional Fish Soup

Escargots Au Pastis — $7.25
Snails in a Tomato Sauce with Pastis

Brandade De Morue — $7.25
Shredded Cod Fish with Potatoes, Olive Oil, Garlic and Parsley

Calamars Grillés — $7.50
Grilled Baby Squid Provencal

Salade D'Haricots Verts Aux Foies De Volailles — $7.25
Sauteed Chicken Livers on a Bed of French String Beans

Mesclun Vinaigrette Gourmande — $6.25
Mixed Wild Baby Lettuce in Fresh Herbs Vinaigrette

72 MacDougal St • Greenwich Village • (212) 505-0727

Nos Hors D'Oeuvres

Frisée Aux Pignons Et Fromage De Chévre $7.50

Chicory Salad with Roasted Pine Nuts and Goat Cheese

Paté De Campagne $6.50

Country Paté

Nos Specialitees

Bourride Provencale $18.50

Seafood Casserole in Light Cream Sauce with Safron and Garlic

Saumon En Papillote $17.50

Broiled Salmon in Parchment Foil

Rognon Á La Moutarde $14.50

Veal Kidneys in a Dijon Mustard, Cognac and Cream Sauce

Foie De Veau Grand-Mêre $14.95

Calves Liver Sauteed in Balsamic Vinegar Garlic and Parsley

Daube Niçoise $15.50

Beef Stew in Red Wine Sauce, Tomatoes and Nicoises Olives

Carré D'Agneau Aux Herbes $19.50

Rack of Lamb Broiled with Provencal Herbs

Filet De Boeuf Au Poivre Vert $19.50

Filet Mignon with Green Peppercorn Sauce

Poussin Rôti Au Romarin $16.50

Roasted Free Range Baby Chicken with Fresh Rosmary

Dinner: Mon - Thurs 6 - 11, Fri - Sat 6 - 11:30, Sun 5:30 - 11

Chez Michallet

This is the kind of place that everyone likes to discover in the Village; a small jewel decorated in toile that's almost hidden among the small houses that surround it. It's very charming and romantic and has highly regarded French food.

chez michallet

Menu Changes Seasonally

HORS D'OEUVRES

Escargots De Bourgogne — ***6.50***
(Traditional snails with a garlic butter sauce)

Raviolis A L'Huile De Truffe — ***8.95***
(Ravioli of wild mushrooms with a perfumed truffle oil broth)

Soupe De Jour — ***4.95***
(Soup of the Day)

Salade Michallet — ***6.00***
(Organic baby lettuces and endives with house vinaigrette)

Quenelle De Fruit De Mer — ***8.75***
(Shrimp and scallop seafood sausage with tomato & caper sauce)

Pate De La Maison — ***P/A***
(Pate or mousse of the day)

ENTREES

Steak Au Poivre **(Grilled shell steak with a green peppercorn cognac cream sauce - Served with pommes frites)**	***19.95***
Filet Mignon De Porc A L'Orange **(Orange marinated pork tenderloin, served with potato and bacon hash)**	***17.95***
Saumon A L'Oseille **(Seared North Atlantic Salmon with a Sorrel Sauce)**	***18.95***
Magret De Canard Au Coulis De Framboise **(Duck breast served with a raspberry and creme de cassis sauce)**	***17.50***
Cotes D'Agneau Au Romarin **(Rack of lamb with a succulent red wine and rosemary sauce, served with bulghur wheat pilaf)**	***19.95***
Poitrine De Poulet Farcie A La Duxelle De Champignons **(Chicken breast stuffed with mushrooms, served with a grain mustard cream sauce and brown rice pilaf)**	***17.25***
Notre Poisson Du Jour **(Our fish of the day)**	***P/A***
Cote De Veau A L'Orientale **(Grilled veal chop marinated in an oriental style spicy mustard, served with roasted creamer potatoes)**	***19.95***

Dinner: 7 Days a Week 5:30 - 11

Cité has an excellent wine list and good French food, including a hearty steak. A popular favorite, especially pre- or post-theater.

Menu Changes Seasonally

APPETIZERS

Carpaccio of Marinated Tuna with Seaweed Wrapped Noodles	11.50
House Smoked Salmon with Warm Corn Blini	12.50
Tuna & Salmon Tartare with Petrossian Caviar	12.50
Hand Made Cavatelli with Wild Mushrooms & White Truffle Oil	11.50/21.00
or	
Simply with Tomato, Basil & Parmesan	9.50/19.00
Barbecued Squab with Foie Gras & Corn Cake	12.50
Asparagus Risotto	11.50

SOUPS & SALADS

Lobster Wonton Soup	9.50
Gazpacho with Smoked Shrimp & Jack Cheese Quesadilla	9.50
Country Salad with Walnuts & Coach Farms Goat Cheese	9.50
Salad of Mixed Organic Greens	7.50

120 West 51st St • Midtown West Side • (212) 956-7100

SIDE DISHES

Whipped Potatoes with Basil Oil	6.50
Stir Fried Vegetables	7.50
Wild Mushroom Hash	6.75
Creamed Spinach & Leeks	6.50

ENTREES

Soy Glazed Brook Trout with Manila Clams, Sticky Rice & Nori	19.50
Park Avenue Cafe Swordfish Chop* Save the Tag...! (Market Availability)	29.50
Seared Salmon with Ginger, Cracked Pepper & Shitake Dumpling	26.50
Sautéed Red Snapper with Shrimp & Lemon Pepper Noodle Cake	27.50
Halibut Steak with Artichoke Ravioli & Shaved Fennel	25.50
Mrs. Ascher's Steamed Vegetable Torte	19.00
Pan Roasted Chicken with Grilled Eggplant "Parmesan" & Balsamic Sauce	19.50
Spiced Veal Chop with Mango, Celery & Leeks	29.50
Rack of Baby Lamb with Honey Mustard & Rosemary	28.50
Sirloin of Aged Beef with Wild Mushroom Hash	29.50

All of Our Entrées are Available Simply Grilled or Steamed.

Dinner: 7 Days a Week 5 - 12

The premier cooking school in the country features four unique restaurants at which students do all the cooking and serving under the direction of chef-instructors. St. Andrews Café features contemporary cuisine; The Caterina de Medici Dining Room — regional Italian cuisine; The Escoffier Restaurant — classical French; and The American Bounty Restaurant showcases American food and wine.

Menus Change Daily

The Escoffier Restaurant

la cuisine d'aujourd'hui

magrêt et confit de canard au poivre vert et miel 22.00
sauteed duck breast, leg confit with honey and green peppercorn sauce

pintade rôtie à l'orientale 19.00
roasted game hen with oriental five spice, garlic and rosemary, carved table side

homard rôtie au Cognac, cerfeuil et ciboulettes 25.00
pan-roasted lobster with Cognac, chervil and chives

entrecôte grillée "marchand de vin" 19.00
broiled strip sirloin with shallot, red wine and parsley sauce

The American Bounty Restaurant

MAIN COURSE

Sauteed Loin of Venison with Wild Mushrooms, Pearl Onions and Butternut Squash on Toasted Pecan Pasta 21.00

Grilled Beef Tenderloin with Cheddar Potatoes, Rapini, Shiitake Mushrooms and Cream 21.00

Sea Scallops, Clams and Shrimp Steamed in a Fennel-Fish Broth with Seasonal Vegetables and Potatoes 15.00

Grilled Tuna with Black and White Beans, Smoked Sweet Peppers, Tomatillo Vinaigrette and Jicama-Mango Salsa 16.00

433 Albany Post Rd • Hyde Park, NY • (914) 471-6608

The Caterina de Medici Dining Room

Antipasti

Insalata di Funghi con Sedano e Parmigiano
Mushroom Salad with Celery and Parmesan Cheese

Secondi Piatti

Costolette d'Agnello Grigliate
Grilled Lamb Chops with Herb Crust and Parmesan

Arista di Maiale con Salsicce e Pesto
Roast Pork Tenderloin with Sausage and Pesto

Tonno con Olive e Patate al Forno
Oven-Roasted Tuna with Olives and Potatoes

Petto di Pollo con Prosciutto
Breast of Chicken with Prosciutto and Mozzarella

St. Andrews Café

Wood-Fired Pizzas

White Beans, Shrimp, Roasted Onions, Mushrooms and Provolone Cheese on Whole Wheat Crust Appetizer 4.25 or Dinner 5.75

Entrees

Stir-Fry of Moulard Duck Breast and Gulf Shrimp with Asian Vegetables 11.95

Pan-Seared Salmon with Herbed Potato Puree and Citrus Chardonnay Sauce 12.25

Mesquite Grilled Tenderloin of Double J Limousin Beef with Barbequed Prairie Beans and Creamy Western Slaw 14.25

Grilled Breast of Chicken with Orechiette Pasta, Asparagus and Mushrooms 10.75

"Buttons and Bows," Breaded Baked Scallops and Spinach Bow Tie Pasta with Tomatoes, Pearl Onions and Yellow Squash 12.25

Dinner: Tues - Sat 6:30 - 8:30

This place is a mecca for francophiles in the Chelsea area. The authentic bistro food and interior are relatively unique in the neighborhood, which makes it doubly welcome.

Gascogne

Menu Changes Seasonally

Prix Fixe Menu

$25

Soupe d'Asperge au Canard et Poivre Vert
asparagus soup with duck tenderloins and green peppercorn

or

Gaspacho du Pays Basque
gaspacho with sauteed salt cod

or

Terrine de Thon Fume aux Aubergines
smoked tuna and eggplant terrine, red pepper coulis

or

Croustillant de Chevre Chaud et puree d'echalote
salad of warm goat cheese

Main Courses

Cuisse de Canard Confite et ragout de Flageolet
duck leg confit with ragout of flageolet

or

Poulet Grille aux Ecrevisses
grilled chicken with crawfish sauce

or

Steak de Porc aux pruneaux et armagnac
pork steak with prunes and armagnac

or

Truite Meuniere aux Poivron Rouge, Ail and Capres
sauteed trout with garlic, capers and pimientos

Desserts and Armangnac V.S.O.P.

Prune Ice Cream

or

Creme Brulee

or

Gateau Basque

158 Eighth Ave • Chelsea • (212) 675-6564

Les Hors D'Oeuvres

Salade d'Endives, Roquefort, Noix et Eguillettes de Canard Chaudes 9.00
endive, walnut and rouquefort salad with warm duck tenderloins

Croustillant de Chevre Chaud et puree d'echalote en salade 8.50
salad of warm goat cheese and puree of shallots in phyllo dough

Salade de St. Jacques, ail confit, petites Tomates et Champignons 8.50
warm salad of scallops, garlic confit, cherry tomatoes and mushrooms

Roulades de Jambon et Haricots 7.50
proscuitto and beans sausages with gribiche sauce

Les Foies Gras

Les Terrines de Foies Gras 16.50
assorted foie gras terrine

Terrine de Canard Confit et foie Gras 16.50
terrine of duck confit and foie gras

Les Viandes et Volailles

Medaillon d'Agneau en Croute d'Ail confit, Jus a l'Estragons 19.50
sauteed Lamb noisette with garlic crust and tarragon jus

Magret de Canard a l'Orange Sanguine et Armagnac 20.00
duck breast with blood orange and armagnac sauce

Longe de Veau Grille aux Oignons, Olives et Jambon 18.00
grilled veal loin with onions, olives ad proscuitto

Poulet Grille aux Ecrevisse 17.00
grilled chicken with crawfish sauce

Les Poissons

Saumon poche au Noilly Prat et Crevettes, sauce creme 19.00
poached salmon with baby shrimp, dry vermouth cream sauce

Sandre Grillee Fondue D'Oignons Rouges et Citron Confit 18.50
grilled walleye with melted red onions and lemon confit

Truite Meuniere aux Poivron Rouge, Ail et Capres 16.50
sauteed trout with garlic, capers and pimientos

Dinner: Mon - Sat 6 - 10:30

Jean-Georges Vongerichten established his reputation as one of the country's best chefs at Lafayette; thus, when he opened his own restaurant, his fans were waiting. They love his delicious bistro and Alsatian-style preparations and the beautiful interior.

APPETIZERS

GOAT CHEESE ***$10.00***
and Potato Terrine with Arugula Juice

ASPARAGUS ***$9.00***
Salad on Mixed Greens, Avocado and Mushroom

SHRIMP ***$12.00***
in a Spiced Carrot Juice with Thai Lime Leaves

FOIE GRAS ***$14.00***
Poached in Sauterne with Braised Fennel and Caramel Pepper

TUNA ***$11.00***
Tartare with Gaufrette Potatoes and Chive Oil

RABBIT ***$10.00***
Confit, Roasted Red Pepper and Arugula Salad

CRAB $12.00
Salad with Zucchini, Tomato and Basil Vinaigrette

SWEETPEA $8.00
Soup, Matignon of Vegetable, Crisp Country Bread

ENTREES

CODFISH $16.00
Sauteed with Aromates and Herb Smashed Potatoes

SALMON $18.00
Slices Between Crisp Potato and Celeriac Threads and Horseradish Condiment

LOBSTER $24.00
Roasted with Garlic, "Pommes Parisienne" and Sweet Corn

CHICKEN $16.00
Roasted in Ginger, Olive and Coriander, Chickpea Fries

LAMB $20.00
Rack with a Spicy Red Pepper Crust, Artichoke and Fava Beans

SQUAB $19.00
Roasted, Morel and Asparagus "Meuniere"

Dinner: Mon - Sat 6 - 11

Located on the ground floor of a townhouse, this charming place has a genuine French ambiance - nothing cutesy, just well-prepared bistro fare in a lace-curtained, plate-decorated series of rooms. Its proximity to Lincoln Center is another reason for its continued popularity.

La Boîte en Bois

MENU CHANGES SEASONALLY

Hors d'Oeuvres et Potages

Endive et Frisée au Roquefort ENDIVE AND CHICKORY WITH ROQUEFORT	5.75
Paté du Chef HOME MADE PATÉ	5.00
Salade de Thon aux Olives Noires TUNA SALAD WITH BLACK OLIVE SALSA	6.00
Saumon Fumé ou Gravlox Maison HOME CURED SMOKED SALMON OR GRAVLOX	7.50
Saucisson Chaud aux Lentilles du Puy WARM SAUSAGE WITH LENTILS	5.50
Coquille d'Escargots aux Cépes SNAILS WITH PORTOBELLO	7.50
Ravioles de Chèvre, Coulis de Tomates GOAT CHEESE RAVIOLI AND TOMATOES	6.50

75 West 68th St • Lincoln Center • (212) 874-2705

Soupe de Poisson Marseillaise 5.50
FISH SOUP MARSEILLE STYLE

Entrées

Saumon Rôti au Miel et Moutarde 18.00
ROAST SALMON GLAZED WITH HONEY MUSTARD

Nage de Crevettes au Fenouil 18.50
SHRIMPS IN A FENNEL BROTH

Red Snapper Grillé aux Poivrons 19.00
GRILLED RED SNAPPER WITH BELL PEPPERS

Tranche d'Espadon Homardine 20.00
SWORDFISH WITH LOBSTER SAUCE

Mignon de Veau au Jus et Confits d'Endive 21.00
SAUTEED LOIN OF VEAL SERVED WITH ENDIVE

Poulet Rôti aux Herbes 16.50
ROAST CHICKEN WITH HERBS

Daube d'Agneau au Coriandre 17.50
BRAISED LAMB WITH CORIANDER

Entrecôte au Poivre 20.00
PEPPER STEAK

Dessert au Choix

PRIX FIXE 30.00, OR À LA CARTE

PLEASE, NO PIPES OR CIGARS

Dinner: 7 Days a Week 5:30 - 12

La Caravelle has been around for a long time, and although it went through a period of decline, it is once again among the top tier of serious classic French restaurants under chef Tadashi Ono. The cuisine is the best quality and the interior is quiet and elegant.

Menu Changes Bi-Annually

Hors d'Oeuvres

Chiffonade de mesclun et son chèvre tiède
baby mixed greens salad with goat cheese

Carrelet mariné aux deux citrons
fluke marinated in lemon and chive oil

Coquilles Saint-Jacques et asperges au piment doux
sea scallops and asparagus with sweet chili sauce

Pâte fine aux crevettes et coquilles Saint-Jacques
shrimps and scallops in thin pasta layers

Chair de crabe Caravelle *supp. $6.50*
crabmeat in a fine herbs dressing

Sélection d'huîtres et palourdes *Belons* *supp. selon arrivage*
selection of oysters and clams

Terrine de cailles aux champignons des bois
quail and wild mushrooms terrine

Navets farcis au canard et foie gras en consommé
turnips stuffed with duck and foie gras in consomme

Saumon fumé par nos soins *supp. $5.00*
our own housesmoked salmon

Ris de veau pané au sésame, sauce Périgourdine
sesame breaded sweetbreads with a foie gras sauce

Caviar russe Malossol *supp. $25 per oz.*
service of russian malossol caviar

33 West 55th St • Midtown West Side • (212) 586-4252

Entrées

Saumon fumé "en famille" au basilic, fondue de tomate
grilled smoked salmon and its roe with basil sauce and tomato fondue

Homard du Maine au beurre de soja Homardine *supp. selon arrivage*
poached lobster with homardine sauce

Quenelles de brochet truffées, salpicon de homard
pike quenelles in a lobster sauce

Tuile de mer et sa compote de légumes au sabayon de limon
tilefish with vegetable compote, lime sabayon

Sole anglaise grillée, sauce moutarde *supp. $5.00*
grilled dover sole, mustard sauce

Mignonettes de chevreuil aux poires et purée d'aubergines
venison steaks with pears, eggplant puree

Magret de canard à la moutarde verte et son gâteau de riz
duck breast with green mustard, rice cake

Canette croustillante aux cousinettes
crispy duck with cranberries

Poularde rôtie au Champagne
roast chicken with champagne sauce

Filet de veau à l'extrait de carottes, galette de nouilles *supp. $6.00*
sliced filet of veal with carrot juice sauce, noodles pancake

Noisettes d'agneau panées aux huit épices, sauce aux haricots noirs
spice breaded lamb medallions with black bean sauce

Tournedos de Black Angus, sauce Vigneronne
black angus filet mignon with wine sauce

Desserts

La carte des desserts Caravelle

Soufflés *supp. $5.00*

Café, Thé ou Infusion *$3.00*

Prix du Dîner *$58.00*
A la carte available *$40.00* *minimum*

Dinner: Mon - Sat 5:30 - 10

La Colombe d'Or

Even though there's not a lot of competition near this French bistro, it would probably do well wherever it was. A charming townhouse setting, consistently and reliable French food, and a history of training great chefs, bring people from all over.

Menu Changes Seasonally

Appetizers

RATATOUILLE 6.50

MIXED GREEN SALAD 5.75
(with goat cheese & roasted red peppers 7.50)

GALETTE OF VEGETABLES & HERBS 7.50

SOUPE DE POISSONS 6.50

BRAISED ARTICHOKES WITH TOMATO & CORIANDER 8.00

SOCCA ROULADE FILLED WITH RATATOUILLE & GOAT CHEESE 8.50

SMOKED DUCK SALAD WITH TURNIPS & HARICOTS VERTS 9.00

HOUSE SMOKED SALMON WITH MESCLUN GREENS 9.50

SEAFOOD SALAD WITH LEMON VINAIGRETTE 11.50

134 East 26th St • Murray Hill/Kips Bay • (212) 689-0666

Entrées

FETTUCINE WITH ROASTED TOMATOES 15.00

CHICKEN WITH ROASTED SHALLOTS & TRUFFLED MASHED POTATOES 18.50

CASSOULET 19.50

BŒUF EN DAUBE ***provençal beef stew*** **18.50**

DUCK: GRILLED BREAST & THIGH CONFIT, SWEET & AROMATIC SPICES 19.50

GRILLED CALF'S LIVER WITH ONION PUDDING 18.50

COD WITH PROVENÇAL BLEND OF WHITE BEANS & ROASTED TOMATOES 17.50

SKATE, PAN ROASTED WITH ZUCCHINI, GREEN BEANS & PLUM TOMATOES 18.50

MONKFISH ROASTED IN HERBS WITH LIMA BEANS & RED PEPPERS 18.75

SALMON WITH LEEK/CARROT FONDUE & BROCCOLI FLEURETTES 21.50

BOUILLABAISSE 24.50

Side Orders:

Truffled Mashed Potatoes 5.00 **Beet Frites 3.00**

Provençal Beans 5.00

✿

George & Helen Studley, Proprietors / Michelle Everett, Mgr.
Jonathan Crayne, Maître d'Hôtel / Naj Zougari, Chef

Dinner: Sun - Thurs 5:30 - 10, Fri - Sat 6 -11

Long a bastion of haute French cuisine, La Cote Basque continues to be one of the most famous and important of all New York French restaurants. No list would be complete without it.

La Côte Basque

DEJEUNER

Les Hors d'Oeuvres

Le Pannequet de Crabe "Côte Basque"

Corolle d'Artichaut au Chèvre

Terrine de Homard aux Concombres

Escargots à la Méridionale

Saucisson Chaud en Croûte Perigourdine

Savouris de Canard, Haricots Verts

Asperges Froides Vinaigrette

Les Entrées

Red Snapper au Grill, Sauce Moutarde

Dover Sole Grillée ou Meunière

Le Cassoulet du Chef Toulousain

Les Noisettes de Veau, Sauce Morilles et Champagne

Les Mignonnettes de Boeuf aux Champignons

Les Escalopes de Veau Arlesienne

Swordfish Sauté Provançale

Le Foie de Veau Lyonnaise

Embeurré de Scallops au Basilic

Les Desserts

Les Mousses au Grand Marnier & Chocolat

La Crème Brûlée

Les Glaces & Les Sorbets

Le Chariot de Patisserie du Chef Pâtissier

Dinner: Mon - Sat 6 - 10:30

La Metairie

Tucked away on a Greenwich Village side street, this exceedingly charming French bistro has the feel of the French countryside. It's very romantic and has excellent food.

Menu Changes Seasonally

Boudin de Fruits de Mer au Safron — *8.00*
SEAFOOD SAUSAGE WITH WHITE WINE AND SAFFRON SAUCE

Petit Flan d'Ail aux Champignons Sauvage — *7.00*
GARLIC MOUSSE WITH SAUTEED WILD MUSHROOMS

Carpaccio de Thon et Saumon aux Herbes du Jardin — *9.00*
TUNA AND SALMON CARPACCIO WITH A FRESH HERB SAUCE

Feuillantine de Courgettes Chaud au Gingembre — *6.00*
WARM GALETTE WITH ZUCCHINI, TOMATO, GINGER BASIL VINAIGRETTE

Galantine de Canard — *6.00*
DUCK GALANTINE OVER SEASONAL GREENS

Escargots de Bourgogne Provençal — *6.00*
SNAILS SAUTEED WITH HERBS, GARLIC, WHITE WINE, ROQUEFORT

Escalope de Foie Gras à la Normande — *18.00*
FRESH FOIE GRAS SAUTEED WITH CALYADOS AND CARAMELIZED APPLES

189 West Tenth St • Greenwich Village • (212) 989-8939

Salade d'Endive au Roquefort 7.00
BELGIAN ENDIVE WITH ROQUEFORT VINAIGRETTE DRESSING

Salade Printanière aux Pois Gourmand à l'Estragon 6.00
GREEN SPRING SALAD WITH SNOW PEAS IN TARRAGON DRESSING

Soupe de Jour Froide ou Chaude suivant le Temps 5.00
COLD OR HOT SOUP OF THE DAY

Poussin Grillé St. Tropez 11.00
GRILLED CORNISH HEN WITH HERBS OF PROVENCE

Supréme de Poulet Rôti aux Shiitake et Miel de Montagne 13.00
ROASTED CHICKEN BREAST STUFFED WITH SHIITAKE AND HONEY

Tranche de Thon Côte d'Azur 17.00
GRILLED TUNA STEAK WITH TOMATOES, OLIVE OIL AND BLACK OLIVES

Darne de Saumon à l'Anise et Gingembre 16.00
ROASTED NORWEGIAN SALMON WITH GINGER AND STAR ANISE

Ragout de Homard aux Nouilles Fraiches P/A
MAINE LOBSTER SERVED WITH WHITE WINE, BASIL SAUCE AND FRESH NOODLES

Suprême de Canard "Metairie" 16.00
SLICED BREAST OF DUCK WITH SAUCE DU JOUR

Escalope de Veau aux Aubergines 18.00
VEAL SCALLOPINI WITH GRILLED EGGPLANT AND TOMATO FONDUE

Carré d'Agneau Provençal 19.00
ROAST RACK OF LAMB WITH GARLIC-POTATO FLAN

Migononnette de Boeuf au Poivre 18.00
FILET OF BEEF FLAMBÉ WITH COGNAC AND PEPPER SAUCE

Dinner: 7 Days a Week 5 - 1

La Panetière is considered the best French restaurant in Westchester County (the top residential community north of Manhattan). The food is on a par with any city restaurant and the Provencal decor is charming.

Menu Changes Seasonally

Pour Commencer

Frivolités de saumon mariné, fumé et de caviar sevruga
Composition of marinated, smoked salmon and caviar 19.50

Crème de choux-fleurs frappée, profiteroles à la chair de crabe
Chilled, satiny cauliflower soup with crabmeat puffs 9.50

Filets de merlan au ragoût fin d'haricots et piments doux
Whiting fillet with seasonal beans and sweet pepper compote 10.50

Terrine de canard truffée et pistachée à l'ancienne
Country style duck paté, truffles and pistachios 15.50

Soupe de tous les légumes du marché liée au pistou
Clear soup of garden vegetables with pesto 8.50

Feuilleté léger de coquilles St. Jacques, foie gras et truffes
Sauteed scallops, foie gras, and truffles with puff pastry 24.00

Mesclun de jeunes pousses de laitues à l'huile de noisette
Assorted leaves of field salad, hazelnut vinaigrette 9.50

530 Milton Rd • Rye, NY • (914) 967-8140

Crustacés et Poissons

Croustade de bar dorée au four avec une sauce au champagne
***Sea bass and spinach mousse wrapped in a crust with champagne sauce** 28.00*

Espadon grillé sur une lasagne de légumes, huile au basilic
***Grilled swordfish on a medley of vegetables, basil emulsion** 26.00*

Volailles et Viandes

Poussin entier au parfum de truffes, petit farci de foie gras
***Roasted baby chicken, truffle sauce, foie gras savoury** 26.00*

Médaillon et ris de veau au porto, risotto au cresson
***Médaillon and sweetbread of veal in port sauce, watercress risotto** 28.00*

Desserts Maison

Pêche pochée à la vanille, sabayon au champagne, glace pistache
***Poached peach in vanilla syrup, champagne sabayon, pistachio ice cream** 10.50*

Trois petits desserts sur un thème à l'abricot
***Three assorted desserts with an apricot theme** 10.00*

Tartelette à la rhubarbe, son ragoût et sorbet au fromage blanc
***Rhubarb-filled tart with its own compote and fresh cheese sherbet** 9.00*

Panier de fruits frais et sorbets du temps
***Pastry basket filled with sherbets and fruits** 8.50*

Dinner: Mon - Sat 6 - 9:30, Sun 5 - 8:30

This is an elegant, refined temple of haute French cuisine. The service, excellent food, and soigne setting make for a very special evening.

Menu Changes Seasonally

LES HORS D'OEUVRES FROIDS

CHAUD-FROID DE HOMARD AUX PETITS LÉGUMES
ET SA QUENELLE AU RAIFORT (8.00)
Lobster with Gelée, Assorted Vegetables and Dumpling with Horseradish

SAUMON FUMÉ MAISON, MOUSSELINE DE CRESSON (5.00)
House Smoked Salmon with Watercress Mousse

TERRINE DE GIBIER FUMÉ
Terrine of Smoked Game with Cumin, Pistachio and Hazel Nuts

ST. JACQUES ET SAUMON FRAIS MARINÉS À L'ANETH
Scallops and Salmon Marinated with Dill

LE FOIE GRAS DE CANARD MAISON, "TRUFFÉ" (7.00)
Truffle Flavored Duck Liver Paté

LES POTAGES ET CONSOMMÉS

BISQUE DE HOMARD ET SA QUENELLE
Cream of Lobster Soup with Lobster Dumpling

CONSOMMÉ DE VOLAILLE AUX CHAMPIGNONS SAUVAGES
Chicken Consommé with Wild Mushrooms

LES HORS D'OEUVRES CHAUD

L'ASSIETTE DE CAILLE GRILLÉE EN CRAPAUDINE
VINAIGRETTE DE CORIANDRE (4.00)
Salad of Grilled Quail with Coriander Vinaigrette

LES HUÎTRES TIÈDES EN CHEMISE, SAUCE SAFFRAN
Warm Oysters with Saffron Sauce

ESCALOPES DE FOIE GRAS DE CANARD COMPOTE DE RHUBARBE (7.00)
Scallops of Duck Livers Sautéed with Rhubarb Compote

4 West 49th St • Midtown West Side • (212) 247-2993

LES POISSONS

SOLE DE LA MANCHE "LA RÉSERVE" (5.00)
Poached Dover Sole with Artichoke Mousse, Basil and Vermouth

FILET DE SNAPPER GRILLÉ VALLAURIS
Grilled Red Snapper with Tomatoes, Capers and Olives

FILET DE BASS AUX TRUFFES NOIRES (3.00)
Filet of Bass with Black Truffle Sauce

PAILLARD DE SAUMON, SAUCE A L'OSEILLE
Filet of Salmon with Sorrel Sauce

TIMBALE DE FRUITS DE MER AU RIS BASMATI
Seafood with Basmati Rice

LES VIANDES ET GIBIERS

CANARD RÔTI AU CHOCOLAT ET KUMQUATS "ANDRÉ"
Roast Duck with Chocolate and Kumquat Sauce

ENTRECÔTE DE BOEUF, BEURRE D'ÉCHALOTE ET MOËLLE (5.00)
Sirloin of Beef with Red Wine, Shallots and Marrow Sauce

MÉDAILLON DE VEAU AU ROMARIN ET MORILLES
Veal Medallion with Rosemary Sauce and Morels

POUSSIN RÔTI AUX GOUSSES D'AÏL ET THYM FRAIS
Roasted Chicken with Thyme and Garlic Clove

ESCALOPE DE RIS DE VEAU, CUMIN, ET ASPERGES
Sweetbreads with Cumin and Asparagus

CARRÉ D'AGNEAU À LA CROUTE MOUTARDÉE
ET AROMATISÉE (For Two, 10.00)
Rack of Lamb with Aromatic Crust

POËLEE DE ROGNON AU FOND DE XÉRÈS
Veal Kidneys with Sherry Sauce

AIGUILLETTE DE CANARD SUR CHOUX AU MIEL ET DEUX VINAIGRES
Sliced Breast of Duck with Cabbage, Honey and Balsamic Vinegar

GIBIER DE SAISON FAÇON DU CHEF (3.00)
Wild Game du Jour

FILET D'AGNEAU MARINÉ EN VENAISON
Lamb Filet, Marinated, Venison Style

RABLE DE LAPIN AU VIN DE PAILLE ET SARIETTE
Saddle of Rabbit, Fresh Savory and Wine Sauce

PRIX FIXE: $49.00

Dinner: Mon - Thurs 5:30 - 10:30, Fri - Sat 5:30 - 11

Since David Ruggerio took over the kitchen of this venerable institution, many people think this is also one of the top haute cuisine French restaurants in town. It appeals to a business and more-sedate crowd who appreciate its reliability and predictability.

Menu Changes Seasonally

Le Diner A La Carte

LES HORS D'OEUVRES

Salade Composée au Fromage de Chèvre 11.00
Salade of Goat Cheese with Roasted Beets, Crispy Potatoes, Basil and Beet Vinaigrette

Papillon de Langoustines 15.00
Grilled Langoustines with Roasted Zucchinis.
Vine Ripened Tomatoes and Virgin Olive Oil

Terrine de Foie Gras et Confit de Canard 22.00
Terrine of Foie Gras and Duck Confit marinated Wild Mushrooms, Haricots Verts and Duck Prosciutto

Salade de Homard 14.00
Chilled Lobster with Baby Lettuce, Cranberry Beans, Tomato and Olive Oil Emulsion

Risotto de Cailles Épicées 12.00
Risotto of Spiced Quails with Grilled Shitakes and Garden Peas

Ravioles de Crabe à L'essence de Kaffir et Citronnelle 12.00
Open Ravioli of Crab in a Lemongrass and Kaffir Bouillon

106 East 57th St • Midtown East Side • (212) 751-2931

LES ENTREES

Filet de Flounder en Papillotte de Choux Craquants 19.00
Casco Bay Flounder, Wrapped in Savoy Cabbage, Braised Endives, Aromatic Sauce and Caviar

Bayaldi de Cabillaud Provencal 19.00
Roasted Filet of Cod Fish with Provencale Vegetables, White Beans and Virgin Olive Oil

Aile de Raie Rotie à la Marjolaine et Capres 19.00
Roasted Skate with Marjoram and Capres with Swiss Chard

Filet de Saumon Rôti au Chermoula 19.00
Oven Roasted Salmon with Moroccan Spices, Herbed Cous-Cous, Roasted Vegetables

Steak de Homard aux Poireaux Croustillants 25.00
Steak of Lobster, Crispy Leeks, Truffles and Lobster Oil

Suprême de Capon en Crêpe Craquante 19.00
Breast of Capon Stuffed with Vegetables and Foie Gras, Wrapped in Crispy Phylo

Selle de Lapin Rissolée à La Mytre 21.00
Roasted Saddle of Rabbit with White Beans, Baby Fennel and Fresh Myrtle

Côte d'agneau et sa Charlotte d'aubergine 25.00
Pan Seared Lamb Chops with Spiced Charlotte of Eggplant and Lamb

Cannette Rôtie au Miel et Lavande 21.00
Roasted Duck with Lavender and Honey

Entrecôte Poëllée au Vin Rouge 25.00
Black Angus Steak Sauteed with Red Wine Sauce, Crispy Shallots and Purée of Potato

Dinner: Mon - Fri 5:30 - 10:30, Sat 5:30 - 11:15, Sun 4:30 - 10

Who could call himself a foodie and not have heard of Le Cirque? This legendary restaurant, orchestrated by master host Sirio Maccioni, continues to reinvent French food with stellar results under the new chef, Sylvain Porter.

NEW YORK

Menu Changes Seasonally

DINER A LA CARTE

LES LEGUMES EN ENTREE

GROSSES ASPERGES VERTES ROTIES, SABAYON CITRONNE
Roasted asparagus with shallots, parmesan and lemon sabayon 17.00

ARTICHAUT VINAIGRETTE OU HOLLANDAISE
Artichoke with vinaigrette or hollandaise sauce 10.00

HORS D'OEUVRES FROIDS ET CHAUDS

MEDAILLON DE SAUMON TIEDE EN SALADE DE LEGUMES CROQUANTS
Warm medaillon of salmon with crispy vegetable salad 14.00

DODINE DE PIGEON A L'ANCIENNE, SALADE DE CONCOMBRES, RADIS ET TOMATES
Squab stuffed with foie gras, truffles, cucumbers, radish and tomato salad 18.00

GRECQUE DE LEGUMES, AILERONS DE VOLAILLE FARCIS, JUS AU GOUT DE PISTOU
Assorted vegetables and chicken wings stuffed with different greens and pesto dressing 14.00

LES PATES

RAVIOLI DE BLETTES, ROQUETTE, ARTICHAUTS ET FROMAGE DE CHEVRE A L'HUILE D'OLIVE
Ravioli with swisschard, arrugula, artichokes and goat cheese with olive oil Apt. 18.00 M.C. 29.00

PATES PAPILLON "MAISON", COQUILLAGES ET CRUSTACES FRENCH RIVIERA
Farfalle with octopus, calamari and squid with fresh basil Apt. 19.00 M.C. 29.00

GNOCCHI DE LAIT CAILLE ROULES AU PARMESAN, LEGUMES MIJOTES "FACON ALAIN DUCASSE"
Ricotta gnocchi with parmesan, vegetables and prosciutto "Alain Ducasse style" Apt. 21.00 M.C.29.50

RISOTTO DE HOMARD DU MAINE, CHIFFONNADE DE CHOUX ET JUS AU ROMARIN
Lobster risotto with shredded green cabbage and lobster sauce with rosemary Apt. 18.50 M.C.28.00

POISSONS ET CRUSTACES

HOMARD DU MAINE CUIT EN CARAPACE, FINE SAUCE NATURELLE AU CORAIL ET ARTICHAUTS
Lobster with artichokes in a natural lobster broth 32.00

PAUPIETTE DE BLACK SEA BASS CROUSTILLANTE AU VIN DE BAROLO
Black sea bass wrapped in a crispy potato crust with red wine sauce and braised leeks 31.00

RED SNAPPER CROUSTILLANT, JUS DE DAUBE CITRON ET ORANGE, PANISSES ET TOMATES
Sauteed red snapper with sweet and sour sauce, baked tomatoes and chick pea fritter 31.00

CABILLAUD DEMI SEL ROTI, HARICOTS BLANCS AU JUS DE PERSIL, CALAMARS ET CLAMS
Roasted codfish with cranberry beans, Italian parsley, calamari and clams 33.00

ST PIERRE EN FILET "LARDE" DE BASILIC FRAIS ET D'OLIVES NOIRES, SAUCE BOUILLABAISSE
Braised John Dorry with basil, black olives and bouillabaisse juice 29.00

TRONCON DE TURBOT ROTI, JUS DE PIPERADE AU JAMBON, PIQUILLOS ET TOMATES VERTES
Roasted turbot with green tomatoes, piquillos, piperade broth and sliced prosciutto 31.00

SAUMON TRANCHE EPAIS ET GRILLE, TOMATES CONFITES, UNE GRENOBLOISE CLASSIQUE
Grilled salmon with baked tomatoes, capers, lemon, parsley and small croutons 28.00

VIANDES ET VOLAILLES

PIGEONNEAU FROTTE D'EPICES ET ROTI, FINE SAUCE DOUCE ET FORTE, NAVETS ET RADIS
Roasted squab with spices, dolce forte sauce, braised turnips and radish 30.00

RIS DE VEAU DE LAIT DORE EN CASSEROLE, JUS DU DEGLACAGE, LEGUMES SAUTES A CRU
Roasted sweetbread with sauteed young vegetable fricassee 28.00

CARRE D'AGNEAU ROTI, VRAI JUS, POMME DE TERRE A LA BOULANGERE ET BATAVIA BRAISEE
Roasted rack of lamb with potatoes, onions and chicken broth with braised lettuce 30.00

RABLE DE LAPEREAU FARCI EN ROGNONNADE, GNOCCHI ET CAROTTES, JUS A LA SAUGE
Roasted stuffed saddle of rabbit with kidneys, mushrooms and gnocchi with carrots and sage sauce 28.00

MIGNONNETTES DE BOEUF AUX ECHALOTES, CROUTON DE MOELLE ET GRATIN DE LEGUMES
Sauteed mignonettes of beef with baked shallots, marrow bone toast and gratin of vegetables 32.00

JARRET DE VEAU BRAISE MOELLEUX ET FEUILLES DE BLETTES MIJOTEES AU JUS VINAIGRE
Braised veal shank with sauteed swisschard, pepper and vinegar sauce (for Two) 33.00 p.p.

FRICASSEE DE POULET AUX OIGNONS, CHAMPIGNONS, POMMES, ARTICHAUTS ET TOMATES
Roasted free range chicken with onions, mushrooms, potatoes, artichokes and baked tomatoes 28.00

NAVARIN D'AGNEAU PRINTANIER
Lamb stew with spring vegetables 27.00

Dinner: Mon - Sat 5:45 - 10:45

Although Le Perigord has been around forever, this restaurant with its Provence-style cooking never seems to go out of style. Restaurant critics and restaurant-goers always like whatever chef Antoine Bouterin dishes out.

Les Hors-D'Oeuvre Froids

Le Buffet Froid

Choose from this selection

Celery root remoulade
Fresh grated carrots
Spring vegetable salad
Pâté of duck maison
Cold ratatouille, Tapenade
Baby artichoke à la Farigoule

Foie Gras à la Gelée de Sauternes ($15.00)
Duck liver with Sauterne jelly

Artichaut ou Asperges Vinaigrette
Artichoke or asparagus vinaigrette

Les Hors-D'Oeuvre Chauds

Tarte Tiède au Saumon Fumé et Poireau Confit + ($5.00)
warm Smoked Salmon Tarte with candy Leeks

Crèpe de Ris de Veau
Crèpe of Sweetbread

Foie Gras chaud, Sauce Périgourdine ($15.00)
Duck liver sauce Périgourdine

Les Pâtes Fraiches

aux Crevettes et Saumon fumé
Noodles with shrimps and smoked salmon

---

405 East 52nd St • Midtown East Side • (212) 755-6244

Les Entrées

Les Poissons

Esturgeon au Beurre Blanc
Fresh Sturgeon with vinegar and shallot sauce

Red Snapper au ragout d'Artichaut
Red Snapper with artichoke stew

Le Plat à Basses Calories
Low calorie specialties

Panaché du Pecheur à la Vapeur de Citronelle
Panache of fish steamed with lemon grass

Le Plat Classique

Boeuf aux carottes, Vieille Façon
Beef stew, country style

Les Plats de la Chasse

Pigeonneau de Ferme aux échalotes et ail confits
Little pigeons with shallots and garlic candy

Les Viandes

Mignon de Veau Normande + ($5.00)
Sliced filet of veal calvados sauce

Rognon, Sauce Bourguignone
Veal kidney with Burgundy sauce

Sélection des Desserts

Chariot à Pâtisserie

Tarte Chaude à la minute

Gratin de Chocolat au citron et Rhum

Prix au Dîner $49.00

Dinner: Mon - Sat 5:30 - 10:30

This is a less expensive offshoot of La Cote Basque, and thus, must be considered an important restaurant. It's more bistro than haute French and has proven extremely popular in the couple of years it's been open.

Lunch

DUCK LIVER PATE WITH CELERY REMOULADE
QUENELLE OF PIKE WITH LOBSTER SAUCE
FRIED CALAMARE WITH TOMATE COULIS
HOT GARLIC SAUSAGE IN BRIOCHE

BRANDADE DE MORUE WITH SHRIMPS
SKATE SAUTE GRENOBLOISE
CHESSE SOUFFLE
HANGER STEAK WITH FRENCH FRIES
ESCALOPINE OF VEAL FORESTIERE
SAUTE CALF'S LIVER WITH SWEET TURNIP PUREE
SUPREME OF CHICKEN SAUTE WITH RIGATONI
NAVARIN OF LAMB PRINTANIER
ROASTED VEAL KIDNEY
CASSOULET DE CHEF

Dinner

COLD POACHED SALMON AND SCALLOPS CEVICHE
ESCARGOTS BOURGUIGNON ($4.00)
TIAN OF MUSHROOMS AND SHRIMP

134 East 61st St • Upper East Side • (212) 838-7987

TERRINE OF SOLE AND LOBSTER
CARPACCIO WITH COLD NOODLES
CHARCUTERIE DU JOUR
ONION OR PISTOU SOUP
MIXED GREEN SOUP

ATLANTIC SALMON STEAK IN A SESAME SEED CRUST
RED SNAPPER SAUTE WITH TOMATO FONDUE
FILET OF SOLE GRILLE SAUCE MOUTARDE
ROASTED MONKFISH MILLEFEUILLE
STEAK AU POIVRE OR GRILLED WITH FRENCH FRIES ($6.00)
POACHED BREAST OF CAPON WITH WILD MUSHROOM TIMBALE
ROAST DUCKLING WITH VEGETABLE FILLED CREPES
TENDERLOIN OF VEAL, HARICOTS BLANCS AU JUS
SADDLE OF LAMB SLICED ON A HERB FOCCACCIO

CHOCOLATE CAKE - MERINGUE DACQUOISE - FRESH FRUITS SHERBETS
TARTE OF THE DAY - CHOCOLATE/GRAND MARNIER MOUSSE
PEACH MELBA - FRESH FRUIT SALAD - CREME BRULEE
SOUFFLE GRAND MARNIER, CHOCOLATE OR RASPBERRY ($4.00)
{Please Order In Advance}

TEA, COFFEE OR DECAF. (2.00)
EXPRESSO (2.50)
CAPPUCINO (3.50)

DINNER PRICE $30.00

Dinner: Mon - Sat 6 - 10

Its location in the Plaza Athenee, a branch of the Paris original, gives this restaurant real French luster. It's an elegant, "Louis- something-or-other" room with authentic haute cuisine.

Menu Changes Seasonally

Déjeuner à la Carte

Préludes

Coquilles Saint Jacques Grillées et Salade de Lentilles Vertes
à la Vinaigrette de Miel et Gingembre
Grilled Sea Scallops with Green Lentil Salad and Honey Ginger Vinaigrette

Salade de Magrets de Canards et Haricots Verts Fins,
Petits Légumes au Vinaigre de Banuyls
Smoked Duck Breast Salad with String Beans and Banuyls Vinegar Dressing

Saumon Mi-Fumé Maison avec sa Galette de Pommes de Terre,
Crème Epaisse aux Oignons
Smoked Salmon with Potato Pancake, Mixed Herbs and Onion Cream

Salade Tiède de Homard, Jeunes Carottes et Petits Artichauts à l'Huile de Basilic
Warm Lobster Salad with Baby Artichokes and Baby Carrots, Basil Oil Dressing

Salade de Volaille Grillée aux Pointes d'Asperges,
Pommes Croustillantes et Huile de Sésame
Grilled Chicken Salad with Asparagus Tips and Sesame Oil

Caviar Beluga Servi sur Glace
Beluga Caviar

Hotel Plaza Athénée • 37 East 64th St • Upper East Side • (212) 606-4647

Entrées

Le Saumon Rôti avec Côtes de Blette et Pommes Maxime, Crème Légère au Coriandre
Roasted Salmon with Swiss Chard, Crispy Potatoes and Coriander Sauce

Le Black Bass au Vapeur avec Petits Artichauts et Fondue d'Epinards, Sauce Pistou
Steamed Black Bass with Baby Artichokes and Spinach, Pistou Sauce

Les Noisettes de Chevreuil en Poivrade, Choux Rouges Croquants, Marrons et Pommes Fruit
Medallions of Venison in Peppery Sauce with Red Cabbage, Chestnuts and Apples

Poissons et Crustacés

Les Filets de Sole aux Champignons Sauvages, Purée de Courgettes et Sauce aux Truffes Noires
Dover Sole Filets with Wild Mushrooms, Zucchini Puree and Truffle Sauce
$28.50

Le Homard et son Gratin de Pâtes Maison au Goût de Citron, Asperges et Petits Légumes
Lobster with Home Made Pasta, Lemon Flavored Sauce, Asparagus and Vegetable Brunoise
$30.00

Viandes et Volailles

Les Noisettes de Chevreuil en Poivrade, Choux Rouges Croquants, Marrons et Pommes Fruit
Medallions of Venison in Peppery Sauce with Red Cabbage, Chestnuts and Apples
$31.50

Le Dos d'Agneau Rôti aux Echalotes Marinées à l'Huile d'Olive
Rack of Lamb with Shallots marinated in Olive Oil
$27.50

Poissons

Bass Noir à la Vapeur avec Petits Artichauts et Fondue d'Epinards, Sauce Pistou
Steamed Black Bass with Baby Artichokes and Spinach Pistou Sauce
$21.00

Red Snapper Grillé à la Crème de Persil, Fenouils Doux et Mousse de Carottes
Grilled Red Snapper with Candied Fennel, Carrot Mousse and Parsley Sauce
$23.50

Dinner: 7 Days a Week 6 - 9:30

The Nikko hotels put tons of money into this exquisite little place in the Essex House. The setting is intimate and elegant, and the French food from chef Christian Delouvrier is spectacular. No wonder it's one of the most expensive in the city.

LES CÉLÉBRITÉS

Menu Changes Seasonally

PRÉLUDES

TARTE DE THON CRU AUX PÉTALES DE POIVRONS VERTS ET JAUNES, ÉMULSION DE TOMATES
Tart of Raw Tuna with Green and Yellow Peppers in a Tomato Emulsion
18.00

SAUMON DE L'ATLANTIQUE FUMÉ MAISON, SALADE DE CONCOMBRES, SAUCE AIGRELETTE AUX ZESTES DE CITRON
House Smoked Atlantic Salmon, Cucumber Salad
with Sour Cream Sauce and Lemon Zest
17.00

SALADE DE CANETTE DE BARBARIE RÔTIE À LA BROCHE, AUX ASPERGES, CAROTTES EN VICHY, POMMES DE TERRE
Salad of Spit Roasted Muscovy Duck with
Asparagus, Carrots and Potatoes
15.00

JEUNES LÉGUMES AUX TRUFFES NOIRES ÉCRASÉES À L'ÉCUME D'HUILE D'OLIVE, VINAIGRE DE BANYULS, FLEUR DE SEL
Young Vegetables with Crushed Black Truffles in
Supreme Olive Oil, Banyuls Vinegar and a touch of Virgin Sea Salt
18.00

BURGER DE FOIE GRAS DE CANARD AUX POMMES VERTES, SON JUS LÉGÈREMENT ACIDULÉ, SALADE FRISÉE
Burger of Fresh Duck Foie Gras with Granny Smith Apples au jus with Frisée Salad
22.00

POISSONS ET CRUSTACÉS

FEUILLANTINE DE SAINT JACQUES AU CURRY, POUSSES D'ÉPINARDS
Curried Sea Scallops in thin light Pastry with Tender Spinach Leaves
32.00

PAVÉ ÉPAIS DE SAUMON AUX ÉPICES CHINOISES AU VERJUS, SA PEAU CROUSTILLANTE, COMPOTE DE POIREAUX
Crispy Skin Salmon Steak with Oriental Spices and Leek Compote
31.00

DOS DE RED SNAPPER POÊLÉ AU BOUILLON DE LÉGUMES,TOMATES CONFITES, SAUTÉ D'AUBERGINES ET COURGETTES, PARFUMÉ À L'ANIS
Braised Red Snapper in a Vegetable Bouillon
with Tomato Confit, Sauteed Zucchini and Eggplant perfumed with Anise
32.00

Hotel Essex House • 155 West 58th St • Midtown West Side • (212) 484-5113

VIANDES ET VOLAILLES

CANARD LAQUÉ AU MIEL ET À L'ORANGE, FRICASSÉE DE PETITS LÉGUMES, PURÉE DE FIGUES
Honey and Orange Lacquered Duck with Young Vegetable Fricassée and a Fig Purée
33.00

PIGEON AUX CHOUX ET À L'ÉCRASÉE DE POMME DE TERRE EN ROBE DES CHAMPS, HUILE DE TRUFFE BLANCHE
Squab with Cabbage and Mashed Potatoes in a White Truffle Oil
36.00

FONDANT DE BOEUF EN DAUBE, TARTE DE CAROTTES CONFITES, CÊPES RÔTIS AU FOUR
Tender Beef Stew with a Tart of Carrot Confit and Roasted Cêpes
31.00

CÔTE DE VEAU POÊLÉE Á L'ETUVÉ RISOTTO AUX CHAMPIGNONS SAUVAGES, JUS NATUREL
Veal Chop with Wild Mushroom Risotto, natural jus
35.00

RÔTISSERIE

HOMARD RÔTI, ASPERGES, POIS GOURMANDS, BEURRE DE PETITS POIS, ÉMINCÉ DE TRUFFES
Lobster with Asparagus, Snow Peas and Sweet Pea Butter with Grated Truffles
42.00

POULET À LA BROCHE, CHAMPIGNONS SAUVAGES ET PELURES DE POMME DE TERRE
Free Range Chicken au jus, Wild Mushrooms and Potato Skins
28.00

CARRÉ D'AGNEAU À L'ÉCRASÉE DE POMME DE TERRE, SALADE D' HARICOTS VERTS ET BLANCS
Rack of Lamb au jus, Mashed Potatoes, Salad of Green and White Beans
33.00

FILET DE BOEUF RÔTI À LA FICELLE AUX CÊPES, ARTICHAUTS, CAROTTES GLACÉES, JUS DE CUISSON À L'ESTRAGON
Spit Roasted Beef Tenderloin with Cêpes, Artichokes and Glazed Carrots, Tarragon jus
33.00

DESSERTS

POIRE MERVEILLEUSE DU GATINAIS
Poached Pear with Honey Ice Cream and Chocolate Sauce
13.00

GRATIN DE POMMES
Hot Apple Gratin
12.00

SOUFFLÉ AU CHOCOLAT, GLACE PRALINE
Chocolate Souffle with Praline Ice Cream
13.00

Dinner: Tues - Sat 6 - 10

Reflecting its Parisian derivation, this noisy spot is full of good food, drink, and bonhomie. You really feel you're in Paris eating a wonderful meal of steak and pommes frites.

Les Halles
Restaurant

Menu Changes Seasonally

Amuses-Gueules

Les Rillettes du Boucher 6.50
(house rillettes)

Tarte de Tomates au Chevre 7.00
(tomato goat cheese tart)

Sabodet aux Lentilles 6.50
(warm sausage w/lentils)

Salade Verte 5.25
(green salad)

Escargots 7.00

Macquereaux Escabeche 6.00
(marinated mackerels)

Terrine du Jour 6.00
(pate of the day)

Gratinee des Halles 5.00
(onion soup)

Frisee aux Lardons 6.75
(frisee, bacon, roquefort croutons)

Salade de Poulpe Nicoise 7.25
(octopus salad)

Assiettes "Fort des Halles"

Assiette de Charcutaille 14.50
(ham, saucisson, pate, etc....)

Assiette de Poisson Fume 15.50
(assorted smoked fish)

Salade de Poulet Grille 12.50
(grilled chicken salad)

Steak, Frites, Salade 15.50

Les Specialites

Boudin aux Pommes 15.00
(blood sausage w/apples)

Moules Marinieres 15.00
(steamed mussels w/wine)

411 Park Avenue South • Murray Hill/Kips Bay • (212) 679-4111

Faux Filet Age 26.00
(American beef French style)

Cassoulet "Toulousain" 18.50
(classic cassoulet)

Steak au Poivre 19.00
(pepper steak)

Cote de Porc "Maison" 16.50
(grilled pork chop w/mustard butter)

Calamari a la Portugaise 14.00
(ragout of squid)

Steak Tartare 14.50

La Rotissoire

Poulet Roti 14.50
(free range chicken)

Gigot d'agneau 14.50
(leg of lamb)

Pommes Frites
Legumes du jour 3.50

Le Poisson Egare .... *ask your waiter*
(the lost fish)

La Grillade

Faux-Filet Bercy 21.00
(N.Y. sirloin)

Bavette a L'echalotte 15.50
(flank steak)

Onglet 18.50
(hanger steak)

Filet Boeuf Bearnaise 22.50
(filet)

Cote de Boeuf 45.00
(for two)

Paillard de Veau 16.00
(veal paillard)

Cotes d'agneau grillees 20.50
(lamb chops)

Les Desserts "Maison"

Fromage, Creme Caramel,
Tartes et Gourmandises du jour 5.75

Private Banquet Facilities Available in our Townhouse

Dinner: 7 Days a Week until 12am

The latest in a series of upgraded hotels and hotel dining rooms. When Lespinasse acquired chef Gray Kunz, one of New York's very best, it succeeded in matching the quality of the food with that of the furnishings. It's a popular power lunch spot.

Tasting Menus

Vegetables and Spices

Mung Bean Crêpes and Sprout Salad

Cassolette of Morels with Petite Arvine

Piperade of Vegetables with a Light Curry Jus

Passion Fruit Soufflé and Grand Marnier Ice Cream

52.00

Springtime

Peeky Toe Crab Meat with Celeriac Remoulade

Sugar Snap Pea Soup with Black Truffle Julienne

Yellow Perch on Bamboo Leaf with Kaffir Court Bouillon

Roasted Lamb Chop on an Eggplant Tart with Spiced Carrot Emulsion

Selection of Desserts

69.00

St Regis Hotel • 2 East 55th St • Midtown East Side • (212) 339-6719

The Cuisine of Lespinasse

Crisped Smelts with Dill and Cucumber Salad 16.00

Lobster Medallions and Morels with Petite Arvine 23.00

Peeky Toe Crab Meat and Celeriac Remoulade 18.00

Herbed Risotto with Spring Mushroom Fricassée 19.00

Salad of Boneless Chicken Wings with Coriander Vinaigrette 15.00

Sugar Snap Pea Soup with Black Truffle Julienne 13.00

Steamed Vegetable Cannelloni in Rosemary Broth 17.00

Roasted Rabbit Loin on Watercress and Tarragon Salad 18.00

Sauteed Foie Gras with Hazelnut Crust and Papaya Compote 21.00

Roulade of Salmon on Artichoke Hearts and Tomato Fondue 32.00

Fanned Yellow Perch and Pickled Ramps with Caviar, Champagne Reduction 30.00

Steamed Black Bass in Bamboo Leaf with Kaffir Court Bouillon 29.00

Sauteed Shrimp and Scallops with Anise Basil and Water Chestnut Ravioli 32.00

Ragoût of Squab with Curry and Mung Bean Crêpes 30.00

Veal Medallion, Sweetbread and Kidney Casserole with Black Pepper Sauce 33.00

Lamb Chop on an Eggplant Tart with Spiced Carrot Emulsion 33.00

Braised Short Rib of Beef, Potato Mousseline and Horseradish-Mustard Sauce 29.00

Selections of Cheese 12.50

Dinner: Mon - Sat 6 - 10

Lutèce has reigned at the top of the French culinary pyramid for years, and it's still going strong. This is the restaurant that sets the standards for others.

CONSUMMÉ DE VOLAILLE, JULIENNE DE LÉGUMES
CONSUMMÉ VEGETABLES JULIENNE

SOUPE DE POISSONS AU CRABE
FISH AND CRAB SOUP

CRÈME SAINT-GERMAIN
CREAM OF PEA SOUP

OU

SAUMON FUMÉ *
SMOKED SALMON

MOUSSE DE CANARD AU GENIÈVRE
MOUSSE OF DUCKLING WITH JUNIPER BERRIES

PÂTÉ EN CROÛTE ET TERRINE MAISON
PATE AND TERRINE

BRIOCHE AUX TROIS POISSONS
THREE FISH IN BRIOCHE

ARTICHAUT GARNI DE CHAMPIGNONS AU SAFRAN
ARTICHOKE STUFFED WITH MUSHROOMS

CAVIAR AUX BLINIS *

TIMBALES D'ESCARGOTS
À L'ALSACIENNE
SNAILS ALSATIAN STYLE

ESCALOPE DE SAUMON FRAIS
À LA MOUTARDE
SALMON, MOUSSE OF MUSTARD

TRUITE FRAÎCHE À LA CRÈME
TROUT IN CREAM SAUCE

PÉLERINES À LA MÉRIDOINALE
BAY SCALLOPS MERIDIONAL

SAUTÉ DE HOMARD (PRIX SELON MARCHÉ)
SAUTE OF LOBSTER

BLANQUETTE DU PÊCHEUR
BLANQUETTE OF ASSORTED FISH

SAUMON OU BASS FARCI EN CROÛTE (Pour 4)
SALMON OR BASS FARCI IN FEUILLETE

FEUILLETÉ DU JOUR
FEUILLETE OF THE DAY

TRUFFE EN PÂTE LUCULLUS *
TRUFFLE WITH FOIE GRAS IN CROISSANT

HOMARD RÔTI AU FOUR,
(PRIX SELON MARCHÉ)
LOBSTER ROTI

CASSOLETTE DE CRABE VIEILLE
FRANCE
CASSEROLE OF CRABMEAT

SOLE DE LA MANCHE BELLE MEUNIÈRE

---

249 East 50th St • Midtown East Side • (212) 752-2225

FILETS D'AGNEAU PANÉS AU POIVRE
FILET OF LAMB WITH PEPPERCORNS

ROGNONS DE VEAU AU VIN ROUGE
VEAL KIDNEYS IN RED WINE SAUCE

MEDAILLONS DE VEAU AUX MORILLES
MEDALLIONS OF VEAL WITH MORELS

COQUELET À LA CRÈME AUX MORILLES
BABY CHICKEN IN CREAM AND MOREL SAUCE

CARRÉ D'AGNEAU AU MIEL, CARAMELISÉ
(Pour 2)
CARMELIZED RACK OF LAMB

MIGNON DE BOEUF IN FEUILLETÉ, LUTÈCE
FILET MIGNON IN FEUILLETE

GIBIER EN SAISON
GAME AND VENISON IN SEASON

POUSSIN RÔTI AUX HERBES
ROASTED BABY CHICKEN WITH HERBS

RIS DE VEAU SAUTÉ AUX CÂPRES
SWEETBREADS WITH CAPERS

TOURNEDOS AUX FOIES DE CANARD
FILET MIGNON WITH DUCKLING LIVERS

CANETON AUX FRUITS DE SAISON
(Pour 2)
DUCKLING WITH FRUITS OF THE SEASON

CÔTE DE BOEUF, AU BEURRE ROUGE
(Pour 2)
SIRLOIN IN RED WINE SAUCE

ENDIVES AU BEURRE *

NOUILLES FRAÎCHES MAISON *

MORILLES À LA CRÈME *

FROMAGES DE FRANCE

FRUITS GLACÉS AU SABAYON
GLAZED FRUITS

MOUSSE CHOCOLAT AU RHUM
CHOCOLATE MOUSSE

GÂTEAU GLACÉ AU PRALIN
PRALIN ICE CAKE

GÂTEAU CHOCOLAT À L'ORANGE
CHOCOLATE ORANGE CAKE

SUCCÈS MAISON
PARFAIT

SORBET AU CASSIS
CASSIS SHERBET

"SOUFFLÉ GLACÈ" AUX FRAMBOISES
FROZEN RASPBERRY SOUFFLE

FRUITS ROUGES AU COULIS DE FRAMBOISES OU À LA CRÈME FRAÎCHE
BERRIES IN RASPBERRY COULIS OR CREME FRAICHE

Prix du Diner 60.00

*supplemental charge

Dinner: Mon - Sat 5:30 - 9:45

This elegant hotel dining room gets rave reviews from restaurant critics. It's really beautiful - quiet, panelled, intimate, and refined. You'll also find chef Philippe Boulot's French food some of the best in NYC.

THE MARK

Menu Changes Seasonally And Monthly

APPETIZERS

SOUPE DU JOUR *7.50*

SELECTION OF FRESH OYSTERS ON ICE
champagne mignonette 10.50

MELANGE OF BABY LETTUCE
sherry vinaigrette 8.50

NEW YORK GOAT CHEESE PARFAIT
farm bread crouton, baby greens, red pepper oil 10.50

KITCHEN-SMOKED SALMON
crisp potato layers 12.50

CRISPY LOBSTER ROLL
carrot vinaigrette, parsley essence 15.00

POACHED SKATE SALAD
sizzled leeks, miso vinaigrette 12.50

CRISP SOFT SHELL CRAB, ROASTED PEPPER SALAD
basil aioli 15.00

FRICASSEE OF ASPARAGUS AND OREGON MORELS
"meuniere" 14.50

HOME-MADE CANELLONI OF WILD MUSHROOMS
braised arugula, real jus 14.00

ENTREES

SEARED SWORDFISH, CORIANDER AND CUMIN CRUST
tapenade and sweet garlic beurre fondue 26.00

GRILLED SEAFOOD RISOTTO
porcini mushrooms, real jus 25.00

BARBEQUED STRIPED BASS
creamed savoy cabbage, wild mushroom packages 26.00

SAUTEED FILET OF SALMON, PESTO CRUST
oven-cured tomatoes, red onions and caper relish 24.00

LOBSTER BAKED POTATO
baby arugula salad 29.00

ROASTED FREE-RANGE CHICKEN (FOR TWO)
mashed potatoes, natural juice 38.00

HOME-MADE AIR-DRIED DUCK
plum wine sauce, sauteed baby bok-choy, shiitake mushrooms 26.00

ROASTED VEAL TENDERLOIN
home-made potato gnocchi, fricassee of wild mushrooms and pea shoots 29.00

GRILLED FILET OF BEEF
truffled pomme croquettes, wild mushroom chopsticks, sherry wine sauce 27.00

ROAST RACK OF LAMB
whipped potato napoleon, thyme jus 28.00

SAUTEED SWEETBREAD
ragout of wild mushrooms, green peppercorn sauce 26.00

PRIX-FIXE DINNER 42.00
Appetizer - Entree and Dessert

prices do not include N.Y.C. sales tax and service gratuity

Dinner: 7 Days a Week 6:30 - 10:30

Maxime's

This classic French restaurant is expensive, but its very good food, elegant atmosphere and lovely country setting make it a favorite.

Menu Changes Seasonally

PREAMBULES

★★★★★

Les Terrines de Carnard et de Gibier Gelée au Porto — Two Patés of Duck and Game in Port Aspic
9.75

Le Saumon Fumé Maison — Our Own Smoked Salmon
10.75

La Salade Paysanne — Salad with Bacon and Rocquefort Cheese
8.75

La Salade Tiède de Confit de Canard — Salad with Warm Duck Confit
10.50

Le Foie Gras Frais de Canard Poëlé — Fresh Sauteed Foie Gras of Duck
16.75

La Bisque de Homard — Lobster Bisque
8.75

Le Zephir de St. Jacques au Vermouth — Soufflé of Sea Scallops
9.75

La Cassolette d'Escargots Bourguignonne — Cassolette of Snails in Creamy Garlic Sauce
9.75

Les Pâtes Fraîches aux Fruits de Mer à la Provençale — Pasta with Fresh Seafood in Wine, Herbs and Garlic
10.75

LES POISSONS ET CRUSTACÉS

★★★★★

Le Rouget Grillé au Coriandre — Red Snapper Grilled with Coriander Sauce
23.50

Le Saumon au Choux Bordelaise — Salmon Grilled with Cabbage and Bordelaise Sauce
22.50

Old Tomahawk St • Granite Springs, NY • (914) 248-7200

Le Homard Maxime's Roasted Lobster with Spinach and Potato Galette
25.75

La Bouillabaisse au Homard — Seafood, Fish and Lobster in Saffron Broth
24.75

LES VOLAILLES

★★★★★

La Poitrine de Poulet Rôtie au Vinaigre de Framboise — Breast of Chicken roasted with Raspberry Sauce
18.75

La Caille Rôtie Périgourdine — Quail with Red Wine and Foie Gras
22.75

LES VIANDES

★★★★★

Le Carré d'Agneau à la Fleur de Thym — Rack of Lamb with Fresh Thyme Sauce
24.75

L'Opéra de Filet de Veau et de Boeuf aux Deux Sauces — Medallions of Veal and Tournedos of Beef with Mushroom and Pepper Sauce
25.75

Notre Menu Dégustation — Our Six Course Tasting Menu
68.00

LES DESSERTS $6.75

★★★★

La Tarte Tatin — Warm Apple Tart

Le Fondant au Chocolat — Chocolate Mousse Cake

Le Crême Brûlée — Caramalized Vanilla Custard

La Terrine au Chocolat — Chocolate Terrine

La Feuillantine à la Mousse de Framboise — Raspberry Mousse Napolean

Les Soufflés: Grand Marnier/Framboise/Noisette/Chocolat

Our Soufflés: Grand Marnier/Raspberry/Hazelnut/Chocolate

Les Cafés, Thés et Infusions : $2.00 *Espresso : $2.50* *Cappuccino : $3.25*

Dinner: Wed - Fri 6 - 9:30, Sat 6 - 10:30

Mirabelle is always at the top of everyone's list of best restaurants on Long Island. Its many fans claim the country French cooking ranks with the finest in Manhattan.

Menu Changes Seasonally

FIRST COURSE

FLAMEKUECHE *$8.50*
(Onion and bacon tart)

SAUMON CRU EN MARINADE DE CITRON ET POIVRE VERT *$10.00*
(Marinated salmon in lime juice, green peppercorn, with potato pancake)

PETITS GRIS A LA CHABLISIENNE ET PAIN AUX POMMES DE TERRE *$11.00*
(Fresh little California snails with garlic, parsley butter, roasted garlic and potato bread)

RAVIOLES DE CHAMPIGNONS ET BOUILLION DE CAROTTE EPICE *$9.00*
(Mushroom ravioli with carrot juice and coriander)

POITRINE DE PIGEONNEAU CARMELIZEE AU MIEL ET ESSENCE DE VIN ROUGE *$13.00*
(Roasted breast of squab with honey, red wine, and shell pasta)

SALADE AU FROMAGE DE CHEVRE TIEDE *$7.75*
(Warm goat cheese salad)

TERRINE AU FROMAGE DE CHEVRE ET LEGUMES GRILLES *$9.00*
(Goat cheese and grilled vegetable terrine)

FOIE GRAS DE CANARD SAUTE AUX RAISINS ET ROULADE DE CONFIT *$20.00*
(Domestic duck foie gras with madeira and raisins, roulade of duck confit)

SOUPE DU JOUR *$6.75*
(Soup of the day)

~~ Prices for our daily specials are similar to our menu prices unless otherwise noted ~~

404 North Country Rd • Long Island • (516) 584-5999

- A LA CARTE -

MAIN COURSE

PATES FRAICHES, SAUMON FUME ET BEURRE DE TOMATE — *$12.00*
(Home-made pasta with smoked salmon & tomato butter sauce)

FILET DE MORUE FRAICHE, RAGOUT DE GRAINES, SAUCE INDIENNE AU TENDORI — *$14.00*
(Seared scrod with wheatberry wrapped in grilled eggplant with a tandoori sauce)

ESPADON GRILLÉ, SALADE D'ASPERGES TIEDES ET POMMES CHIPS HOMARDINE — *$16.50*
(Grilled swordfish with warm asparagus salad and potato chips cooked in lobster oil)

SALADE AU BLANC DE VOLAILLE A L'ORIENTALE — *$11.00*
(Chicken salad with sesame dressing)

L'ASSIETTE DU PERE JOSEPH — *$13.00*
(Mirabelle's seasonal vegetarian tasting)

PIECE DE BOEUF DU BOUCHER APPRETEE A LA FACON DU CHEF — *$20.00*
(The Chef's beef preparation of the day)

FILET D'AGNEAU "MEZZALDI" A LA MAROCAINE — *$20.00*
(Loin of lamb and lamb chop with saffron, cinnamon and ginger sauce and couscous)

~ ~ ~ ~ ~ ~ ~ ~

DESSERTS	*$5.00*
CAFE FILTRE, TEA & HERBAL TEA	*$2.50*
SPARKLING WATER	*$3.00*

~ ~ ~ ~ ~ ~ ~ ~

Dinner: Tues - Sat 6 - 10, Sun 5 - 10

Montrachet

Chef Debra Ponzek puts her own stamp on the French classics and she happens to be one of the country's top award-winning chefs. The restaurant itself is rather spare; the emphasis is on the superlative food and the excellent wine list, which has won a few awards, also.

MONTRACHET

Menu Changes Daily

Menu 28.

Salad of Field Greens

*

Buckwheat Pasta with Grilled Artichokes, Chorizo and Tomatoes

*

Creme Brulee

Menu 36.

Chilled Cucumber Soup

*

Pan Seared Duck Breast with Spring Vegetable Ragout

*

Banana and Chocolate Gratin

Menu 60.

Soft Shell Crabs with Fennel, Kumquats and Red Onion

*

Maine Halibut with Fiddleheads and Morels, Lobster Essence

*

Grilled Quail Salad with Balsamic Vinaigrette

*

Saddle of Lamb with Fava Beans and Basil Oil

*

Warm Apricot Tart with Amaretto Ice Cream

*

Coffee or Tea

Tasting Menu Available for Table Monday - Friday

239 West Broadway • TriBeCa/Downtown/Chinatown • (212) 219-2777

Chilled Cucumber Soup with Maine Shrimp	11.
Seared Sashimi Tuna with Marinated Cucumber	13.
Baby Octopus and Squid Salad with Citrus Vinaigrette	12.
Fennel Cured Salmon with Mustard Dill Sauce	13.
Vegetable Terrine with Herbes de Provence	11.
Grilled Quail Salad with Balsamic Vinaigrette	13.
Arugula Salad Composée with Pecorino Romano	12.
Salad of Field Greens with Hot Chevre	11.
Hot New York Foie de Canard with Glazed Shallots	22.
Maine Halibut with Fiddleheads and Morels, Lobster Essence	26.
Red Snapper with Roasted Peppers and Lemon	25.
Roasted Chicken with Potato Puree and Garlic Sauce	23.
Tripolini with Wild Mushrooms and Truffle Juice	21.
Squab with Foie Gras Flan, Game Consomme	29.
Pan Seared Duck Breast with Spring Vegetable Ragout	24.
Roasted Veal Kidney with Sherry Vinegar Sauce	21.
Grilled NY Strip Steak with Eggplant Pancake, Pepper Chutney	29.
Fiddlehead Ferns	6.
Whipped Potatoes	6.
Roasted Beets	6.
Asparagus Vinaigrette	8.
Haricots Verts	6.
Coconut Flan with Caramelized Pineapple	9.
Warm Apricot Tart with Amaretto Ice Cream	9.
Banana and Chocolate Gratin on Linzer Crust	9.
Creme Brulee	8.
Special	9.

Debra Ponzek, Chef
Chris Gesualdi, Sous Chef
David Blom, Pastry Chef

Dinner: Mon - Thurs 6 - 10, Fri - Sat 6 - 11

A sibling of Les Halles across the street, it shares the same quality bistro food and bustling, Parisian ambiance.

PARK BISTRO

Menu Changes Seasonally

Jean Michel Diot vous propose:

Pétatou de Chèvre Frais au Thym et Pitchoulines 8.00
(Warm potato salad w/goat cheese & fresh herb dressing)

Crabe en Salade et Macédoine, Sauce Maltaise au Basilic 10.50
(Crab Salad and vegetable macedoine, citrus & Basil dressing)

Terrine de poissons Fumés, Pommes de terre au Raifort 9.50
(Terrine of Smoked fish, Potato salad w/horseradish)

Jambon de Parme, Huile de Truffe et Vieux Parmesan 12.50
(Prosciutto, Arugula & old Parmesan cheese w/white truffle oil)

Asperges Blanches, Raviole de Morrilles, bouillon d'herbes 13.50
(Asparagus and Morels Ravioli, in a light herb broth)

Bouquet de Mesclun à l'Huile d'Olive 7.00
(Mesclun Field green salad & olive oil dressing)

Raie au Vieux Vinaigre de Vin, Cocos au Persil Plat 19.00
(Sauteed skate, old wine vinegar sauce and white beans)

414 Park Ave South • Murray Hill/Kips Bay • (212) 689-1360

Snapper Pané d'Herbes fraiches, carrottes au Cumin 21.50
(Roasted Snapper w/fresh herbs, Sauteed carrots & Cumin)

Cabillaud, Pomme Purée au Jus d'oignons et Poireaux frits 22.00
(Fresh codfish, on mashed potatoes, onion sauce w/fried leeks)

Langoustines à la Planche, riz aux Poivrons et Piments P/A
(Sauteed Langoustines, Rice w/sweet peppers)

Selle D'Agneau rotie au Romarin, Tian Niçois et Panisses 24.00
(Roasted Lamb saddle w/Rosemary & nocoise vegetables)

Onglet de Boeuf Poêlé, Moëlle au gros sel, Sauce "Mode" 23.00
(Hanger steak w/Sauce "Mode" and Bone Marrow)

Jarret De Veau en Osso Bucco, Petits oignons et Basilic 22.50
(Osso Bucco a la Provencale)

Suprême de poulet de ferme, Coucous à L'Orientale 20.50
(Breast of farm raised chicken w/Lemon sauce & Couscous)

Private banquet facilities available in our townhouse

Jean Michel Diot, Philippe Schmit, Patrick Jehano
et leur équipe vous souhaitent un bon Appétit.

Dinner: 7 Days a Week 6 - 11

Laurent Manrique is the young southwestern French chef who is bringing new life to this handsome, old-fashioned hotel dining room. It's a very popular hotel and a great location; the critics are enthusiastic.

Peacock Alley®

Menu Changes Seasonally

Hors d'Oeuvres Froids

Salade de Haricots Verts et Béatilles de Canard,Tuiles D'Ail au Paprika
French Bean Salad with Assortment of Sauteed Duck
9.50

Coquilles-Saint-Jacques Mi-Fumées et Grillées,Galette de Morue aux Tomates
Smoked and Grilled Sea Scallops, Salt Codfish Tart with Yellow and Red Tomato
11.50

Homard à la Façon du Pays Basque, Œufs de Caille Mollets au Jambon de Bayonne
Lobster Basque Style, Poached Quail Eggs and Cured Ham of Bayonne
13.50

Grosses Asperges Tièdes au Parmesan et Huile de Truffes Blanches, Jeune Bouquet de Salade aux Herbes
Jumbo Asparagus with Parmesan and White Truffle Oil, Mesclun Salad with Fresh Herbs
9.75

Hors d'Oeuvres Chauds

Foie de Canard Gras Poché et Grillé à la Rubarbe Poivrée, Coulis d'Oignons Blancs
Duck Foie Gras Poached and Grilled with Rhubarb, Pearl Onion Coulis
14.50

Casserole de Légumes Frais à l'Huile d'Olive, Ecrevisses et Gnocchis au Parmesan
Fresh Vegetable Casserole with Olive Oil, Louisiana Crayfish and Parmesan Gnocchis
10.75

Maltalialté Fraiches à la Ventrèche Seiche, Tomates Confites, Olives Noires et Fleur de Brocoli Amer
Fresh Pasta with Tomato Confit, Pancetta and Broccoli Rabe
9.50

Waldorf-Astoria Hotel • 301 Park Ave • Midtown East Side • (212) 872-4895

Poissons et Crustacés

Bar Pôelé à L'Huile D'Olive, Piperade, Emulsion de Jus de Moules au Safran
Sea Bass Sauteed with Mixed Vegetables, Shell Fish Broth Emulsion with Saffron
25.00

Cabillaud Frais Rôti à l'Origan, Pommes Nouvelles Ecrasées à l'Huile d'Olive Vierge et Persil, Tomates Confites et Pétales d'Ail
Roast Codfish with Oregano, Potato Hash with Parsley, Tomato Confit and Garlic Chips
24.00

Filet de Vivaneau Grillé sur la Peau et Parfumé au Laurier, Jeunes Artichauts aux Olives Noires et Tartelettes aux Deux Tomates
Grilled Red Snapper on the Skin with Laurel, Baby Artichokes with Black Olives and Tartelettes with Two Tomatoes
28.00

Saumon Cuit sur l'Arête, Poires et Pommes Nouvelles Grillées au Coulis de Citron Confit
Sauteed Filet of Salmon, Grilled Pear and New Potato, Candied Lemon Coulis
26.00

Viandes et Volailles

Rable de Lapereau aux Figues Marinées au Vinaigre, Petit Piment Doux, Friture de Polenta
Saddle of Rabbit Stuffed with Sweet Pepper, Figs Marinated in Vinegar and Polenta Fries
26.00

Pigeonneau de Ferme en Croute de Sel de Mer, Petits Pois Cuits Comme Autrefois
Roast Squab in Sea Salt Dough, Casserole of Young Peas
25.00

Côte de Veau Mijotée à la Fleur de Thym, Fricassée d'Asperges, Oignons Grelots, Pommes Nouvelles au Beurre Frais et Nouilles
Slowly Sauteed Veal Chop with Fresh Thyme, Fricassee of Asparagus and Pearl Onion
29.00

Tranche de Bœuf Black Angus Grillée à l'Huile de Poivre Noir, Croustillant de Légumes Nouveaux
Grilled Black Angus Sirloin with Black Pepper Oil, Napoleon of Baby Vegetables
30.00

Chef de Cuisine Laurent Manrique

Dinner: Tues - Sat 5:30 - 10:30

Although Petrossian is synonymous with caviar, which, of course, is served in a number of different ways, the restaurant serves an excellent French/Continental menu. It also happens to be elegant, draped and candlelit.

Menu Changes Seasonally

TEASERS

The Petrossian Teasers are a unique combination of classic French & Russian Zakouski inspired recipes. These recipes have been executed featuring Petrossian products & are offered as an assortment or individually.

Large Sampling $24.00
Small Sampling $19.00

Fillet of Smoked Eel Rolled with Ratatouille & Aged Balsamic Vinegar

**

Smoked Sturgeon with Cucumber, Radish & Roasted Tomato Salad

**

Smoked Cod Roe with Waffle Potato Chips

**

Smoked & Fresh Salmon Tartare in Choux Puffs

SPECIALTIES

Sevruga Caviar(30g) $24.50

Sevruga Caviar(50g) $39.00

Our Whole Foie Gras $25.00
Our Premier Smoked Salmon $25.00

Salmon Tasting
Small $19.00
Large $30.00
Our Premier Smoked Salmon, Tsar Cut Salmon, Salmon Marinade, Arctic Char & Salmon Roe

Zakouski $28.00
A Sampling of Smoked Cod Roe, Smoked Eel, Our Smoked Salmon & Sturgeon

Pressed Caviar, Smoked Cod Roe & Russian Salmon Roe with Blini & Crème Fraîche $18.00

Russian Salmon Roe(50g) with Blini & Crème Fraîche $18.00

Smoked Cod Roe(50g) with Blini & Crème Fraîche $18.00

APPETIZERS

Borscht with Crème Fraîche & Pirojkis $6.50

Petrossian Duck Foie Gras with Sweet Lettuces, Haricot Vert & Nut Oil $14.00

Salad of Sweet Baby Lettuces, Soft Herbs & Mushroom Vinaigrette $7.50

Roasted Eggplant, Zucchini & Yellow Squash Terrine with Black Olive Tapenade Roasted Garlic Puree, Saffron & Red Pepper Sauce $14.00

Smoked Salmon Salad with Frisee, Bitter Greens & Aromatic Herbs $12.00

MAIN COURSES

Roasted Monkfish Loin with Braised Savoy Cabbage & Tomato Saffron Sauce $22.00

Roasted North Atlantic Salmon with Vegetable Fricassee, Italian Rice & Lobster Consomme $25.00

Fricassee of Maine Lobster & Spring Vegetables with Potato Puree & Mushroom Juices $28.00

New York State Organic Chicken with a Gratin of Potato, Leek & Dried Cranberries $22.00

Roasted Breast of Duck with Soft White Wheat Berries, Tart Apples, Dried Winter Fruits & Sweet Corn $24.00

Griddled Prime T-Bone Steak with Creamed Spinach $28.00

Penne with Gulf Coast Shrimp, Plum Tomatoes, Mediterranean Oil Cured Olives, Whole Basil & Roasted Garlic with Extra Virgin Olive Oil $20.00

Chef de Cuisine Joseph Pace

KINDLY REFRAIN FROM CIGAR & PIPE SMOKING

Dinner: 7 Days a Week 5:30 - 12

Poiret

Poiret is an excellent French bistro on the Upper West Side and is extremely popular with people in and out of the neighborhood. They do a perfect job with the classics: roast chicken, steak and pommes frites, etc.

MENU CHANGES SEASONALLY

SOUPES

GRATINEE AUX TROIS OIGNONS 4.95
Classic onion soup with shallots, red and white onions

CREME DE CHAMPIGNONS 4.95
Smooth mushroom soup with creme fraiche and chives

POTAGE DE LEGUMES AUX MOULES ET ST. JACQUES 5.95
Carrot, leek, mussel and scallop soup with saffron

HORS D'OEUVRES

TERRINE DE FOIES DE CANARDS 6.95
Duck liver pate with brandied prunes, garnishes

CHEVRE CHAUD AUX TOMATES CONFITES 7.95
Warm mild goat cheese with home cured tomatoes and fresh basil

MOULES PROVENCALE 7.95
Canadian mussels steeped in chardonnay with garlic, herbs, tomatoes and extra virgin olive oil

TARTINE CHAUDE AU BLEU DE BRESSE ET DE CANARD FUME 5.95
Grilled mild blue cheese and smoked duck breast on garlic croutons

ASSIETTE DE SAUMON FUME 9.95
Petrossian smoked salmon, creme fraiche, horseradish, garnishes

BAIGNETS DE CABILLAUD ET COURGETTES 5.95
Fresh cod and zucchini fritters, with olive oil tapenade and red roasted pepper sauce

SALADES

SALADE VERTE AUX TOMATES 4.95
Bibb lettuce, frisee and tomato salad, shallot vinaigrette

SALADE DE MESCLUN AUX NOISETTES 7.95
Mixed baby greens salad with toasted hazelnuts

PANACHE DE SALADES AMERES 5.95
Mixed bitter greens with sherry wine vinaigrette

474 Columbus Ave • Upper West Side • (212) 724-6880

ENTREES SALADES

SALADE NICOISE COMME EN PROVENCE 12.95
Nicoise salad with grilled tuna, raw vegetables and garlic dressing

SALADE DU SUD OUEST 13.95
Smoked duck breast salad with white beans, greens, vegetables and shallot pickles

CHEVETTES GRILLEES, SALADE AU GINGEMBRE 13.95
Grilled shrimp with garlic olive oil, served with a ginger, leek, celery and mixed green salad

SALADE DAUPHINOISE AU POULET GRILLE 9.95
Grilled chicken breast salad with frissee lettuce, endives, walnuts, apples and a creamy blue cheese walnut oil dressing

ENTREES

POULET ROTI AUX HERBES JUS A L'AIL 13.95
Roast chicken with herbs, garlic infused pan juice, straw potatoes

COUSCOUS MAISON 15.95
North African style lamb and chicken stew, with vegetables and spices, lamb sausage, chick peas, and spicy sauce

CASSOULET AU CONFIT DE CANARD 16.95
Traditional cassoulet with moulard duck leg confit, duck sausage and white beans

FRICASSEE DE CUISSE DE LAPIN A LA SAUGE 16.95
Braised rabbit legs with wine, mustard, fresh sage, served with pasta

COTES D'AGNEAU GRILLEES, BEURRE MOUTARDE 19.95
Charcoal grilled lamb chops, served with a dijon mustard garlic butter

STEAK FRITES, BEURRE MAITRE D'HOTEL 19.95
Charcoal grilled sirloin steak with straw potatoes

FILET DE SAUMON A L'OSEILLE 19.95
Sauteed salmon filet, finished with a fresh sorrel cream sauce

COQUILLES ST. JACQUES AU SAFRAN ET GINGEMBRE 19.95
Sauteed sea scallops with ginger, saffron and ginger butter cream sauce

ASSORTIMENTS DE LEGUMES 13.95
A selection of baked vegetables, mushrooms, mashed potatoes and fresh steamed vegetables

We Welcome the American Express Card, VISA/Mastercard and Diner's Club Card

Dinner: Sun - Thurs 5:30 - 11, Fri - Sat 5:30 - 12

As you would expect from its name, Provence features hearty specialties from the Provence region of France. It's a small restaurant and always crowded with fans of the country French cuisine.

Menu Changes Seasonally

Dinner

Pissaladiere *provençal onion & anchovy tart* 5.

Moules Gratinées Catalane *gratin of mussels w/ almonds & garlic* 6.

Caviar d'Aubergines *roasted eggplant purée with assorted provençal toasts* 7.

Petits Rougets au Escatéche *fillet of red mullet in saffron, onion, & white wine marinade* 9.

Paté du Chef *Homemade Paté w/ cured vinegar fruits* 7.

Fleurs de Courgettes Farcies *stuffed zucchini flowers* 8.

Ravioles d'Escargots *raviolis stuffed w/ snails, herb garlic & olive oil sauce* 9.

Galette des Bergeres *goat cheese & potato cake on mesclun salad* 8.

Soupe de Poissons avec sa garniture *provençal fish soup w/ rouille and gouyere* 6.

Soupe du Jour *soup of the day* 5.

Lotte Rotie au Safran *monkfish roasted w/ saffron sauce* 17.50

Joues de Monie St. Tropez *cod cheeks baked with tomato, potato, garlic & olives* 18.50

Bar au Morilles et Asperges *poached bass w/ morels & asparagus risotto cake* 18.50

---

38 MacDougal St • SoHo • (212) 475-7500

Bourride Setoise *poached fish in an aioli thickened broth* **15.50**
Aioli Arlésien *steamed vegetables garnished with cod, mussels, garlic mayonnaise* **16.50**
Assiette Vegetarienne *roasted & grilled vegetables w/ aioli or herb emulsion* **14.50**
Tian d'Agneau Ratatouille *pan roasted lamb w/ ratatouille* **17.50**
Poussin Rôti gousses d'ail en chemise *roast baby chicken w/ whole roasted garlic cloves* **15.00**
Lapin Jardiniere *braised rabbit w/ stuffed loin, fava beans, olives* **17.50**
Bouillabaisse de la Ferme *free range chicken in bouillabaisse sauce* **17.50**
Steak Frites *broiled shell steak with french fries* **19.50**

Tuesday: Loup de Mergrillé au fenouil *sea bass grilled & flambéed with Pastis and fennel* **P.A.**
Friday: Bouillabaisse Façon Provence *poached fish and shellfish in a tomato, saffron pastis broth w/ rouille* **18.00**
Sunday: Cous Cous Marocain *traditional Moroccan lamb, chicken & vegetable stew over semolina grain* **17.50**

Desserts

Tarte Maison *fruit tart of the day* **6.**
Marquise au Chocolat *chocolate terrine w/coffee creme angaise* **6.**
Creme Brulée Catalane *light custard under burnt sugar crust* **6.**
Ile Flottante *poached meringues with cream anglaise* **7.**
Sorbets Assortis *different flavored fruit sorbets* **6.**
Sorbets Arrosés *fruit sorbet with its corresponding eau de vie or liqueur* **7.**
Assiette de Fruits Frais *fresh fruit plate* **P.A.**

Dinner: Mon - Thurs 6 - 11:30, Fri - Sat 6 - 12, Sun 5:30 - 11

This outstanding French restaurant has brought authentic bistro cuisine to its neighborhood. You really feel you are in some small town in France.

Menu Changes Seasonally

– WINES –

	glass	bottle
Pinot Blanc (Trimbach) "Selection QUATORZE" 1990	4.50	15.00
Côtes-du-Rhône (Château d'Aigueville) 1990	4.50	15.00
Crémant d'Alsace (sparkling)	6.50	26.00

Kir Crémant d'Alsace	7.00
Kir Pinot Blanc	5.25
Kir Cardinal	5.25
St Raphaël (white / red)	5.50
Lillet (white / red)	5.50
PASTIS (PERNOD, RICARD)	5.50

Perrier	½ 3.50	full 6.00
Evian		full 6.00

MENU

OYSTERS various / please ask

APPETIZERS

Marinated herring	7.00
Pâté maison	6.50
Bacon, leek & Gruyère tart	6.95
Seafood sausage	7.95
Saucisson de Lyon	6.50
Smoked salmon (Petrossian)	9.00

SOUP OF THE DAY please ask

323 East 79th St • Upper East Side • (212) 535-1414 • (Call For Other Locations)

SALADS

Mixed green salad	(mustard vinaigrette)	6.50
	with grilled goat cheese	8.25
Petite Salade Niçoise		7.50

CHICORY WITH BACON AND HOT VINAIGRETTE 8.50

ENTREES

CHOUCROUTE GARNIE (Specialty) 17.95

Braised Duck, notre façon	18.50
Fish filet of the day, grilled or sautéed (meunière, amandine, grenobloise)	please ask
Grilled Salmon, sauce Choron	22.00
Sautéed Calf's Liver, shallot sauce	17.50
Sautéed Brook Trout	16.50
Grilled Black Angus Sirloin, pommes frites & sauce Béarnaise	24.00
Half Chicken, grilled with herbs	18.95
"Bouillabaisse" QUATORZE	19.50
Cassoulet	19.95

SUNDAY, MONDAY

Roast Chicken, mashed potatoes	18.95

TUESDAY, WEDNESDAY

Boeuf Bourguignon	18.95

THURSDAY

Duck Confit, notre façon	18.50

FRIDAY, SATURDAY

Braised Lamb Shank, flageolets verts	18.00

Dinner: Mon - Sat 6 - 11:30, Sun 5:30 - 11

Raoul's was one of the first bistros to open in SoHo and it still gets a large share of the business. It's always bustling with the type of person you imagine would smoke a Gauloise.

Restaurant

Menu Changes Seasonally

SOUPE DU JOUR 5.50

ASSIETTE DE CRUDITÉS 6.50

ARTICHAUT VINAIGRETTE 8.50

PATÉ MAISON 6.50

ASPERGES VINAIGRETTE 9.50

AVOCAT AUX CREVETTES 8.50

THON OU SAUMON FUMÉ 13-

HUITRES DE BELON 13-

CAVIAR DE OSETRA 35-

RIS DE VEAU EN SALADE 9.50

FOIE GRAS MAISON 19-

CELERI REMOULADE 6.50

180 Prince St • SoHo • (212) 966-3518

ESPADON AU FROMAGE DE CHEVRE	23-
SAUMON GRILLÉ BEARNAISE	23-
THON AU POIVRE	23-
CREVETTES AU BEURRE D'AIL	25-
FILET DE VEAU FORESTIERE	25-
COTE DE VEAU AUX TROMPETTES	26-
COTES D'AGNEAU AUX HERBES	27-
STEAK AU POIVRE	24-

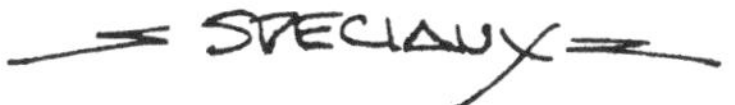

= SPECIAUX =

STRIPED BASS AUX CREVETTES	25-
SNAPPER AUX CAVIARS	24-
MEDAILLONS DE BOEUF AU MIEL	25-
SOLE DE DOUVRES MEUNIERE	25-

Dinner: Sun - Thurs 6 - 11:30, Fri - Sat 6 - 2am

Although Restaurant Daniel is not scheduled to open until the middle of May 1993, it will be THE most important restaurant of the year in New York when it does. Boulud was chef at Le Cirque for many years, and his own restaurant promises to be the culinary event of the year, and for a long time to come.

Menu Changes Seasonally And Daily

APPETIZERS

Warm Asparagus, Artichoke, and Herb Salad with Cured Lemon and Sweet Pepper Confit
Asperges, artichauts, salade d'herbes et citron confit aux poivrons doux — $12.00

Thin Layer of Salmon and Crispy Garlic Toast with Avocado, Black Olive and a Chive Dressing
Sandwich de saumon à l'avocat, olives noires et huile de ciboulette — $10.00

Curried Tuna Tartare with Pink Radishes in a Celery Sauce
Thon cru au curry, radis roses et coulis au vert de céleri — $13.00

Rillettes of Squab, Duck, Foie Gras, Rabbit, Pork, and Black Truffle with Spring Greens
Rillettes fermière à la truffe noire, mesclum et pain de campagne à l'ail — $17.00

Spring Greens and Vegetables with an Herbed Goat Cheese in a Parmesan Shell
Mesclum aux crudités du marché, fromage blanc et tuiles de parmesan — $9.50

Salad of Maine Crab, Mango, and Cucumber with a Mint, Coriander and Lime Dressing
Crabe du Maine, mangue, et concombre à la menthe, coriandre et citron vert — $15.00

Chilled Spring Peas Soup with a hint of Rosemary Cream and Bacon
Soupe glacée de pois frais, crème de romarin et lard fumé — $9.50

Nine-Herb Raviolis in a Pool of Fresh Tomatoes with Parmesan Shavings
Raviolis de neuf herbes à la tomate fraiche et tranches fines de parmesan — $12.50

Poached Foie Gras in a Duck Broth with Morels and Cranberry Beans
Foie gras poché dans un bouillon de canard aux morilles et cocos frais — $19.00

ENTREES

Poached Cod in a Cockle Broth with Parsley, Potatoes and Leeks
Marinière de cabillaud au persil plat, pommes de terre et poireaux — $26.00

Black Sea Bass in a Crispy Potato Shell with Scallions in a Red Wine Sauce
Sea Bass enrobé de pomme de terre croustillante a la ciboule et sauce au Pinot Noir — $29.50

Grilled Salmon Tournedos with Garlic, Zucchini and Stuffed Sweet Pimentos in a Red Pepper Sauce
Tournedos de saumon grillé à l'ail, courgettes et piments doux farcis au jus de piperade — $27.75

Swordfish Wrapped in Eggplant with Basil in Bouillabaisse Sauce flavored with Garlic and Saffron
Espadon enrobé d'aubergine et basilic au jus de bouillabaisse parfumé de rouille — $28.50

Crayfish and Quail Casserole with Wild Mushrooms, Asparagus, and Chervil
Fricassée d'ecrevisses et cailles aux champignons des près, asperges et cerfeuil — $28.00

Roasted Chicken Breast with Creamer Potatoes, Wild Morels, and Watercress
Poitrine de volaille rôtie aux pommes de terre nouvelles, morilles, et jus aux pluches de cresson — $27.50

Roasted Loin and Braised Legs of Rabbit with Truffles and a Zucchini filled Pasta
Filet et cuisses de lapin braisés à la truffe noire et ravioles de courgette — $30.00

Roasted Veal Chop and Sweetbread with Fresh Chamomile, Spring Vegetables, and Porcini
Côte et ris de veau rôtis à la camomille fraiche, légumes du printemps et cepes
(2 person minimum) — per person $31.00

Sautéed Beef Tenderloin with a Crispy Potato Purse filled with Spinach, Morels, and Marrow
Filet de boeuf poelé au croustillant de pommes de terre farci de pousses d'épinard, morilles, et moelle — $29.00

Roasted Duck with Spicy Spring Fruits and a Stuffed Vidalia Onion with Swiss Chard
Canard rôti aux fruits épicés et oignon de Georgie farci de blettes — $28.75

Roasted Loin of Lamb with Savory and Nut Crust, Spring Bean Casserole with Tomatoes
Canon d'agneau rôti à la sariette, casserole de haricots frais et tomate confite — $29.50

Dinner: Mon - Sat 6 - 10:30

Along with Bertrand, Jean-Louis is the top French restaurant in Connecticut. The restaurant is charming and the cuisine more contemporary than haute.

Menu Changes Seasonally

MENU DEGUSTATION

"Menu Degustation" is a five course menu designed to acquaint our guests with Jean Louis' special brand of cuisine. It is specially meant to tempt while allowing to explore a broad range . . . as the menu changes daily. It is also an attempt to nurture and nourish the senses while satisfying the appetite.

$60.00 per person - two person minimum

LES CLASSIQUES

HORS D'OEUVRE - SOUPES ET POTAGES

MARINADE D'ENDIVE AUX CAVIARS AMERICAINS POUR LINDA
created for my wife, this salad accents American Caviars
and Belgian Endive folded in Creme Fraiche 16.00

TERRINE DE FOIS GRAS FRAIS MAISON EN SALADE
Fresh Duck Foie Gras Terrine
on a bed of Salad - with Raisin Bread Toast 16.00

SOUPE DE MOULES ET SAFRAN FLEUR AUX LEGUMES
Fresh Mussels and Diced Vegetables in Saffron
Creme Fraiche and Lobster Broth 7.00

LES CREATIONS

HORS D'OEUVRE - SOUPES ET POTAGES

**TRIO DE LENTILLES TIEDES
AUX FEUILLES DE FOIE GRAS**
Three kinds of lentils, served warm with leaves of Terrine of Foie Gras 18.00

SALADE DE HOMARD TIEDE AU JUS DE CORAIL
Warm Lobster tossed in Corail Vinaigrette Served with Mesclin Salad 16.00

LES CLASSIQUES

LES POISSONS

POELEE DE HOMARD, POMMES DE TERRE, ET SALADE TIEDE EMULSION DES JUS A L'HUILE D'OLIVE
Sauteed Lobster on a bed of Crisp Thin-Sliced Potatoes and Salad
Dressed with a Veal and Lemon Emulsion 27.00

ESCALOPE DE SAUMON AU COULIS DE PERSIL PLAT
Sliced Filet of Salmon - Sauteed
Finished in Italian Parsley Sauce 25.00

VIANDES ET VOLAILLES

AIGUILETTES DE CANARD ET FOIE GRAS DE POELE GASTRIC AU JUS D'ORANGE
Sliced Breast of Duck and Foie Gras sauteed
Served on a Bed of Spinach Salad
Dressed with Orange and Sherry Vinegar Reduction 28.00

MEDAILLONS DE FILET DE BOEUF SAUCE AU VIN ROUGE CALIFORNIEN
Filet of Beef Medallions in a California Red Wine Sauce
Served with Gratin of Potatoes and Vegetable 29.00

RILLONS DE RIS DE VEAU CROQUANT - GARNIS DE CHAMPIGNONS - SAUCE FOIE GRAS ET TRUFFE
Crisp Sauteed Sweetbread Morsels
Wild Mushrooms with an Emulsion of Veal Juice,
Fresh Foie Gras and Black Truffle Essence 28.00

LES CREATIONS

LES POISSONS

SELECTION DU JOUR

LES VOLAILLES

BLANC DE FAISAN AUX TROIS LENTILLES
Roast Breast of Pheasant
served with a trio of Lentils baked in Pheasant Juice 28.00

PALOMBE D'ECOSSE EN SALMIS CLASSIQUE ET CHUTNEY
Scotch Wood Pigeon, Flambee with a salmis of Truffles and Foie Gras 30.00
served with Chutney

MEDAILLONS DE CHEVREUIL A LA GRAND VENEUR
Medaillons of Fresh Venison
served with traditional Sauce and Garnishes 28.00

Dinner: Mon - Sat 6 - 9

There's been a series of chef turnovers at Lafayette the past couple of years, but the decor and service are still top-notch. It's an elegant hotel dining room, and as such, has stayed popular and busy.

Menu Changes Seasonally

Executive Chef
John Di Leo

- Appetizers -

House Smoked Atlantic Salmon
Served Warm on a Risotto Cake with Truffles
12.00

Grilled Barbecued Prawns
Mango/Green Peppercorn Vinaigrette & Basmati Rice Salad
13.00

Mesclun Salad
Roast Shallots and Sherry Vinaigrette
7.50

Spit-Roasted Muscovy Duck Breast
Wheatberry and Corn Salad with Cilantro Oil
12.00

Charred Lamb Tenderloins
Morel Mushrooms and Mustard Oil
11.00

Maine Crabmeat & Asparagus Salad
With Truffle Oil Vinaigrette
13.50

Seared Skate
Salad of White Beans, Olives, Dried Tomatoes and Lime Juice
9.00

Seared Sea Scallops and Hudson Valley Foie Gras
With Sauternes, Corn and Shallots
16.00

65 East 56th St • Midtown East Side • (212) 756-3910

- *Main Courses* -

Seared Loin of Tuna
Quinoa and Indonesian Plum Wine Sauce
26.00

Pan Roasted Atlantic Salmon
Red Onions, Dried Tomatoes and Jicama Puree
24.00

Grilled Halibut
Lemon, Basil and Tomato Broth
24.00

Soft Shell Crabs
Wild Rice, Wilted Greens and Corn Broth
26.00

Grilled Lobster
Foie Gras, Artichoke Chips and Braised Cabbage
30.00

Roast Loin of Veal
Lemon Pasta, Fava Beans and Morels
26.00

Seared Loin of Lamb
Roasted Vegetable Tart and Tomato Oil
25.00

Spit-Roasted Saddle of Rabbit
Asparagus, Rosemary and Natural Jus
25.00

Black Angus Filet
Mushroom/Potato Cake, Crisp Shallots and Catamount Porter Sauce
27.00

Spit-Roasted Muscovy Duck
With a Crisp Noodle Cake and Figs
25.00

Dinner: Sat 6 - 10

Chef Jean-Michel Bergounoux has breathed new life into this elegant, intimate restaurant tucked away in a townhouse just off Fifth Avenue. It's very popular with patrons and critics.

Restaurant Raphaël

Chef de Cuisine: JEAN MICHEL BERGOUGNOUX

Menu Changes Seasonally

LUNCH

HORS D'OEUVRE

Tarte à la confiture d'oignon, ciboulette et maïs -- 8.00
Tarte of onion confit chives and corn

Pain aux olives et tomates séchées aux sardines grillées et basilic -- 10.50
Bread with olives and sundried tomatoes and grilled sardines with basil

Les escargots de Bourgogne au shiitake et beurre d'escargot -- 9.00
Escargots with wild mushrooms and snail butter

Un glacé d'aubergines et agneau confit au fromage de chèvre -- 9.00
confit of eggplant and lamb, warm goat cheese

Saumon fumé maison, salade de navets chinois marinés -- 10.50
House smoked salmon marinated chinese turnips

Soupe du Jour -- 7.00

POISSONS

Steak de thon aux galettes de pomme de terre, poivre gris et vinaigre de vin -- 20.00
tuna steak with crisp potatoes and grey peppercorns

Pavé de saumon croustillant, aux épinards et vinaigrette de champignons des bois -- 19.00
pan seared salmon with spinach and wild mushroom sauce

Darne de Raie rôtie aux câpres, salade de légumes d'hiver tièdes a l'échalotte -- 18.00
Skate roasted with capers, salad of warm winter vegetables and shallots

VIANDES ET VOLAILLES

Poulet rôti aux cêpes purée de pommes de terre à l'huile de noisette -- 20.00
Roasted free range chicken with cêpes, potato mousseline with hazelnut oil

Pavé de foie de veau aux poireaux frits, compote d'oignons acidulés -- 21.00
Calf's liver with fried leeks and onion compote

Sauté de veau fondant, parfumé a l'anis étoilé, risotto à la coriandre -- 22.00
Risotto with braised veal perfumed with star of anise and cilantro

Entrecôte marchand de vin, gratin de salsifis au jambon de Bayonne -- 24.00
Sirloin steak with red wine sauce, salsify gratin and prosciutto

DINER

HORS D'OEUVRE

Tarte à la confiture d'oignon, ciboulette et maïs -- 8.50
Tarte of onion confit chives and corn

Pain aux olives et tomates séchées aux sardines grillées et basilic -- 10.50
Bread with olives and sundried tomatoes and grilled sardines with basil

Les escargots de Bourgogne au shiitake et beurre d'escargot -- 9.50
Escargots with wild mushrooms and snail butter

Un glacé d'aubergines et agneau confit au fromage de chèvre -- 9.50
confit of eggplant and lamb, warm goat cheese

Saumon fumé maison, salade de navets chinois marinés -- 10.50
House smoked salmon marinated chinese turnips

Gnocchi de pommes de terre aux cêpes et crevettes, salade de roquette -- 11.50
Potato gnocchi with cêpes and shrimps, arugula salade

POISSONS

Steak de thon aux galettes de pomme de terre, poivre gris et vinaigre de vin -- 22.00
tuna steak with crisp potatoes and grey peppercorns

Pavé de saumon croustillant, aux épinards et vinaigrette de champignons des bois -- 21.00
pan seared salmon with spinach and wild mushroom sauce

Red snapper fumé et poëlé au basilic et gratin de courgettes -- 24.00
house smoked red snapper with basil and zucchini gratin

Noix de Saint Jacques caramélisées aux betteraves rouges a l'huile de noix -- 22.00
Jumbo Maine sea scallops with red beets and walnut oil

VIANDES ET VOLAILLES

Poulet rôti aux cêpes purée de pommes de terre à l'huile de noisette -- 22.00
Roasted free range chicken with cêpes, potato mousseline with hazelnut oil

Poitrine de canard sautée au chutney de coings et airelles -- 25.00
Sauteed duck breast with chutney of quince and cranberries

Carré d'âgneau rôti au romarin, vin rouge, confit d'aubergines -- 28.00
Roasted rack of lamb with rosemary, red wine and eggplant confit

DESSERTS

Le mousseux aux fruit exotiques, granité au coco -- 8.00
mousse of exotic fruits with coconut granité

La soupe de fraises, glace a la mascarpone, gauffre a la vanille -- 9.00
strawberry soup with mascarpone ice cream, vanilla waffles

Crème caramel parfumée a l'expresso -- 8.00
creme caramel perfumed with espresso

Dinner: Mon - Fri 6 - 9:30, Sat 6 - 10

The Ryland Inn

This lovely old country inn is a popular destination for its elegant, refurbished interior, excellent contemporary French cuisine by chef Craig Shelton, and extensive wine list; one of the best in the metropolitan area.

THE
RYLAND
INN

Menu Changes Seasonally

APPETIZERS

SOUPS

• Creamless Purée of Asparagus with Maine Crabmeat & Fava Beans	9.50
• Garbure of New Jersey Spring Vegetables and fresh herbs	7.25

COLD

Avocado and Leek Terrine with Gazpacho Sauce and Shrimp	12.95
Chilled Brandade of fresh Maine Cod and Black Truffles	11.50
Terrine of Foie Gras with Sauternes	18.95
Russian Osetra Caviar, the ounce	45.00

HOT

Ragoût of Cock's Combs, Sweetbreads, Crayfish, and Morels	13.95
• Mussels in herb broth Côte d'Azur	12.50
Maine Sea Scallops and Caviar with Chive Cream	18.50
Grilled Foie Gras, Baby Turnips, local Wildflower Honey	19.25
• Tagliatelle with Tomatoes, Basil, and Parmesan Shavings	9.50
Mixed Garden Vegetables à la Greque	10.95

Route 22 West • Whitehouse, NJ • (908) 534-4011

Entrees

Fish

• Grouper with Orange Crust, Artichokes, grilled Shallots, and Beef Bouillon	24.50
• Atlantic Salmon, cooked on one side, marinated Vegetables	24.95
• Sliced Maine Codfish with quick Ratatouille	23.95
• Seared Rare Tuna in Shallot Broth	25.95
• Grilled Monkfish with Tomato-Fennel Salad, Black Olive Sauce	24.50
• Steamed Black Sea Bass with Seared Oysters, Chablis, and Garden Herbs	28.95
• Sautéed Soft Shell Crabs with Garden Vegetables à la Grecque	28.50
Roasted Maine Lobster and Cockles with Orange, Saffron, and Ginger	32.50
• Poached Maine Lobster à la Nage	31.00

Meats

• Roasted Chicken and Vegetables with Rosemary	21.50
Tender Duck with Wildflower Honey and Turnips	24.50
Roasted Pigeon and Grilled Foie Gras, Asparagus, and Morels	32.50
• Young Rabbit with Wild Mushrooms and Spring Vegetables	24.95
Pan roasted Veal Chop with Fava Beans, Sweet Peas, and Carrots	31.95
• Confit of Pork Loin with Thai Vegetables	23.50
Pan roasted dry-aged Sirloin with Aligot and String Beans	27.95
Dry-aged Côte de Boeuf with Cèpes, Salsify, and roasted Shallots	28.95
Rack of Lamb Gasconny Style	29.50
Roasted Sweetbreads with Spanish Paprika, Spring Onions, Carrots, and Crayfish	24.95
Sliced Veal Kidneys with Tagliatelle and Green Mustard	22.50

Grills

Any entree item can be prepared grilled with classic garnishes

Dinner: Mon - Fri 5:30 - 10, Sat 5:30 - 11, Sun 2 - 8

The Terrace is the only fine restaurant north of 96th Street on the West Side. Located on the top floor of a Columbia University building, it has dramatic views of the city and offers good French cuisine.

Menu Changes Daily And Seasonally

FIRST COURSE

Ravioli of Shrimp Provencal with Red and Yellow Tomato Coulis 11.oo

Panache of Marinated Norwegian Salmon and Yellowfin Tuna with Herb Salad 10.oo

Duck Pate with Foie Gras and Truffles, Chives Balsamic Vinaigrette 9.oo

Escargot with Basil and Pancetta in an Herb Crust with Fried Leeks 10.oo

Homemade Fine Pasta with Basil and Tomato Concassees 9.oo

Seared Roulade of Montrachet Cheese and Smoked Salmo Salad with Herb Infused Olive Oil 10.oo

New York Foie Gras with Wild Mushroom Crumble and Thyme Scented Duck Jus 18.oo

Terrine of Roasted Eggplant, Sweet Peppers, Smoked Porcini and Shiitake Mushrooms with Beet Coulis 11.oo

400 West 119th St • Upper West Side • (212) 666-9490

SECOND COURSE

Seared Tuna Aux Poivre with Vegetable Cannelloni in a Black Bean and Saffron Sauce 24.oo

Red Snapper Adriatic Style with Braised Leeks 25.oo

Poached Medallions of Norwegian Salmon with Seasonal Vegetables and Fish Consomme 24.oo

Grilled Swordfish with Mussels Vinaigrette and Roasted Garlic Potato Puree 26.oo

Sauteed Loin of Veal with Sweetbreads Strudel and Morel Sauce 25.oo

Honey Roasted Poussin with Herb Butter and Whole Garlic 20.oo

Grilled Filet Mignon with Green and Pink Peppercorn Sauces and Pommes Darphin 27.oo

Herb Crusted Rack of Lamb with Roasted Eggplant and Zucchini, Rosemary Lamb Jus 30.oo

Assiette of Venison and Grilled Foie Gras Sausage in a Cherry and Tarragon Game Jus 24.oo

Sliced Breast of Muscovy Duck and Leg Confit with Savoy Cabbage Timbale and Fig Sauce 25.oo

Dinner: Tues - Sat 6 - 10

Trois Jean is a dream restaurant of three best friends from France. Its warm welcome, stylish bistro fare and fabulous pâtisserie has made habitués of the chic Upper East Side crowd.

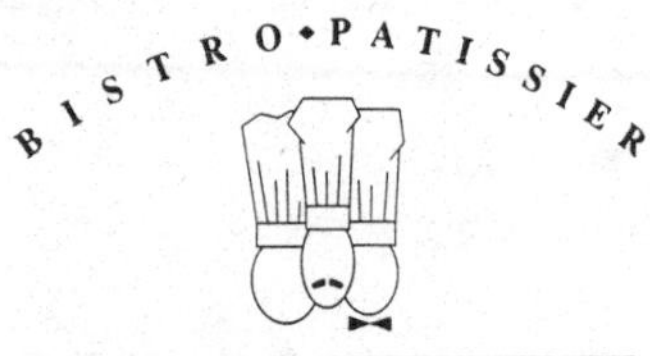

Trois Jean

Menu Changes Seasonally

Hors d'oeuvre

***Pot de harengs salade tiède de pommes de terre* 9.00**
Smoked and marinated herrings with a warm potato salad

***Salade de ris-de-veau et artichauts confits, poireaux frits** 9.50**
Sauteed sweetbreads and artichokes scented with cumin and served on mixed greens with fried leeks.

***Saumon frais d'Atlantique fumé par Jean-Louis** 11.50**
Our own smoked salmon from the Atlantique

***Macédoine de légumes aux crevettes grillées* 10.00**
Fresh grilled shrimp and "macédoine" of spring vegetables over mixed salad

***Salade de mesclun aux herbes fraîches* 7.00**
Mixed organic salad greens and herbs with Autumn dressing

***Tartare de thon au pommes gaufrettes* 11.50**
Fresh tuna tartar between "gaufrettes potatoes"

****The Favorites***

Chef Jean-Louis suggests

Hors d'oevre	***Entree***
$18.00	***$20.00***
Foie Gras de canard au Naturel	***Cassoulet "Jean Dumonet"***
Home made Hudson Valley "Foie Gras" terrine	*Crusty traditional stew of Toulouse sausage duck confit, smoked ham, garlic and white beans braised with duck broth*

154 East 79th St • Upper East Side • (212) 988-4858

Entrées

Coquilles Saint-Jacques rôties, ratatouille niçoise* 18.50
Roasted jumbo sea scallops served with "ratatouille" and black olive coulis

Saumon rôti, moules marinières et petits raviolis 19.50
Roasted filet of salmon with mussels "marinières" and raviolis

Steack de thon grillé, céleri et pommes pailles 19.50
Grilled Yellow fin tuna steak served over a bed of crispy potato and celeriac with a warm sesame vinaigrette

Aile de raie poelée au jus de viande* 16.50
Skate, pan-seared with beef juice and sauteed potatoes

Tartare "Trois Jean", pommes frites* 16.50
Hand chopped beef Tartar, pommes frites, a specialty

Onglet au poivre, gratin Dauphinois* 18.50
Black angus hanger steak in a pepper sauce and scalloped potatoes

Coquelet grillé et purée de pommes de terre 17.50
Grilled cornish hen served with mashed potatoes

Feuilleté de petits légumes et asperges à la nage de persil 13.00
Baby vegetables and asparagus in puff pastry with a parsely broth

Desserts

Pyramide au Chocolat* 9.00
Jean-Marc's specialty, a chocolate ganache made from three imported chocolates formed into a pyramid and served with fresh raspberries

Assiette dégustation de Jean-Marc* 9.00
A delectable assortment of miniature pastries, a chocolate basket with passion fruit bavarian and fresh fruits

Crème brûlée à la réglisse 7.50
Licorice flavored crême brulée

Paris-Brest 7.00

Dinner: Mon - Sat 5:30 - 11

This was the most eagerly awaited restaurant-opening of the year and it has not disappointed. Master chef Jean Georges Vongerichten serves a unique blend of French and Thai cuisines in a dramatic new space. It's a real hot spot.

Menu Changes Seasonally

APPETIZERS

SHRIMP SATAY WITH FRESH OYSTER SAUCE $12

RAW TUNA AND VEGETABLES WRAPPED IN RICE PAPER $10

CRAB SPRING ROLL WITH TAMARIND DIPPING SAUCE $10

GREEN PAPAYA SALAD WITH CASHEW NUTS $8

SAUTEED FOIE GRAS WITH GINGER AND MANGO $14

LOBSTER AND TURNIP SALAD WITH HONEY-GINGER VINAIGRETTE $14

GRILLED SQUID ON ORIENTAL GREENS WITH CUCUMBER-PEANUT RELISH $9

CHARRED LAMB SALAD $12

CHICKEN IN COCONUT MILK AND GALANGA SOUP $8

SHRIMP WITH LEMON GRASS AND BERGAMOT LEAF BROTH $9

EGG NOODLE SOUP WITH SHREDDED DUCK AND PRESERVED LIME $8

ENTREES

SPICY MAINE SCALLOPS WITH RICE
NOODLES AND VEGETABLES $17

BLACK BASS WITH WOK FRIED NAPA CABBAGE,
WATER CHESTNUTS AND CHILLIS $20

SPICED CODFISH WITH CURRIED ARTICHOKE $16

SALMON IN CARDAMON, TOMATO, AND TURNIP BROTH $19

LOBSTER WITH THAI HERBS $22

STEAMED SQUAB IN CABBAGE LEAVES WITH HOLLY BASIL $19

RABBIT CURRY $18

DUCK ORIENTAL $20

GRILLED BEEF IN A GINGER BROTH $19

ROASTED POUSSIN WITH LEMON GRASS, SWEET RICE $17

RICE AND VEGETABLE

PINEAPPLE FRIED RICE $4
VEGETABLE PHAD THAI $5
GRILLED ASIAN EGGPLANT $4

JAMES CHEW-CHEF

Dinner: Mon - Fri 6 - 11, Sat 5:30 - 11

This is about the only upscale Greek restaurant in NYC; it serves the standards, like moussaka, and creative specials as well. It's nicely decorated and is the one place to go in Manhattan for serious Greek food.

Periyali

APPETIZERS

Paradosiaka Orektika 9.50
Traditional greek, regional appetizers on display

Fava Me Kremidaki 7.00
Pureed yellow split peas with onion and olive oil

Gigandes Skordalia 8.00
Giant white beans with garlic sauce

Oktapodi Scharas 9.50
Octopus in red wine marinade, grilled over charcoal

Calamarakia Tiganita 8.00
Tossed salad greens with crisp calamari

Sikotakia Me Fakes 8.50
Sauteed chicken livers served over warm lentils with onions and carrots

Tiropita - Spanakopita 8.00
Blended feta and graviera cheeses baked in fillo pastry
Fresh spinach and feta cheese baked in fillo pastry

Kotopoulo Souvlaki me Maratho 9.00
Chicken and fennel brochette with eggplant and semolina salad

Soupa Avgolemono 6.00
Rich chicken soup finished with egg and lemon

Soupa Epochis 6.00
Seasonal soup

MAIN COURSES

Moschari Scharas Me Rigani 19.50
Grilled escallopes of veal with oregano and olive oil

Solomos Exochiko 21.00
Filet of salmon baked in fillo with spinach and feta cheese

Paidakia Thendrolivano 23.00
Lamb chops grilled over charcoal with fresh rosemary

Kotopoulo Fournou 19.00
Roasted "naturally farmed" chicken with oregano and country rice

Souvlaki Arnisio 20.00
Shish Kebob of lamb grilled over charcoal

Moussaka 17.00
Casserole dish with layers of eggplant, ground lamb, bechamel

Kouneli Stifado 20.00
Rabbit stewed in tomato with red wine and tiny onions

Lavraki Plaki 21.00
Striped bass filet baked with white wine, tomato, onion and garlic

Glikadakia kai Sikoti Moscharisio 19.50
Pan braised calves liver and sweetbreads with red wine vinegar natural sauce

Fileto Scharas 23.00
Charcoal grilled filet mignon with brown butter

Garides Periyali 19.50
Grilled shrimp with olive oil, lemon and herbs

Horta 3.00
Steamed greens with olive oil and lemon

Dinner: Mon - Thurs 5:30 - 11, Fri - Sat 5:30 - 11:30

Darbar has ranked among the top Indian restaurants for years. The food is excellent and the decor is subtly exotic; it's also in a prime business and shopping district.

Darbár
Indian Restaurant

Tandoori Dasterkhawan

Specialties from the charcoal clay oven

RESHMI KEBAB 17.95

Boneless dark chicken pieces flavoured with fresh herbs and spices and grilled on skewers in our tandoor.

CHICKEN DARBARI 19.95

Chef's favorite preparation. Boneless chicken marinated in yogurt, fresh garlic and ground spices, carefully broiled in the tandoor.

Tarkaree Ke Pakwaan

Vegetarian Specialties

MALAI KOFTA 12.95

Mixed vegetable balls cooked in an onion and tomato sauce.

SHAHI SABZ KORMA 13.95

A royal entree. Garden fresh vegetables and cheese gently cooked in spice-laced cream, sprinkled with nuts.

44 West 56th St • Midtown West Side • (212) 432-7227

Special Presentations

LAMB KEBAB PUNJABI 22.95

A specialty from Punjab. Lamb marinated in chef's special marinade and broiled in our tandoor.

SHAHI LAMB CHOPS 22.95

Lamb chops marinated in yogurt, garlic, ginger and delicately flavored with chef's special spices and carefully broiled in the tandoor. Served with Basmati Rice.

Samundaree Dasterkhawan

Seafood Specialties

LOBSTER MALAI KHASA 22.95

Lobster gently cooked in a cream flavoured with coconut.

CRAB MALABAR 22.95

A specialty of Malabar. Succulent pieces of crab meat simmered in onions, tomatoes, and fennel seed, sprinkled with coconut.

Gosht Ke Pakwaan

Lamb/Beef Specialties

KHARA PASANDE 18.95

A northern delicacy, juicy slices of lamb marinated overnight then simmered in light sauce with yogurt, onions, tomatoes and mild spices.

ROGAN JOSH 18.95

Tender morsels of lamb cooked in an onion sauce, with yogurt, almonds, cream and a unique blend of spices.

Dinner: Mon - Thurs 5:30 - 10:30, Fri - Sat 5:30 - 11, Sun 5:30 - 10

Unlike most Indian restaurants, Dawat has a striking, modern decor with few traces of filigree and mirrored fabrics. The food is also very upscale; Madhur Jaffrey was the original consultant. All the traditional dishes are delicious too.

Dishes perfected by **MADHUR JAFFREY**, world famous actress, author and authority on the cuisines of India. In our continuing effort to bring you exciting new dishes these recipes have been gathered from the four corners of the Subcontinent and represent the culinary tradition of both the royal table and family meals.

RAAN 21.95

A whole, small tender leg of lamb is first marinated in a chili-garlic paste and then twice-cooked: first braised with ginger and whole spices, then roasted in the tandoor oven until it is crisp outside and meltingly tender inside.

MURCH JEHANGIRI 16.95

Chicken pieces marinated in yogurt and roasted in the tandoor oven with lavish bastings of chili-coriander sauce.

WHOLE TANDOORI FISH 21.95

Whole fish and fiery, quick cooking tandoor ovens aré meant for each other. The fish is marinated in yogurt and flavored with dill-like ajwain seeds before it is roasted.

STARTERS

SHAMI KABAB **$6.25**

Patties of finely ground lamb stuffed with fresh mint

MADHUR JAFFREY'S BAGHARI JHINGA **9.95**

Succulent shrimp, flavored with garlic, mustard seeds and curry leaves

BHEL POORI **6.25**

A melange of assorted crisps and noodles, smothered in sweet, sour and spicy chutneys

DAHI ALOO POORI **6.25**

A mouth-watering mixture of crisps, potatoes and chick peas in yogurt and tamarind sauces

SPECIAL DINNERS

MADHUR JAFFREY'S VEGETARIAN THALI **$22.95**

Miss Jaffrey's selection of vegetables, split peas, rice, breads, chutneys and relishes

TANDOORI MIXED GRILL **22.95**

Tandoori chicken, Muradabadi boti kabab, Tandoori shrimp, Reshmi kabab and Nan, served with Kali dal

MADHUR JAFFREY'S LIGHT PLATTER **22.95**

Miss Jaffrey's low-calorid combination of chicken or fish, assorted vegetables, salad, chutneys relishes and bread

210 East 58th St • Midtown East Side • (212) 355-7555

SEA FOOD

MADHUR JAFFREY'S KERALA-STYLE KONJU PAPPAAS **$21.95**
Shrimp in a coconut milk sauce, flavored with aromatic curry leaves and smoked tamarind

MADHUR JAFFREY'S PARSI-STYLE PATRA-NI-MACHHI **22.95**
Salmon smothered in a fresh corinander chutney wrapped in a banana leaf and steamed. Served with basmati rice

FISH IN A MUSTARD SAUCE **18.95**
Chunks of tile fish in a spicy sauce of crushed mustard seeds and mustard oil

GOAT AND LAMB DISHES

HOME-STYLE ROGAN JOSH **$16.95**
Succulent pieces of baby goat (with bone), in a cardamom flavored sauce

LAMB VINDALOO **16.95**
Lamb in a hot, tangy sauce

SHABDEG **16.95**
A mild sixteenth century Mughlai dish of lamb and turnips, stewed gently in yogurt

LAMB PASANDA **16.95**
Lamb scallops in a rich creamy sauce

KEEMA MATAR **16.95**
Ground lamb cooked with green peas ginger and browned onions

SAG GOSHT **16.95**
Cubes of lamb in a spicy spinach puree

BOTI KABAB MASALA **16.95**
Cubes of lamb roasted in a clay oven and then folded into a delicately spiced sauce

CHICKEN DISHES

CHICKEN KEEMA MASALA **$15.95**
Ground chicken, deliciously flavored with browned onions and cardamom

CHICKEN SAG **15.95**
Chicken pieces smothered in a spicy spinach puree

CHICKEN MAKHANI **15.95**
Chicken pieces roasted in a clay oven and then folded into a creamy tomato sauce

CHICKEN TIKKA MASALA **15.95**
Chunks of chicken, roasted in a clay oven and then folded into a cream sauce

CHICKEN BADAMI **15.95**
Chicken pieces in a rich almond-flavored sauce

TANDOOR

CLAY OVEN SPECIALTIES

TANDOORI SHRIMP **$21.95**
King-size shrimp marinated in mild spices, roasted in a clay oven

TANDOORI FISH TIKKA **16.95**
Chunks of seasonal fish, marinated in an aromatic herb mixture, roasted in a clay oven

TANDOORI CHICKEN (whole) **16.95**
Chicken marinated in yogurt **(half)** **10.95**
and mild spices, roasted in a clay oven

CHICKEN TIKKA **15.95**
Boneless chunks of chicken, marinated in yogurt and mild spices, roasted in a clay oven

VEGETARIAN SPECIALTIES

PANEER BHURJI **$11.95**
Fresh home-made cheese, grated and cooked with green peppers, tomatoes and onions

MATAR PANEER **11.95**
Fresh home-made cheese cubes cooked with green peas

SAG PANEER **11.95**
Fresh home-made cheese cubes in a spicy spinach sauce

BHINDI MASALA **11.95**
Okra flavored with browned onions and dried mango

MADHUR JAFFREY'S BAKED EGGPLANT **11.95**
Thin slices of young eggplant coated with a mild sweet-and-sour tamarind sauce and baked

Dinner: 7 Days a Week 5:30 - 11

Located downtown in TriBeCa, Arquá is in an open, airy space with ochre-colored sponged walls that makes you feel you are in an Italian villa. People love the simple and authentic Tuscan-style cooking.

Menu Changes Seasonally Along With Specials

DINNER

ZUPPA DEL GIORNO (Soup of the Day)	$5.00
ZUPPA DI PESCE ALLA VENEZIANA (Venetian Fish Soup)	8.00
CARPACCIO (Thin Sliced Raw Beef with Lemon and Olive Oil)	8.00
CARCIOFI RIPIENI AL FORNO (Stuffed Baked Artichokes)	8.00
TORTINO DI RISOTTO RIPEINO CON FONTINA (Risotto Pancake with Fontina)	8.00
FRESH MOZZARELLA WITH ROASTED PEPPERS AND ROASTED EGGPLANT & PROSCIUTTO	10.00
CALAMARI IN PADELLA (Sauteed Fresh Calamari)	8.00
SARDINE IN SAORA (Fresh Sardines with Sweet and Sour Onions)	8.00
CAPESANTE IN PADELLA (Seared Sea Scallops with Anchovies and Capers)	10.00

PASTA

GNOCCHI (Homemade Gnocchi with Tomato and Fresh Herbs)	$14.00
MATTONELLA (Homemade Lasagna with Fresh Baby Artichokes and Béchamel)	14.00

PAPPARDELLE CON SALSICCIA E FUNGHI (Pappardelle with Sausage & Mushroom)	14.00
TAGLIENINI ALLE VONGOLE (Homemade Pasta with Imported Clams)	14.00
TAGLIENINI ALLA PUTTANESCA (Homemade Pasta with Black Olives and Capers)	14.00
RAVIOLI DI PORRI (Leek Ravioli in a Brown Butter Sauce)	14.00
RAVIOLI DI ZUCCA (Butternut Squash Ravioli with Cream and Pistachio)	14.00
TAGLIENINI AL PESTO (Homemade Pasta with Fresh Spring Basil Sauce)	14.00
RISOTTO DEL GIORNO (25-30 Minutes)	14.00

SECONDI PIATTI

DENTICE IN BRODETTO (Sauteed Red Snapper in a Pungent Tomato Sauce)	$18.00
SALMONE ALLA GRIGLIA (Grilled Salmon Glazed with Balsamic Vinegar)	18.00
STINCO D'AGNELLO AL BAROLO (Braised Spring Lamb Shank with Barolo Wine)	16.00
CARRÉ DE MAIALE ARROSTO (Roasted Loin of Pork with White Wine & Fennel)	16.00
GALETTO ALLA GRIGLIA (Marinated Grilled Baby Spring Chicken)	16.00
CONIGLIO BRASATO AL FORNO (Braised Rabbit with White Wine and Herbs)	18.00
FEGATO VENEZIANA (Calf's Liver Sauteed with Onions and White Wine)	15.00

INSALATE

CAESAR SALAD	$7.00
MIX OF ORGANICALLY GROWN BABY LETTUCE	7.00
RUGOLA SALAD WITH SHAVED PARMESAN	7.00
FENNEL SALAD WITH SHAVED PARMESAN AND PINK GRAPEFRUIT	7.00

Dinner: Mon - Thurs 5:30 - 11, Fri - Sat 5:30 - 11:30, Sun 1:30 - 9:30

People (i.e., tourists) go to Barbetta for its location (in the Theater District), its decor (very romantic, with crystal chandeliers and elegant table settings) and its garden. They've just renovated their kitchen, so maybe the traditional Italian food will improve.

BARBETTA

Menu Changes Seasonally Along With Daily Specials

* Specialties of Piemonte

HORS D'OEUVRE

Antipasto Piemontese* 8.50
Field Salad Piemontese* 8.50
Insalata di Carne Cruda alla Monferrina* 14.00
Roast Fresh Peppers Alla Bagna Cauda* 8.50
Salads of the Day 8.50

PASTA
(half portions)

Tajarin with salsa di campagna* 13.00
Agnolotti - made by hand 13.00
Linguine al Pesto 13.00
Lingue di Passero al Paté di Olive 14.00
Canelloni alla Savoiarda 13.00
Tortellini alla Panna 13.00
Pasta taken as a main course will be served as a full portion and charged from 22.00

Fonduta Valdostana* 13.00

RISOTTI
(half portions)

Risotto alla Piemontese* 15.00
Risotto al Rosé Champagne 14.00
Risotto con le Seppioline, served only when the seppie are running very small. 17.00
Risotto di Gamberetti, served only when tiny fresh gamberi are available. 18.00
Risotto taken as a main course will be served as a full portion and charged from 22.00

FISH

The Fish Specialties of the day 28.00
Fresh Crabmeat sautéed in Moscato d'Asti with Wild Rice 29.00

ENTREES

varying daily:

Bolliti Misti Piemontesi* served from the silver wagon 27.00
Bue al Barolo, Beef braised in red wine with Polenta* 26.00
Rabbit in the mode of the day* 27.00
Pollo al Babj* 27.50
Free Range Organic Chicken in the mode of the day 27.00
Scaloppine with Wild Porcini Mushrooms 28.00
Rack of Veal Chop al Verde 28.00
Veal Kidneys Trifolati 24.00
Fegato Veneziana 28.00
Tagliata of Sirloin of Beef alla Fiorentina 29.00

GAME

varying daily:

Charcoal-grilled Squab with cranberry beans and red beet olive oil* 28.00
Cervo (Venison) alla moda del giorno 29.00
Quail with Polenta in the mode of Venice 28.00
Lepre (Wild Hare) in Civet 29.00
Pheasant - alla moda del giorno 29.00

SALADS

Field Salad Piemontese* 8.00
Mesclun Greens 7.50
Rugola and Bibb 7.50
Cremini Mushrooms 8.00
Salads of the Day 8.50
Bibb and Belgian Endive 7.50

DESSERTS

Panna Cotta* 7.95
Monte Bianco* 7.95
Torta di Nocciole* 7.95
St. Honoré 7.95
Fruit Tarts of the day 7.95
Mousse of Bittersweet Chocolate
Red Fruits Soup 7.75
Creme Brulée 7.75
Chocolate Cake 7.75
An assortment of Cooked Fruits - from the wagon 7.95
Fuga di Dolci 12.00

Dinner: Mon - Sat 5 - 12

A hip, trendy, noisy, TriBeCa Italian restaurant that also happens to serve excellent, uncomplicated, authentic food.

BAROCCO

Menu Changes Seasonally

Dinner

CALAMARI FRITTI deep fried squid	8.00
FETTUNTA homemade Tuscan bread, grilled w/garlic & olive oil	2.00
BRUSCHETTA al POMODORO fettunta, fresh tomato & basil	4.50
BRUSCHETTA alla ROMANA fettunta, anchovy & mozzarella	5.00
ANTIPASTO MISTO prosciutto, coppa, salami, Tuscan pecorino	12.00
INSALATA MISTA salad of organic greens	7.00
INSALATA di VERDURE organic greens, beets, asparagus & peppers	8.00
INSALATA di FINOCCHIO fresh fennel, arugula & parmigiano	7.50
INSALATA di GAMBERI white beans, cilantro & shrimp salad	8.00
GRILLED SHIITAKE MUSHROOMS with garlic & fresh herbs	10.50
CARPACCIO with ARUGULA and shaved parmigiano	12.00

301 Church St • TriBeCa/Downtown/Chinatown • (212) 431-1445

RAVIOLI VERDI homemade spinach pasta filled with fresh ricotta & swiss cheese chard; tomato and sage	15.00
PAPPARDELLE with rabbit, squab and black olive sauce	14.00
RIGATONI with pureed eggplant, roast peppers, tomato & basil	13.00
LASAGNA with meat and porcini, bechamel & parmigiano	16.00
RISOTTO of the DAY	p.a.

BRAISED LOIN of RABBIT with spinach and olives	21.00
ROAST ORGANIC CHICKEN with mashed potatoes & greens	18.00
ROAST RACK of LAMB with rosemary roast potatoes	27.00
GRILLED NEW YORK STRIP STEAK and rosemary potatoes	26.00
GRILLED NORWEGIAN SALMON with/salsa verde & spinach	20.00
WHOLE ROAST SEA BASS with greens and roast pototoes	24.00

SAUTEED MIXED GREENS	6.00
ROAST POTATOES	5.00

Dinner: 7 Days a Week 6 - 11

People consider this the best restaurant in Southampton; the well-known watering hole of the rich. It serves a light menu, highlighted by pastas, grills and salads, using the bounty provided by local farms.

Menu Changes Daily And Weekly

Antipasti

Panzanella 8.50
Tuscan bread, cucumber, tomato salad seasoned with virgin olive oil, red wine vinegar and fresh basil

Funghi Misti alla Griglia 9.50
assorted mushrooms grilled and deglazed with balsamic vinegar

Caprese di Buffalo 9.50
fresh Itallian buffalo mozzarella, vine ripened tomato, basil and virgin olive oil

Ostrica Naturale 2.00ea
local oysters served on the half shell with a balsamic, chive vinaigrette

Tonnacio con Arrugola 9.50
sushi quality tuna, thinly sliced, marinated in mustard and balsamic vinegar served over arrugola

Pasta

Spaghetti al Granseola 22.00
pasta tossed with Dungeness crab, tomato, crushed red pepper, herbs, garlic and a small touch of cream

Penne ai Spinaci 14.00
quill pasta tossed with a light sauce of blended spinach, ricotta cheese and prosciutto

Spaghetti basilico 15.00
pasta tossed with tomatoes and fresh basil

Orecchiette con Cime di Rape 16.00
little ears tossed with bitter broccoli rabe, garlic, extra virgin olive oil and crushed red pepper

Rigatoni con Sugo di Maiale e Piselli 16.00
pasta tossed with a sauce of smoked sausage and peas with a touch of cream and tomato

Spaghetti alle Vongole 16.00
pasta tossed with small clams, crushed red pepper, garlic, herbs and virgin olive oil

10 Windmill Lane • Southampton, NY • (516) 283-7987

Pizze

Pizza basilico — 15.00
pizza topped with tomato, basil and cheese

Pizza con Rugola e Prosciutto — 16.00
pizza topped with tomato, mozzarella cheese, arugola and prosciutto

Pesce

Pesce del Giorno — 22.00
fresh local fish of the day

Dentice Arrosto — 26.00
whole roast striped bass, served in it's entirety, accompanied with roast potatoes and steamed vegetables

Carne

Tagliata alla Fiorentina — 26.00
certified Angus rib-eye steak grilled rare, sliced and seared with virgin olive oil, herbs, garlic, accompanied with roast potatoes and steamed vegetables

Lombatina di Vitello — 22.00
pounded and breaded veal chop, sauteed in virgin olive oil, topped with arrugola and tomato salad

Petto di Pollo alla Griglia — 22.00
grilled breast of chicken accompanied with mashed potatoes and steamed vegetables

Costeletto di Angello — 24.00
lamb chops pounded, marinated with garlic and rosemary, served with roast potatoes and sauteed spinach

Insalata

Mista della Casa — 8.00
mixed local greens tossed with house vinaigrette

Insalata di Carciofini — 8.50
salad of shaved baby artichokes and shaved Parmesan cheese tossed with house vinaigrette

Contorni

Broccoli Affogati - sauteed broccoli rabe and garlic — 5.50

Spinaci al Profumo di Aglio - sauteed spinach and garlic — 5.50

Dinner: Mon - Thurs 6 - 10, Fri - Sat 6 - 11:30

Its location (Theater District) and lineage (the same family as Felidia) make this an important restaurant. The gutsy, peasant-style Italian fare and flexible menu have made it a winner.

Menu Changes Daily

With the concept of BECCO, we would like to share with the diner a part of the Italian culinary heritage that is not often experienced. In Italy, as one travels in the countryside, especially on weekends, the Trattorie/Fattorie (basically farmhouses) open their doors and share their products (wine, prosciutto, vegetables, meats) with their guests.

Usually there is an antipasto served, then either a minestra and/or a pasta. Following this is the main course, a meat either roasted or braised. The main course could either be lamb, goat, suckling pig or game, whatever the season offers. The ending is usually a fruit crostata or dolce al cucchiaio (spoon dessert) such as tiramisu or panna cotta.

The experience is always a warm one; it is like being at a friend's home. This is the concept and feeling that we would like you to experience at Becco.

DINNER

MENU I (antipasto and pasta) **$19.00**	**A LA CARTE**
ANTIPASTI ASSORTITI A spread of mixed grilled vegetables, legumes and fish	**$ 7.00**
SINFONIA DI PASTE Pastas of the day	**$14.00**

MENU II (antipasto, pasta and entree) (not available pre-theater)	Price includes **Menu I**	**A LA CARTE** (with salad)
OSSOBUCO Braised veal shank	**$27.95**	**$18.00**
AGNELLO ALLO SPIEDO Spit-roasted lamb	**$28.95**	**$19.00**
GALLETTO AL MATTONE Grilled young game hen	**$23.95**	**$16.00**

355 West 46th St • Theater District • (212) 397-7597

MENU II (antipasto, pasta and entree)
(not available pre-theater)

	Price includes **Menu I**	**A LA CARTE** (with salad)
BISTECCA FIORENTINA ALLA BECCO Steak florentine alla "Becco"	**$29.95**	**$20.00**
PETTO DI POLLO ALLA GRIGLIA CON ARUGULA Grilled chicken breast with arugula	**$28.95**	**$19.00**
ROMBO AI FERRI CON POMODORO E BASILICO Broiled halibut with tomato and basil	**$28.95**	**$19.00**
PEPERONI RIPIENI Stuffed peppers	**$23.95**	**$16.00**
TRIPPA ALL'ISTRIANA CON PATATE Braised tripe Istrian style with potatoes	**$23.95**	**$16.00**
CONIGLIO IN SGUAZET Rabbit in squazet	**$28.95**	**$19.00**
PORTOBELLO ALLA GRIGLIA Grilled portobello with polenta	**$25.95**	**$17.00**
SALSICCIA FATTA IN CASA ALLA PIZZAIOLA BIANCA Sausages made in house with roasted peppers and onions	**$23.95**	**$16.00**
QUAGLIA IN SGUAZET Quail in squazet	**$28.95**	**$19.00**
PESCE SALTATO IN PADELLA Red Snapper in a thyme sauce	**$28.95**	**$19.00**
PESCE SPADA AGRODOLCE Swordfish in a sweet and sour sauce	**$28.95**	**$19.00**
SALMONE ALLA SALSA DI SENAPE Salmon with mustard sauce	**$28.95**	**$19.00**
CARPACCIO DI SALMONE CON ARUGULA Cured salmon over arugula	**$26.95**	**$17.00**

SALATA MISTA ITALIANA - a la carte Mixed salad of Italian greens	**$ 5.00**
MINESTRONE DI VERDURA Minestrone soup	**$ 5.00**

Dinner: Mon - Sat 5 - 12, Sun until 10

When it first opened, Bice was super trendy, but it has since settled into middle-age. No longer quite the scene, the quality Milanese-style Italian food and chic decor have shown staying power.

Menu Changes Daily

ANTIPASTI

CARPACCIO DI MANZO CON RUCOLA, PALMITO E PARMIGIANO
Beef carpaccio with arrugola, hearts of palm & parmesan 13.--
BRESAOLA DELLA VALTELLINA CON CARCIOFINI E GRANA
Dried beef with baby artichokes and parmesan cheese 11.--
CESTINO DI PROSCIUTTO CON MELONE E VERDURE
Parma prosciutto with sweet melon and vegetables 15.--
VITELLO TONNATO CON INSALATA DI CAROTE
Cold sliced veal with carrot salad 14.--

GIARDINETTO D'ARAGOSTA CON VINEGRETTE AI LAMPONI
Lobster salad with raspberry vinaigrette 18.--
SALMONE MARINATO CON ARANCE E SONCINO
Marinated salmon with orange and mash 15.--
CALAMARETTI FRITTI CON ZUCCHINE E BASILICO ROSSO
Fried calamari with zucchini and red basil 15.--
CARPACCIO DI PESCE SPADA CON ASPARAGI E MELE VERDI
Swordfish carpaccio with asparagus and green apples 15.--
CAPPESANTE GRIGLIATE CON FAGIOLINI E POMODORI GIALLI
Grilled scallops with green beans and yellow tomatoes 15.--

SFORMATINO DI MELANZANE E ZUCCHINE ALLA PARMIGIANA
Eggplant and zucchini with mozzarella and tomato 12.--
INSALATINA CAPRESE
Tomato and mozzarella salad with basil 12.--
VERDURA ALLA GRIGLIA CON OLIO LIGURE EXTRA VERGINE
Grilled vegetables with Ligurian virgin olive oil 13.--
MISTICANZA ALL'OLIO AFFIORATO ED ACETO BALSAMICO
Organic salad with olive oil and balsamic vinegar 9.--
ASPARAGI TIEPIDI CON UOVA DI QUAGLIA E PARMIGIANO
Warm asparagus with quail eggs and parmesan cheese 14.--
INSALATA DI CAPRINO CALDO CON TAGLIATELLE DI VERDURE
Warm goat-cheese salad with vegetables 13.--

7 East 54th St • Midtown East Side • (212) 688-1999

PRIMI PIATTI

PENNE ALL'ARRABIATA
Penne with a spicy tomato sauce 19.--
RIGATONI CON MELANZANE, POMODORI E RICOTTA SARDA
Rigatoni with eggplant, tomato and aged ricotta 19.--
LINGUINE ALLE VONGOLE CON BROCCOLETTI
Linguine with baby clams and broccoli 20.--
FARFALLE CON SALMONE ED ASPARAGI
Bow-tie pasta with salmon and asparagus 20.--
MALLOREDDUS CON SALSICCIA E ROSMARINO FRESCO
Sardinian pasta with Italian sausage and rosemary 20.--
***PAPPARDELLE AL TELEFONO**
Large noodles in tomato sauce with mozzarella and basil 20.--
***SPAGHETTI ALLA CHITARRA CON RAGU' ALLA BOLOGNESE**
Spaghetti with meat sauce Bolognese style 20.--
***AGNOLOTTI DI CARNE E SPINACI CON SALSA AI FUNGHI**
Veal and spinach ravioli with mushroom sauce 20.--
***FETTUCCINE CON ARAGOSTA DEL MAINE E FUNGHI SELVATICI**
Fettuccine with Maine lobster and wild mushrooms 24.--
***TAGLIOLINI NERI CON CAPPESANTE E ZAFFERANO**
Black tagliolini with scallops and saffron 22.--

RISOTTO CON COZZE E PISELLI
Risotto with mussels and peas 22.--
RISOTTO AI FUNGHI PORCINI SECCHI
Risotto with dry porcini mushrooms 20.--

PIATTI DEL GIORNO

CARRE' D'AGNELLO AL FORNO IN CROSTA DI PANE E BASILICO
Roasted rack of lamb in bread and basil crust 28.-
ENTRECOTE ALLA ROBESPIERRE
Sliced New York steak with arrugola 25.--
FILETTO DI MANZO CON SPUGNOLE E PISELLI
Sauteed beef filet with morel mushrooms and peas 28.--
COSTOLETTA DI VITELLO ALLA MILANESE
Classic breaded veal chop, thinly pounded Milanese style 26.--
FEGATO DI VITELLO ALLA VENEZIANA CON POLENTA
Sauteed calves liver with onions and polenta 22.--
LASAGNETTE DI VITELLO CON ZUCCHINE E SCAMORZA
Veal scaloppine with zucchini and smoked mozarella 24.--
GALLETTINO MARINATO ALLA GRIGLIA
Grilled cornish hen with fresh herbs 20.--
PAILLARD DI POLLO CON BURRO ALL'ERBE
Grilled chicken breast with herb butter 20.--

PESCI

DENTICE AL FORNO CON PATATE E FUNGHI
Roasted red snapper with potatoes and mushrooms 25.--
SALMONE A VAPORE CON SALSA DI RUCOLA
Poached salmon with arrugola sauce 24.--
TONNO ALLA PAPRICA CON LENTICCHIE E CIPOLLE ROSSE
Tuna in paprika crust with lentils and red onions 25.--

***We make our fresh pastas daily**

Dinner: 7 Days a Week 6 - 12

Rather than a tourist destination, neighborhood people come here for consistent northern Italian food, friendly service, and the warm, comfortable atmosphere. It's highly rated by local restaurant critics.

Specials Change Daily

Assorted Antipasto 7.50

Melon and Prosciutto 8.75

Bresaola (Cured Beef) 8.50

Mozzarella and Tomatoes 8.75

Tortellini in Brodo 5.00

Clams on Half-Shell 9.75

Baked Clams 9.75

Mussels in White Wine 7.50

Vegetable Soup 5.00

Canelloni with Meat Sauce 14.50

Ravioli with Tomato Sauce 14.75

Spaghettini Puttanesca 15.75
(tomatoes, anchovies, capers, olives)

Spaghettini with Clam Sauce 17.25

Penne All'Arrabiate 15.75
(with spicy Red Sauce)

Tortellini with Cream 14.75

Fettuccine Alfredo 14.75

Tagliolini Al Pesto 14.75

Penne with Fresh Vegetables 15.75

1570 First Ave • Upper East Side • (212) 249-0040

Half Pasta 9.75

Fried Squid 15.50

Calamari Fra Diavolo 15.75
(Squid in Spicy Red Sauce)

Broiled Shrimp 21.50
with herbs

Mussels Marechiara 15.00

Carpaccio - Sliced Raw Beef 17.50

Veal Pizzaiola 18.50

Veal Piccata 18.50

Veal Parmigiana 18.50

Bocconcini Di Vittello 18.50
(Veal Stew with Vegetables)

Veal Milanese 18.50

Chicken Piccata 15.25

Broiled Veal Chop 23.50

Veal Chop Valdostana 24.75

Broiled Lamb Chops 23.50
(Rosemary Balsamic)

Broiled Chicken 15.25

Breast of Chicken stuffed with Prosciutto and Cheese 18.50

Breast of Chicken with Artichoke Heart 18.50

Fried Zucchini 5.00

Spinach Sauteed 5.00

Caesar Salad 7.50

Italian Salad 6.50

Desserts 7.00

Strawberry Zabaglione 7.50

Coffee 2.00 *Espresso 3.00* *Cappuccino 3.50* *Tea 2.00*

This has long been the best northern Italian restaurant in the Village. The decor is more refined than you'll find in most places around here, and the food is consistently excellent.

CENT'ANNI

Menu Specials Daily

DINNER MENU

ANTIPASTI

INSALATA CAPRICCIOSA 5.00
Rucola, Lettuce, Peas, Carrots, Mushrooms and Beans

INSALATA di PESCE 9.00
Lobster, Shrimp, Bay Scallops and Squid

ANTIPASTO ITALIANO 9.00
Prosciutto, Salami, Cheese, Pimiento and Olives

ZUCCHINI RIPIENI 6.00
Stuffed with Meat, Cheese, and Broiled with Butter, Spices, Consomme

PEPERONI ARROSTITI CON ACCIUGHE 7.00
Roasted Red Peppers with Anchovy

FUNGHI PORTOBELLO 9.00
Portobello Mushrooms Broiled with Olive Oil, Garlic and Fresh Basil

MOZZARELLA di BUFFALO 9.00
Mozzarella di Buffalo with Sliced Tomato and Basil

PASTE

RIGATONI ZUCCHINI 13.00
Tubular Pasta in a Sauce of White Wine, Onions, Tomatoes and Zucchini

FETTUCINE AL SALMONE AFFUMICATO 16.00
Homemade Green and White Fettucine in a Sauce of Cream, Butter and Smoked Salmon, Sun Dried Tomatoes, Mint and Onions

RIGATONI ALLA MEDICI 13.00
Tubular Pasta in a Sauce of Butter, Chopped Chicken Breast, Onions and Carrots, Cream and Dried Porcini Mushrooms

PAPPARDELLE AL CONIGLIO 13.00
Thick, Flat Pasta in a Sauce with Rabbit, Onions, Carrots and Tomatoes

CAPELLINI CON ARAGOSTA 16.00
Angel Hair Pasta in a Light Tomato Sauce with Lobster Meat and Clams

LINGUINE ALLA VODKA 13.00
Thin Flat Pasta in a Tomato Sauce with Vodka and Red Pepper

PENNE ALLA GRAPPA 13.00
Tubular Pasta in a Sauce of Olive Oil, Grappa, Shitaki Mushrooms and Basil

ALL HALF PASTAS 8.50

50 Carmine St • Greenwich Village • (212) 989-9494

PIETANZE NOSTRANE

CONIGLIO ALLA FIORENTINA 15.00
Rabbit with White Wine, Onions, Carrots and Tomatoes

ARISTA di MAIALE 18.00
Double Cut Loin of Pork Roasted with White Wine, Garlic and Rosemary Served in a Brown Sauce

FAGIANO ARROSTO 22.00
Baby Pheasant Marinated, Split then Roasted Served with a Brown Sauce

TRIPPA ALLA FIORENTINA 13.00
Honeycomb Tripe Sauteed in Butter, Onion, Celery, Black Olives, Carrots, Tomatoes and Parmigiano Cheese

POLLO ALLA DIAVOLA 15.00
Broiled Game Hen, Marinated in Oil, Garlic, Balsamic Vinegar and Rosemary

POLLO FUNGHI e POMODORO 16.00
Chicked Breast Sauteed in White Wine, Garlic, Butter, Basil, Wild Mushrooms and Fresh Tomatoes

COSTOLETTE di AGNELLO 22.00
Baby Rack of Lamb, Split and Grilled

VITELLO ALLA GIOVANNI 18.00
Veal Scaloppine Sauteed in Oil, Mushrooms, Artichokes, Tomatoes and Spices

VEAL CHOP SALVIA 26.00
A Double Cut, Milk Fed Veal Chop, Broiled then Sauteed in Wine and Fresh Sage

GRIGLIATA MISTA 24.00
Mixed Grilled Plate (Rabbit, Lamb, Sausage and Quail)

BISTECCA FIORENTINA (for two) 45.00
Large Porterhouse Steak Grilled

CALAMARI CON AGLIO 14.00
Tender Squid Sauteed in Oil, Garlic, Tomato and Spices

SCAMPI AND SCALLOPS-AL-TIMO 20.00
Shrimp and Bay Scallops Sauteed with Butter, Garlic, Thyme, Cognac and a hint of Tomato

RED SNAPPER ALLA GRIGLIA 22.00
A Whole Red Snapper, Basted with Oil, Garlic, Lemon, Spices and Broiled

ARAGOSTA COMBINATA 26.00
Half a Lobster Sauteed in a Red Sauce Served with Shrimp, Bay Scallops, Calamari, Mussels and Clams

VERDURA MISTA SAUTEE 14.00
Mixed Seasonal Vegetables Sauteed with Olive Oil and Garlic

INSALATA CENT' ANNI 14.00
Vegetarian Salad with Seasonal Vegetables

Dinner: 7 Days a Week 5:30 - 11:30

Pino Luongo's reputation for serving excellent, authentic Italian specialties has led to this being one of the most popular, hard-to-get-into places on the Upper East Side. The decor is extremely attractive, as is the clientele.

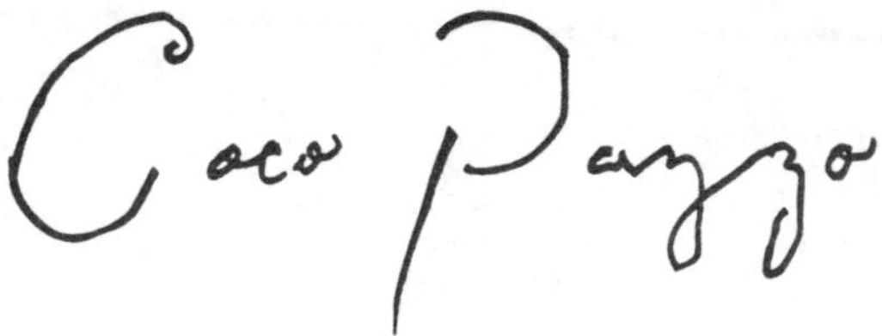

Menu Changes Seasonally

Antipasti

Antipasto Pazzo **8.00**
A tasting of cold appetizers from the crazy chef

Misto di Mare **8.50**
Selection of marinated and cured fish with sliced tomato and arugula

Funghi alla Griglia Con Insalatina di Patate e Caprino **9.00**
Grilled assorted mushrooms served on a salad of curly endive, potatoes and goat cheese

Spiedino di Calamari **8.50**
Skewers of squid lightly breaded, roasted and garnished with marinated tomatoes

Gnocchi alla Romana con Funghi e Olio di Tartufo **9.00**
Semolina dumplings with sauteed mushrooms and truffle oil

Salsiccia Fatta in Casa con Broccoli di Rape **8.00**
Assorted homemade sausages with broccoli rabe

Pasta *served in appetizer portions*

Spaghetti all' Aglio, Olio e Pomodoro **10.50**
...with olive oil, garlic, crushed red pepper and tomato

Orecchiette con Salsiccie e Broccoli di Rape **11.50**
...with hot and sweet sausage, broccoli rabe and garlic

Tagliolini ai Funghi e Vegetali **11.50**
Fresh homemade pasta with sauteed mushrooms and spring vegetables

Spaghetti alla Sapore di Mare **12.50**
Assorted seafood sauteed with olive oil, garlic, crushed red pepper and a splash of tomato

Full portions of pasta available

Secondi Piatti

Pesce

Pesce Arrosto del Giorno Roasted fish of the day	**24.00**
Fettina di Tonno Scottato con Salsa di Mostarda Carpaccio of seared tuna topped with salad and balsamic and mustard dressing	**24.00**
Acquapazza Assorted shellfish in a spicy broth of tomato, white wine, olives and capers	**24.00**
Cous Cous con Brodo di Pesce Steamed cous cous with poached fish and shellfish	**24.50**

Carne

Faraona con Cipolla e Pancetta con Vino Rosso Breast of guinea hen, roasted then braised in red wine with onions and pancetta	**28.00**
Osso Buco con Erbe e Pure di Patate Traditional braised veal shank with white wine and fresh herbs, served with mashed potatoes	**24.00**
Tagliata alla Fiorentina Black Angus rib-eye steak seared with olive oil and grilled with rosemary	**28.50**
Polletto alla Campagnola Spicy grilled baby chicken with zucchini, onion, potatoes and pancetta	**23.00**
Costolette di Agnello con Carciofi alla Giudea Roasted rack of lamb seasoned with garlic and herbs served with Roman Jewish style baby artichokes	**28.50**

Contorni Caldi

Rapine Saltate in Padella Broccoli rabe sauteed with garlic, olive oil and hot pepper	**6.00**
Patate Paesana Sauteed potatoes with onions, peas, pancetta and zucchini	**4.50**
Asparagi con Burro e Parmigiano Steamed spring asparagus with butter and parmesan cheese	**7.00**

Chef: Mark Strausman

Dinner: Mon - Sat 6 - 12, Sun 6 - 11

A good location near museums, hotels, shopping and Carnegie Hall, plus quality northern Italian cooking and a sleek interior have added up to a winning ticket. There aren't many other "modern" Italians in the immediate area.

CORRADO

Menu Changes Seasonally Along With Daily Specials

First Course

Minestrone
$5.50

Garden Salad
Mixed Greens With Basil and a Sherry Vinaigrette $6.95

Crispy Roast Duck Salad
with Cucumber, Arugula, Endive , Caramelized Onions, and a Walnut Vinaigrette $7.95

Arugula Salad
Wrapped in Grilled Eggplant, with a Balsamic Tomato Vinaigrette and Shaved Parmesan $7.95

Caesar Salad Frisee
with Pumpernickel Croutons $7.50

Bruschetta
Grilled Bread with Tomatoes, Mozzarella, Garlic and Basil $6.95

Homemade Mozzarella
with Roasted Peppers $7.95

Grilled Portabello Mushrooms
with an Herbed Garlic Sauce $7.25

Cornmeal Crusted Calamari
Spicy Red Sauce $7.95

Warm Seafood Salad
with Scallops, Shrimp, Calamari, Mussels Sundried Tomatoes, Fennel and Lemon $9.95

Goat Cheese and Broccoli Salad
with Potato Crisps, Crispy Greens and a Sherry Vinaigrette $7.95

Entrees

Gnocchi of the Day
$14.50

Wild Mushroom Risotto
$18.95

Risotto Arrabbiata
with Fresh Mozzarella $17.50

Rigatoni Salsicce
Hot and Sweet Sausages, Tomatoes, Peppers, and Cream $14.75

Manila Clam Linguine
with Grilled Vegetables and White Wine $15.50

Penne With Mozzarella
Tomatoes, Crushed Red Pepper and Basil $13.95

Farfalle
Bow Tie Pasta with Grilled Chicken, Grilled Vegetables
Smoked Mozzarella and a Spicy Garlic Sauce $14.95

Grilled Salmon
with Grilled Polenta and Black Bean Salsa $19.95

Grilled Aged Strip Loin
with Steamed Spinach and a Caper Vinaigrette $21.50

Sea Scallops
with a Corn, Cumin and Cilantro Salad, Grilled Asparagus $18.50

Grilled Yellowfin Tuna Ceviche
Served Rare with Julienne Vegetables and a Jalepeno, Cilantro,
Lime Barbeque Sauce $21.00

Herbed Chicken Paillard
with Grilled Potatoes, and a Vegetable Ragout $17.50

Tiger Shrimp With Grilled Polenta
Tomatoes, Crushed Red Pepper and Garlic $19.50

Roasted Breast of Duck
with Mashed Potatoes, Vegetable Flan and a Black Currant Sauce $19.50

Roasted Loin of Lamb
with Sauteed Wild Mushrooms, Sweet White Runner Bean Salad
and a Black Pepper Balsamic Vinegar Sauce $20.95

Dinner: 7 Days a Week 5:15 - 11:15

This storefront space, decorated in charming Provencal prints, serves Italian food that's as good as anything in or out of Connecticut. It's always packed, especially on weekends.

Menu Changes Seasonally

APPETIZERS

Insalata Di Frutta Dimare
Hot seafood salad.
$9.95

Insalata Della Casa
DaPietro's special salad prepared with radicchio, baby bib lettuce, arugula, gorgonzola cheese, finished with imported olive oil and balsamic vinegar.
$7.95

PASTA

Fettucine Alla Caterina
Fettucine prepared with smoked salmon, fresh tomatoes, basil, dill and creme fraiche.
$19.95

Capellini Alla Pietro
Grilled sea scallops, fresh spinach, green onions served over capellini, finished with imported olive oil.
$17.95

36 Riverside Ave • Westport, CT • (203) 454-1213

Coccioline Arrabbiata
Shells with fresh tomatoes, garlic, hot crushed pepper and imported olive oil.
$17.95

ENTREES

Noisette D'Agneau Provencal
Braised loin of lamb with garlic, imported olive oil, finished with white wine and fresh herbs.
$23.95

Crevettes Au Marsielles
Sauteed shrimp, finished with fresh fennel, pernot and saffron.
$19.95

Saumon Grillè
Grilled Norwegian salmon, finished with balsamic vinegar, olive oil and fresh mint.
$21.95

Scaloppini Di Vitello Ai Tre Moschettieri
Sauteed veal with pistachio nuts, shallots, finished with light cream and cognac.
$22.95

DESSERTS

Profiteroles Au Chocolat
Puff pastry filled with ice cream, covered with hot chocolate sauce.
$6.95

Torta Di Cioccolata
A very special chocolate velvet cake.
$6.95

Dinner: Mon - Sat 5 - 10

As common a practice as it is now, a waiter reciting a long list of the day's specials originated with Da Silvano - as well as high prices for those specials. Even so, the restaurant remains a popular Village standby for well-prepared Italian food.

Da Silvano

Menu Changes Seasonally

Antipasti

Crostini
chicken liver, capers, anchovies & onions
sauteed, roughly chopped, served on Italian bread **5.50**

Carpaccio
mixed fish or meat **10.50**

Panzanella
cold bread salad with roasted peppers, tomatoes,
cucumbers & onions, seasoned with herbs, oil/vinegar **5.50**

Insalata di polpo
fresh octopus with olive oil, hearts of celery, diced
fresh tomato **7.50**

Pesce

Langostine catalana
large prawns sauteed in olive oil topped
with a julienne of fennel, celery, scallions
& tomatoes **24.50**

Pesce del giorno
fish of the day **A.T.**

Pasta

Rigatoni focaccia
rigatoni, double smoked bacon, sage, garlic, white wine, cream, tomato & parmigiano **12.50**

Spaghettini puttanesca
"spaghettini whore style." chunks of tomatoes, garlic, black olives, capers & anchovies **12.50**

Tortellini alla panna
meat filled tortellini sauteed with heavy cream, parmigiano & butter **12.50**

Carni

Pollastrello all diavola
roast cornish hen, cracked open, marinated in olive oil & cayenne pepper **14.50**

Fegato alla salvia
a very thin slice of calf's liver sauteed with butter & sage **15.50**

Scaloppine Silvano
veal scaloppine, cream & mushrooms **16.50**

Controfiletto Robespierre
grilled boneless shell steak, sliced, topped with green pepper corns & fresh rosemary **19.50**

Lombatina alla griglia
grilled rack of veal chop **24.50**

Dinner: Mon - Fri 6 - 11, Sat - Sun 6 - 11:30

Da Umberto continues the latest trend in Italian restaurants of sponged ochre walls, a mouth-watering antipasto display and a simple, authentic menu. The restaurant critics love it.

RISTORANTE daUMBERTO

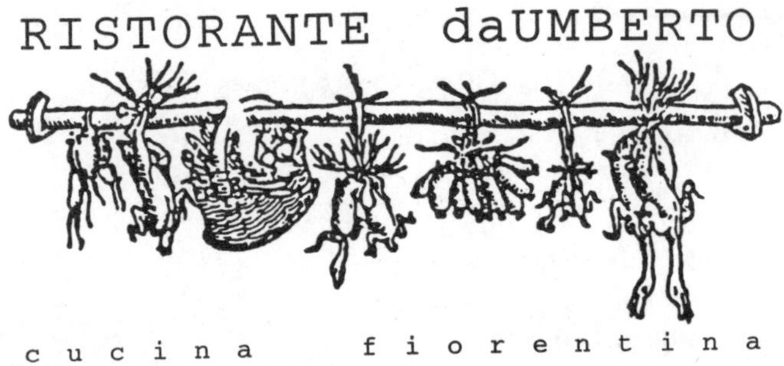

c u c i n a f i o r e n t i n a

Menu Specials Change Daily

Bresaola con carciofi
Carpaccio con parmigiano
Proscíutto con melone
Insalata di pesce
Crostini del giorno
Antipasto della casa
Insalata capricciosa

9.00

Ribollita Minestrone

5.75

Lasagne del giorno 16.00
Gnocchi all'arrabbiata 14.00
Farfalle al pesto 14.00
Capellini con aragosta 16.00

107 West 17th St • Chelsea • (212) 989-0303

Coniglio al forno 20.00
Veal Chop con cognac 26.00
Quaglie farcita 22.00
Pollo Val'dostana 18.00
Trippa Fiorentina 15.00
Zuppa di pesce 22.00
Pesci del giorno p.a.
Spiedini di scampi 20.00

Veal Scaloppine all'Umberto 18.00
Fegato di vitello alla salvia 16.00
Bistecca alla Fiorentina per due 48.00
Paillard di Pollo con Erbe 16.00
Paillard di vitello 18.50
Calamari affogati 15.00

Indivia con gorgonzola 7.50
Insalata tricolore 5.00

Dinner: Mon - Thurs 5:30 - 11, Fri - Sat 5:30 - 11:30

Adman Jerry Della Femina and restaurateur Drew Nieporent opened this contemporary Italian restaurant and Chef Pat Trama creates the innovative menu of pastas and grills to immediate acclaim and success. Reservations are the most difficult ticket in town.

Della Femina

Menu Changes Daily

Soup of the Day	7.
Sweet Stuffed Red Pepper	8.
Romaine Lettuce with Parmesan, Caesar Dressing	9.
Endive, Watercress & Roquefort with Bacon	9.
House Cured Duck Prosciutto with Grilled Mushrooms	9.
Field Green Salad, Red Wine Vinaigrette	7.
Crab Cake with Tomato & Balsamic Vinegar	9.

Orecchiette with Broccoli Rabe, Crushed Red Pepper & Garlic	19.
Penne with Sausage, Peas, Tomato and Cream	18.
Spaghetti with Shrimp, Baby Artichokes & Basil	19.

Rigatoni with Spring Lamb Bolognese	17.
Barbecued Duck with Whipped Sweet Potatoes	22.
Roast Chicken with Baby Artichokes & Soft Polenta	21.
Fish of the Day with Warm Vegetable Tart	P/A.
Grilled Salmon with Lentils & Beets	22.
Grilled Rib Eye Steak with Roast Potato & Porcini Butter	26.
Roasted Quail with Black Truffles & Baby Leeks	24.

Warm Valrhona Chocolate Cake	7.
Frozen Passionfruit Souffle	6.
Creme Brulee	6.
Sarsaparilla Float	6.
Banana Financier with Blueberries	6.

Chef Pat Trama

Pastry Chef Kevin Penner

Dinner: Mon - Thurs 6 - 10, Fri - Sat 6 - 11, Sun 5:30 - 10

Many New Yorkers travel to the Bronx for the traditional family atmosphere and "red sauce" Italian cooking here. In fact, it's just about the only place Manhattanites do go in the Bronx. It's what you think of when you want old-fashioned Italian.

Menu Changes Daily

When you "come home" to Dominick's, the dining is unique. No written menus, no chalk boards with specials, and no waiters with attitudes. There are **no rules to dining** at Dominick's.

2335 Arthur Ave • Brooklyn • (718) 733-2807

Some of the most popular dishes you can ask for include Stuffed Artichokes, Baked Clams, and our sumptuous Antipasto. Dominick's delicious entrees include:

Linguini with Shrimp
Linguini Alla John
Chicken Scarpariella
Roast Pork
Stuffed Veal
Shrimp Oreginati
Zuppa Di Pesce
and
on Sundays only, our famous Pasta Platter

At Dominick's there are no menus, and remember, its **no rules dining!**

Dinner: 7 Days a Week until 10

Ecco opened downtown near City Hall before TriBeCa existed and became trendy. It's housed in a 19th-century bar; the food has always been considered excellent, though expensive for the neighborhood.

Menu Changes Seasonally

Antipasti Freddi

Antipasto Assortito — From 9.95
Assorted antipasti from our table

Bufala Mozzarella Campagnola (Ecco) — 9.95
Imported mozzarella, tomato, onion, roasted peppers

Prosciutto Di Parma E Melone — 9.95
Imported parma, prosciutto and melon

Pasta

Penne Arrabiata — 15.95
Spiced marinara with dry porcini mushrooms

Linguine Ai Frutti Di Mare — 16.95
Seafood on light marinara sauce

Spaghetti Bolognese — 16.95
Bolognese meat Sauce

Pesce

Zuppa Di Pesce Alla Livornese — 27.95
Italian bouillabaisse with lobster

Pescato Del Giorno — P.A.
Catch of the day from Fulton Fish Market

124 Chambers St • TriBeCa/Downtown/Chinatown • (212) 227-7074

Veal Scaloppine

Al Limone 20.95
Lemon, butter and white wine

Alla Pizzaiola 20.95
Tomato, black olive, garlic, oregano and parsley

Alla Ecco 21.95
Artichokes, grated cheese, cream and white wine

Pollo

Pollo Campagnola 18.95
Sausage, peppers, mushrooms and artichokes

Pollo Con Carciofi E Prosciutto 18.95
Artichokes, prosciutto and white wine

Pollo Alla Scarpariello 18.95
Sausage, garlic and rosemary

Pollo Alla Salvia 18.95
Chicken breast, sage and white wine

Costoletta

Alla Griglia 26.95
Best grilled in New York

Con Salvia 26.95
Sage, butter, garlic and white wine

La Famosa Valdostana 26.95
Stuffed with prosciutto, mozzarella, in mushroom sauce

Paillard 24.95
Rosemary, garlic and black peppers

Bistecca

Alla Griglia 28.95
Grilled shell steak, steak-house style

Alla Pizzaiola 28.95
Tomato, black olives, garlic, oregano and parsley

Dinner: Mon - Sat 5 -12

Although it's usually panned for its uninspired Italian food, none of the regulars care. This is a mecca for several generations of the famous and would-be famous, where artists, writers, and movie stars have hung out for 25 years.

Elaine's

APPETIZERS

Grilled Shrimp on Garlic Toast 8.00

Clams on the Half Shell 6.50

Antipasto 8.75

Melon & Prosciutto 7.50

Calamari Fritti (For Two) 10.75

Prosciutto, Buffalo Mozzarella Roasted Peppers 9.50

Baked Clams 7.00

Seafood Salad 8.00

Zucchini Fritte 6.00

Steamed Mussels (For Two) 10.75

Beef Carpaccio 10.75

Grilled Vegetables with Goat Cheese 7.75

PESCE

Shrimp Fra Diavolo 18.00

Zuppa di Pesce 19.75

Broiled Scallops with Butterflied Zucchini 19.75

1703 Second Ave • Upper East Side • (212) 534-8103

CARNE

Veal Scallopini Piccata 15.75

Veal Marsala with wild mushrooms 16.00

Veal Saltimbocca 16.75

Veal Milanese & Tri-Color Salad 17.75

Chicken Limone with Rosemary 15.75

Broiled Veal Chop 23.75

Broiled Sirloin Steak 21.75

Shrimp & Scallops Provencale 18.75

PASTA

Capellini with Roman Mushrooms & Sage Butter 15.75

Fettuccine Primavera 12.00

Linguini with Clam Sauce... 12.50

Tortelloni with Peas & Prosciutto 13.00

Spaghetti Bolognese 12.00

Spaghetti Squash Vegetable Marinara 13.00

VEGETABLES

Spinach 5.75

Asparagus 6.75

Broccoli 5.75

String Beans 5.75

Potato Fritti 6.00

7 Days a Week 5:30 - 2am

Erminia is one of those little places on the Upper East Side that tourist don't know about. But it has great, hearty food, a warm atmosphere, and the feeling that you are in on a secret.

Menu Changes Seasonally

Antipasti

Mozzarella Erminia *8.95*
(Homemade mozzarella with roasted peppers and tomatoes)

Carciolfi alla Giudia *8.95*
(Artichokes completely cooked in olive oil, garlic, in earthenware pan)

Grigliata di Vegetali *8.95*
(Assorted grilled vegetables)

Carpaccio Affumicato *9.95*
(Sliced smoked filet mignon)

Pasta

Orecchiette Erminia *15.95*
(Small shells with sausage and broccoli sauce)

Capellini Primavera *15.95*
(Very fine spaghetti with vegetables)

Fusilli con Radicchio *15.95*
(Spiral pasta with a sauce of sauteed radicchio)

Pappardelle Campagnola *16.95*
(Homemade noodles with artichokes, sausage, porcini and tomato)

Rotolo *16.95*
(Homemade pasta rolls stuffed with spinach, ricotta and mozzarella in a light tomato sauce)

Fettuccine Porcini *16.95*
(Homemade fettuccine with procini mushrooms and cream)

Fettuccine con Peperoni *16.95*
(Homemade fettuccine with roasted peppers, shallots and sun-dried tomatoes)

250 East 83rd St • Upper East Side • (212) 879-4284

Primi Piatti

Zuppa di Pesce 26.95
(Combination of snapper, scampi, squid, lobster, mussels in a marinara sauce)

Calamari in Cartoccio 18.95
(Calamari with tomato, garlic, basil and wine in a pouch)

Orata Erminia 24.95
(Snapper with balsamic vinegar, wine, carrots and shallots)

Orata al Balsamico 24.95
(Snapper with onions sauteed in balsamic vinegar, olive oil, garlic and white wine)

Pesce Spada alla Guidia 24.95
(Swordfish steak with onions, raisins and pine nuts)

Scampi Angela 20.95
(Jumbo scampi sauteed with white wine and served on arugula salad)

Scaloppina Ripiena di Funghi 19.95
(Veal scaloppine filled with mushroom duxelle in white wine sauce)

Scaloppine con Carciofi e Funghi 19.95
(Veal scaloppine sauteed with mushrooms, artichokes and rosemary)

Scaloppina Piccata 19.95
(Veal scaloppine sauteed with lemon and wine)

Pollo e Salsiccia 17.95
(Boneless chicken and sausage sauteed with fresh herbs and balsamic vinegar)

Grigliata

All Entrees are Grilled on Mesquite Wood

Pollo alla Legna 16.95
(Half boneless chicken)

Lombata di Vitello 23.95
(Veal Chop)

Costolette di Agnello 23.95
(Baby lamb chop)

Rollatini di Vitella allo Spiedo 21.95
(Stuffed veal rolls grilled on skewers)

Spiedino di Carne 19.95
(Skewers of Seafood)

Aragosta .... *priced accordingly*
(Grilled Lobster)

Dinner: Mon - Sat 5 - 11:30

Felidia introduced New Yorkers to a new level of Italian cuisine (it could now properly be called cuisine, not cooking). It has continued to offer a challenging combination of ingredients and preparations, all matched by an outstanding wine list.

Menu Changes Daily

MINESTRE & ANTIPASTI

MINESTRA DI VERDURE AL FINOCCHIO -
Vegetable stock with diced vegetables and fresh fennel $7.00

MINESTRA DI RISO E ASPARAGI -
Spring asparagus soup with rice and cheese crisps $8.00

CALAMARI FRITTI -
Pan fried calamari with spring greens $10.00

INSALATA DI PORCINI -
Fresh porcini salad with shaved parmigiano reggiano, rughetta, dressed with Ligurian olive oil $14.00

GAMBERONI ALLA GRIGLIA -
Spicy grilled large shrimp with braised radicchio trevisano $15.00

PORTOBELLO & PORCINI FRESCHI TARTUFATI ALLA GRIGLIA -
Sauteed portobello caps, procini, truffle paste and grilled polenta $14.00

PROSCIUTTO DI PARMA, MELONE E FRUTTI TROPICALI -
Prosciutto di Parma, melon, mango & papaya $12.00

INSALATA DI RADICCHIO PRIMO TAGLIO -
Radicchio and bean salad $9.00

243 East 58th St • Midtown East Side • (212) 758-1479

RISOTTI E PASTE

FUZI CON BROCCOLI DI RAPE -
Individually hand shaped (low egg) bow-tie pasta served in olive oil, garlic, crumbled sausage and broccoli di rape $18.00

TORTELLACCI ALLE ERBE E ORTICA -
Pillows of fresh pasta stuffed with nettle, scallions, swisschard, thyme and fresh ricotta cheese in a fresh sage sauce $18.00

PAGLIA E FIENO CAPRICCIOSE -
Egg and spinach trenette with guanciale, onion, fresh tomato and Tuscan peperocino $18.00

TORTELLINI ALLA FELICE -
Pasta hats stuffed with chicken, veal and vegetables in a light sauce of porcini, chicken liver, cream tomato and peas $18.00

All fresh pastas are made daily on premises.

PESCI E CARNI

PIANUZZA AL VAPORE -
Steamed halibut served with spicy vinaigrette, marinated cucumbers and red cabbage $28.00

SALMONE ALLA SENAPE -
Filet of atlantic salmon in a light dijon mustard sauce served with fennel and mashed potatoes and beets $29.00

PICCIONE AL FEGATO D'OCA -
Braised squab over savoy cabbage topped with foie gras $29.00

COSTOLETTA DI VITELLO CAPRICCIOSA -
Butterflied and breaded veal chop, pan fried served with a mountain of garden green and tomato $29.00

VALDOSTANA CON ASPARAGI -
Veal chop stuffed with spring asparagus and fontina cheese in a light carrot and lemon sauce, served with asparagus gratinati $29.00

OSSOBUCO CON RISOTTO D'ORZO -
Braised veal shank in a light tomato, white wine, celery and carrot sauce, flanked with barley risotto, zucchini, carrot specks and peas $28.00

Dinner: Mon - Sat 5 - 11

Although it's relatively new, Follonico has received excellent reviews from critics and patrons for the lovely, warm setting and excellent Tuscan food.

F O L L O N I C O

Menu Changes Daily

ANTIPASTI

Seared Diver Scallops with Blood Orange Vinaigrette and Marinated Fennel	$9.00
Baby Octopus under a Black Pasta Net	$9.50
Grilled Portobello Mushrooms with White Truffle Oil	$7.00
Deep-Fried Calamari with Crispy Mizuna and Capers	$7.00
Fiori di Zucca Stuffed with Ricotta and Fresh Mint	$8.50
Wood-Roasted Langoustines with Chervil and Lime	$10.00
Salad of Mixed Baby Lettuces with Extra-Virgin Olive Oil and Balsamic Vinegar	$5.50

PRIMI

Penne with Spicy Tomato Sauce	$8.50
Tortelli of Fresh Fava Beans with Butter and Parmigiano	$11.00
Orecchiette Tossed with Sweet Sausage and Bitter Broccoli	$9.00
Shellfish Ragout under Herb-Printed Fazzoletto	$11.00
Spaghetti with New Zealand Cockles, White Wine and Fresh Tomato	$11.00

6 West 24th St • Murray Hill/Kips Bay • (212) 691-6359

SECONDI

"Minute Steak" of Tuna with Caponata and Baby Red Mustard Greens	$18.50
Basil-Perfumed Baby Chicken with Roasted Vegetables	$17.50
Halibut Filet with Baby Artichokes and Fresh Thyme	$19.00
Whole Red Snapper Roasted in a Rock Salt Crust (For Two)	$44.00
Roast Turbans of Salmon and Asparagus	$18.00
Pan-Roasted Medallions of Veal with Morels and Fiddlehead Ferns	$24.00

CONTORNI
(Side Dishes)

Broccoli di Rape Sauteed with Garlic and Hot Pepper	$4.50
Mashed Yukon Gold Potatoes	$4.50
Cannellini Beans "all'Uccelletto"	$4.00
Wood Roasted Spring Vegetables	$5.00
Schiacciata with Rosemary	$4.00

WINES BY THE GLASS

White
Verdicchio dei Castelli di Jesi 1991, Colle Solato (Marches) — $5.00

Red
Salice Salentino 1987, Cantele (Puglia) — $5.50

Sparkling
Blanc de Blancs 1988, Scharffenberger (Mendocino County, CA) — $8.00

Dinner: Mon - Thurs 6 - 10:30, Fri - Sat 6 - 11

In a little over a year, Gabriel's has become a Lincoln Center hot spot. They serve excellent and original northern Italian cuisine, with lots of pastas and simple grilled meats in a spacious room decorated with huge modern paintings.

Bar and Restaurant

Menu Changes Seasonally

Specials

APPETIZERS

Buckwheat Polenta w/ Roasted Corn & Truffle Oil 10.00

PASTA

Rye Flour Agnolotti Stuffed w/ Lamb Topped w/ Rosemary Olive Oil 17.00
Taglitelle Pesto 14.00

ENTREES

Roasted Kid w/ Rosemary & White Wine 25.00

APPETIZERS

Vitello Tomato 10.00
Grilled Sea Scallop Tart w/ Tomato Oil & Sundried Tomatoes 12.00
Soft Polenta w/ Braised Mushrooms 9.00
Spicy Mussel Soup 9.00
Grilled Portobello Mushrooms with Garlic and Olive Oil 9.00
Mixed Lettuces w/ Sherry & Shallot Vinaigrette 6.5o
Arrugla w/ Balsamic Vinegar, Olive Oil & Parmesan Cheese 6.5o
Roasted Beets & Onions w/ Pea Sprouts & Walnut Dressing 7.5o

11 West 60th St • Lincoln Center • (212) 956-4600

PASTAS

Homemade Gnocchi with Tomato and Basil 13.00
Wild Mushroom filled Lasagne w/ Tomato & Romano Cheese 14.00
Half Moon Pasta stuffed w/ Spinach, Pine Nuts & aged Ricotta, in Tomato Sauce w/ Oregano 15.00
Pappardelle w/ Artichokes 17.00
Sweet Potato Agnolotti w/ Fresh Herbes 16.00
Risotto of the day P/A (approx. 30 min.)

ENTREES

Grilled Baby Chicken Marinated with Buttermilk & Rosemary 19.00
Grilled Calves Liver w/ Roasted Onions, Sage & Mashed Potatoes 23.00
Grilled Veal Chop w/ Mustard & Balsamic Vinegar 25.00
Roasted Salmon w/ Mixed Citrus Orange Oil & Asparagus 23.00
Whole Roasted Fish w/ White Wine, Fresh Herbs 24.00
Grilled One Pound Angus Strip Steak w/ Potato Cakes & Fresh Horseradish 26.00

Desserts

Chocolate & Caramel Flan w/ Fresh Berries 7.00
Peach & Poppyseed Upsidedown Cake w/ Raspberry Coulis 8.00
Chocolate Espresso Torte w/ Unsweetened Whipped Cream 8.00
Red Wine Roasted Pears w/ Sweet Polenta & Parmesan 8.00
Chocolate & Cherry Bread Pudding 8.00
Fresh Strawberries w/ Cream 7.00
Gelato, 6.00
(Chocolate, Vanilla, Lemon, Ricotta, Hazelnut) & Espresso
Toppings for Gelato: Hot Fudge, Warm Caramel, Brandied Fruit 1.00 Additional
Fresh Fruit Bellini 7.00

Dinner: Mon - Thurs 5:30 - 11, Fri - Sat 5:30 - 12

Girafe

This is a solid and dependable northern Italian place near Bloomingdale's that still pleases a loyal following of mostly older New Yorkers. The interior is sedate and comfortable and the food is very good.

Menu Changes Seasonally

Antipasti

Antipasto Caldo Della Casa	14.00
Melone e Prosciutto	11.00
Vongole Cassino	10.50
Shrimp Cocktail	13.00
Caprese	10.50
Spedino di Mozzarella	11.50

Farinacei

Spaghetti Carbonara	18.00
Fettuccine Alfredo	18.00
Paglia e Fieno	18.00
Spaghetti Bolognese	17.00

Pesce

Salmone alla Griglia	24.00
Zuppa di Pesce Veneziana	23.00
Scampi Fra Diavolo	26.00
Spigola al Brodetto	24.00

208 East 58th St • Midtown East Side • (212) 752-3054

Pollo

Scallopine di Pollo Umberto 19.50
Pollo Peperonata 19.50
Pollo Cacciatora 19.50
Pollo Scarpariello 19.50

Vitello

Saltinbocca alla Romana 21.50
Scallopine Martini 21.50
Cotoletta Parmigiana 21.50
Vitello Peperonata 21.50
Cotoletta Magenta con osso 25.00
Costoletta Del Priore 25.00
Scallopine Gracchi 21.50

Vegetali

Scarola 7.00
Fagiolini 7.00

Dolci

Fragole 8.00
Zabaglione al Marsala 10.00
Coppa ai Marroni 8.00
Melone in Stagione 8.00
Tartufo 7.50
Marchese di Salambo 6.00

Dinner: 7 Days a Week 5:30 - 10:30

Very European and elegant. Now that Cipriani has taken it over again, he has put new life in the food and decor and the location is one of the best in the city - on Fifth Avenue overlooking the Plaza and Central Park.

HARRY CIPRIANI

Menu Changes Daily

TONIGHT WE SUGGEST

MENU NO. 1 $ 42.95
Traditional fish soup
Veal spezzatino with asparagus
Choice of homemade cakes

MENU NO. 2 $ 49.95
Cold marinated salmon
Prime sirloin steak with red wine sauce
Choice of homemade sherbets

MENU NO. 3 $ 49.95
Tagliolini with fresh peas
Red snapper alla Milanese
Crepes a la creme

THE CLASSICS OF HARRY'S BAR IN VENICE

Pasta e fagioli	$ 10.95
Traditional fish soup	$ 13.95
Baked tagliolini with ham	$ 19.95
Risotto alla Primavera	$ 21.95
Riso pilaf alla Valenziana	$ 23.95
Fish of the day alla Carlina	$ 32.95
Calves liver alla Venziana	$ 28.95
Chicken curry with rice pilaf	$ 25.95
Carpaccio alla Cipriani	$ 27.95
Crepes a la creme	$ 12.95

HARRY'S GRILL

Half free range chicken
$ 25.95

Calves liver
$ 28.95

Prime Beef Sirloin
or Lamb chops
$ 31.95

Fish of the day
$ 32.95

All served with vegetables

APPETIZERS AND FIRST COURSES

Fresh polenta with veal ragu'	$ 10.95
Carrot soup	$ 10.95
Minestrone soup	$ 10.95
Fagioli in saor	$ 10.95
Asparagus vinaigrette	$ 10.95
Vegetables ratatouille	$ 10.95
Tomato and fresh mozzarella	$ 11.95
Cold marinated salmon	$ 20.95
Prosciutto di Parma with rucola or melon	$ 21.95
Special lobster and shrimp salad	$ 23.95

PASTA

Tagliardi with veal ragu'	$ 19.95
Tagliolini with fresh peas	$ 19.95
Tagliatelle alla Sbiraglia	$ 19.95
Spinach and cheese Cannelloni with eggplant	$ 21.95
Basked veal ravioli with ham	$ 21.95
Risotto with Mushrooms	$ 21.95

MAIN COURSES

Fried calamari with a green salad	$ 25.95
Salmon in wine with zucchini	$ 29.95
Sword fish alla Livornese	$ 29.95
John Dory with artichokes	$ 32.95
Red snapper alla Milanese	$ 32.95
Free range chicken in umido	$ 25.95
Veal spezzatino with asparagus	$ 25.95
Veal farfalle alla Pizzaiola	$ 30.95
Veal chop with butter and sage	$ 33.95
Veal Milanese with vegetables	$ 33.95
Veal kidney saute' with risotto alla Milanese	$ 28.95

DESSERTS

Choice of home made ice cream	$ 8.95
Choice of home made cakes	$ 10.95

Dinner: Mon - Sat 6 - 10:45, Sun 6 - 9

You feel you are in a Tuscan farmhouse when you dine at Il Cantinori: "charming" and "rustic" come to mind immediately. The food continues this theme, with hearty, authentic pastas and grills that have made this a popular spot for years.

IL CANTINORI

Menu Changes Weekly

ANTIPASTI

CARPACCIO E SEDANI IN BAGNACAUDA 11.00
(CELERY WRAPPED WITH RAW FILET MIGNON WITH A GARLIC DIP)

CALAMARI ALLA GRIGLIA 9.50
(FRESH SQUID SEASONED WITH BREADCRUMBS AND GRILLED)

GRIGLIATA DI FUNGHI E VERDURE MISTE 9.00
(GRILLED WILD MUSHROOMS AND VEGETABLES)

INSALATA DI MARE 12.50
(SEAFOOD SALAD, TUSCAN STYLE)

FUNGHI MISTI CON RUGOLA 9.50
(SAUTEED WILD MUSHROOMS OVER ARRUGOLA)

CAPESANTE AL LIMONE 9.50
(SCALLOPS SAUTEED WITH WINE, LEMON, AND BUTTER)

FEGATINI DI POLLO CON FINOCCHI 9.00
(CHICKEN LIVERS SAUTEED WITH BROWN BUTTER)

MINESTRE

CREMA DI OSTRICHE 10.75
(OYSTER STEW)

CACCIUCCO AI FUNGHETTO 9.75
(MUSHROOM SOUP)

PASTE

FETTUCCINE ALL'ARAGOSTA 23.50
(PASTA WITH LOBSTER)

SPAGHETTI ALLA RUSTICA 17.50
(PASTA WITH TOMATO SAUCE)

GNUDINI ALLA FIORENTINA 17.50
(SPINACH AND RICOTTA DUMPLINGS WITH BROWN BUTTER)

FARFALLE CON PUMATE 19.00
(BOWTIE PASTA WITH SUN-DRIED TOMATOES)

RAVIOLI AL FUNGHETTO 21.00
(RAVIOLI IN A CREAM AND MINCED MUSHROOM SAUCE)

PAPPARDELLA CON FAGIOLI E PESTO 21.00
(PASTA WITH CREAM, BEANS, AND PESTO)
RIGATONI AL SUGO DI RAGU 18.00
(PASTA WITH A MEAT SAUCE)
RISOTTO CON ASPARAGI 22.00
(RICE STEW WITH ASPARAGUS)

SECONDI PIATTI
CARNE

PETTO DI POLLO AL FUNGHETTO 22.00
(BREAST OF CHICKEN STUFFED WITH PROSCIUTTO)
POLLETTO AL LIMONE 24.50
(FREE RANGE CHICKEN BROILED WITH LEMON AND SAGE)
OSSOBUCO AL TARRAGONE CON RISO 23.00
(VEAL SHANK STEWED WITH TARRAGONE)
FEGATO DI VITELLA ALLA SALVIA 19.50
(CALF'S LIVER WITH BROWN BUTTER AND SAGE)
COSTOLETTE DI AGNELLO A SCOTTADITO 24.50
(RACK OF LAMB, BROILED)
ARISTA DI MAIALE AL FORNO CON PATATE 19.00
(LOIN OF PORK ROASTED SERVED WITH POTATOES)
SCALOPPINE ALLE ERBE FRESHE 22.00
(VEAL MEDALLIONS SAUTEED WITH FRESH HERBS)

PESCE

PESCE DEL GIORNO
(FISH OF THE DAY)

INSALATE

INSALATA ALLA PAESANA 9.00
(RUGOLA SALAD WITH ONIONS AND BEANS)
INSALATA TRICOLORE 9.00
(RUGOLA, ENDIVE, AND RADICCHIO)
INSALATA DI INDIVIA 9.00
(ENDIVE SALAD)

DOLCI

(YOUR WAITER WILL DESCRIBE THE DESSERTS)

PLEASE NO CIGAR OR PIPE SMOKING.

Dinner: Sun - Thurs 6 - 11:30, Fri - Sat 6 - 12

Il Giglio

Playing on its relationship with the ever-popular Il Mulino, this gentrified Italian restaurant way downtown draws a mostly male crowd of business types. In the evening, limos from New Jersey line up at the door.

IL GIGLIO

Menu Changes Seasonally

—— ANTIPASTI ——

Prosciutto e Melone 7.25 Antipasto Freddo 7.25 Vongole Oreganata 9.00

Vongole Cassino 9.00 Scampi Oreganata 12.75 Antipasto Caldo 9.00

—— ZUPPE ——

Stracciatella Fiorentina 6.25 Pastina in Brodo 6.25

Tortellini in Brodo 6.25

—— PASTA ——

Spaghettini Carbonara 14.00 Spaghettini Alle Vongole 16.75

Paglia Fieno Papalina 14.00 Spaghettini Bolognese 14.00

Tortellini Alla Panna 14.00

—— PESCE ——

Vongole Posillipo 19.75 Calamari Fradiavolo 17.50

Scampi Fradíavolo 20.75 Scampi Alla Romana 20.75

Scampi Alla Francese 20.75 Snapper Marechiaro 19.75

81 Warren St • TriBeCa/Downtown/Chinatown • (212) 571-5555

CARNI

Saltimbocca Alla Fiorentina 18.75
Veal sautéed with Sage & Prosciutto

Pollo Alla Romana 17.25
Morsels of Chicken braised in Wine & Artichokes

Piccata Di Vitello Al Limone 18.75
Veal sautéed in Lemon & Butter

Pollo Scarpariello 17.25
Morsels of Chicken sautéed with Garlic & Wine

Scaloppine Di Vitello Pizzaiola 18.75
Veal sautéed with Tomato, Mushrooms, Peppers

Petto Di Pollo Sorrentina 17.25
Breast of Chicken with Prosciutto, Eggplant & Fontina

Costoletta Di Vitello Parmigiana 22.75
Breaded Veal Chop, Tomato Sauce & Mozzarella

Pollo Al Cognac 17.25
Morsels of Chicken with Cream, Mushrooms & Cognac

Scaloppine Alla Romana 18.75
Veal sautéed with fresh baby Artichokes

Vitello Alla Zingara 18.75
Spicy Veal sautéed with Anchovies, Capers & Mushrooms

Scaloppine Di Vitello Alla Marsala 18.75
Veal sautéed with Mushrooms & Marsala

Ceasar Salad 7.00 Rugola 7.00 Endive 7.00 Insalata Mista 7.00

Spinaci All' Aglio e Olio 7.00 Zucchini Fritti 7.00

Broccoli All' Aglio e Olio 7.00

Dolci Assortiti Frutta Di Stagione

Zabaglione (per 2)

Caffé Thé Expresso

Dinner: Mon - Fri 5 - 10:30

Il Nido has been one of the top Italian restaurants for years, with dependable quality, huge portions, and an established crowd.

ANTIPASTI

SALAME e PEPERONI 12.00
Salami and roast peppers

INSALATA di FUNGHI FRESCHI 12.00
Fresh mushroom salad

BRESAOLA 14.00
Fine sliced air dry special beef

MELANZANE PARMIGIANA 11.00

CARPACCIO ASSORTITO 16.00

IL GIARDINO alla GRIGLIA 15.00

MINESTRE

PASTA e FAGIOLI 8.00
Macaroni and bean soup

CAPPELLETTI in BRODO 8.00
Dumplings in broth

ZUPPA di SPINACI 8.00
Spinach in broth

PASTA

FETTUCCINE "IL MONELLO"............ 20.00
RISOTTO con PORCINI 24.00
TORTELLINI ai QUATTRO FORMAGGI 20.00
RAVIOLI MALFATTI 20.00
RISOTTI "NIDO" 24.00
SPAGHETTI a PIACERE 20.00

251 East 53rd St • Midtown East Side • (212) 753-8450

CARNI

SALCICCIA PIZZAIOLA 26.00
Italian sausage

INTERCOSTA di MANZO 30.00
Prime sirloin steak

PAILLARD di MANZO 30.00
Butterflyed Sirloin Steak

COSTOLETTA BOLOGNESE 30.00

FRITTO MISTO ALL'ITALIANA per 2 .... 60.00
Fried meats for 2

COSTOLETTE D'AGNELLO MILANESE ... 29.00

COSTATA D'AGNELLO per 2 .... 60.00

LEGUMI

FUNGHETTI TRIFOLATI 7.00
Mushroom saute

CARCIOFINI DORATI 6.00
Artichokes golden saute

SPINACI SALTATI 6.00
Spinach saute

TESTE di FUNGHI DORATI 6.00
Mushroom caps

INSALATE

ENDIVIA BELGA (in season) 7.00

FAGIOLINI e BARBABIETOLE 6.00
String Beans and Beets

INSALATA di POMODORI 6.00
Sliced tomato

DOLCI

TORTA di CIOCCOLATO 7.00

TORTA ST. ONORATO 7.00
Gatteau St. Honore

ZUPPA INGLESE 7.00
English trifle

TORTA di FORMAGGIO 7.00
Cheese Cake

CREPES SUZETTE (for two) 26.00

Dinner: Mon - Sat 5 - 11

People who wonder what New York-style pizza is all about must try John's. It's baked in a blackened wood-burning brick oven and emerges with a thin, crisp crust and tasty, fresh toppings. That's why the line always snakes down the block.

John's of Bleecker St.

Original Brick Oven Pizza

Pasta Specialties

Home Made Stuffed Shells $6.25

Shells stuffed with fresh Ricotta and Mozzarella cheese, cooked with plum tomatoes

Home Made Stuffed Shells and Meatballs $7.25

Home Made Stuffed Shells and Sausage $8.00

Home Made Ravioli $5.75

Home Made Ravioli and Meatballs $6.75

Home Made Ravioli and Sausage $7.50

Home Made Manicotti $6.25

Long Noodles filled with Ricotta and Mozzarella cheese with savory sauce baked in the oven.

Home Made Manicotti and Meatballs $7.25

Home Made Manicotti and Sausage $8.00

Home Made Cavatelli $5.75

Home Made Cavatelli and Meatballs $7.25

Home Made Cavatelli and Sausage $8.00

Please specify Marinara or Bolonase sauce

Garlic Bread .... Sm. $2.50 Lg. $5.00

408 East 64th St • Greenwich Village • (212) 935-2895 • (Call For Other Locations)

Salad of the Day

Fresh crisp salad served with croutons and red onions, fresh mushrooms and a special House dressing. Served with fresh crisp Italian bread (on Request) $4.25

Extras

Sausage Rolls (6) $4.00

Spinach Rolls (6) $5.50

Calzoni

A half moon-shaped pocket of dough stuffed with fresh Ricotta and Mozzarella cheese and pieces of sausage baked to perfection $11.00

Pizza

"All Pizzas are Made to Order Please be Patient."

Items on 1/4 or 1/2 Part of Pizza as Listed Extra • Cheese 1.00 • Essence 75¢ (Garlic)

54 varieties of Pizza - a sampling follows:

Pizza Bianca (no tomatoes) $8.50

Marinara (no cheese) $3.50

Cheese, onions & tomatoes $8.75

Cheese, sliced meatballs & tomatoes $10.00

Cheese, tomatoes, anchovies, & peppers $10.50

Cheese, tomatoes, mushrooms & sausage $10.50

Cheese, tomatoes, sausage, onions & peppers $10.75

Cheese, tomatoes, sausage & meatballs $10.50

Cheese, tomatoes, onions & peppers $10.25

Cheese, tomatoes, onions, meatballs & peppers $10.75

Cheese, tomatoes, anchovies, sausage, peppers & mushrooms $11.50

Cheese, tomatoes, anchovies, sausage, peppers & onions $11.25

Cheese, tomatoes, anchovies, sausage, peppers, mushrooms & sliced meatballs $12.00

Cheese, tomatoes, anchovies, sausage, peppers, meatballs, onions & mushrooms $12.25

We also have pepperoni, black olives, spinach

Dinner: Sun - Thurs until 11:30, Fri - Sat until 12:30

A warm, congenial, family-run atmosphere and unfancy Italian food draw lots of people to this Theater District restaurant. However, what makes it unique is the menu of Roman Jewish specialties that it serves after 8 pm.

LATTANZI

Specials Change Daily

ANTIPASTI

Carciofi alla Giudia 9.95
(artichoke cooked in olive oil, garlic)

Carne secca e concia 11.95
(homemade dry beef with marinated zucchini)

Caponata Ebraica, Mozzarella in carrozza, Supplì al telefono 10.95
(combination of marinated eggplants, fresh mozzarella and rice ball)

Stracciatella 8.95
(egg drop soup)

Boccette 10.95
(veal and chicken cooked in broth)

Zuppa di Broccoli 8.95
(broccoli, garlic, oil, fish stock)

PASTE

Bigoli con Salsa di Carciofi 14.95
(homemade pasta with artichoke sauce and pecorino)

Tortelloni di Pesce con Finocchio 14.95
(homemade seafood ravioli with braised fennel and raisins)

Penne con Zucchine 13.95
(short pasta with sautéed zucchini in olive oil)

Fettuccine allo stracotto 14.95
(homemade noodles, beef, tomatoes, onion)

Orecchiette al Tonno 13.95
(little ears with tomato, olive oil, garlic, tuna fish)

361 West 46th St • Theater District • (212) 315-0980

CARNE

Scaloppine ai Carciofi 18.95
(veal scaloppine with artichokes, garlic, onion)

Stinco di Manzo Brasato con Polenta 21.95
(braised beef shank with corn meal)

Arrosto di Vitello con Cipolla e Piselli 20.95
(veal roast with braised onions and peas)

Stracotto 17.95
(beef, tomatoes, onions)

Pollo Arrosto 15.95
(roast chicken with rosemary, garlic)

Agnello al Rosmarino 23.95
(lamb chops grilled, rosemary, garlic)

PESCE

Sogliola con Indivia 20.95
(fillet of sole with endive and vinegar)

Trigliette all' Ebraica 21.95
(red snapper, raisin, vinegar)

Scalopine di Salmone al Finocchio 20.95
(salmon scaloppine with fennel)

Zuppa di Pesce e Fagioli alla Veneta 23.95
(Venetian style fish stew)

DOLCI

Chocolate Mousse ... 6.45

Zabaglione Freddo .. 6.45

Napoleone 6.95

Tiramisu 6.95

Tartufo 6.45

Frutta Fresca 6.95

Fragole con Zabaglione 6.95

Dinner: Mon - Thurs 5 - 11, Fri - Sun 5 -12

Le Madri

When owner Pino Luongo was searching around for a new concept, he decided to import some of the great chefs from Italy—four mothers. Marta Pulini oversees the robust home-cooking that continues to remain a hit.

le Madri

R E S T A U R A N T

Spring Menu
Dinner

Menu Changes Seasonally

ANTIPASTI

Gelato di Parmigiano con Pere e Uva 7.50
Parmesan cheese "gelato" served with fresh pears and grapes

Insalata di Rucola e Indivia con Crostino al Caprino Caldo 8.00
Arugola and endive salad with a warm goat cheese crouton

Portobello e Cipolle Grigliati con Pomodori Marinati 8.00
Grilled portobello mushrooms with oven dried tomatoes and grilled red onion

Scaloppa di Salmone al Dragoncello con Insalatina di Finocchi 8.50
Seared salmon served with a fennel and orange salad in a black olive vinaigrette

Tonno Scottato con Lattughette e Olio All'Erba Cipollina 8.00
Seared fresh tuna carpaccio and baby greens dressed with chive oil

Quaglia alla Griglia con Polenta, Funghi e Porri Croccanti 8.50
Grilled quail with soft polenta, mushrooms and crispy fried leeks

Calamari e Zucchini Fritti 8.00
Squid and zucchini, lightly dusted in flour and deep fried

PASTA *In the Italian tradition... pasta is served as a first course*

Appetizer portion

Penne con Melanzane, Pomodoro e Provola Affumicata 11.50
...with eggplant, tomato and fresh herbs with diced smoked mozzarella

Panzotti di Ricotta e Spinaci con Burro e Pinoli 11.50
Homemade ravioli filled with ricotta cheese and spinach, tossed with butter and pine nuts

Gnocchetti del Giorno 11.50
Homemade potato dumplings, preparation changes daily

Garganelli con Zucchini, Radicchio e Speck 11.50
Homemade fresh pasta with julienned zucchini, radicchio and smoked prosciutto

Tagliolini allo Zafferano con Gamberi e Asparagi 12.50
Homemade thin saffron fettuccine with shrimp and asparagus, olive oil and garlic

Mezzaluna di Vitello con Sughetto al Rosmarino e Funghi 11.50
Half moon shaped ravioli filled with veal, in it's own juices with rosemary and mushrooms

168 West 18th St • Chelsea • (212) 727-8022

SECONDI PIATTI

Pesce del Giorno Arrosto . . . . P.A
Whole roasted fish of the day, served with roasted potatoes

Pesce del Giorno al Vapore 19.50
Fresh fish of the day steamed between lemon leaves, served with steamed vegetables

Guazzetto di Cernia con Verdurine, Vongole e Crostino all'aglio 22.00
Fillet of grouper braised with vegetables, clams and garlic croutons

Tagliata di Tonno con Insalata Tiepida di Melanzane e Peperoni 24.00
Fresh tuna steak grilled with crushed black peppercorns, served with a warm grilled eggplant and roasted pepper salad

Ossobuco con Risotto all'Ortolana 24.00
Veal shank, stewed with white wine, tomato and herbs, served with spring vegetable risotto

Costolette di Vitello alla Salvia con Stufatino di Carciofi e Patate 28.50
Veal chop seared with fresh sage, mushrooms, braised artichokes and potatoes

Fegato di Vitello al Balsamico con Cipolle e Polenta Grigliata 19.00
Calf's liver sauteed with balsamic vinegar, with onion compote and grilled polenta

Carre d'Agnello con Spinaci e Carciofi Fritti 28.50
Grilled rack of lamb in it's own juice with thyme, wilted spinach and crispy fried artichokes

From the Wood Burning Oven...

Polletto al Forno con Cime di Rape 19.50
Whole baby chicken, split and roasted, served with broccoli rabe and roast potatoes

CONTORNI CALDI

Patate Novelle Arrosto 4.50
Roasted new potatoes

Spinaci all'Aglio e Olio 5.50
Spinach sauteed with garlic and olive oil

Verdure al Vapore 6.00
Steamed vegetables

Broccoli di Rape in Padella 6.00
Broccoli rabe steamed with garlic and oil

INSALATA

Insalata di Stagione 6.50
A salad of seasonal greens

Insalata di Carciofini 8.00
Shavings of baby artichokes with lemon, olive oil and parmesan

****

Executive Chef: Marta Pulini   Chef di Cucina: Gianni Scappin

All major credit cards accepted

Cigar smoking allowed in the bar and lower level lounge

Dinner: Mon - Sat 6 - 12:30, Sun 6 - 10:30

You get the feeling you are in a '90s version of La Dolce Vita here. It has a classy clientele, authentic pastas and pizza, and a clean, bright interior accented with colorful Italian pottery.

MEZZOGIORNO

Menu Changes Seasonally

ANTIPASTI

Polpettine di melanzane al caprino con insalatina di campo **9.00**
eggplant croquettes with goat cheese and field salad

Carpaccio di salmone all'aneto e mostarda di miele **13.00**
salmon carpaccio with dill and honey mustard sauce

Carpaccio di pesce spada affumicato al salmoriglio **14.00**
smoked swordfish carpaccio with salmoriglio sauce

Pesce d'uovo alla Pontormo **9.00**
omelette with fontina cheese and fine herbs

INSALATE

Insalata tiepida calamari con avocado e pomodoro	**10.00**	*calamari sauteed with tomato and avocado*
Insalata Pollanca	**10.00**	*grilled chicken, frisee, celery, apple*
Insalata del contadino	**9.00**	*pear, caciotta, rucola, with champagne vinaigrette*
Insalata mediterranea	**10.00**	*tuna, potato, tomato, capers and onions with ginger oil*

IL CARPACCIO

Rucola e parmigiano	**13.00**	*rucola and parmesan*
Avocado e palmito	**13.00**	*avocado and hearts of palm*
Carciofi e parmigiano	**13.00**	*artichokes and parmesan*
Margherita	**13.00**	*mozzarella, tomato, basil*

LA GRIGLIA

Battuta di pollo alle erbe aromatiche e aceto balsamico	**14.00**	*chicken paillard with herbs and balsamic vinegar*
La tagliata alla Robespierre	**20.00**	*sliced sirloin steak with rucola and peppercorns*
Grigliata mista mare al salmoriglio	**18.00**	*grilled seafood combination with salmoriglio sauce*

195 Spring St • SoHo • (212) 334-2112

PRIMI PIATTI

Strozzapreti coi peperoni rossi e gialli **13.00**
with yellow and red peppers

Fusilli con lattuga e punte di asparagi **13.00**
with lettuce and asparagus tips

Cavatelli con tonno e piselli **13.00**
with tomato, tuna and green peas

Farfalle al pesto di melanzane e pecorino pepato **12.00**
with eggplant thyme sauce and peppery pecorino

Minigonne piccanti **12.00**
spicy sauce with fresh herbs, tomato, olives, capers

Maccheroncini alla crudaiola **13.00**
diced tomato, celery, fresh herbs, pecorino cheese

Tagliolini con gamberetti, rucola e pomodoro fresco **14.00**
with shrimp, fresh tomato and rucola

Penne alla Bisanzio **12.00**
with fresh tomato, basil and mozzarella

Trenette prezzemolate con vongole e olive alla maniera sarda **16.00**
with clams and olives sardinian style

Linguine nere sciué sciué **13.00**
black linguine in spicy sauce

Risotto del giorno **28.00**
risotto of the day (minimum 2 persons)

Raviolo dello chef del giorno **14.00**
raviolo of the day

Lasagna del giorno **13.00**
pasticcio of the day

La minestra regionale del giorno **8.00**
regional soup of the day

LA PIZZA

Pizza marinara .... **11.00** *with tomato, garlic, anchovy*
Pizza pugliese .... **11.00** *with tomato, onions, pecorino*
Pizza bianca al prosciutto crudo **14.00** *white pizza with prosciutto*
Pizza margherita .... **11.00** *with tomato, mozzarella and basil*

Dinner: Mon - Fri 6 - 1, Sat - Sun until 1

You could call Nanni's a golden oldie. It is one of the old school of Italian restaurants, serving quality standard fare rather than innovative anything. But it's still very popular with the businessmen's lunch crowd.

NANNI

Specials Change Daily

ANTIPASTI

Carpaccio a Piacere 12.00
(Raw beef any style)

Prosciutto e Melone 9.00
(Prosciutto with Melon)

Bresavalo al Olio Vergine 10.00
(Dry beef with virgine oil)

Insalata di Mare 9.00
(Roast Peppers with anchovy)

ZUPPE (Soup)

Pasta e Fagioli 8.00
(Pasta and bean soup)

Capellini in Brodo 8.00
(Angel hair in consumme)

PASTE (Macaroni)

Capellini alla Nanni 18.00
(Angel hair with Nanni sauce)

Tortellini Mantecati 18.00
(Tortellini with white sauce and prosciutto)

Fettuccine alla Bolognese 18.00
(Fettuccine with meat sauce)

Gnocchi alla Piemontese 18.00
(Potato dumpling with tomato and cheese)

Fusilli Puttanesca 18.00

Spaghetti al Filetto di Pomodoro 18.00

Rigatoni all'Arrabiata 18.00
(Pasta with tomato and basil 'spicy')

Risotto ai Porcini 23.00
(Rice with wild mushrooms)

Pasta served with salad.

146 East 46th St • Midtown East Side • (212) 697-4161 • (Call for Seasonal Hours)

PESCE (Fish)

Gamberi alla Basque 25.50
(Shrimp sauteed, garlic, tomato and mushrooms)

Calamari alla Luciana 22.00
(Squid in casserole)

Vongole alla Oreganate 8.50
(Clams oreganata)

Linguine alla Vongole 18.00
(Pasta with clam sauce)

Pesce Spada con Capperi 24.50
(Swordfish with capers)

Salmone al Barolo e Funghi 24.50
(Fresh salmon with barolo and mushrooms)

POLLAME (Chicken)

Pollo Scarpariello 23.50
(Chicken with lemon and garlic)

Scaloppine di Polla Pizzaiola 26.00
(Breast of Chicken with red spicy sauce)

VITELLO E MANZO (Veal and Beef)

Scalloppine Sorrentina 24.50
(Veal with eggplant and cheese)

Saltimbocca Romana 24.50
(Veal with prosciutto and sage)

Fegato alla Veneta 24.50
(Calf liver saute with onions)

Costolette di Vitello Sorpresa 27.00
(Veal chop with cheese and prosciutto)

Filetto di Manzo ai Ferri 27.00
(Broiled filet mignon)

Bistecca di Manzo ai Ferri 27.00
(Broiled sirloin steak)

Payllard di Manzo 26.00
(Beef Payllard)

Medaglioni di Filetto Nanni 26.50

CACCIA/STAGIONE (Game in season)

Quaglie
(Quail)

Cervo in Salmi con Polenta
(Venison with polenta)

Dinner: Mon - Fri 5:30 - 11

Orso is probably the most popular spot on Restaurant Row, located in the Theater District. It serves a lightish Italian menu specializing in salads, pastas, and pizza. It's also pretty good for celebrity-spotting.

Menu Changes Daily

APPETIZERS

Chicken soup with escarole and spinach	5.00
Grilled oyster mushroom and red onion salad with herbs and balsamic vinegar	8.00
White vegetable and lettuce salad with shaved parmesan	8.00
White anchovies and sicilian vegetable salad	8.00
Grilled bread with fontina cheese, chopped tomatoes and olives	7.00
Asparagus, gorgonzola and roasted pepper salad	8.00
Baby eggplant, endive, tomato and scallion salad	8.00
Mozzarella, basil and tomato salad	8.00
Arugula, radicchio and tomato salad with peppered sheep cheese	8.00
Grilled baby mozzarella wrapped with prosciutto and sage	8.00

PIZZA

Pizza bread with rosemary and oil	6.00
Pizza bread with garlic and oil	6.00
Flat pizza with mussels, anchovies, peppers, olives, tomatoes and onions	11.00
Small pizza with goat cheese, roasted garlic, chopped tomato and parmesan	11.00
Small pizza with eggplant, onions, mozzarella, parmesan and spicy tomato sauce	12.00
Small pizza with roasted peppers, sundried vegetables, provolone and sage	11.00

FIRST COURSE

Flat spaghetti with octopus, mussels, fava beans, olives, potatoes, garlic and tomatoes	14.50
Thin noodles with basil, garlic, tomato sauce, parmesan and pecorino	14.50

322 West 46th St • Theater District • (212) 489-7212

Spiral-shaped pasta with porcini mushrooms, broccoli rabe, plum tomatoes, butter and parmesan	14.50
Flat noodles with goat cheese, escarole, cream and parmesan	14.50

ENTREES

Grilled guinea hen with grilled oyster mushrooms	19.00
Grilled marinated lamb chops with three bean sautee	20.00
Spicy sausage with roasted peppers & ricotta cheese potatoes	17.00
Pork tenderloin scaloppine w/figs, marsala, tomatoes & scallions	18.00
Sliced pan-fried calves liver with pancetta and onions	18.00
Grilled marinated chicken with grilled vegetables	17.00
Grilled tuna with spinach, artichokes and cream	19.00
Braised Atlantic salmon w/sea beans, tomatoes & olives	19.00

VEGETABLES

Mixed green salad	4.00
Escarole with hot pepper flakes & garlic oil	4.00
Grilled zucchini with black olive butter	4.00
Roasted garlic potatoes	4.00

FRUIT

Capuccino gelato	4.00
Raspberry ice	4.00
Fresh fruit	4.50
Hazelnut biscuits with dessert wine	4.50

CHEESE

Parmesan	4.00
Gorgonzola	4.00

DESSERT

Chocolate hazelnut cake	5.50
Zabaione with blueberries	5.00
Risotto pudding with chocolate sauce	5.00
Cheese and fruit plate	6.00
Tirami su	6.50
Sabbiosa sponge cake w/brandied mascarpone and berries	5.50
Drunken figs in vanilla custard	5.00

Please refrain from cigar or pipe smoking

Visa and Mastercard only

Dinner: 7 Days a Week until 11:45

The exceptional food and decor here combine to make this an important NYC restaurant. There's a striking wraparound mural in the bar area that's a draw in itself. It's popular for lunch and pre-theater.

Menu Changes Seasonally

PRIX FIXE

You may choose an appetizer, pasta, main course, and dessert from the a la carte menu for $65.00

ANTIPASTI CALDI

CROSTONE DI POLENTA CON RAGOUT DI FUNGHI
Polenta crouton with wild mushroom ragout $19.00

"PANSOTI"
Homemade rye flour "pansoti" filled with ricotta and spinach $18.00

CALAMARETTI IN GUAZZETTO
Casserole of baby squid $18.00

RISOTTI

RISOTTO ALLO CHAMPAGNE AL PROFUMO DI TARTUFO BIANCO
Champagne risotto with white truffle flavor $ 26.00

RISOTTO CON ARAGOSTA
...with lobster $26.00

CARNE POLLAME SELVAGGINA

FILETTO DI BUE GRATINATO, ALLO SCALOGNO E SENAPE, CON ORTAGGI VARI
Filet of beef with a shallot and mustard sauce gratin
and a variety of vegetables $34.00

PICCATA DI VITELLO CON PROSCIUTTO E FUNGHI
Veal piccata with prosciutto and mushroom $37.00

MEDAGLIONI DI CAPRIOLO RIPIENI, CON SALSA DI CRANBERRY CON SPAETZLE
Stuffed medallions of venison with a cranberry sauce served
with spaetzle $37.00

PESCE

INVOLTINI DI SALMONE CON SALSA DI POMODORI SECCHI E SPINACI
Rollatine of salmon with a sun dried tomato sauce and spinach $33.00

PESCE SPADA ALLA GRIGLIA, CON SALSA GHIOTTA
Grilled swordfish with fennel, olive sauce, capers and tomato
$36.00

PASTA

SPAGHETTINI CON SALSA AL POMODORO FRESCO E BASILICO
...with fresh tomato and basil $23.00

PASTA DEL PALIO CON SALSA D'ARROSTO DI VITELLO AL DRAGONCELLO
Homemade pasta with a tarragon flavored veal sauce $23.50

TAGLIATELLE VERDI ALL' AMATRICIANA
Homemade green tagliatelle with tomato,
bell peppers and bacon $23.50

Dinner: Mon - Sat 5:30 - 11

Eating in Paola's is like eating in the dining room of a fabulous Italian cook. The food and decor are warm, hearty, and friendly. Paola herself comes out of the kitchen to make sure everything is all right. She has legions of admirers.

Paolas Restaurant

Menu Changes Seasonally

Appetizers

Misticanza con Pere e Pecorino — 7.95
(mixed baby greens with pears, walnuts and shaved sweet pecorino cheese)

Panzanella — 6.95
(Cannellini beans, chopped tomatoes, basil, extra virgin olive oil over mesclum salad)

Melanzana a Scapece — 6.95
(Grilled marinated eggplant, extra virgin olive oil, mint and balsamic vinegar)

Insalata di Gamberi — 7.95
(Grilled shrimp served with sliced tomatoes and bean salad)

Mozzarella della casa — 6.95
(Home made mozzarella served with tomatoes, basil, extra virgin olive oil)

Carpaccio di Filetto — 8.95
(Carpaccio of Fillet Mignon with arugula, capers, onions and shaved parmesan cheese)

Pasta

Capellini Primavera — 14.95
(Angel hair pasta with vegetables and fresh chopped tomatoes)

Malfatti — 14.95
(Dumplings of spinach and ricotta in light tomato, basil sauce)

Trofie Genovesi — 14.95
(Home made pasta with pesto sauce)

Tortelloni della Casa — 14.95
(Tortelloni stuffed with veal and chicken in a light tomato sauce)

Spaghettini Marechiara — 14.95
(Thin spaghetti with mussels, clams, shrimp and tomatoes)

Tonnarelli al Ragu di Scampi e Fagioli — 15.95
(Home made spaghetti with shrimp, & a sauce of fresh chopped tomatoes and beans)

Gnocchi — 13.95
(Potato dumplings with a light marinara sauce)

Risotto a Piacere — 15.95
(Seafood, primavera, porcini mushrooms, etc)

Fettuccine all'Aragosta — 18.95
(Home made pasta with shallots, brandy, tomatoes, touch of cream and 1/2 lobster)

347 East 85th St • Upper East Side • (212) 794-1890

Main Courses

Pesce Spada alla Griglia — *19.95*
(Grilled swordfish steak served with rugola salad & vegetables)

Capesante — *15.95*
(Grilled scallops served with rugola, endive and red onion salad)

Salmone con salsa cruda — *19.95*
(Grilled salmon steak with fresh chopped tomatoes, basil)

Gamberoni della casa — *18.95*
(Grilled shrimps served with peppers, onions, mushrooms and zucchini)

Aragosta estiva — *25.95*
(1 and 1/2 lb. lobster broiled and served with fresh salsa and melted butter)

Petto di pollo alla griglia — *15.95*
(Grilled paillard of chicken breast with light pesto)

Pollo Boscaiola — *15.95*
(Boned chicken with peppers, mushrooms, olives, capers, tomatoes, basil)

Pollo e Salciccia — *15.95*
(Boned chicken and sweet italian sausages sauteed with white wine)

Involtini con spinaci e porcini — *19.95*
(Veal stuffed with spinach & prosciutto, sauteed with porcini mushrooms)

Scaloppine con carciofi — *18.95*
(Veal scaloppine with artichokes, mushrooms and white wine)

Costoletta di Vitello alla griglia — *23.95*
(Grilled veal chop served with vegetables)

Fegato di Vitello Veneziana — *15.95*
(Calves liver with sweet onions and balsamic vinegar)

Desserts

Torta di Ricotta — *5.95*
(Home made ricotta cheese cake)

Tiramisu — *5.95*
(trifle-like dessert with custard, cream cheese, chocolate shavings and cocoa)

Mousse di Cioccolata — *5.95*
(Home made chocolate mousse)

Fagottini di Mele — *5.95*
(Apple turn-overs with chocolate sauce)

Pere Al Vino Rosso — *5.95*
(Pears cooked in red wine)

Sorbetti Vari — *5.95*
(Lemon, Mango, Melon Raspberry)

Frutta Fresca e Zabaione — *5.95*
(Fresh fruit with zabaione sauce)

Dinner: Mon - Sat 5 - 11, Sun 5 - 10

This expensive Italian restaurant is very popular with people of a certain age and stature who don't mind spending the money for the predictably excellent food, elegant decor, and formal service. It's been one of the top Italian restaurants for years.

Parioli Romanissimo

Menu Changes Seasonally

Branzino in carpione 15.50
Poached striped Bass, with a vegetable vinagrette

Scampi alla Romana 14.75
Sauteed scampi

Carpaccio di agnello 14.75
Filet of baby lamb cooked to a turn and served with a cream of red peppers

Carciofini Cassino 14.50
Delicate baby artichockes, cooked with wine, herbs and bacon

Fedelini al jalapeño 21.50
Fedelini with Jalapeños, prosciutto and tomatoes

Trenette ai funghi Porcini 24.75
Thin fettuccine in a wild mushroom sauce

Tortelloni salsa "Baby" 21.60
Cheese tortelloni in a marjoram and tomato sauce

Fusilli ai broccoletti 21.50
Fusilli with olive oil, garlic and broccoli florets

Risotto ai funghi Porcini 26.00
Risotto with wild Porcini mushrooms and safron

"Dover Sole" alla griglia 32.50
Grilled Dover Sole perfumed with herbs

Branzino al forno; condito al vino bianco 32.50
Balked St. Bass with wine and fennel, tarragon sauce

Trancia di "Halibut" grigliata al dragoncello 32.50
Halibut grilled with tarragon

24 East 81st St • Upper East Side • (212) 288-2391

Pulcino arrosto al tartufo 32.00
21 day-old chicken roasted with black truffles

Pollo ai peperoni e melanzane 29.50
Morsels of chicken sauteed with peppers and eggplants

Suprema di pollo al cognac 29.50
Breast of chicken braised with Calvados and cream

Pollo alla Giardiniera 29.50
Morsels of chicken sauteed with herbs and mushrooms

Medaglioni di vitello alla crema di champagne 29.50
Veal sauteed in a cream of champagne and a julienne of vegetables

Noce di vitello, salsa mostarda 32.00
Filet of veal braised in wine and mustard

Costoletta alla Giardiniera 33.00
Veal chop served in a tarragon sauce

Costoletta alla Milanese 30.00
Thin veal chop, breaded and sauteed

Costoletta alla Valdostana 39.50
Stuffed veal chop, breaded and sauteed with black truffles

Carré di vitello al rosmarino (per due) 68.00
Roasted rack of veal, served with purée of broccoli (for two)

Carré di agnello marinato alla Romana 35.50
Rack of baby lamb marinated and grilled, served with a mustard of candied fruit

Filetto di manzo alla Lombarda 34.00
Filet of beef served in a truffled sauce

Bistecca alla Pizzaiola 34.00
Sirloin Steak with tomatoes, basil and peppers

Dinner: Mon - Sat 6 - 11

Petaluma

This attractive, spacious restaurant survived being one of the hottest restaurants in town and has settled down to being a neighborhood favorite, maintaining its very good and well-priced foods. Wonderful pastas, pizzas from a wood-fired brick oven, good grills and salads.

Daily Specials

ANTIPASTI	MINESTRONE DI VERDURE	5.50
	INSALATA DI FUNGHI E FINOCCHIO *Salad of mushrooms and fennel with shavings of parmesan*	7.00
	INSALATA CAPRESE *Buffala mozzarella with tomatoes and basil*	8.00
	INSALATA CON FORMAGGIO DI CAPRA *Baked goat cheese salad*	7.50
	CARPACCIO RUGOLA E PARMIGIANO	9.00
	CARPACCIO SALSA VERDE	9.00
	ANTIPASTO MISTO PETALUMA	8.00
	VITELLO TONNATO	7.50
	SALMONE AFFUMICATO *Home-smoked chunk of salmon with rugola, oil and lemon*	9.00
	MOZZARELLA IN CARROZZA *With julienne of fried zucchini*	8.50
	SPIEDINI DI POLLO CON SALSA VERDE *Grilled chicken on skewers with rugola salad*	8.00
PASTA	SPAGHETTI POMODORO *Tomato sauce and basil*	12.00
	SPAGHETTI PESCATORE *Clams, mussels, scallops and shrimp*	17.50
	LINGUINE ALLE VONGOLE *Clams, olive oil and garlic*	15.00
	LINGUINE AL PESTO	13.50
	FETTUCINE AL SALMONE *Home-smoked salmon, asparagus and cream sauce*	16.50
	PENNE INDIAVOLATE *Spicy tomato sauce, olive puree, capers and garlic*	13.00
	FUSILLI CON SALSICCE *Sausage, tomatoes and garlic*	14.00
	GNOCCHI VERDI AURORA *Tomato, basil and a touch of cream*	14.00
	SPAGHETTI PRIMAVERA *Fresh vegetables and a light tomato sauce*	14.50

1356 First Ave • Upper East Side • (212) 772-8800

SECONDI	FRITTO MISTO DI CALAMARI E GAMBERI *Fried calamari and shrimp*	18.00
	POLLO SCARPARIELLO *Pieces of chicken on the bone with garlic, rosemary and lemon*	14.00
	POLLO ORTOLANA *Chicken sauteed with zucchini, carrots, mushrooms, peas and broccoli*	14.50
	POLLO EUROPEO *Chicken sauteed with Marsala, shallots, mushrooms, prosciutto and fontina cheese*	14.50
	FEGATO VENEZIANA O ALLA GRIGLIA *Calves liver sauteed with onions, vinegar and bay leaf or grilled, both served with polenta*	16.50
	PICCATA CON LIMONE E CAPPERI *Veal scaloppine with lemon and capers*	15.00
	COSTOLETTA CAPRICCIOSA *Veal milanese with tomato, basil, rugola and onion salad*	21.00
ALLA GRIGLIA	SALMONE CON VERDURE AL VAPORE *Salmon with steamed vegetables*	19.50
	PESCE SPADA CON CAPPERI E POMODORI *Swordfish with tomatoes, capers and olives*	20.00
	DENTICE AL SALMORIGLIO *Red snapper with olive oil, lemon and herbs*	19.50
	GALLETTO CON SENAPE *Baby chicken with a light mustard sauce*	15.00
	COSTOLETTE DI AGNELLO CON MENTA *Lamb chops with a fresh mint sauce*	21.00
	BISTECCA ALLA GRIGLIA *Sirloin steak*	21.00
	LOMBATA DI VITELLO *Veal chop*	21.00

INSALATE E CONTORNI	INSALATA MISTA	5.50	ZUCCHINI FRITTI	6.00
	INSALATA TRICOLORE *Rugola, endive and radicchio*	7.50	SPINACI AGLIO E OLIO	5.00
			BROCCOLI AGLIO E OLIO	5.00
	INSALATA SPECIALE PETALUMA	8.00	POTATO OF THE DAY	4.00

PIZZA	PIZZA MARGHERITA *Tomato sauce, mozzarella and basil*	12.00
	PIZZA QUATTRO STAGIONI *Prosciutto, artichokes, olives and mushrooms*	13.00
	PIZZA BIANCA *Four cheeses*	13.00
	PIZZA CAMPAGNOLA *Ham. leeks, tomato sauce, rugola and mozzarella*	13.00

Dinner: Mon - Sat 5:30 - 11:30, Sunday 5 - 11

Positano

Positano was one of the first upscale Italian restaurants to venture down to lower Park Avenue and it has withstood the test of time. If anything, the food has gotten better and it's a reliable, popular place.

Antipasti, Insalate e Zuppe

SELEZIONE DI OSTRICHE DEL GIORNO
oysters of the day on the half shell

FOCACCIA CON PROSCIUTTO... 10.00
grilled focaccia • tomatoes, basil, mozzarella, prosciutto and truffle oil

CALAMARI FRITTI... 8.00
crispy rings of calamari • spicy tomato sauce and fresh lemon

CAPRINI ALLE ERBE CON PEPERONI E PATATE... 9.00
herb goat cheese • warm potato and olive salad and roasted peppers

MELANZANE... 8.00
baked italian eggplant • tomato, mozzarella and pesto sauce

INSALATA GABRIELLA... 9.00
curly spinach, radicchio and frisee • braised seafood and a balsamic- mint vinaigrette

INSALATA PASTORELLA... 8.50
arugula, cremini mushrooms, parmesan shavings, sundried tomatoes and an imported olive paste dressing

Le Paste

CAPELLINI AI GAMBERI ... 15.00
angel hair pasta with shrimp, arugula and fresh tomato

TORTELLI DI POLLO CON SALSA DI PISELLI... 14.00
pasta stuffed with chicken and ricotta with split pea puree and sundried tomato sauce

RIGATONI AMBROSIANA... 14.00
rigatoni with a lightly spiced tomato-cream sauce

RISOTTO AL NERO CON SALSA DI LAMPONI... 15.00
italian rice simmered with calamri and seppia ink • raspberry jus

SPAGHETTI ALLE VONGOLE... 15.00
spaghetti with italian clams, garlic, olive oil and peperoncino

250 Park Ave South • Gramercy Park/Union Square • (212) 777-6211

Secondi Piatti

SALMONE ALL'AGRODOLCE... 19.00
sauteed salmon • white wine, capers and pearl onions • zucchini pappardelle

POLLASTRINO ALLA SATANA... 18.00
grilled free range chicken • hot peppers and citrus • mustard sauce

MERLUZZO AL SOLE MIO... 18.00
pan seared almond coated filet of cod • orange sauce and cous-cous

BISTECCA ALLA GRIGLIA CON VERDURE... 21.00
grilled rib eye steak • rosemary and seasonal vegetables

COSTATA DI VITELLO AI FUNGHI... 21.00
grilled veal chop • wild mushrooms and wine sauce

Pizze Positano

Served After 5:00 p.m.

SEMPLICE... 9.00
fresh tomato, garlic, oregano, and parmesan

MARGHERITA... 9.00
classic... with tomato, mozzarella and basil

VEGETARIANA... 9.00
tomato, seasonal vegetables and cheese

BIANCA/NERA... 10.00
eggplant with mozzarella and ricotta

FUNGHI... 11.00
mushrooms, tomato, basil and mozzarella

TRIO... 11.00
onions, peppers, sausage and cheese

VULCANO... 14.00
fresh tomato, shrimp and olive paste

Dinner: 7 Days a Week 5 - 11

This Upper East Side northern Italian has been top-rated for years. The creative dishes are always distinctive, as are the service and ambiance - a genteel, panelled room. It's expensive, but well worth it.

Specials Change Daily

Storione ai Gamberetti 16.50
Sturgeon with baby shrimps

Ravioli di Carne alla Salvia 19.50
Meat ravioli with sage

Tagliolini "Casanova" 19.50
Tagliolini with mushroom

Crostone di Anguillette*
Baby eels with oil & garlic

Risotto Primavera 24.50
Risotto with fresh vegetables

Carpaccio alla Toscana 16.50
Sliced raw filet of beef with basil sauce

Vongole Oreganata 12.50
Baked clams

Cappelletti in Brodo 7.50
Meat dumplings in broth

Trenette al Pesto 19.50
Taglierini with fresh basil

Torellini della Nonna 19.50
Tortellini with peas and prosciutto

Linguine alle Vongole 22.50
Linguine with clam sauce

Paglia & Fieno alla Romana 19.50
White & green noodles with peas & ham

Fusilli alla Fiesolana 19.50
Fusilli in a white meat sauce

Fettuccine Alfredo 19.50
Fettuccine with cream & cheese

Penne all'Arrabbiata 19.50
Penne with spicy red sauce

Penne alla Russa 24.50
Penne with vodka and caviar

Risotto ai frutti di Mare 24.50
Risotto with seafood

1578 First Ave • Upper East Side • (212) 861-8608

Cappesante in Umido 26.50
Scallops sauteed with herbs and wine

Pesce Spada al Salmoriglio 28.50
Grilled swordfish with lemon, oil & oregano

Costoletta Valdostana 29.50
Veal chop stuffed with cheese, prosciutto & truffles

Scaloppine al Cuore 26.50 di Carciofo
Veal sauteed with artichoke hearts

Medaglioni di Bue alla 29.50 Lombarda
Beef medallions sauteed with sage and shallots, red wine

Bistecca alla Boscaiola 29.50
Sirloin sauteed with mushrooms and red wine

La Cassola 28.50
Assorted fresh fish in a light red sauce

Filetto di Sogliola Primavera 26.50
Filet of sole stuffed with shrimp, sauteed with cream and mushrooms

Pollo alla Griglia 24.50
Broiled Chicken

Costoletta alla 29.50 Mostarda & Funghi
Veal chop with mushrooms and mustard

Costoletta alla Griglia 29.50
Broiled veal chop

Fegato alla Veneziana 26.50
Calf's liver sauteed with onion and white wine

Battuta di Manzo 29.50 alla Griglia
Paillard of beef

Costolette di Agnello 29.50 al Balsamico
Baby lamb chop with balsamic vinegar

Grigliata Mista alla Tirolese 28.50
Assorted grilled meat

Scampi Aromatici 26.50
Shrimp sauteed with herbs, butter, lemon and white wine

Salmone allo Champagne 28.50
Salmon sauteed with champagne

Pollo Forestale 24.50
Breast of chicken, sauteed with peas, prosciutto & mushrooms

Costoletta alla Milanese 29.50
Breaded Veal Chop

Saltimbocca alla Fiorentina 26.50
Veal sauteed with prosciutto and spinach

Uccelletti alla Finanziere 26.50
Rolled veal stuffed with prosciutto and spinach

Dinner: 7 Days a Week 5:30 - 12

In only a few years, this beautiful Italian serving Venetian-style food has become a popular and reliable classic. There's a mural of Venice curving along one side of the room, and the furnishings and clientele are elegant and classy.

REMI

Menu Changes Seasonally
Along With Daily Specials

DINNER
ANTIPASTI

RUCOLA CON SCALOGNO
Arugola with Sweet and Sour Shallots
and Parmiggiano Slices with
a Walnut-Olive Dressing
$ 8.50

ENDIVIA CON ALICI
Endive Salad With Silversides
Served in a Mustard Dressing
$ 7.50

FEGATO DI ANITRA CON POLENTA
Fresh Duck Foie Gras
with Carrot Mustard
$14.00

POLPETTE DI GRANCHIO E GAMBERI
Crabmeat and Shrimp Cakes With
Lentil Salad and Baby Greens
$11.00

ENTREES
PESCE

SALMONE IN SALSA DI RAFANO
Sauteed Salmon with Horseradish Sauce,
Herb Potato Cake, Red Beets
and Sauteed Zucchini
$23.00

TONNO AI SAPORI DEL MEDITERRANEO
Seared Medium Rare Tuna with
Tomatoes, Black Olives
and a Mustard Sauce
$24.00

DINNER
PASTA E RISOTTO

TAGLIOLINI CON SEPPIE E RICOTTA
Homemade Pasta Served with
Calamari, Black Ink and Ricotta
$18.00

RISOTTO DEL GIORNO
Risotto of the Day

RAVIOLI "MARCO POLO" CON TONNO E ZENZERO
Filled with Fresh Tuna and Crispy Ginger
in a Light Tomato Sauce
$17.00

ENTREES

PETTO DI POLLO CON PANCETTA
Breast of Free Range Chicken Wrapped in
Bacon Served with Braised Endive,
Wild Mushrooms and Roasted Potatoes
$21.00

CONIGLIO AL FORNO
Roast Loin of Rabbit Served with
Mashed Potatoes in a Vegetable Sauce
$24.00

COSTOLETTA DI AGNELLO ALL'AGLIO
Rack of Lamb with a Pistachio Herb Crust
Served with a Goat Cheese and Eggplant
Timballo
$24.00

DOLCI

CIOCOLATISSIMO
Warm Chocolate Souffle Cake with
Cappuccino Parfait
$ 7.50

TORTA DI BANANA
Carmelized Banana Tart
Served with Toasted Almond Ice Cream
and Caramel Glaze
$ 7.50

Dinner: 7 Days a Week 5:30 - 11

Rosemarie's

Not many tourists know about this gracious, quiet Italian in TriBeCa. Excellent northern Italian food is served by a warm, attentive staff.

ROSEMARIE'S

Menu Changes Seasonally

ANTIPASTI

Salmone Marinato 9.00
Marinated salmon with corn crèpes

Melanzane con Caprino 8.00
Eggplant and goat cheese fritters with tomato vinaigrette

Trifolata 10.00
Wild mushrooms with polenta, pancetta and sage

Gamberi 9.00
Grilled shrimp with artichoke and tomato

Calamari Fritti 8.00
Deep fried calamari with anchovy lemon mayonnaise

PRIMI

Mezza Rigatoni con Salsiccia 14.00
Mezza rigatoni with sausage, peperonata and black olive

Ravioli di Ricotta e Spinaci 13.00
Ricotta and spinach ravioli with fresh tomato

Risotto con Funghi 17.00
Risotto with wild mushrooms, mascarpone and red wine

Pasta con Gamberi e Asparagi 14.00
Pasta ribbons with shrimp and asparagus

Spaghetti con Broccoli di Rape 14.00
Spaghetti with broccoli di rape, pancetta and pecorino

145 Duane St • TriBeCa/Downtown/Chinatown • (212) 285-2610

SECONDI

Razza 18.00
Crisp skate with sweet and sour onions and red wine

Salmone 19.00
Grilled salmon with spinach, corn and roast garlic

Dentice 19.00
Pan-roasted red snapper with artichokes, capers and tomato

Tonno 19.00
Rare pepper-seared tuna with fennel, white beans and lemon confit

Pollo Arrosto 18.00
Roast farm-raised chicken with whipped and shoestring potatoes

Ossobuco 19.00
Braised veal shank with vegetable risotto

Petti di Anitra 18.00
Roast breast of duck with brandied cherries and soft polenta

Costolette di Vitello 21.00
Sautéed veal chop with asparagus and wild mushroom ragù

Costolette d'Agnello 21.00
Rack of lamb with sage whipped potatoes and black olives

INSALATA

Insalata della Casa 6.00
Mixed seasonal greens

La Caprese 6.50
Fresh mozzarella and roast red pepper with basil oil

Insalata di Caprino 7.00
Roast beets and mâche with warm goat cheese and crisp leeks

DOLCI

Napoleone di Crema al Banane 7.00
Banana cream napoleon with caramel sauce

Tiramisu 6.50
Espresso-soaked ladyfingers with mascarpone and shaved chocolate

Dinner: Mon - Thurs 5:30 - 10:30, Fri - Sat 5:30 - 11

San Domenico is probably the finest Italian in this part of midtown Manhattan. Both the food and decor are elegant and understated.

Menu Changes Daily And Seasonally

ANTIPASTI

SALMONE MARINATO CON SALSA AI TRE CAVIALI $14.50
House marinated salmon with three caviars

RANE BRODETTATE ALLE ERBE $14.00
Frogs legs in a light white wine sauce

POLIPETTI AFFOGATI CON CAPPERI E OLIVE $12.50
Baby octopus with tomatoes olives and capers

COZZE E CANNELLINI ALLE ERBE $10.50
Mussels and cannellini in herb broth

TEGAMINO DI LUMACHE CON FUNGHI E ROSMARINO $16.50
Braised snail casserole with mushrooms and rosemary

MEDAGLIONI DI ANIMELLE ARROSTITE CON SALSA ALL'AGLIO $12.50
Pan-fried sweetbreads with baby greens and garlic oil

CARPACCIO DI BUE CON FEGATO D'OCA $17.50
Beef carpaccio with fresh goose liver

FARINACEI E MINESTRE

CREMA DI FAGIOLI BORLOTTI CON FARRO $8.50
Creamy bean soup with unshelled spelt

UOVO IN RAVIOLO CON BURRO NOCCIOLA TARTUFATO $21.00
Soft egg yolk filled raviolo with truffle butter

SPAGHETTI ALLA CHITARRA CON POMODORO E BASILICO....$16.50
Home made spaghetti with tomatoes and basil

GARGANELLI AL PETTINE CON ERBA CIPOLLINA PUNTE $25.00
DI ASPARAGI E CAVIALE
Hand made pasta quills with chives, caviar and asparagus tips

240 Central Park South • Midtown West Side • (212) 265-5959

PESCE

ASTACO IN FRICASSEA DI CARCIOFI $32.50
Lobster and artichoke fricassee

GAMBERI DELL'ALASKA CON FAGIOLI CANNELLINI $29.50
ROSMARINO
Alaska spot-prawns with cannellini beans with rosemary

TRANCIO DI SALMONE NORVEGESE ALLA GRIGLIA $29.50
CON CREMA ACIDA E CAVIALE
Grilled Norwegian salmon on a potato and leek tart, served with caviar and sour cream

BRANZINO ALL'ACQUAPAZZA $24.50
Poached sea-bass in a herb tomato broth

CARNE

FEGATO D'OCA CON CIPOLLA DORATA $42.50
Sauteed goose liver with three variations of golden onions

NODINO DI VITELLO "NINO BERGESE" $32.50
Roasted veal chop with braised radicchio in smoked bacon cream

FIORENTINA ALLA SALVIA E ROSMARINO....$32.00 (per person)
Broiled prime rib of beef marinated in sage and rosemary
(for two)

MEDAGLIONI DI AGNELLO SU CROSTONE DI POLENTA $29.50
ALL'ACETO BALSAMICO
Roast saddle of lamb on polenta crouton with balsamic vinegar sauce

MENU DEGUSTAZIONE
$55.00

LET CHEF THEO SCHOENEGGER GUIDE YOU THROUGH
A SERIES OF DISHES WITH DIFFERENT TASTES AND TEXTURES
WHICH REPRESENT SAN DOMENICO CUISINE.
IF YOU WOULD LIKE TO TRY A 5 COURSE TASTING MENU,

OR

ESQUIRE GRAND DINNER
$60.00

A FIVE COURSE DINNER INCLUSIVE OF WINES

ask your Captain for details

Dinner: 7 Days a Week 5:30 - 11:30

Sapore di mare

As he does in his other successful restaurants in Manhattan, Pino Luongo serves a contemporary interpretation of Italian basics. The upscale Tuscan farmhouse theme brings every Hamptonite to his door on weekends.

Sapore di mare

Specials Changes Daily

ANTIPASTI

INSALATA CAPRESE **8.00**
Fresh tomato, mozzarella fior di latte and basil

ANTIPASTO SAPORE DI MARE (MISTO DI TERRA) **7.50**
A selection of earth products from the display table.

CALAMARI ALLA GRIGLIA **8.50**
Fresh squid, breaded and grilled, served with marinated tomatoes

CARPACCIO DI MANZO CON FUNGHI E PARMIGIANO **12.50**
Thinly sliced raw filet mignon with mushroom and shaving of parmigiano cheese seasoned with truffles oil

VEGETALI ALLA GRIGLIA **8.00**
A variety of fresh grilled vegetables

FEGATINI DI POLLO AL BURRO NERO E SALVIA **7.50**
Sauteed chicken livers in brown butter and fresh sage served on toasted bread

PORTOBELLO ALLA GRIGLIA **10.50**
Grilled fresh portobello mushrooms seasoned with garlic and rosemary served with marinated tomatoes

MINESTRONE **7.00**
Fresh vegetable soup

FROM OUR WOOD BURNING OVEN - TEGAMINO DI PROSCIUTTO E MOZZARELLA **10.50**
Daily special appetizer served in a terracotta dish with mozzarella, prosciutto di Parma, bread crumbs seasoned with garlic, tomato and herbs.

Montauk Hwy, Box 1357 • East Hampton • (516) 537-2764

PASTE

RIGATONI ALLA BUTTERA (THE ORIGINAL) **16.50**
Rigatoni tossed with hot and sweet sausages, tomato, cream, parmigiano and fresh peas

LASAGNA AL SUGO DI AGNELLO **17.50**
Homemade lasagna filled with lamb ragu', besciamelle sauce and parmigiano cheese

SPAGHETTI AGLIO OLIO E POMODORO **16.50**
Spaghetti tossed with garlic, extra virgin olive oil and fresh tomato and crushed red pepper

GNOCCHI VERDI AL GORGONZOLA **17.50**
Homemade potato and spinach dumplings finished with gorgonzola cheese and fresh cream

SPAGHETTI ALLE VONGOLE **18.00**
Spaghetti with little neck clams, garlic and arrugola

ORECCHIETTE CON RAPINE **17.50**
Ear shaped pasta tossed with broccoli rabe seasoned with olive oil, garlic and crushed red pepper

Half orders of pasta are available **10.50**

PESCE

TONNO ALLA GRIGLIA CON SALMORIGLIO **26.00**
Roasted fresh tuna steak, finished with herbs and olive oil

PESCE DEL GIORNO ALLA LIVORNESE **24.00**
Fresh fish of the day in a tomato, capers, garlic and olives sauce

CACCIUCCO ALLA TOSCANA **28.00**
Spicy seafood stew with fresh fish and shellfish, served with garlic flavored toasted bread

CARNE

TAGLIATA ALLA FIORENTINA **32.00**
Certified Black Angus steak grilled, sliced, seared with extra virgin olive oil, rosemary and sage served with sauteed spinach and roasted potatoes

PETTO DI POLLO ALLA GRIGLIA **21.50**
Grilled breast of chicken, marinated with extra virgin olive oil, balsamic vinegar, herbs and served with vegetables of the day

INSALATE

INSALATA DI STAIONE **6.50**
Assorted seasonal green salad

INSALATA TRICOLORE **7.00**
Attugola, endive and radicchio salad

INSALATA DI CARCIOFINI **8.00**

Dinner: Sun - Thurs 6 - 11, Fri - Sat 6 - 12

Scarlatti has been a reliable, consistent businessmen's expense account lunch place for years. The food is good and the quiet comfort of the dining room is perfect for conversation.

Menu Changes Daily

ANTIPASTI

FREDDI

Prosciutto e Melone 11.00
Salmone Affumicato 13.00
(Imported Smoked Salmon)
Carpaccio 13.00
(Thinly Sliced Beef with Green Herb Sauce)
Cocktail di Gamberi 16.00
(Shrimp Cocktail)
Antipasto Freddo del Giorno 11.00
Bresaola 12.00
(Cured Imported Beef)

CALDI

Vongole Aromatizzate 11.00
(Clams Baked with Mediterranean Herbs)
Crostini di Mozzarella 10.00
Scampi Grigliati 14.00
Antipasto Misto 14.00
Vongole Posillipo 12.00
(Steamed with Marinara Sauce)
Insalata di Mare 16.00
Peperoni Freschi Arrostiti 10.00

ZUPPE

Del Giorno ....
Zuppa Paradiso 8.00
Stracciatella Romana 8.00
Pasta e Fagioli 8.00

FARINACEI

Del Giorno ....
Fettuccine Campagnola 18.00
Linguine ai Frutti di Mare 22.00
Malfatti con Carciofi 18.00
Fettuccine con Zucchini e Broccoli 18.00
Tortellini Bolognese 18.00
Paglia e Fieno al Filetto 18.00
Spaghettini Carbonara 18.00
Tortellini Belvedere 18.00
Spaghettini alle Vongole 22.00
Risotto Primavera 22.00
Risotto ai Frutti di Mare 25.00

PESCE

Filetti di Soglia Favorita 23.00
Scampi Grigliati 26.00
Calamari Fritti 24.00
Scampi Ribelli 26.00
(Baked in Mozzarella)
Scampi Infernali 26.00
(Spicy Tomato Sauce)
Dover Sole Fresca .... ****
Pesce Spada 25.00
(Sword Fish)
Salmone Al Pepe Verde 25.00
(Salmon in wine - green peppercorn)
Filetto di Dentice Marechiaro 25.00
(Red Snapper & Clams in a Red Sauce)
Filetto di Dentice Livornese 25.00
(Red Snapper, olives, capers and tomato)

34 East 52nd St • Midtown East Side • (212) 753-2444

POLLO

Pollo Contadina 23.00
(Sausages and Artichokes)
Pollo Scarpariello 23.00
(Garlic and Wine)

Pollo Cipriani 23.00
(Wine, Shallots & Asparagi)
Pollo Pappagallo 23.00
(Mushrooms, olives, capers and tomato)

PIATTI DELLA CASA

Zuppa di Pesce Mediterranea 34.00
(Mixed Seafood in Light Red Sauce)

****In Season

Carre' D'Agnello Arrosto 52.00
(Roast Rack of Lamb with Mustard and Fine Herbs) [For Two]

VITELLO

Piccata Ambrosiana 24.00
Scaloppine Santa Elena 24.00
(Artichokes, Mushrooms and Wine)
Salti in Bocca Romana 24.00
Fegato alla Veneziana 24.00
(Liver, Wine and Onions)
Scaloppine Vesuviana 24.00
(Tomatoes, Mushrooms and Garlic)

Scaloppine Castellana 24.00
Medaglioni della Casa 26.00
(Garlic, Tomatoes and Imported Mushrooms)
Costoletta Milanese25.00
Costoletta Parmigiana 26.00
Scaloppine Boscaiola 25.00
(Marsala, Prosciutto, Dry Porcini)
Costoletta Capriciosa 25.00

GRIGLIATE

Battuta di Vitello 26.00
(Veal Paillard)
Bistecca Di Manzo 28.00
(Sirloin Steak)
Costoletta di Vitello 30.00
(Veal Chop)

Filetto de Centro alla Griglia 28.00
(Broiled Filet Mignon)
Fegato ai Ferri 24.00
(Broiled Calf's Liver)
Battuta di Pollo 23.00
(Chicken Paillard)

VEGETALI

Broccoli 7.00
Funghi 7.00
(Mushrooms)
Zucchini Fritti 7.00
Asparagi .... ****

Fagiolini 7.00
(String Beans)
Spinaci 7.00
Carciofi 7.00
(Artichokes)

INSALATE

Verde Mista 7.00
Rugola 7.00

Artichoke 7.00
Endive 7.00
Cesare (For two) 14.00

DOLCI

Dolci Assortiti 6.00

Zabaglione al Marsala 8.00

GELATI

Vari 5.00

FORMAGGI

Assortiti 6.00

Dinner: 7 Days a Week 5:30 - 10:30

Across the street from Carnegie Hall, Trattoria dell'Arte greets you with an extensive antipasti selection arrayed on the bar. The generally simple decor is highlighted by huge, dramatic drawings of body parts, mainly noses.

Menu Changes Monthly

ENTREE ANTIPASTO PLATTERS

all are accompanied by an assortment of vegetables from the antipasto bar

HALF ROASTED ROSEMARY CHICKEN *15.95*

HOME-SMOKED SALMON *with capers, onions and black olive pesto crostini* *16.95*

SHRIMP AND SCALLOP SALAD WITH ENDIVES AND BASIL *17.95*

ROASTED SALMON WITH FRESH HERBS *17.95*

HALF LOBSTER WITH SHRIMP, SCALLOPS, ENDIVE AND BASIL SALAD *20.95*

FOCACCIA SANDWICHES AND PIZZA

IL PROSCIUTTO *prosciutto sandwich with roasted peppers, zucchini, eggplant, fontina cheese and watercress* *9.75*

IL TACCHINO *smoked turkey breast sandwich with smoked mozzarella, roasted eggplant, zucchini, rucola and tomato* *9.95*

PIZZA MARGHERITA *tomatoes, mozzarella, oregano, basil* *13.75*

PIZZA CORTINA *tomato, smoked mozzarella, bbq chicken, sundried tomatoes* *14.95*

PASTA

SPAGHETTINI AL POMODORO *thin spaghetti with fresh tomatoes and basil* *14.75*

PINCI CON BROCCOLI *hand made pasta dumplings with broccoli, zucchini and roasted garlic and parmigiano* *15.25*

GNOCCHI AL TELEFONO *with tomato, mozzarella and basil* *15.95*

RAVIOLI AL MAGRO *spinach and goat cheese ravioli with a tomato basil sauce* ... *15.95*

PENNE ALLA ZAMPOGNARA *veal bolognese with wild mushrooms, sundried tomatoes and basil* *16.75*

PIATTI DEL GIORNO

Order a platter of polenta for the table to accompany your entree

CHICKEN PAILLARD *grilled double breast of chicken with grilled vegetables* *17.95*

CLAY POT ROASTED BABY CHICKEN *with rosemary, thyme, whole roasted garlic cloves and assorted vegetables* *18.50*

900 Seventh Ave • Midtown West Side • (212) 245-9800

GRILLED DOUBLE VEAL CHOP (H.S.) *sage mushroom sauce, shoestring potatoes* *32.50*

VEAL SCALOPPINE GREMOLATA *with sauteed artichokes, green olives, capers, lemon and orange zest, sage and rosemary* *18.95*

OSSOBUCO ALLA NOVESE *braised veal shank with green olives, capers, tomatoes and rosemary* *22.95*

ROASTED FILET MIGNON OF TUNA *roasted medium-rare with lentils, endive, artichokes, corn and a tomato infused olive oil* *23.95*

SAUTEED SOFT SHELL CRABS *with lemon, butter and capers* *21.95*

ANTIPASTO PLATTER

(HOUSE SPECIALTY)

Vegetable abondanza from our Antipasto Bar:
a selection of any seven vegetables of your choice - or allow us to choose them for you.

12.95

*******SEAFOOD ANTIPASTO PLATTER** *a seafood abondanza - shrimp and scallops salad, home smoked salmon, calamari, crab claws, polpetti, bacala Mantecato, etc...*

14.95

ANTIPASTI

RIBOLLITA TUSCAN BEAN SOUP *7.00*

MESCLUN GREEN SALAD WITH SHAVED GRANA CHEESE *8.00*

FRESH MOZZARELLA WITH ANY VEGETABLE FROM THE ANTIPASTO BAR *our mozzarella is made fresh three times daily* *7.95*

PROSCIUTTO CARPACCIO *with shaved parmigiano* *10.95*

HOME SMOKED TUNA CARPACCIO *with arugola and carrots* *12.95*

HALF LOBSTER SHRIMP, SCALLOPS AND ENDIVE *12.95*

ANTIPASTI FOR THE TABLE

family style

FRIED ARTICHOKES ALLA GIUDEA *12.95*

PADELLATA DI COZZE *large platter of mussels, garlic, basil, olive oil* *14.75*

POLENTA WITH FRESH TOMATOES AND VEGETABLES *13.95*

POLENTA WITH VEAL BOLOGNESE AND WILD MUSHROOMS *13.95*

****TRIO OF PASTA ALLA TRATTORIA*** *28.00*

Charge Lun Din Sun Bru

Dinner: Mon - Thurs 5:30 - 11:30, Fri - Sat 5:30 - 12:30, Sun 5:30 - 10:30

For a unique experience, New Yorkers have been patronizing this delightful Japanese noodle shop, but one with a twist: fresh soba noodles are actually made on the premises in full view of diners and served in a variety of filling, hearty soups. The decor is very sleek and sophisticated.

本むら庵

Honmura An

Menu Changes Seasonally

SMALL TASTING PLATES

SALMON OROSHI *$5.50*
Small dish of salmon caviar and strips of smoked salmon mixed with fresh grated Daikon radish.

SEAWEED SALAD *$5.50*
With mustard vinegar Miso dressing.

ATSUYAKI TAMAGO *$5.50*
Thick Japanese omelettes flavored with Mirin (sweet sake).

MOMIJI TATAKI *$8.00*
Carpaccio-style Japanese rare roast beef.

KAMO *$8.25*
Sliced smoked duck.

SMOKED SALMON *$9.50*
Served on a bed of sweet onion and dill.

TORI DANGO *$7.00*
Fried, ground chicken meatballs with Japanese herbs, served with mustard.

EBI TOFU OTOSHIAGE *$7.00*
Crisp fried tofu with mashed prawns and ginger.

ISO AGE *$7.25*
Small prawns rolled with Soba, Shiso leaf and Nori, then deep fried.

PRAWN TEMPURA *$17.75*
Two giant prawn tempura.

SPECIAL APPETIZERS

SOBA GAKI — *$9.00*
Soba gnocci served served in bamboo lacquerware box with a dipping sauce. Very healthy and esoteric. (Extra dipping sauce 50¢)

SOBA SUSHI — *$24.00*
Sushi thick roll made of Soba with mashed prawns, omelette, Shiitake and Mitsuba herb. Made to order and takes 40 minutes (serves 2 to 4 persons; advance order requested).

RICE DISHES

TENJU — *$19.75*
Two giant prawn Tempura dipped in a special sauce and served over rice in a lacquerware box with soup and pickles. The one rice dish served in authentic Soba restaurants.

TEMPURA GOHAN — *$19.75*
Two giant prawn Tempura dinner, served with soup and pickles.

All of our noodles, both Soba and Udon, are handmade on the premises.

COLD SOBA

KAMO SEIRO — *$13.75*
Seiro Soba with a hot, duck based, dipping sauce.

TEN SEIRO — *$16.75*
Seiro Soba with giant prawn Tempura

HOT SOBA
(served in a bowl)

OKAME ('Rosy Cheek') — *$13.75*
Topped with seafood, vegetables and fillet of chicken in a rosy cheek figure.

TEMPURA SOBA — *$19.75*
With two giant prawn Tempura.

All Hot Soba dishes can also be served with Udon noodles

UDON

GOMA DARE UDON — *$12.75*
Plain cold Udon noodle with sesame based dipping sauce.

NABEYAKI UDON — *$16.75*
Sizzling hot Udon in a clay dish with prawn tempura and topped with chicken, fish cake and vegetables.

Dinner: Tues - Thurs 6 - 10, Fri - Sat 6 - 10:30, Sun 6 - 9:30

Nippon has a long track record of serving top-quality sushi; it was one of the first in the city and has remained one of the best. You'll see lots of Japanese businessmen there at lunchtime, which says something because there are quite a number of other Japanese restaurants in the area.

Nippon

Appetizer

Tempura 天 婦 羅 10.50
Shrimp, fish and vegetables gently fried with a uniquely delicate batter in sesame oil

Kara-Age 平目唐揚つゆ張り 7.50
Filet of fluke gently fried and dipped in Nippon's delicate sauce

Sashimi 刺 身 9.50
Filet of thinly sliced fresh raw fish served with Wasabi mustard and piquant soy sauce.

Sushi 寿 司 9.50
Popular Japanese delicacy. 3 pcs of Sushi and 2 pcs of roll sushi

A La Carte Sea Food

Sashimi 刺 身 20.00
Filet of thinly sliced fresh raw fish served with Wasabi mustard and piquant soy sauce

Lobster-Ikizukuri 伊勢海老活造り

Sushi 寿 司
Popular Japanese delicacy

Sushi & Sashimi Combination 寿司、刺身盛り合わせ 32.00

Tempura 天 婦 羅
Shrimp, fish and vegetables gentlly fried with a uniquely delicate batter in sesame oil

Kara-Age 平 目 唐 揚 21.00
Filet of fluke gently fried and dipped in Nippon's unique delicate sauce

155 East 52nd St • Midtown East Side • (212) 758-0226

Dinner

御定食

Traditional soybean soup of the day
a choice of small dish below, rice
pickled vegetable, green tea and dessert

味噌椀、下記の前菜一品、香の物
御飯、デザート付

Clams or Oysters 生蛤、生牡蠣
Served with Japanese ponzu sauce consisting of vineger, Japanese hot pepper and radish

Asatsuki-Ae 蛤浅月和え
Clam marinated with seasoned soybean puree and scallion

Awabi-Momijioroshi-Ae 鮑もみじおろし和え
Abalone marinated with ponzu sauce and accented with Japanese hot pepper

Yakitori 焼鳥
Charcoal broiled chicken on bamboo skewers

Nasu-Dengaku 茄子田楽
Traditional Zen dish. Eggplant baked with Miso puree

Aemono 和え物
Marinated vegetable of the day

Sunomono 酢の物
Cucumber and wakame seaweed from Japan in vinegar

Salad with sesame 日本サラダ

Dish of the day *(Ask server)*

Tempura
天婦羅 **32.00**
Shrimps, fish and vegetables gently fried with a uniquely delicate batter in sesame oil

Shabu-Shabu
しゃぶしゃぶ **34.00**
Traditional beef and vegetable dish cooked at your table

Teriyaki
照焼
Filet of beef 特選牛 **36.00**
Chicken 鳥 **30.00**
Marinated in Nippon's special sauce

Negima-Yaki
牛葱間焼 **30.00**
Nippon's original. Created by ***N. Kuraoka*** *in 1963 at valuable suggestion of* ***Mr. Craig Claiborne*** *of New York Times*

Tonkatsu
とんかつ **29.00**
Popular pork dish in Japan

Aigamo Yuan-Nabe *(Duck)*
合鴨柚奄鍋 **33.00**
Nippon's newly created dish with tender duck

Dinner: Mon - Thurs 5:30 - 10, Fri - Sat 5:30 - 10:30

Many people think this is the top sushi restaurant in the city; the fish is always fresh and the staff helpful. It's also popular with Japanese businessmen, who know best about these things.

SUSHISAY

APPETIZERS

Nama Uni 生うに...... **$8.00**
Fresh sea urchin

Yamakake 山かけ..... **8.00**
Tuna & grated Japanese yam

Negi Maguro ねぎまぐろ **7.50**
Ground tuna & scallion

Negi Hamachi ねぎはまち **7.50**
Ground yellowtail & scallion

Ikura Oroshi いくらおろし **8.50**
Salmon roe & grated Japanese radish

Ika Uni Ae いかうに和え **8.50**
Squid & sea urchin

Unagi Yaki うなぎ焼... **8.00**
Broiled eel

Unagi Kyuri Maki ... **9.00**
うなぎきゅうり巻
Eel & cucumber roll

Komochi Kombu **$10.00**
子持ちこんぶ
Herring roe & seaweed in sauce

Shiokara 塩から........ **4.50**
(季節もの)
Fermented squid **(in season)**

Ika Ume Ae いか梅和え **5.00**
Squid & plum paste

Ika Natto いか納豆..... **5.50**
Squid & fermented soy beans

Maguro Natto まぐろ納豆 **8.00**
Tuna & fermented soy beans

Usuzukuri 平目薄造り.. **11.00**
Thin sliced fluke served with vinegar sauce

Ankimo あん肝......... **8.00**
(季節もの)
Steamed monk fish liver **(in season)**

★ Dinner Time Only

★印はディナータイムのみとさせていただきます。

★ Geso Shio Yaki **$5.00**
げそ塩焼
Salted grilled squid legs

★ Geso Shoyu Yaki **5.00**
げそしょうゆ焼
Grilled squid legs with soy sauce

★ Hamachi Kamayaki .. **$6.00**
はまちかま焼
Grilled yellowtail gill

★ Sake Kamayaki 鮭かま焼 **6.00**
Grilled salmon gill

38 East 51st St • Midtown East Side • (212) 755-1781

SASHIMI 刺身

An artfully arranged selection of fresh fillets served with a garnish

Sashimi Regular さしみレギュラー **$14.00**
Assortment

Sashimi Deluxe さしみデラックス **24.00**
Our chef's choice assortment

Sushisay Sashimi 寿司清さしみ .... (三人前) **48.00**
Our chef's colorful arrangement of specially selected Sashimi (For 3)

SUSHI 寿司

An artfully arranged selection of fresh fillets with vinegared rice balls

Sushi Cooked **$16.00**
Cooked assortment 生ものぬき

Sushi Regular 寿司レギュラー **16.00**
Assortment

Sushi Deluxe 寿司デラックス **19.00**
Assortment

Sushi Special Deluxe 寿司スペシャル **22.00**
Our chef's choice assortment

Sushi & Sashimi Combination 寿司と刺身盛り合せ **21.50**
Our chef's colorful arrangement of specially selected sushi & sashimi

Tekka Don 鉄火丼 **17.50**
Fresh tuna fillets artfully arranged on a bed of vinegared rice

Sushisay Chirashi 寿司清ちらし **19.00**
Our chef's special selection of fresh fish fillets on a bed of vinegared rice

Bento 弁当 **19.50**
Sashimi with rice, fruit and green salad

Sushisay Bento 寿司清弁当 **30.00**
Our chef's special selection of sushi, sashimi and special appetizers arranged in a lacquer box

Sushisay Special Makimono 寿司清自選巻物三種 **16.00**
Three kinds of sushi rolls
Eel • California • New York (Smoked salmon & sliced onion)

Dinner: Mon - Fri 5:30 - 10, Sat 5 - 9

Largely a neighborhood spot on the Upper East Side, it has consistently turned out quality meals for a long time. The decor is comfortable and the food is creative and up-to-date.

MENU CHANGES BI-WEEKLY

Artichaut Vinaigrette 6.00
Champignons w/ Roast Garlic & Extra Virgin Olive oil 6.50
Marinated Calamari Salad 7.50
Duck & Foie Gras Sausage w/ French Flageolets beans 8.50
Pasta du Jour P/A
Chicory Salad w/ Bacon Roquefort & Croûtons 7.50
Alexandria Quartet (assorted Mediterranean starters) 8.50

Soupe du Jour 5.50
Salade Crocodile (beets, erbin, greens & chèvre w/ walnuts) 8.00
Pissaladière Provençale pizza w/ goat cheese, tomato & olives) 8.50

354 East 74th St • Upper East Side • (212) 249-6619

Poisson du Jour P/A
Seared Tuna w/ Ginger & Leeks 17.50
Shrimp Couscous Méditerranéen 18.50
Roast Chicken Grand-Mère 14.50
Navarin d'Agneau Printanier (Spring lamb stew) 16.50
Pork Chops Charcutière 15.50
(w/ shallots & French pickles)
Roast Beef Forestière 17.50
(w/ wild mushrooms)
Couscous Marocain (beef, lamb, chicken) 18.50

Guava or Mango Sorbet 4.50
Crème Caramel 4.00
Glacé au Mocha 5.00
Wild Cherries Clafoutis 5.00
Choc au Chocolat 5.50
Pears in Chablis 4.50

$18.50
Prix Fixe

Appetizer
Soup, Salad, Hummus, or Baba Gannouj

Entrée
Chicken Couscous, Striped Bass in Phyllo, Moussaka Moustaki, or Roast Lamb Shank with Orzo

Dessert
Creme Caramel, Pears in Chablis, Chocolate Mousse, or Mediterranean Fruit Salad

Dinner: Mon - Sat 5:30 - 11

Nick & Toni's

Weekending New Yorkers, as well as locals, obviously love chef Paul Del Favero's full-flavored food because it is always packed.

Menu Changes Weekly

APPETIZERS

Soup of the Day $6.00

Mixed Leaf Salad with Citrus-Ginger Vinaigrette $5.50

Caesar Salad $6.50

Mediterranean Antipasto $8.00

Deep Fried Calamari with Ponzu Sauce $7.50

Warm White Bean Salad w/ Arugula, Red Onion & Shaved Parmesan $7.50

Wood Roasted Salmon Salad w/ Rice Beans & Cilantro-Mint Vinaigrette $8.50

Steamed Mussels & Littleneck Clams w/ Merguez Sausage & Spicy Tomatoes $8.50

136 North Main St • East Hampton • (516) 324-3550

PASTA

Penne alla Vecchia Bettola $15.00

Linguine w/ Spicy Spinach & Whole Roasted Garlic $16.00

Fettuccine w/ Grilled Shiitake Mushrooms, Fresh Rosemary & Cream $17.00

Orecchiette w/ Eggplant, Plum Tomatoes & Homemade Mozzarella $17.00

MAIN COURSES

Grilled Calves Liver w/ Carmelized Onions & Sauteed Spinach $19.00

N.Y. Strip Steak w/ Roasted Portobello Mushrooms & Rosemary Potatoes $24.00

Potato Crusted Halibut w/ Haricot Verts & Wood Roasted Shiitake Mushrooms $22.00

Grilled Swordfish w/ Black Olive Puree, Grilled Leeks & Roasted Beets $23.00

Grilled Louisiana Prawns & Scallops w/ Fresh Tomato-Basil Vinaigrette $21.00

EXTRAS

Seasonal Vegetable $5.00

Zucchini Chips $6.50

WOOD BURNING OVEN SPECIALS

Roasted Free Range Chicken w/Roasted Potato,Pancetta,Garlic & Rosemary $18.00

Wood Roasted Spring Lamb w/ Fresh Herbes de Provence $24.00

Roasted Free Range Quail w/ Wood Roasted Vegetables $21.00

Whole Roasted Red Snapper w/ New Potatoes, Roasted Peppers & Artichokes $23.00

Dinner: 7 Days a Week 6 - 11

This charming brick-walled Mexican "bistro" serves some of the best Mexican food in the city. Not touristy, it's packed with locals.

Menu Changes Seasonally
Along With Daily Specials

EMPANADITAS DE PICADILLO
Plump baked turnovers filled with a flavorful beef with raisins and olives. $ 4.95

CAMARONES EN ADOBO PICOSO
Sauteed shrimps in a spicy chiles adobo with steamed spinach. $ 6.95

POLLO EN MIXIOTE
Chicken pieces coated with an aromatic chile sauce, wrapped in parchment and steamed in beer. $ 6.95

CALAMARES JAROCHOS
Golden crisp fried calamari in a Mexican beer batter with salsa ranchera and lime. $ 5.95

CEVICHE DE CALAMARES
Spicy calamari rings with red onions, tomato and cilantro in a garlic-lime marinade. $ 4.95

GUACAMOLE
Hass avocado with tomato, onion, serrano chile and cilantro. Served with warm tortilla chips. $ 5.95

TAMAL DE ACELGAS
Tender steamy corn masa filled with flavorful spicy pork wrapped with swisschard leaves. $ 5.95

FRIJOLES CON CHORIZO Y QUESO
Refried pinto beans with homemade chorizo and cheese with pickled jalapenos and homemade tortilla chips. $ 4.95

SIDE ORDERS

Tortilla chips with salsa ranchera or salsa verde $ 2.00
Tortilla chips with both salsas $ 2.95
Sauteed mixed vegetables $ 2.95
Mexican or white rice $ 1.75
Black or refried beans $ 1.75
Tossed salad $ 2.95
Steamed spinach $ 2.25
Crispy potatoes $ 1.75

57 Jane St • Greenwich Village • (212) 627-8273

ENCHILADAS VERDES CON CREMA
A fresh tomatillo and poblano chile sauce to coat corn tortillas filled with chicken or cheese with cream. $ 10.95

ENCHILADAS ROJAS CON ACELGAS
Swisschard and vegetables rolled into corn tortillas covered with a roasted tomato and chipotle sauce. $ 10.95

ENCHILADAS DE MOLE POBLANO
Just like my grandmother's traditionally prepared mole poblano to dress corn tortillas filled with chicken topped with rings of onion and sesame seeds. $ 13.95

TACOS AL CARBON
Soft corn tortillas with charbroiled meats or vegetables and salsa. Seasoned beef, Chicken or Vegetables $ 8.95

BURRITO
A homemade flour tortilla, black beans, salsa verde, with your choice of grilled vegetables and cheese, grilled chicken or beef $ 8.95

PASTA FRESCA CON SALMON Y RAJAS
Fresh homemade noodles with grilled salmon and rajas in a fresh cream sauce. $ 12.95

CAMARONES ENCHIPOTLADOS
Tender shrimp cooked in a sauce of roasted tomato, chipotle and white wine with spinach. $ 14.95

PECHUGA CON RAJAS A LA CREMA
Grilled breast of chicken with roasted poblano strips and onions in a light cream sauce with crisped potatoes $ 13.95

STEAK QUERETARO
Grilled N.Y. strip steak seasoned with roasted garlic. Served with grilled scallions and black beans. $ 14.95

PESCADO DEL DIA
Fish specialty of the day. Priced accordingly.

FAJITAS DE MI COCINA
Grilled skirt steak or breast of chicken with onions and peppers, black beans and flour tortillas. $ 13.95

CAZUELA DE VEGETALES
Daily regional specialty of vegetables. $7.95

ENSALADA DE CAMARON
Shrimp salad with a mustard-jalapeno dressing. $ 12.95

ENSALADA DE POLLO
Crisp salad greens with tender grilled breast of chicken with avocado and spicy cilantro dressing. $ 8.95

Dinner: Sun - Thurs 5 - 10:45, Fri - Sat 5 - 11:45

Rosa Mexicano

This vies with Zarela as the best Mexican restaurant in the city. It is purely Mexican - what you'd eat in Mexico City without the "Tex" part. The decor, too, is upscale and classy.

Aperitivos

appetizers

Guacamole en Molcajete 9.00
Prepared fresh at the table.

Xalapeños Rellenos 5.75
Roasted and pickled green chiles filled with sardines.

Ostiones Enchilados. De Sinaloa 8.50
Oysters sauteed and served chilled in a marinade of chiles and spices.

Taquitos de Moronga 6.75
Small tortillas filled with blood pudding, fresh coriander and sliced onions.

Taquitos de Tinga Poblana 7.75
Small tortillas filled with sauteed shredded pork, smoked chile chipotle, onions and tomato.

Salpicon de Jaiba 11.00
Jumbo lump crabmeat sauteed with onions, celery, fresh coriander and chiles. Served chilled.

Ceviche 9.75
Fresh fish marinated in lemon juice with chopped onions, tomatoes, green chiles and fresh coriander.

Ceviche of Bay Scallops 9.75
Bay scallops marinated in lemon juice with chopped onions, tomatoes, green chiles and fresh coriander.

Camarones Nayarit 9.75
Small shrimp sauteed, marinated in a mustard and chile vinaigrette and served cold.

Raviolis Poblanos 6.50
Raviolis filled with chicken sauteed with tomato and onion. Served with chile poblano sauce, and manchego cheese.

Cold Seafood Platter per person 15.00
Shrimp, oysters, fish ceviche, scallop ceviche, lump crabmeat, sweetwater prawns and xalapenos filled with sardines and garnished with chile poblano mousse.

soups

Sopa de Pescado 5.00
Mexican soup made with a variety of fresh fish.

Sopa de Poblano y Queso 5.00
A poblano cream soup with cheese.

1063 First Ave • Midtown East Side • (212) 753-7407

Platillos Principales

main dishes

Sweetwater Prawns — 23.00
Sauteed with garlic and parsley and served with black squid rice.

Crepas Camarones — 21.50
Crepes filled with shrimp, covered with a chile pasilla sauce and sprinkled with cheese. Served with rice.

Mixiote de Pollo de Tlaxcala — 16.50
Pieces of chicken coated with chile sauce, wrapped in parchment paper and steamed in beer.

Budin Azteca — 17.50
Multi-layered tortilla pie with shredded chicken, cheese, and chile poblano sauce.

Enchiladas de Mole Poblano — 15.50
Two tortillas dipped in mole sauce, filled with shredded chicken, topped with more sauce, sliced onions and crumbled cheese. Served with rice.

Pescado en Cilantro — 20.50
Baked filet of fish with fresh coriander, tomato and onion. Served with rice.

Menudo Norteno — 16.50
A stew of tripe served with an array of garnishes.

Pozole — 16.50
A stew made with various cuts of pork, chicken, and hominy served with an assortment of condiments.

Tamal en Cazuela — 16.50
Corn meal with chicken breast dipped in mole poblano sauce.

from the grill

Tablas — 19.50
Beef short ribs, marinated in beer and lemon.

Pollo a la Parrilla — 15.00
Skewered boneless chicken, marinated in lemon, garlic, olive oil and spices.

Huachinango — 24.00
Grilled whole red snapper. Served with white rice and black beans.

Alambres a la Mexicana — 19.00
Skewered pieces of filet, chorizo, onion, tomato and chiles serranos. Served on white rice with red and green salsas.

Alambres de Camarones — 20.00
Skewered marinated shrimp with onions, tomatoes and chiles serranos. Served with vinaigrette sauce and white rice.

Carne Asada con Rajas — 21.00
Grilled filet topped with a mixture of sauteed chiles poblanos and sliced onions. Served with Mexican rice and fried beans.

Chuletas de Puerco Adobadas — 17.00
Pork chops marinated with a paste of ground chiles and spices. Served with Mexican rice and fried beans.

Because Rosa Mexicano presents classic Mexican cuisine, some of the popular Americanized dishes often associated with Mexican food are not included on our menu.

Dinner: 7 Days a Week 5 - 12

Zarela

Charming and crowded, Zarela serves serious Mexican (NOT Tex-Mex) food. Owner Zarela Martinez is on hand to oversee the operation and her countless fans return again and again.

ANTOJITOS

Poblano Relleno	*Poblano chile stuffed with a chicken and dried fruit picadillo & served with a roasted tomato sauce.*	*$8.95*
Flautas	*Rolled chicken tacos, crisply fried & served with guacamole.*	*$7.95*
Enchiladas de Mole	*Chicken and cheddar cheese enchiladas in Oaxacan mole sauce.*	*$8.95*
Salpicón de Pescado	*Snapper hash cooked with tomato, scallion, jalapeño and aromatic spices.*	*$8.95*
Chilaquiles	*Crisp corn tortilla strips, shredded sautéed chicken, sour cream and white cheddar cheese baked in a casserole with either tangy tomatillo sauce or salsa ranchera.*	*$8.95*

CALDO

	Caldo of the Day	*Priced Daily*

ENSALADAS

Ensalada de Jícama	*Watercress and jícama salad in Zarela's vinaigrette.*	*$4.95*
Jícama Eschabechada	*Jícama, zucchini and carrots in chipotle vinaigrette with Mexican spices.*	*$4.95*
Ensalada Cesar	*Romaine lettuce and toasted bread cubes in a garlic, anchovy, lemon and egg dressing.*	*$4.95*
Ensalada de Chicharron	*Avocado and pork crackling salad with tomatoes, jalapeños, scallions, cilantro and mayonnaise dressing.*	*$6.95*

953 Second Ave • Midtown East Side • (212) 644-6740

PLATOS FUERTES DEL MAR

Camarones con Coco	*Shrimps sautéed in a spicy jalapeño, onion and cilantro sauce. Garnished with fresh coconut.*	*$13.95*
Atún con Mole	*Tuna marinated in Oaxacan mole sauce and seared rare.*	*$15.95*
Salmon Ahumado	*Salmon grill-smoked and served at room temperature with chipotle mayonnaise and cucumber relish.*	*$15.95*

DEL GALLINERO

Manchamanteles de Pato	*Roasted half duck served with a tomato red chile sauce with dried apricots, prunes, raisins and pineapple.*	*$15.95*
Pollo Borracho	*Half a chicken cut in pieces and braised in a tequila, white vinegar sauce with green olives, golden raisins and almonds.*	*$12.95*
Pollo en Pepian Verde de Tampico	*Chicken braised in a creamy pumpkin seed sauce with cilantro and jalapeño chiles.*	*$12.95*

DEL CORRAL

Puerco con Rajas	*Grilled pork tenderloin, served with poblano and marinated ancho chile strips and a roasted tomato-nata sauce.*	*$12.95*
Fajitas	*Grilled marinated skirt steak, served with salsa, guacamole and flour tortillas.*	*$16.95*
Hígado Encebollado	*Pan-fried liver marinated in pickled jalapeño juice and worchestershire sauce. Served with onions and bacon.*	*$11.95*

VERDURAS Y MÁS

Pozole Guisado	*Hominy sautéed with tomatoes, onions, garlic & jalapeños seasoned with spices.*	*$3.75*
Quelites	*Greens sautéed with bacon, tomato, scallions & jalapeños.*	*$3.95*
Coliflor	*Golden sautéed cauliflower served in salsa ranchera.*	*$3.95*
Arroz con Crema	*Rice baked with sour cream, white cheddar cheese, poblanos and corn.*	*Small $3.50* *Large $5.50*
Verdura Del Día	*Fresh, seasonal vegetable of the day.*	*Priced Daily*
Frijoles Refritos	*Refried black beans.*	*$3.00*
Torta de Arroz	*Bread made with rice flour, corn, poblanos and cheese. Per slice.*	*$2.00*
Plántanos	*Fried plantain slices served with mole sauce.*	*$3.75*
Tortillas de Harina	*Homemade miniature flour tortillas. 4 per order.*	*$1.50*

Dinner: Mon - Thurs 5 - 11, Fri - Sat 5 - 11:30, Sun 5 - 10

Who hasn't heard of the Russian Tea Room. It's maintained the same tinselly, Russian Christmas decor for years and served the same Russian classics for as long. It's still very popular with residents and tourists.

The Russian Tea Room

Menu Changes Daily

Prix Fixe Dinner Menus

Choice of: Hot or Cold Borscht or Soup of the Day
or Caesar Salad

***

Chicken Marechale
Boned Breast of Chicken Filled with Mushrooms, Onions and Herbs

Caucasian Shashlik
Marinated Leg of Lamb en Brochette with Tomatoes, Green Peppers and Onions

Salmon Pojarsky
Cotelettes of Norwegian Salmon Lightly Breaded and Sauteed, Red Caviar Garnish

***

Russian Cream
Sacher Torte
36.50

Choice of: Hot or Cold Borscht or Soup of the Day
or Blini with Red Caviar
or Seared Marinated Mushrooms with Chevre Crouton

***

Cotelette a la Kiev
Boned Breast of Chicken Filled with Herb Butter, Breaded and Baked

Tobermory Scottish Smoked Salmon with Blini
Cucumber and Red Onion Salad

Beef a la Stroganoff
Strips of Seared Filet Mignon in Fresh Mushroom, Onion and Sour Cream Sauce

***

RTR Cheese Cake with Compote of Three Fruits
Strawberry Soup
Assorted Ices and Rhubarb Compote
43.50

All menus include RTR House Blend Coffee or Russian Tea

---

150 West 57th St • Midtown West Side • (212) 265-0947

DINNER

Zakuski
(Appetizers)

Caviar or Smoked Salmon with Blini or Toast Points

Sevruga Caviar 49.75 **Osetra Caviar** 54.50 **Beluga Caviar** 65.50
(One Ounce)
Nova Scotia Smoked Salmon 23.50 **Scottish Smoked Salmon** 27.50
Imported Russian Salmon Caviar (Two Ounces) 28.75

	For One	For Two
RTR Zakuska Plate - An Assortment of Seasonal Russian Hors D'Oeuvres	11.75	19.50

Hot or Cold Borscht with Sour Cream and Pirojok 7.25

Charred Karsky Salad - *Beets, Walnuts and Spicy Lentil Vinaigrette* 9.25

Herb Roasted Mushrooms - *With Frisee and Shell Bean Salad* 8.25

Smoked Salmon Rosette - *With Warm Scallion Potato Cake, Black Caviar, Chive Oil* 10.25

Salad of Mesclun - *With Coriander Vinaigrette* 8.75

Entrees

Kasha Roasted Salmon - *On Sauteed Swiss Chard, Red Caviar Sauce* 28.75

Grilled Sea Scallops - *With Shrimp and Blini Gateau, Lemon Vodka Mignonette* 28.75

Salmon Pojarsky - Cotelletes of Norweign Salmon Lightly Breaded and Sauteed 28.75

Provencale Vegetable Tart - Baked Eggplant, Zucchini, Tomato, Couscous 23.75

Cotelette a la Kiev - Boned Breast of Chicken Filled with Herb Butter, Breaded and Baked 28.75

Pan Roasted Breast of Magret Duck - *Savoy Cabbage Timbale, Lingonberry Sauce* 29.75

Beef a la Stroganoff - Strips of Seared Filet Mignon in Mushroom Sour Cream Sauce 29.75

Pan Roasted Filet Mignon - *With Grilled Foie Gras, Forest Mushroom Ragout* 32.50

Karsky Shashlik Supreme - Grilled Marinated Loin of Lamb, Armenian Pilaf 34.50

Dinner: 7 Days a Week until 11:30

This is the only quality Scandinavian restaurant in New York and is located in a dramatically soaring townhouse setting. Due to Christer Larsson's innovative food, it's been extremely popular since the day it opened.

AQUAVIT

Menu Changes Daily

First Course

Smörgåsbord Plate
Assorted Scandinavian Hors d'Oeuvres
($4.00 suppl.)

Herring Plate
Baltic, Matjes, Gentlemen's Delight,
Västerbotten Cheese

Traditional Gravlax
Mustard Sauce and Dill

Smoked Swedish Salmon
Fennel Salad and Horseradish Cream

Pyramid of Scandinavian Shrimp
Avocado, Tomato Sauce and Dill

Seasonal Salad
with Oyster Mushrooms, Goat Cheese
and Toasted Walnuts

Buckwheat Blini
with Smoked Salmon, Creme Fraîche and Caviar

One Side Sautéed Salmon
Chive Butter Sauce, Mushrooms and Salsify

Pacific Oysters
with Mignonette Sauce

13 West 54th St • Midtown West Side • (212) 307-7311

Second Course

Poached Salmon
Asparagus and Hollandaise

Arctic Char with Horseradish Crust
Braised Greens and Zucchini

Seared Sea Scallops
Fennel, Artichoke, Basil and Vinaigrette

Fillet of Red Snapper with Potato Crust
Cucumber and Tomato Concasse

Poached Halibut
Drawn Butter, Egg, Shrimp and Dill

Roasted Snow Grouse
Cream Sauce, Mushrooms and Potato-Carrot Cake

Loin of Arctic Venison
Apple and Juniper Sauce
"Hasselback" Potato

Rack of Lamb
Red Wine Sauce, Haricots Verts and Salsify

Desserts

Lingonberry and Blueberry Sorbet
Vanilla Sauce

Swedish Pancakes
with Punsch Raisin Ice Cream

Warm "Tosca" Pear
with Coffee Ice Cream

Prix Fixe Three Courses
$62.00

Dinner: Mon - Sat 5:30 - 10:30

Claire

Claire is not only one of the best seafood houses outside of midtown, but it comes with a twist: a Key West influence with bright, splashy colors, waiters in wildly printed shirts, and a sizable gay crowd.

Menu Changes Daily

APPETIZERS

****

FLOWER (LONG ISLAND) OYSTERS ON THE HALF SHELL	*7.95*
SQUID SALAD MARINATED IN OLIVE OIL & LIME JUICE	*6.50*
GRAVLAX (FRESH SALMON CURED IN SALT, HERBS & SPICES) W/MUSTARD MAYONNAISE SAUCE	*7.95*
SMOKED MOZZARELLA W/TOMATO, FRESH BASIL & OLIVE OIL	*5.95*
BAYOU CRAWFISH PATTY (1)	*4.95*
SMOKED HALF BROOK TROUT W/SOUR CREAM HORSERADISH SAUCE	*5.95*
ROASTED ANDOUILLE SAUSAGE W/CREOLE MUSTARD SAUCE	*6.50*
ROASTED PORTOBELLO MUSHROOMS W/PESTO VINAIGRETTE	*5.95*
BLACKENED TUNA SASHIMI W/JAPANESE HORSERADISH MUSTARD (WASABI) & SOY SAUCE	*8.95*
****SPECIAL - SAUTEED MEDALLIONS OF ALLIGATOR TAIL W/HOT PEPPER, BASIL & OYSTER SAUCE****	*8.95*

SOUPS

*****

BAHAMIAN CONCH CHOWDER	*3.95*
CARROT GINGER	*3.50*

SALADS

******

HOUSE SALAD	*3.95*
SPINACH SALAD W/MUSHROOMS, BACON, TOMATO & MUSTARD DRESSING	*6.95*
GREEN SALAD W/GORGONZOLA & VINAIGRETTE DRESSING	*4.95*
AVOCADO, TOMATO & RED ONION SALAD W/VINAIGRETTE DRESSING	*5.95*

DESSERTS

****

KEY LIME PIE	*4.25*	*MISSISSIPPI MUD CAKE W/WHISKEY SAUCE*	*4.95*
ICE CREAM	*3.50*	*PECAN PIE*	*4.95*

156 Seventh Ave • Chelsea • (212) 255-1955

ENTREES
****

LINGUINI IN WHITE CLAM SAUCE W/FRESH LITTLE NECK CLAMS	13.95
STIR-FRY VEGETABLES W/RICE FETTUCINE NOODLES	11.95
FISHERMAN'S HARVEST W/SHRIMP, SNAPPER, MUSSELS & SCALLOPS SERVED OVER LINGUINI IN A FRESH MARINARA SAUCE	15.95
BROILED COHO SALMON STUFFED W/CRABMEAT	14.95
BROILED SWORDFISH (STEAK) "TERIYAKI" W/STIR-FRY VEGETABLES	17.95
BROILED KEY WEST GROUPER "PROVENCAL"	15.95
BROILED MAINE COAST SALMON W/CUCUMBER DILL SAUCE	15.95
BROILED NEW BEDFORD SEA SCALLOPS W/LEMON, BUTTER & WHITE WINE	14.95
BROILED FLOUNDER W/BREAD CRUMBS & PESTO SAUCE	14.95
SPECIAL - SEARED TUNA STEAK W/CREOLE MUSTARD SAUCE	17.95
SPECIAL - ROASTED GOLDEN BROWN TILAPIA W/COUSCOUS & JULIENNED VEGETABLES	14.95
SPECIAL - ROASTED TIGER PRAWNS W/BACON, COGNAC & CHOPPED SCALLIONS	16.95
SAUTEED SHRIMP & LOTTE (MONKFISH) W/HOT PEPPERS & FRESH BASIL	15.95
BAYOU CRAWFISH PATTIES (3) MADE W/CRAWFISH TAILS FROM LOUISIANA W/CAYENNE & CILANTRO SAUCE	14.95
PAN-FRIED VIRGINIA RIVER CATFISH W/JALAPENO PEPPER SAUCE	13.95
PAN-FRIED "CRISPY" PACIFIC SNAPPER W/HOT CHILI SAUCE ON A SIZZLING PLATTER	16.95
BLACKENED BLUEFISH..........................A CLAIRE SPECIALTY	14.95
SAUTEED BREAST OF CHICKEN W/CHOPPED SHRIMP "BAYOU STYLE"	13.95
WARM GRILLED CHICKEN BREAST ON A BED OF WATERCRESS, RADICCHIO & ENDIVE W/PESTO VINAIGRETTE	12.95
BROILED CORNISH GAME HEN "GAI YANG"	12.95
ROASTED BONED DUCKLING W/FRESH PLUM & HOT PEPPER SAUCE	15.95
BROILED FILET MIGNON WRAPPED IN BACON W/MUSHROOM CAP	19.00
NEW YORK SIRLOIN STEAK	18.00
CHOPPED STEAK W/MUSHROOM & ONION SAUTE	9.95
HAMBURGER SERVED W/LETTUCE, TOMATO & COLE SLAW	6.95
HAMBURGER SERVED W/JARLSBURG OR CHEDDAR CHEESE	7.95

Dinner: 7 Days a Week 5 - 12

Dock's Oyster Bar

These bustling seafood houses feature a long menu of only what's fresh that day, written on boards on the wall. The decor is understated, but who cares - the fish is fresh and the staff is friendly.

Menu Changes Daily

Starters

Soup of the Day	P/A
Docks Chowder	4.50
Steamers in Beer Broth	9.00
Mussels in Tomato and Garlic	7.00
Fried Calamari	6.00
Maryland Crabcake	8.00

The Shell Bar

Clams on the Half Shell	P/A
Oysters on the Half Shell	P/A
Shrimp in the Rough: 1/4 lb.	7.00
1/2 lb.	12.00
1 lb.	22.00
Lobster Cocktail	P/A

Chilled Entrees

Cold Poached Salmon Filet	18.50
Chilled Stuffed Lobster	P/A

Land Locked

Grilled N. Y. Shell Steak	21.00
Grilled Chicken	14.50

633 Third Ave • Murray Hill/Kips Bay • (212) 986-8080 • (Call For Other Locations)

Grilled Seafood

Fresh Norwegian Salmon Steak 18.00
Fresh Swordfish 18.50
Fresh Tuna 18.00
Fresh Red Snapper 19.50
Barbequed Seafood Grill 17.50
Fresh Specials of the Day . . . . . P/A

Above Served with Docks Slaw and choice of Potato or Rice

Lobsters

Steamed Lobsters: 1-9 LBS. . . . P/A
Larger sizes available upon request
Two Lobster Special:
two 1 lb. steamed Lobsters . . . P/A
Three Lobster Special:
three 1 lb. steamed Lobsters . . P/A

Fried Seafood

Fried Sole (Broiled upon request) 16.00
Fried Scallops (Broiled upon request) 16.50
Fried Shrimp (Broiled upon request) 16.50
Fried Ipswich Clams 16.50
Fried Oysters 16.00
Fried Seafood Platter 18.00

Above Served with Docks Slaw and choice of Potato or Rice

Side Orders

Fresh Vegetable of the Day . . . . P/A
French Fried Potatoes 2.75
French Fried Yams 2.75
Steamed New Potatoes 2.75
Baked Potato 2.75
Brown Rice Pilaf 2.75
Docks Slaw 2.75

Desserts

Ice Creams and Sherbet 4.00
Fresh Fruit in Season . . . . P/A
Hot Fudge Ice Cream Sundae . . 5.50
Chocolate Mud Cake 5.00
Docks Mud Fudge 6.50
Homemade Key Lime Pie 4.00
Coffee / Brewed Decaf 1.50

Charge Lun Din Sun Bru

Dinner: Sun - Thurs until 11, Fri - Sat until 12

Manhattan Ocean Club

Usually ranked among the top two or three seafood houses in New York. You can always depend on the quality and the execution of the meals here. Also, owner Alan Stillman is an important restaurateur.

The Manhattan Ocean Club

Menu Changes Seasonally Along With Daily Specials

Blackfish 25.75

Roasted with Shitake Mushrooms and Penne

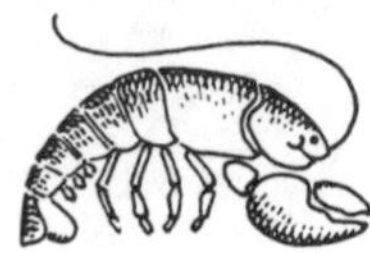

Lobster 2 1/2LB or 4LB 16.75/LB

Live Maine Lobster Steamed or Broiled, or with Crabmeat Stuffing

Shrimp 27.50

Fresh Louisiana Shrimp Saute' with Potato Puree and Sauce Bouillabaisse

Swordfish 29.75

Grilled with A Cream of Lentils, Curry and Crisp Onions

Salmon 27.75

Grilled with Marinated Vegetables and Olive Puree

Soft Shell Crabs 26.75

Saute' with Thai Curry Potato Dumplings and Fresh Peas

57 West 58th St • Midtown West Side • (212) 371-7777

SOUPS

Ocean Club Clam Chowder 6.75
Fish Soup with Saffron and Rouille 6.75

COLD APPETIZERS

Marinated Sardines Escabeche 8.50
Ceviche of Sea Scallops 9.50
Rare Seared Tuna, Lattice Potatoes and Salsa Verde' 11.50
Marinated Smoked Salmon and Gravlax with Fennel Oil 9.75
Lobster Salad with Cous Cous, Corn,
and Lobster Curry Vinaigrette 11.75
Asparagus Spears and Artichoke with
Walnut Oil Vinaigrette 10.50

HOT APPETIZERS

Warm Potato and Smoked Salmon Tart 11.50
Grilled Sea Scallops with Marinated Seaweed
Salad and Oranges 11.75
Baked Oysters with Morel Cream 12.50

MAIN COURSES

Medallions of Swordfish with Lemon Grass,
Carrot Sauce and Bok Choy 24.50
Crispy Salmon with Basil Pistou and Gnocchi 28.75
Roasted Blackfish with Shitake Mushrooms and Penne 25.75
Red Snapper with Rosemary Crust and Beurre Blanc 28.75
Ocean Club Crabcakes 28.50
Swordfish au Poivre 28.75
Post House Filet Mignon, Sauce Bearnaise 28.50

VEGETABLES

Asparagus 7.75
Sugar Snap Peas with Pine Nuts 6.75
Spinach Steamed in Sesame Broth 6.75
Shoestring Potatoes 6.75
California New Potatoes 6.75

Dinner: 7 Days a Week until 11:30

Oceana opened a couple of years ago in the elegant space vacated by a prominent French restaurant. It serves very high quality seafood with a Greek accent (the reincarnation of a popular Greek seafood place that closed) and gets excellent reviews from the press.

RESTAURANT

Menu Changes Weekly

Three Course Price-Fixed Dinner

●●●●●●●●●●●

APPETIZERS

Soup du Jour

Mixed Green Salad with Beets
Lemon, Mustard & Chive Dressing

Salmon Trio
Hickory Smoked Salmon, Tartar with American Sturgeon Caviar
Rillettes with Crisps; Mesclun Salad with Creme Fraiche

Watercress & Endive Salad
Cod Fritters, Gaeta Olives, Roasted Peppers, Artichokes & Green Beans
Shallot Sherry Vinaigrette

Salmon Gravlaks with Black Bean Fritters
Cilantro & Creme Fraiche Mousse; Vegetable Chips

Tuna & Scallop Carpaccio
Green Horseradish Oil & Ginger; Scallion Won-Ton

Parfait of Maine Crab, Avocado & Roasted Peppers
Sweet Pepper Cilantro Vinaigrette

Rock Shrimp & Snapper Cake
Soya & Mirin Ginger Broth with Wasabi

ENTREES

Roast Salmon Roulade
Tomato & Lobster Bouillon with Orzo
Garlic, Gaeta Olives, Horseradish, Frizzled Shallots & Red Mustard Greens

Atlantic Skate Filet
Risotto with Spicy Tuna Sausage & Escarole
Tomato Fines Herb Vinaigrette

Roast Florida Grouper
Thyme & Roast Garlic Vinaigrette
Polenta with Spinach, Zucchini & Roasted Peppers

Atlantic Monkfish Medallions
Lyonnaise Potatoes
Mustard Caper Vinaigrette

Roast Maine Cod
Miso Broth with Turnips, Bok Choy, Trumpet Mushrooms & Spicy Ginger Ravioli

••••••••••

Dessert Selection

••••••••••

$38

Crisp Florida Red Snapper
Mashed Potato Brandade
Roasted Peppers & Parsley Oil

Grilled Gulf Stream Swordfish Steak
Pumpkin & Goat Cheese Ravioli, White Beans & Caramelized Onion Broth

Oceana Bouillabaisse
Daily Selection of Fish & Shellfish
Lobster Tomato Broth with Leeks & Fennel; Sourdough Crouton with Rouille

Grilled Yellowfin Tuna Steak with Foie Gras
Pearl Onions, Crisp Potato Tart with Parsnips
Juniper Vinaigrette

Tournedos of Beef
Asparagus, Mashed Potatoes & Wild Mushroom Ragout

••••••••••

Dessert Selection

••••••••••

$44

Dinner: Mon - Sat 5:30 - 10:30

One Fifth Avenue

The team from Gotham Bar & Grill around the corner does double duty at this new seafood place located in a wonderful old nautical-themed space. It can't help but be a success.

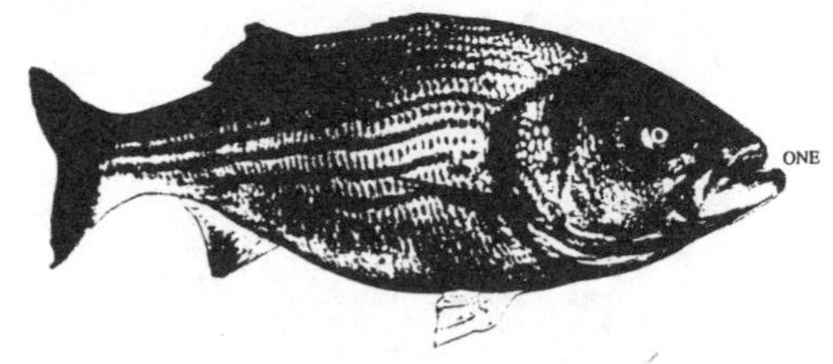

ONE FIFTH AVENUE

Menu Changes Seasonally

Le Plateau Oysters, Clams and Chilled Shellfish Composed according to Market P.A.

Select Oysters and Clams on the Half Shell 1/2 dzn. P.A.

Florida Snapper Ceviche Avocado, Cucumber, Cilantro and Tomato $9.50

House Smoked Salmon Grilled Leeks, Potatoes, Creme Fraiche and Caviar $11.00

Garden Salad with Chianti Vinaigrette $7.50

One Fifth Caesar Salad Romaine and Frisee Lettuces, Anchovy Vinaigrette $8.50

Belgian Endive Salad with Roquefort and Walnut Vinaigrette $8.00

Grilled Octopus Panzanella Salad and Red Wine Vinaigrette $10.00

"Divers" Scallops with Greens, Sea Urchin Roe and Lobster Vinaigrette P.A.

Grilled Shrimp Salad with White Beans, Arugula and Caponata $12.00

Deep Fried Squid with Lemon and Tartar Sauce $8.00

'Cataplana' Manila Clams, Fennel and Linguica sausage $10.50

Fifth Avenue Soup Composed Daily P.A.

Linguini with Clams Garlic, Flat Parsley and Extra Virgin Olive Oil $11.50

Alaskan Spot Prawn Risotto with Swiss Chard, Chives and Chervil P.A.

1 Fifth Ave • Greenwich Village • (212) 529-1515

Grilled Yellow Fin Tuna Yellow Finnish Potatoes, Scallions and Grilled Onions $24.00

Roast Maine Monkfish White Beans, Swiss Chard and Confit Tomato $21.50

Red Snapper Fennel, Potatoes, Whole Garlic and Kalamata Olives $24.50

Atlantic Salmon Lightly Cured, with Savoy Cabbage, Cardamom and Mashed Potatoes $23.50

Steamed Lobster with Braised Vegetables, White Beans, Manila Clams and Lobster Broth P.A.

Roast Chicken with Polenta, Salsify and Mustard Greens $19.00

Bouillabaisse Market Fish and Shellfish with Rouille and Croutons $24.00

Halibut Braised with Baby Artichokes, Haricots Verts and Rosemary Vinaigrette $24.00

Poached Skate Steamed Spinach, Brown Butter and Caper Berries $18.50

Penobscot Bay Cod Manila Clams, Mustard Greens and Chorizo Sausage $21.50

Grilled Swordfish with Wild Mushroom Ragout, Leek, and Mushroom Vinaigrette $25.00

Roast Duck with Wheat Berries, Root Vegetables, Duck Stock and Toasted Celery Essence $23.50

Grilled Sirloin Steak with Roasted Potato Cake and Red Wine Sauce $24.00

Mashed Potatoes $5.00 **Steamed Spinach** $5.00 **Creamy Polenta** $5.00

Certain fish can be simply grilled and served with Herb Vinaigrette.

Chef de Cuisine: KERRY HEFFERNAN

Executive Chef: ALFRED PORTALE

Dinner: Sun - Thurs 5:30 - 10, Fri - Sat 5:30 - 11

Yes, the legendary Oyster Bar, the cavernous, loud, vaulted white-tile room beneath Grand Central, is still considered one of the best seafood restaurants in the city.

Menu Changes Daily

APPETIZERS

FRIED OYSTERS 7.50 FRIED CLAMS 9.95
CAVIAR (STURGEON) SANDWICH . . 8.95
NEW ZEALAND GREENLIP MUSSELS IN DIJON SAUCE . .
MARINATED HERRING WITH MUSTARD DILL SAUCE . . 4.25
SHRIMP COCKTAIL 9.25
IMPERIAL BALIK SALMON . . . 8.95
SMOKED SALMON 8.75
SMOKED STURGEON 7.75
SMOKED RAINBOW TROUT . 6.75
POACHED WELLFLEETS ON WILD MUSHROOMS, BEURRE BLANC . . 9.50
BAKED CLAMS (3) 4.75
DUNGENESS CRABMEAT COCKTAIL . 7.95

SOUPS

MANHATTAN CLAM CHOWDER . . 2.85
NEW ENGLAND CLAM CHOWDER . 2.85
MARYLAND SHE CRAB SOUP . . 4.75
MOUSSES OF SCALLOPS A LA NAGE . .

COLD BUFFET

A MEDLEY OF COLD SHELLFISH . 23.45
COLD WHOLE MAINE LOBSTER . . 24.50
FRESH SALMON SALAD . . . . .
A FOURSOME OF SEAFOOD SALADS.
CAPE MAY SQUID SALAD WITH AVOCADO . 20.45
WHOLE MAINE LOBSTER CLUB SANDWICH, CAYENNE MAYONNAISE . . . 24.95
POACHED SALMON WITH CUCUMBER SALAD 23.95
SCALLOPS AND MUSSELS IN MUSTARD VINAIGRETTE ON ASPARAGUS . .
SHRIMP SALAD, SAUCE PIQUANTE . 24.50
SMOKED RAINBOW TROUT . . . 13.50
TUNA SALAD NICOISE, FRESH ATLANTIC TUNA 19.95

LOBSTER

THE LIVE LOBSTERS IN OUR TANKS ARE SHIPPED DIRECTLY FROM MAINE TO US. PICK YOUR OWN, OR TELL US WHAT SIZE YOU PREFER. TODAY'S PRICE $24.50 PER LB

CLAMS

LITTLE NECK . . . PER PIECE . . 1.25
CHERRYSTONE . . . . " . . 1.15
CASINO 9.25
STUFFED AND BAKED . . . 9.25
FRIED WITH TARTAR SAUCE . . 19.95
STEAMED WITH BROTH 13.45
STEAMED MUSSELS IN WHITE WINE 8.95

OYSTERS

PER PIECE
BELON (PACIFIC) . . . . " . 2.05
BLUEPOINT (LONG ISLAND) " . 1.25
ALUTIIQ PRIDE (ALASKA) " . 1.85
MOBJACK BAY (VIRGINIA) . " . 1.75
FISHERS ISLAND (NEW YORK) " . 1.95
HALIFAX (NOVA SCOTIA) . . " . 1.95
COTUIT (MASSACHUSETTS) " . 1.95
ROBBINS ISLAND (NEW YORK) " . 1.65
SISTER POINT (WASHINGTON ST) " . 1.85
MALPEQUE (P.E. ISLAND) . " . 1.95
MARTHA'S VINEYARD (MASS.) " .
WELLFLEET (CAPE COD) . . " . 1.85
WESTCOTT BAY PETITES . " . 2.05

MAY WE SUGGEST OUR OWN SHALLOT SAUCE WITH YOUR OYSTER SELECTION

BLANQUETTE DE BELONS AUX POIREAUX 10.95
OYSTERS ROCKEFELLER 13.95
FRIED WITH TARTAR SAUCE . . 14.95
BROILED WITH ANCHOVY 9.45
POACHED WELLFLEETS ON WILD MUSHROOMS, BEURRE BLANC . . . 9.50

Grand Central Terminal • Lower Level • Midtown East Side • (212) 490-6650

TODAY'S CATCH

BLUEFISH, FILET, BAKED . . . 18.95
BROOK TROUT
CATFISH, FILET, FRIED . . . 19.95
CHANNEL BASS, FILET
DOVER SOLE, MEUNIERE
FINNAN HADDIE
FLOUNDER, WHOLE . . . 19.95
GROUPER, FILET, SNOWPEAS . . . 22.95
HALIBUT, FILET
LOTTE, TOURNEDOS, BÉARNAISE . . . 22.95
MACKEREL, WHOLE
MEDITERRANEAN BASS, FILET
PERCH, YELLOW, FILET
PIKE, WALLEYE
POMPANO
RAY, FILET, STEAMED
RED SNAPPER, FILET, MALTAISE . . . 23.95
SALMON, NORTH ATLANTIC . . . 23.95
SALMON, FILET, POACHED, CHAMPAGNE . . . 24.45
SCALLOPS, SEA, FRIED . . . 23.95
SCROD, FILET . . . 19.95
SCALLOPS, SEA, BROILED . . . 23.95
SEA TROUT, FILET
SHAD 22.95 AND/OR ROE . . . 24.95
SHARK, MAKO, PICCATA, LEMON, CAPERS 23.95
SMELTS, FRIED, CANADIAN . . . 19.95
SOLE, LEMON, BR. OR PANFRIED . . . 24.45
SQUID, FRIED . . . 19.95
STRIPED BASS, FILET
STURGEON, WILD, STROGANOFF . . . 23.95
SWORDFISH, STEAK . . . 26.95
TILEFISH
TUNA, STEAK, SALSA . . . 23.45
TURBOT
VIRGINIA SPOTS
WHITEFISH
WHITEBAIT
WOLFFISH (LOUP), FILET . . . 22.45

HOLLANDAISE OR BEARNAISE SCE. 1.50

STEWS AND PANROASTS

	STEW	PANR.
OYSTER	8.95	9.45
CLAM, IPSWICH	15.25	15.75
CLAM, CHERRYSTONE	11.75	12.25
SHRIMP	18.45	18.95
LOBSTER	19.45	19.95
COMBINATION	19.45	19.95
SCALLOP	18.45	18.95

MAIN DISHES

MARYLAND SHE CRAB SOUP . . . 4.75
CHILLED: FRESH FLORIDA STONE CRAB CLAWS, MUSTARD MAYONNAISE . 26.95
ESCALOPES OF WILD PACIFIC WHITE STURGEON STROGANOFF . . . 23.95
POACHED FILET OF NORTH ATLANTIC SALMON IN CHAMPAGNE SAUCE WITH SALMON CAVIAR . . . 24.45
BROILED FILET OF FLORIDA RED SNAPPER, SAUCE MALTAISE . . . 23.95
PICCATA OF CAPE HATTERAS MAKO SHARK WITH LEMON AND CAPERS . . 23.95
BAKED FILET OF CAROLINA BLUEFISH, TOMATO, ONION AND HERBS . . 19.95

SPECIALTIES

BOUILLABAISSE . . . 24.45
COQUILLE SAINT JACQUES . . . 23.95
MAKO SHARK STEAK AU POIVRE
PANFRIED FILET OF POMPANO WITH RUM RAISINS
SAUTEED FILET OF FLORIDA PINK SNAPPER IN KEY LIME CREAM
PAUPIETTES OF SOLE DUGLÉRÉ
IMPERIAL BALIK SALMON . . . 8.95
AN ENSEMBLE OF SALMON & TURBOT
POMMEPADOUR OF SEABASS ON A BED
STURGEON TONNATO WITH DILLED CUCUMBER SALAD

EGG DISHES

EGG BENEDICT W. SMOKED SALMON AND SALMON CAVIAR . . . 11.75

HOMEMADE DESSERTS

CHOCOLATE AMARETTO MOUSSE TORTE . . 5.50
SILHOUETTE OF PEAR WITH PEAR SHERBET . 5.50
PEACH MOUSSE IN A GLASS . . . 5.45
FRENCH LEMON TARTELETTE WITH FRESH RASPBERRIES . . . 5.50
TANGERINE LAYER CAKE WITH TANGERINE COULIS . . . 5.45
STRAWBERRY CREAM TART . . . 5.35
CHOCOLATE BANANA CREAM PIE . . . 5.50
FLORIDA KEY LIME PIE . . . 4.75
OAT BRAN APPLE PIE . . . 4.75
CHEESE CAKE . . . 4.85
PEAR SHERBET . . . 4.50
VERY FRESH FRUIT SALAD . . . 4.75
FRESH FLORIDA STAR RUBY GRAPEFRUIT . 2.75
MAYAN MELON . . . 4.25
FRESH CALIFORNIA STRAWBERRIES . . . 5.35

Dinner: Mon - Fri until 9:30

Situated next to the Rockefeller Center Skating Rink, this top-of-the-line seafood restaurant has a view of ice skaters in winter and, when the doors are open in summer, of Rockefeller Center. Chef Seppi Reggli creates some of the best, albeit pricey, seafood dishes in the city.

Menu Changes Daily

Complete Dinner

First Course

Chicken and Vegetable Curry Soup

Salad of Field Greens and Focaccia Toast

Penne Pasta with Basil Pesto

Carmenet, Colombard 1990 *or* Mont St. John, Pinot Noir 1989

Main Course

Chilled Salmon Filet, Dilled Cucumber & Lemon Mayonnaise

Grilled Breast of Free Range Chicken, Red Pepper Aioli

Shad and Roe, Topped with Hickory Smoked Bacon

R.H. Phillips, Chardonnay 1991 *or* Groth Sauvignon 1988

Dessert Course

Key Lime Pie with Fresh Blackberries

Prometheus Gold Dusted Chocolate Cake

29.50 Two Course or 35.00 Three Course Complete Dinner

"Thumbs Up", Late Harvesting Riesling 1990

19 West 49th St • Midtown West Side • (212) 246-9201

First Courses

Chicken and Vegetable Curry Soup 6.50

Salad of Field Greens, Focaccia Toast 7.50

SeaGrill Chowder, Lobster, Shrimp and Clams 8.50

Beefsteak Tomato and Buffalo Mozzarella 9.00

Maryland Crabcake, Lobster and Chive Sauces 9.50

Oysters and Clams on the Half Shell, Three Dipping Sauce 11.50

Gold and Red Seafood Gazpacho 12.50

Pasta Courses

Farfalle Primavera, Fresh Spring Herbs, Tomato Cream Broth 10.50 half 18.50

Pipe Rigate with Littleneck Clams and Cannellini Beans 11.50 half 21.50

Penne with Grilled Shrimp and Basil Pesto 13.50 half 25.50

Grilled Specialties

Crispy Skin Salmon, Dijon Mustard Sauce 21.00

Halibut "T-Bone" Steak, Mediterranean Orzo Pasta 22.00

Swordfish Steak, Blackened Tomatoes and Fresh Basil Coulis 24.00

Yellowfin Tuna, Pickled Ginger and Sesame Snow Peas 26.00

Loin of Spring Lamb, Seared Eggplant and Garlic Flan 27.00

Today's Market Specialties

Breast of Free Range Chicken, Grilled Vegetables and Red Pepper Aioli 19.50

Sauteed Grey Sole, Pipe Rigate Pasta and Cannellini Beans 24.00

Sauteed Soft Shell Crabs, Lemon Butter 26.00

Maryland Crabcakes, Lobster and Chive Sauces 26.50

Iced Plateau of Lobster, Shrimp Clams and Mussels, Three Dipping Sauces 27.50

Side Orders

Grilled Zucchini & Peppers

Penne Parmesan

Sauteed Sesame Snow Peas

5.50

Dinner: Mon - Sat 5 - 11

This is the best seafood restaurant on the Upper East Side. It's in a clean, airy space, the staff is congenial and the fish is very fresh and beautifully prepared.

Menu Changes Seasonally

Appetizers

Maryland Jumbo Lump Crab Cake with Red Pepper Coulis	11.
Cumin Smoked Salmon Salad with Lemon Thyme Vinaigrette and Couscous	8.
Fried Calamari with Mango, Jicama and Black Bean Salsa	7.
Seared Yellowfin Tuna with Star Anise Sauce and Soba Noodles	8.
Gulf Shrimp Salad with Orange Poppyseed Vinaigrette, Mizuna Lettuce and Artichokes	9.
Soup of the Day	6.

Entrees

Sautéed Red Snapper with Black Pepper Orange Aioli, Squid Ink Fettucine and Asparagus	22.
Pan-Seared Tuna with Miso Sauce, Sesame Seeds, Wasabi Paste and Cucumber Carrot Salad	22.
Grilled Jumbo Sea Scallops with Spinach Morel Sauce and Mashed Sweet Potatoes	22.
Grilled Swordfish Steak with Eggplant, Olive and Sundried Tomato Relish and Italian Parsley Salad	23.

1573 York Ave • Upper East Side • (212) 535-5454

Basil Parsley Linguini with Rock Shrimp, Salmon Roe and Creme Fraiche	22.
Sautéed Shrimp with Lobster Sauce and Wild Rice Pancakes	23.
Grilled Norwegian Salmon with Sweet Corn Basil Sauce and Grilled Baby Vegetables	22.
Pan Roasted Lobster with Tequila Orange Sauce and Corn Poblano Pancake	29.
Soft Shell Crab of the Day	22.
Sautéed Breast of Chicken with Asparagus, Morels and Fried Leeks	19.
Grilled Shell Steak, with Roasted Garlic Chive Butter and Roasted Shallots	24.

Salads

Mixed Seasonal Greens with Sherry Chive Vinaigrette	6.
Arugula Salad with Goat Cheese, Roasted Peppers, and Sun Dried Tomatoes	8.
Spinach Salad with Wild Mushrooms and Warm Caramelized Shallot Vinaigrette	7.

Dessert

Chocolate Mousse Cake with Raspberry Puree	6.
Blackberry Cobbler	6.
Profiteroles with Chocolate Sauce	6.
Fresh Fruit Sorbet	5.
Hazelnut Roulade with Strawberries	6.
Coffee Crème Brûlée	5.

Dinner: 7 Days a Week 6 - 10:30

New York has few authentic Spanish restaurants, and Solera is probably the best of them; largely because chef Dominick Cerrone is one of New York's most talented chefs. It's located in a townhouse and offers a gracious respite to the hassles of midtown.

Menu Changes Seasonally

DINNER

CENA

APPETIZERS

Today's Soup
Sopa del dia

Stewed Clams in Montilla Wine, Roasted Garlic and Pepper Purees
Almejas con montilla y un puré de ajo asado y pimienta

Garlic Shrimp with Parsley
Gambas al ajillo con perejil

Smoked Salmon Terrine with Green Peppercorns, Sherry-Lemon Sauce
Terrina de salmon ahumado en salsa de jerez y limon

An Assortment of Vegetables and Grains in a Coriander Bouillon
Surtido de vegetales y cereales en su caldo

Spicy Pasta Roll with Braised Duck and Chorizo, Cumin Lentils
Canalon de pato asado y chorizo, lentejas con comino

Country Terrine of Duckling and Pistachios
Terrina casera de pato y pistachos

Catalan style Salt-Cod Salad
Esqueixada de bacalao

Marinated Salt-Cod on Chicory with Romesco
Xato de bacalao

Serrano style Ham, Loin and Chorizo with Country Bread
Jamon serrado, lomo y chorizo con pan y tomate

Roasted Peppers stuffed with Grilled Vegetables, Tomato Consomme
Pimientos del Piquillo rellenos con escaliuada, consomé de tomaté

Griddled Mackerel over Stewed Vegetables, Spicy Oil
Caballa sobre pisto, aceite de adobo

Semi-Boneless Quail with Foie Gras Couscous, Port Wine Glaze
Cordoniz lustrada de oporto, con couscous al foie

Catalan style Mussels
Suquet de mejillones

MAIN COURSES

Filet of Grouper, Peppery Shellfish Essence, Eggplant-Spinach Roll
Filete de mero, esencia de mariscos pimentada, rollito de berenjena y espinaia

Roasted Loin of Monkfish, Blood Orange-Coriander Vinaigrette, Arugula
Lomo de rape, vinagreta de culantro y naranjas sanguinas, rucola y endibia asada

Griddled Salmon, Smoked Tomato Sauce, Vegetable Compote
Salmon a la plancha con salsa de tomate ahumado, pisto sencillo

Salt-Cod in an Aioli Broth with Stewed Vegetables and Mussels
Bacalao en caldo de aioli con vegetales estofados y mejillones

Stew of Codfish Filet, Tongue and Cheek with Herb Emulsion, Asparagus
Filete y cocochas de merluza en salsa verde, esparragos y guisantes

Shellfish Paella (minimum of two) 4.00 supp.
Paella de pescado y marisco

Vegetable Paella with Grains (minimum of two)
Paella de vegetales y cereales

Poached Fish and Shellfish in an Aromatic Broth
Zarzuela de pescado y marisco

Lamb Chop and Merguez with Spring Vegetables
Chuleta de cordero y merguez con vegetales de primavera

Breast of Duck* with Olives and Pimientos
Pato con accitunas y pimiento

Medallions of Veal with Mushrooms and Roasted Salsify
Medallines de ternera con bongos y salsifi

NO BUTTER OR CREAM ****ORGANIC***

38.00 PER PERSON

DESSERTS

Assorted Fruits in Sangria Soup
Sopa de fruta in sangria

Apricot-Ginger Rice Pudding and Rice Wafers
Pudín de arroz al jenjibre y giruela

Mocha-Banana Burnt Cream
Crema Catalana de moca y platano

Flan of Lemon Thyme, Berries
Flan al tomillo con frutas silvestres

Dinner: Mon - Sat 6 - 10:30

Christ Cella

Christ Cella is a traditional New York steakhouse on the order of the Palm and Sparks, with starched table linens and stiff waiters. It's very dependable for quality steaks and chops.

APPETIZERS

CANAPES 4 PER PERSON	6.50	MELONS	5.50
CRAB MEAT COCKTAIL	18.25	SEA FOOD COCKTAIL	19.75
GRAPEFRUIT	6.50	SHRIMP COCKTAIL	18.75
LOBSTER COCKTAIL	19.75	SOUPS	6.00

FISH

CRABMEAT AU GRATIN	32.00	SEA FOOD NEWBERG	34.00
CURRIED SHRIMP	32.00	SHAD	29.00
FILET OF SOLE	31.00	SHAD ROE	33.50
LOBSTER	41.00	SHAD AND ROE	33.50
LOBSTER/SHRIMP		SHRIMP	29.75
NEWBERG	34.00	SHRIMP CREOLE	29.75
RED SNAPPER	29.75	SOFT SHELL CRAB	29.75
SALMON	31.00	SWORD FISH	31.00
SCALLOPS	33.00	TUNA	29.00

ENTREES

BEEF TONGUE	24.75	FILLET MIGNON	31.00
CALF'S LIVER	25.25	FILLET MIGNON SLICED	30.50
CHICKEN	22.75	LAMB CHOPS	28.50
CHOPPED STEAK	18.50	LAMB CHOP SINGLE	18.50
CORNED BEEF	25.25	LIVER STEAK	23.00
DUCK	28.75	MEAT LOAF	23.75

160 East 46th St • Midtown East Side • (212) 697-2479

MINUTE STEAK	20.00	ROAST LOIN OF PORK	25.25
OMELETS	18.50	SAUSAGE	19.50
PORK CHOPS	26.50	SIRLOIN STEAK	33.75
POT ROAST	26.00	STEAK TARTAR	27.00
ROAST BEEF	29.75	STEWS	26.50
ROAST BEEF HASH	26.50	VEAL CHOPS	30.00
ROAST LAMB	28.50	VEAL CUTLET	28.50
		VEAL STEAK	29.00

SALADS

CAESAR SALAD	10.50	GREEN TOSSED FRENCH	9.25
CHEF'S SALAD	18.75	SEA FOOD SALAD	28.75
CHICKEN SALAD	18.75	SHRIMP SALAD	28.50
COLD SALMON	28.00	SPECIAL SALAD	10.50
CRABMEAT SALAD	29.50	SPINACH SALAD	10.00
LOBSTER SALAD	32.75	TOMATO SALAD	7.75

VEGETABLES

ASPARAGUS	10.50	COTTAGE FRIES	8.50
BAKED POTATOES	5.00	FRIED ONIONS	8.50
BROCCOLI	8.50	GREEN VEGETABLES	8.75
		HASHED BROWNS	8.75

DESSERTS

BLUEBERRIES	8.00	MELONS	6.75
CHEESECAKE	8.00	MILLEFEUILLE	7.75
COFFEE, TEA, MILK	2.50	RASPBERRIES	8.00
ESPRESSO	3.00	FRUIT TART	8.00
ICE CREAM	4.75	STRAWBERRIES	8.00

MINIMUM PER PERSON 12.00

Dinner: Mon - Sat 5 - 10:45

Off the beaten path, and unknown to most tourists, this oldtimer is located in the wholesale meat district and, of course, serves great steak. The atmosphere is somewhat macho, with cigars and all, but it's fun and different.

Frank's
RESTAURANT

Menu Changes Weekly And Seasonally

~ Appetizers ~

Tripe 7.00
Stewed with Onions & Tomatoes

Sweetbreads Vin Blanc 7.00
Sauteed in White Wine & Parsley

Veal Kidney Saute 6.00
With Cognac & Cream

Escargots Bourguignonne 7.00
Snails saute with Garlic, Cognac & Red Pepper

~ Pasta For Two ~

Tagliarini Putanesca 18.00
Long Pasta with Tomatoes, Olives, Capers & Anchovies

Fettuccine Shrimp Marinara 21.00
Light Tomato Sauce with Shrimp & Garlic

~ Side Orders ~

Block Potatoes for Two 6.00
Mashed Potatoes Baked with Cheese and Prosciutto

Hand Cut Steak Fries 4.00

Bacon 3.00

431 West 14th St • Greenwich Village • (212) 243-1349

~ Entrees ~

Broiled Shell Steak 25.00

Hand Picked, Dry Aged, 16 ozs. Boneless Cut
One of the Finest Cuts of Beef

Filet Mignon 25.00

The Tenderest Cut of All, Served 12-14 ozs.

Broiled Skirt Steak 20.00

One of the Tastiest Cuts

Beef Bordalaise 17.00

Pieces of Sirloin Steak with Red Wine and Mushrooms

T-Bone Steak 45.00

Cut 35 ozs. for Two

Sweetbreads Eugenia 20.00

In a Cream and Cognac Sauce served on a Slice of Smoked Ham

Scallopine of Veal Piccata 20.00

Thin Slices in a Light White Wine Sauce

Calves Liver 18.00

Grilled and served with Sauteed Onions

Nature Veal Chop 25.00

Loin of Veal Cut Thick and Grilled

~ Dessert ~

Cheese Cake 5.50

Tirami Su 5.50

Dinner: Mon - Thurs 5 - 10, Fri - Sat 5 - 11

Although no longer considered in the top rank of New York steakhouses, Gallagher's is still a popular old-timer in the Theater District, with an original interior of wood floors, checked tablecloths and lots of memorabilia on the walls.

DINNER

CHERRYSTONE OR LITTLENECK CLAMS 8.25

JUMBO SHRIMPS 10.95

BLUEPOINT OYSTERS 8.25

CHARCOAL BROILED 8.95

CHOPPED CHICKEN LIVERS 7.75 MARINATED HERRING 7.95
SLICED GREAT TOMATO AND BERMUDA ONION 6.50
SMOKED SALMON 10.75

VICHYSSOISE 4.25 GAZPACHO 4.25
ONION SOUP 4.25 OXTAIL SOUP 4.50
THE OTHER SOUP 4.50

SPINACH SALAD 5.95

CAESAR SALAD 5.95

MIXED GREEN SALAD 4.95

WATERCRESS SALAD 5.50

BROILED OVER HICKORY LOGS

THE SIRLOIN STEAK 29.75
FILET MIGNON STEAK 28.75
CALF'S LIVER STEAK 21.25
SLICED BEEFSTEAK 19.50
CHOPPED SIRLOIN STEAK 16.95
SALMON STEAK 26.50
SWORDFISH STEAK 25.50
RED SNAPPER STEAK 27.95
ROAST PRIME RIB OF BEEF 27.75
DOUBLE RIB LAMB CHOPS 25.75
PORK CHOPS 19.95
VEAL CHOP 24.95
HALF CHICKEN 14.95
STEAMED OR BROILED MAINE LOBSTER 44.00
FRIED SHRIMP IN BEER BATTER 26.95
SCALLOPS 25.95 DOVER SOLE 27.75

"GALLAGHER'S OWN" POTATOES 4.75
HASH BROWN POTATOES 4.75
COTTAGE FRIED POTATOES 4.75
LYONNAISE POTATOES 4.75
FRENCH FRIED POTATOES 4.75
BAKED POTATO 4.75
MASHED POTATOES 4.75

FRENCH FRIED ONION RINGS 5.25
BROILED MUSHROOM CAPS 5.25
FRIED ZUCCHINI 5.25
BUTTERED STRING BEANS 5.25
SPINACH, CREAMED OR PLAIN 5.25
JUMBO ASPARAGUS 6.50
POTATO SHELL 4.75

ICE CREAMS AND SHERBETS 3.95
RICE PUDDING 3.95
CHEESE CAKE 4.95
STRAWBERRY SHORTCAKE 5.25

VARIETY OF FRUIT 5.95

CHOCOLATE MOUSSE CAKE 5.25
APPLE PIE 4.95
MELON IN SEASON 4.25
FRESH STRAWBERRIES 5.25

GALLAGHER'S IRISH COFFEE 5.95

COFFEE 1.75
ESPRESSO 1.75
BREWED DECAFFEINATED COFFEE 1.95
DECAFFEINATED ESPRESSO 1.95

Dinner: 7 Days a Week 4 - 12

The Palm is a legendary, quintessential New York steakhouse that has spawned duplicates in other cities around the country. It is a no-frills, male-type place; the walls are lined with caricatures of former newspapermen and serves humongous steaks, chops, and 22 lb. lobsters.

Menu Changes Seasonally

APPETIZERS

ANCHOVIES & PEMENTOS 7.00

CLAMS/BAKED/CASINO/OREG 10.00

CLAMS ON THE HALF SHELL 7.00

CRAB MEAT COCKTAIL 14.00

SHRIMP COCKTAIL 12.00

LOBSTER COCKTAIL 14.00

ENTREES

BEEF

BEEF A LA DUTCH 22.00

CHOPPED STEAK 14.50

FILET MIGNON 27.50

ROAST BEEF 26.00

STEAK 27.00

STEAK A LA STONE 29.00

DOUBLE STEAK 56.00

FISH

SWORD FISH 22.00

FILET OF SOLE 22.00

FRIED SHRIMP 24.00

ALL SHRIMP DISHES 24.00

RED SNAPPER 24.00

SALMON 22.00

LOBSTER

VARIOUS SIZES 55.00 & UP (ask waiter for prices)

CHICKEN

BROILED 16.00

CHICKEN BRUNO 16.50

CHICKEN SAUTE 17.00

CHICKEN SCARPIELLA 17.00

837 Second Ave • Midtown East Side • (212) 687-2953

PORK

PORK CHOPS 18.00

LAMB

LAMB CHOPS 26.00

VEAL

VEAL CHOP 27.00

ALL VARITIES 19.50

PASTA

SPAGHETTI/TOMATO SAUCE 14.00

SPAGHETTI/MARINARA SAUCE 14.00

SPAGHETTI/MEAT SAUCE 14.00

SPAGHETTI/WHITE CLAM SAUCE 18.00

FETTUCINI ALFREDO 18.00

SALADS

ALL VARIETIES SALAD 6.00

STRINGBEAN 6.00

TOMATO/ONION 6.00

SLICED TOMATO 6.00

GIGI SALAD 11.00

SPINACH SALAD 7.50

MONDAY NITE 7.50

VEGETABLES

STRINGBEANS & SPINACH (2) 6.00

SPECIAL VEGETABLE 6.00

F.F. ONIONS (FOR TWO) 6.00

ALL POTATOES FOR TWO 6.00

1/2 ONIONS - 1/2 POTATOES 6.00

CREAMED SPINACH FOR TWO 7.00

BAKED POTATO 2.00

DESSERTS

CHEESECAKE 5.00

MELON 5.00

TARTUFO 5.00

STRAWBERRIES 6.00

CHOCOLATE 6.00

BEVERAGES

COFFEE 2.00

TEA 2.00

MILK 1.50

EFFECTIVE JUNE 1992
PRICES SUBJECT TO CHANGE WITHOUT NOTICE

Dinner: Mon - Sat until 11:30

Peter Luger

Manhattanites travel to the Williamsburg section of Brooklyn (right over the Williamsburg Bridge) to eat what is generally acknowledged to be one of the best steaks in New York. There are no frills here - it's a rather plain German beer-hall - just incredible prime steaks, creamed spinach, beefsteak tomato salad, and home fries.

Famous For Over 100 Years

STEAK FOR TWO	53.90
STEAK FOR THREE	80.85
STEAK FOR FOUR	107.80
STEAK SINGLE	26.95

STEAK SANDWICH,
With French Fried Potatoes, Lettuce & Tomato 18.95

LAMB CHOPS, 2 DOUBLE LOIN,
Extra Large 23.95

ROAST PRIME RIBS OF BEEF, WHEN AVAILABLE
Extra Heavy Cut 19.95

FRESH FISH IN SEASON 18.95

178 Broadway • Brooklyn • (718) 387-7400

★LUGER'S OWN EXCLUSIVE

STEAK HOUSE SAUCE

NOW BOTTLED AND AVAILABLE FOR TAKE HOME SALES

Appetizers

Sliced Tomatoes, With Luger's Own Sauce (for 2) 5.95
Sliced Tomatoes & Onions, With Luger's Own Sauce (for 2)..... 6.95
Salad, Large Bowl Mixed Green (for 2) 6.95

With Choice of Dressing
French — Garlic — Russian
Blue Cheese — .75 extra

Jumbo Shrimp Cocktail (4) 10.75
Jumbo Shrimp Cocktail, Extra Large Portion (6) 15.50

Grapefruit or Melon, according to season

Vegetables

Potatoes, French Fries (for 1)............................ 3.50
Potatoes, French Fries Platter (for 2)...................... 5.95
Potato, Idaho, Baked, when available...................... 2.95
Potatoes, Luger's German Fried Platter (for 2)................ 6.95
Creamed Spinach 3.75

Desserts

A Fine Selection of Delicious Desserts Available, Including:

Chocolate Mousse Cake

Cheese Cake
Ice Cream
Melon in Season
Pecan Pie
Strawberries, in Season
Strudel

Available with "Schlag" (Whipped Cream)

Dinner: Sun - Thurs until 9:45, Fri - Sat until 10:45

Post House, The

This is probably the best-looking steakhouse in New York, which is not to imply that the meat isn't of the best quality. It is. The wine list is also a top priority, as it is at all of Alan Stillman's restaurants.

THE POST HOUSE

Menu Changes Seasonally

APPETIZERS

COLD

Clams 9.50
Oysters 12.50
Maryland Crab Cocktail 12.50
Jumbo Gulf Shrimp 12.50
Whole Chilled Baby Lobster 13.50
Carpaccio 11.00
Gravlax 10.50

HOT

Cornmeal Fried Oysters 10.50
Oysters Rockefeller 10.50
Fried Calamari with Smoked Red Pepper Aioli 10.50
Maryland Crab Cakes 13.00/25.50
Coconut Shrimp with Curry and Tomato Basil Chutney 12.00

Today's Soup 6.00

SALADS

Caesar Salad 8.50
Post House Salad 8.50
Mixed Green Salad 7.50
Spinach Salad 8.50

ENTREES

Stone Crab Claws (In Season) 13.50/27.00
Broiled Sole with Lemon Butter 21.50
Grilled Shrimp Creole 25.00
Filet Tips with Vegetables in an Herb Crust 25.00

28 East 63rd St • Upper East Side • (212) 935-2888

Roast Chicken with Chestnut Stuffing 20.50
Lemon Pepper Chicken 20.50
Medallions of Veal with Stuffed Shiitake Mushrooms 28.00
Lobster (Broiled or Steamed) 16.00/lb
Today's Fish

POST HOUSE CLASSICS 29.75

Prime Rib
Post House Sliced Steak
Sirloin Steak
Filet Mignon or Filet au Poivre
Rack of Baby Lamb
Veal Chop
Triple Lamb Chops

SIDE DISHES 6.50

Onion Rings
Cottage Fries
Fried Zucchini
Hash Browns
Seasonal Vegetables

DAILY SPECIALS

MONDAY	Pan Roasted Double Pork Chop with Apples	22.00
TUESDAY	"Chick'n Fried" Quail with Sweet Potatoes and Pecans	26.00
WEDNESDAY	Tea Smoked Muscovy Duck Breast with Duck Confit and Wheatberry Stir Fry	26.00
THURSDAY	Herb Roasted Rack of Lamb with Vegetable Hash Browns and Garlic Mint Jam	28.00
FRIDAY	Shellfish Stew	27.00
SATURDAY	Beef Wellington	29.75
SUNDAY	Grilled Rack Veal Chop with Buttered Egg Noodles and Pear Chutney	28.50

Charge Lun Din

Dinner: 7 Days a Week 5:30 - 12

This is another highly successful, excellent midtown steakhouse with a bustling, macho air. It has the feel of a real old-timer and has an extensive and well-respected wine list to boot.

Steak & Chop House

Prosciutto di Parma with Melon	$ 11.50
Shrimp Cocktail	12.75
Fresh Lump Crabmeat	12.75
Lobster Cocktail	13.50
Stone Crabs (In Season)	- -
Soup du Jour	4.75
Artichoke	5.50
S&W Famous Pea Soup	4.50
Asparagus	7.50

****

Salads	7.00
Vegetables	7.00
Potatoes	4.00
Cottage Fries, Onion Rings, Hashed Browns or Fried Zucchini	7.00

797 Third Ave • Midtown East Side • (212) 753-1530

THE S & W CLASSICS

Sliced Steak Wollensky	29.75
Sirloin	
Filet Mignon	
Filet au Poivre	
Prime Rib of Beef	
Triple Lamb Chops	
Veal Chop	

****

Veal Dishes	19.50
Chopped Steak	15.50
Calf's Liver	17.50
Sole	19.50
Scallops	- -
Fish	23.50 to 28.50
Stone Crabs	- -
Lobster 4 to 13 lbs	- -
Lemon Pepper Chicken	19.50
Double Sirloin or Chateau Briand (for two)	30.00 per person

****

DESSERTS

Cheese Cake	$ 6.50
Homemade Fresh Fruit Tart	7.50
Napoleon	7.25
Homemade Austrian Strudel	7.50
Hot Deep Dish Apple Pie with vanilla sauce	6.75
Wollensky's Basket	7.50
Pecan Pie	6.75

Dinner: 7 Days a Week 5 - 11:30

Sparks Steak House

Always one of the top-rated steakhouses, it's more infamous as the place where a mob boss was rubbed out a number of years ago. An extensive wine list (which is partially displayed in racks along the front wall) and a plush, gas-lit setting add to the difficulty in getting a reservation.

Fresh Halibut Steak 22.95

Fresh Filet of Tuna 23.95

Fresh Rainbow Trout 19.95

Fresh Filet of Salmon 24.95

Fresh Swordfish 24.95

Special Lump Crab Meat & Bay Scallops 26.95

Special Hot Appetizers

Lump Crab Meat & Bay Scallops 12.95

Combination of Baked Clams & Shrimp Scampi 10.95

Chunks of Lobster Meat & Broiled Shrimp
in Lemon Butter Sauce
29.95

Appetizers

Shrimp Cocktail 11.95

Lump Crabmeat Cocktail 14.50

Broiled Shrimp (Lemon Butter) 12.50

Clams on the Half Shell 7.95

Baked Clams 8.95

Oysters on the Half Shell 9.50

Melon in Season 5.95

Prosciutto with Melon 8.95

Any Appetizer as Entree 16.95

Salads

Mixed Greens with Tomato Wedges 6.95

Roquefort Cheese Dressing 1.75

Sliced Tomato and Onion 6.95

Spinach Salad 8.95

Any Salad as Entree 14.95

Vegetables

Hash Brown Potatoes 3.95 *Baked Potato 3.95* *Spinach 5.95* *Broccoli 5.95*

210 East 46th St • Midtown East Side • (212) 687-4855

Entrees

Extra Thick Veal Loin Chop	*28.95*
Extra Thick Rib Lamb Chops (3)	*29.95*
Sliced Steak	*26.95*
Medallions of Beef *Served with Bordelaise sauce, fresh mushrooms*	*26.95*
Sliced Steak with Sauteed Onions & Peppers	*26.95*
Beef Scaloppini *Thick slices of filet mignon, peppers and mushrooms*	*26.95*
Steak Fromage *Topped with Roquefort cheese*	*29.75*
Prime Sirloin Steak *A boneless shell steak from premium steers*	*29.95*
Filet Mignon *From beef tenderloin, a gourmet's delight*	*29.75*

Sea Food

Fresh Flounder (Lemon Sole)	*21.95*
Striped Bass	*25.95*
Red Snapper	*24.95*
Broiled Bay Scallops	*24.95*
Broiled Shrimp *with lemon butter, a hint of garlic, a pinch of thyme and a little white wine*	*24.95*

Large Live Lobsters

3 - 3 1/2 lbs. *4 - 4 1/2 lbs.* *5 - 5 1/2 lbs.*

No Pipe Smoking Allowed - Thank You

Dinner: Mon - Fri 5 - 11, Sat 5 - 11:30

This top-rated Thai has a genteel decor, suitable for its neighborhood clientele. The food is authentic and spicy.

BANGKOK HOUSE

THAI RESTAURANT

hot and spicy
very hot and spicy
extremely hot and spicy

APPETIZERS

		small	large
YUM-NUR	barbecued beef quickly cooled and delicately balanced with onion, ground chili and lime		8.75
PLA-PA-MUOK	squid briefly plunged into boiling water, then quickly cooled and subtly balanced with onion, ground chili and lime		8.75
PLA-KOONG	shrimp briefly plunged into boiling water, then quickly cooled and exquisitely balanced with onion, ground chili and lime		9.75
PLA MUOK TOD	deep-fried breaded squid, served with traditional hot sauce	4.95	9.50
HAE-KUN	ground shrimp wrapped in bean curd skin and deep-fried served with plum sauce	5.50	10.50
LAAB	stir-fried ground meat (choice of pork, chicken or beef) quickly cooled and delicately balanced with ground chili pepper, onion and lime served with fresh vegetables		9.75

BANGKOK HOUSE SPECIALTIES

PLA LAD PRIK	sizzling deep-fried whole fish, topped with chili and garlic sauce	17.25
NUR YANG	the popular treat from Northeastern Thailand: sliced beef marinated in Thai spices, then grilled served with chili and garlic sauce	15.25
GAI-TA-KRAI	Lemon-Grass Chicken: sautéed marinated breast of chicken, rolled in crispyfried chopped lemon-grass and scallions topped with ground peanuts	13.50

1485 First Ave • Upper East Side • (212) 249-5700

PED YOD PAK — sautéed tender boneless half-duck with Chinese broccoli in oyster sauce served with mixed vegetables 16.50

BEEF

GANG NUR — sautéed beef with coconut milk, bamboo shoots and chili in red curry 9.75

GANG KYO WAN NUR — sautéed beef with coconut milk, string beans and chili in green curry 9.75

NUR PAD PRIK — sautéed beef with chili, onion and scallions 9.75

CHICKEN

GANG GAI — sautéed sliced chicken breast with coconut milk, bamboo shoots and chili in red curry 9.75

GANG KYO WAN GAI — sautéed sliced chicken breast with coconut milk, string beans and chili in green curry 9.75

SEAFOOD

KOONG PAD PRIK — shrimp sautéed with chili and onion 10.50

KOONG MASAMAN — shrimp, cashews and chunks of avacado sautéed with coconut milk in masaman curry 11.50

PORK

GANG MU — sautéed pork with coconut milk, bamboo shoots and chili in red curry 9.75

MU PAD PRIK — sautéed pork with chili, onion and scallions 9.75

VEGETABLES

PAD RUOM-MIT — sautéed mixed vegetables and bean curd in oyster sauce 7.95

PAK PAD KRUONG-GANG — sautéed mixed vegetables in red curry sauce 7.95

NOODLES AND RICE

MEE KROB — sweet crisp noodles with shrimp, pickled garlic and tamarind sauce 8.75

PAD THAI — rice noodles sautéed with shrimp, egg, bean sprouts and ground peanuts 8.75

Dinner: 7 Days a Week 5 - 11:30

Index

- *Cuisine*
- *Geographical*
- *Alphabetical*

American

American Southwest

Chinese

Continental

MANHATTAN

Chelsea

Gramercy Park/Union Square

Greenwich Village

Lincoln Center

Midtown East Side

Midtown West Side

Murray Hill/Kips Bay

SoHo

Theater District

TriBeCa/Downtown/ Chinatown

E

F

H

I

J

L

M

T

U

V

W

X

Z

Gift Order Form

THE MENU is the perfect gift for every food lover, and is available at bookstores and gift shops everywhere. If you would prefer to order copies by mail, please fill out the form below, and return it to us with your payment. For gift purchases, a personalized card announcing your gift will be enclosed.

The Menu, New York City & Vicinity, 448 pgs. $12.95 x Qty = ____________

The Menu, Chicago & Vicinity, 448 pgs. $12.95 x Qty = ____________

The Menu, Los Angeles & Vicinity, 448 pgs. $12.95 x Qty = ____________

The Menu, San Francisco Bay Area, 448 pgs. $12.95 x Qty = ____________

Subtotal = $ ____________

Postage & Handling (each book) $2.00 x Qty = ____________

Total Order = $ ____________

☐ I enclose payment of $ ____________ payable to **Menubooks, Inc.**

☐ Please charge this order to my credit card. Total order = $ ____________

MasterCard # ______________________________ Exp. Date ____________

VISA # ______________________________ Exp. Date ____________

American Exp. # ______________________________ Exp. Date ____________

Approval Signature ______________________________

Name ______________________________ Phone ____________

Address ______________________________

City ____________________ State __________ Zip __________

Payment must accompany order. Please allow up to four weeks for delivery.
Rush/overnight delivery available. Call for details.

Menubooks, Inc.
David Thomas Publishing
733 NW Everett St., Box 12
Portland, Oregon 97209
(503) 226-6233

(Please fill out shipping instructions on reverse side.)

Gift Order Form

Please Send:
❑ New York City ❑ San Francisco ❑ Chicago ❑ Los Angeles
To:
Name ____________________ Phone ____________
Address ______________________________
City __________________ State ______ Zip ______

Please Send:
❑ New York City ❑ San Francisco ❑ Chicago ❑ Los Angeles
To:
Name ____________________ Phone ____________
Address ______________________________
City __________________ State ______ Zip ______

Please Send:
❑ New York City ❑ San Francisco ❑ Chicago ❑ Los Angeles
To:
Name ____________________ Phone ____________
Address ______________________________
City __________________ State ______ Zip ______

Please Send:
❑ New York City ❑ San Francisco ❑ Chicago ❑ Los Angeles
To:
Name ____________________ Phone ____________
Address ______________________________
City __________________ State ______ Zip ______

Please Send:
❑ New York City ❑ San Francisco ❑ Chicago ❑ Los Angeles
To:
Name ____________________ Phone ____________
Address ______________________________
City __________________ State ______ Zip ______

Gift Order Form

THE MENU is the perfect gift for every food lover, and is available at bookstores and gift shops everywhere. If you would prefer to order copies by mail, please fill out the form below, and return it to us with your payment. For gift purchases, a personalized card announcing your gift will be enclosed.

The Menu, New York City & Vicinity, 448 pgs. $12.95 x Qty = ____________

The Menu, Chicago & Vicinity, 448 pgs. $12.95 x Qty = ____________

The Menu, Los Angeles & Vicinity, 448 pgs. $12.95 x Qty = ____________

The Menu, San Francisco Bay Area, 448 pgs. $12.95 x Qty = ____________

Subtotal = $ ____________

Postage & Handling (each book) $2.00 x Qty = ____________

Total Order = $ ____________

❑ I enclose payment of $ ____________ payable to **Menubooks, Inc.**

❑ Please charge this order to my credit card. Total order = $ ____________

MasterCard # ______________________________ Exp. Date ____________

VISA # ______________________________ Exp. Date ____________

American Exp. # ______________________________ Exp. Date ____________

Approval Signature ______________________________

Name ______________________________ Phone ____________

Address ______________________________

City ______________________________ State __________ Zip __________

Payment must accompany order. Please allow up to four weeks for delivery.
Rush/overnight delivery available. Call for details.

Menubooks, Inc.
David Thomas Publishing
733 NW Everett St., Box 12
Portland, Oregon 97209
(503) 226-6233

(Please fill out shipping instructions on reverse side.)

Gift Order Form

Please Send:

❑ New York City ❑ San Francisco ❑ Chicago ❑ Los Angeles

To:

Name ______________________ Phone ______________

Address ______________________________________

City ______________________ State ________ Zip ________

Please Send:

❑ New York City ❑ San Francisco ❑ Chicago ❑ Los Angeles

To:

Name ______________________ Phone ______________

Address ______________________________________

City ______________________ State ________ Zip ________

Please Send:

❑ New York City ❑ San Francisco ❑ Chicago ❑ Los Angeles

To:

Name ______________________ Phone ______________

Address ______________________________________

City ______________________ State ________ Zip ________

Please Send:

❑ New York City ❑ San Francisco ❑ Chicago ❑ Los Angeles

To:

Name ______________________ Phone ______________

Address ______________________________________

City ______________________ State ________ Zip ________

Please Send:

❑ New York City ❑ San Francisco ❑ Chicago ❑ Los Angeles

To:

Name ______________________ Phone ______________

Address ______________________________________

City ______________________ State ________ Zip ________